Social Networks Around The World
How is Web 2.0 changing your daily life?

*By **An De Jonghe***

Table of Contents

New developments p494

Conclusion p510

I Introduction

How this book came about

As a headhunter in Information Technology, I started using social networks a couple of years ago in my professional surroundings. Networking became increasingly important in my job, and ICT people – being in their natural habitat – have been early adopters of the phenomenon.

Intrigued by the untapped potential of these networks, I decided in December 2006 to write a book on the subject for which the research phase ended in May 2007.

Scope & Definition

The social networking sites that are covered are all online or mobile community sites where users create their profile to be shared with friends or acquaintances for social or business purposes. They can blog, chat, send pictures or video, upload their cv, reconnect with old friends or classmates...

All social networks have been classified into six different categories: business, friends, dating, special interest (e.g. hobbies), video/ photo, and mobile, in order for you to find what you're looking for easily. I have made the decision to classify networks under a country, based on where this network's headquarters were located. Obviously this doesn't exclude a network being used elsewhere as well. Most social networks are free of charge, with or without the possibility to upgrade to a paying account. Similarly, most networks are open to new members without prerequisites other than filling out a form with some personal details. Only a small percentage are so-called "gated communities" where you need an invitation to become a member. This approach seems to be less attractive to new networks, and some of the older communities, which were gated to begin with, have become unrestricted today.

Sources

The book's content has come together through the input from the founders of the different social networks themselves, expert opinions ("testimonials") from topnetworkers, bloggers, and speakers with a penchant for the subject, and ordinary users. I have contacted 266 networks directly through a personalized e-mail; these are indicated with the letters (LS) next to their address. Generally speaking, these were the networks I came across first where an e-mail address was available. I have voiced my opinion only in areas where it seemed relevant, but I have otherwise abstained from giving a colored version, preferring instead that the reader makes up his or her own mind as to what is useful to him or her and what is not.

Whenever possible, I have tried to list the source of the material I have consulted or mentioned the author of an opinion. At the end of the book you'll find a list of websites and articles which have been particularly helpful to me during the research phase of this book.

I have tried to be as exhaustive as possible in the number of social network sites covered, but due to the sheer number and constant arrival of new players on the market it is entirely possible that a site has not been mentioned, for which I offer my apologies. Also I have sourced the Internet in Dutch, French, English, and Spanish, which may account for a slight dominance of sites coming from these countries.

If your site has not been mentioned or you would like to get in touch for any other reason, you can do so online at **http://worldwidenetworking.blogspot. com** or **http://worldwidenetworking.ning.com** . Likewise, if you're new to social networking and would like to connect, or you would like to invite me to a new social network, feel free to do so at **adj@ulysses-consulting.com** .

I hope you'll enjoy this book as much as I have enjoyed writing it!

An De Jonghe
October 2007

THANK YOU !

This book would not have been realized without the help of all the people who were willing to send their feedback and share their passion in creating a social network.

All of you founders who have responded have been given a place in this book — I hope it will help in a small way in enhancing the popularity of your networks.

Also I would like to thank the following experts for lending their credibility to this project:
Shally Steckerl (USA)
Vanessa diMauro (USA)
Hugo Antonio Reyes (Argentina)
Igor Kovalev (Russia)
Daisuke Kano (Japan)
Idan Gafni (Israel)
Geert Conard (Belgium)
Michiel Gerbranda (the Netherlands)
David Long (United Kingdom)

As well as the people who have endorsed me.

But also Hendrik, Carl, Vadim, Thomas, Bart, Marcin, Nathalie, Noel, Bas, Marga, Frans, Laurent & Betty, who have kept me updated on new developments.

The Booksurge team (thank you Sarah & Kenneth!) who have done a wonderful job in making this book come to life.

A special thank you to my partners, who have backed this adventure financially and who make a habit of supporting my crazy ideas.

To my husband and family, who see the least glamorous part of writing a book: the grumpy, sleep-deprived author!

2 A North-America: the Godmother of all social networking sites

USA

As is often the case in all things technology, the United States is leading the pack on the social networking scene. With MySpace and YouTube, they have started the social network craze both technologically as well as financially. Not only have these two sites (one geared to interaction between friends on the Internet, the other to video exchange) led the way in terms of building a faithful userbase, they have also opened the gate to social networks that are no longer the brainchilds of an enthusiastic bunch of friends but big bucks media concerns or venture capitalists instead. There is no doubt that the United States represents the best and the worst in what social networks stand for today, as well as some of their more bizarre eccentricities. Given the more mature market, the US offers subcategories such as religion or politics, which you do not encounter (or only marginally so) in other continents. Secondly, we see an important difference in the way commercial companies react to and anticipate the social networking trend, in a much more advanced way than any of the other countries. Examples include such diverse companies as Sheraton hotels, Dell or Disney (more about this later on). About one half of all networks dicussed in this book are located in the USA with a large majority located in San Francisco, California. Despite the very nature of Web 2.0 enterprises, where developers do not need to be physically present in order to create a network, it seems that the creative presence of Silicon Valley inspires many – or is it the number of VC capital around?

BUSINESS

http://www.60secondnetworking.com (LS)
The 60 Second Network was started to help individuals do extreme networking. The bottom line of this organization is to help individuals meet a lot of people in a selected venue or online. It's up to you to make the quantity into quality. All you have to do is subscribe or come to an event, network with people and find out who to know.

Want to get started?

Option 1. Subscribe to the database and start searching instantly for contacts and leads for businesses or referrals.

Option 2. Subscribe and attend one of the local events in your city.

Founder: Dakotta J.K. Alex
411@60secondnetworking.com
PO Box 23311, Seattle, WA 98121

http://www.globalurbanites.com/

Founded by Beth A. Di Santo & Marcelo Rivero in 2005, Global Urbanites has quickly expanded into an exclusive community of business owners, executives, artists, professional advisors and entrepreneurs. Global Urbanites Network (GUN) is a private international social and networking community, which is not open to the public. Our organization is intended for those who already have strong connections with one another, and those who want to create new connections. Our events and website allow our members to interact more effectively with compatible individuals with common interests, objectives, and colleagues.

Global Urbanites Network, Inc.
555 Washington Avenue, Suite 200
Miami Beach, FL 33139
info@globalurbanites.com

275 Madison Avenue, Fourth Floor
New York, NY 10016

http://ziffdavisitlink.leveragesoftware.com/

Online social network for information technology (IT) professionals created on April 16th 2007.

Ziff Davis Media Inc.
Corporate Headquarters28
East 28th Street
New York, NY 10016
Phone: 212-503-3500

Ziff Davis Media Inc.
101 Second Street
San Francisco, Calif. 94105
Phone: 415-547-8000

Ziff Davis Media Inc.
500 Unicorn Park Drive
Woburn, Mass. 01801
Phone: 781-938-2600

http://bizpreneur.com/
Business Entrepreneur is an online community that lets you market your business/company for free!
Create a personal community on BizPreneur, and you can promote your business with free marketing and advertisement, make company profiles and develop agreements between other companies, find jobs through our classifieds section, and with your growing network you will be able to generate a great magnitude of hits to your site.
You may also see what business is affiliated with other businesses, or how they are connected. Find out if you really are a multi-million dollar company!

Business Entrepreneur is for everyone:
People who want to find a job, growing businesses who want to affiliate with other growing businesses, companies who want to connect their companies with other companies, business people, and co-workers interested in networking.

Contact: webmaster@bizpreneur.com

Based in Texas.

http://www.barcardz.com/
BarCardz is the world's first Truly Social Network. It is our objective to encourage real life social interaction. We feel BarCardz is the world's first Truly Social Network. We provide all of the fun benefits of other social networks, with one twist... You must actually meet somebody in the real world in order to interact with them on BarCardz.

The BarCardz Team
President/CEO: Alex Lubyansky
Vice President of Operations/ Strategic Planning: Joe Shargorodsky
Director of Web Applications: Bill Johnson
Graphic Design Specialist: Derek Billings
Card Printing Guru: Slava Apel

http://www.yopro.com
Chicago based, professional network. Members are able to search for other members based on a variety of categories such as name, city, company, industry, profession, and school. YoPro gives its members the option of filling out three different profiles (general, dating, and professional services), which other members have the ability to search.

Mike Zeinfeld - mzeinfeld@yopro.com
Co-Founder. Responsible for marketing information, media inquiries, technology & advertising opportunities

http://www.fastpitchnetworking.com (LS)
Fast Pitch! Online provides a one-stop shop for business professionals to network and market their business. Each member builds a Profile (one-page website), which outlines his/her business including what he or she buys and sells. Once the profile is connected into the Fast Pitch! Network, members can begin to build a referral network and promote their business. Over 2.5 million introductions have been made using our innovative online lead exchange system that analyzes profiles and matches professionals based on what they buy and sell.

Bill Jula, CEO and Founder

Also:

www.fastpitchpress.com
Fast Pitch! Press is a Press Distribution website that promotes press releases issued by Fast Pitch! members. Fast Pitch! Press has built a strong network of affiliates and channels to syndicate news throughout the web.

www.fastpitchradio.com
Fast Pitch! Radio is an interactive website that publishes PodCast Interviews of business professionals and brings to life the profiles of Fast Pitch! Members.

Headquarters:
6580 Palmer Park Circle
Sarasota, FL 34238
Phone: (941) 684-3271

E-mail: info@fpnetworking.com

http://networkingforprofessionals.com/
We believe in networking because we understand the power of people. That's why our mission is to bring together successful, motivated professionals and help them become more successful by creating connections that take their careers to the next level and beyond!

Networking for Professionals was started by a group of professionals who saw the limitations of traditional networking. We wanted to provide a better alternative to building business contacts, quickly and efficiently.

Founded in New York City in 2002, NFP has already grown throughout the Tri-state area, with NFP branches in Manhattan, Long Island, and Atlanta and Chicago.

Membership-based service.

http://www.experience.com
Experience has been a pioneer and innovator in the educated talent recruiting market since 1996. Our university-powered recruiting solutions help employers connect to the nation's largest network of diverse and educated candidates. Over the past nine years, Experience has re-invented the recruiting process for universities, employers, students, and alumni. The company pioneered the first web-based college recruiting platform, which has since become the standard in the college market. With the acquisition of eProNet in

2002, Experience added the exclusive alumni recruiting service that serves mid- and senior-level professionals. Today Experience offers employers the university advantage across all stages of recruiting, from entry-level to experienced.

www.ziki.com
Ziki was founded by Olivier Ruffin (former CTO of Amen) and Patrick Chassany (founder of Amen and co-founder of Fotolia) in New York on January 2006. Ziki addresses three simple needs:
How to optimize visibility on the Internet for a person or a small business? (How can I be found? How can my web site be found?)
How to network and exchange for free with like-minded or complementary people?
How to gather in one place information and content and still be free to choose different publishing services?

Ziki can be dubbed "a light social network" since it does not require a member to invite friends to benefit from the service, like most of the existing social networks. Networking between members is done through keywords, which members select to describe themselves. Ziki is an open social network. It does not yet offer a publishing tool; only syndication is available at the moment. You are free to publish your content where you wish: your blog (blogger, typepad, msnspaces..), your photos (flickr, fotolog..), your videos (youtube, dailymotion, vpod.tv..), your favorites (delicious, blogmarks.net, blinklist), and you can automatically gather all this content on your ziki.

http://www.vshake.com/ (LS)
Vshake is short for Virtual Hand Shake

Vshake was created by two founders: Sagi Richberg and Sergey Gribov. The original idea was conceived by Sagi Richberg in the year 2001 and presented to friends who claimed that social networking services on the internet would never work. Mr. Richberg decided to abandon the project after receiving his friends' criticism, only to find out, to his surprise after two years, that social networking websites for business and dating were springing up like mushrooms after rain. Luckily for him, these websites did not possess the technology or the business models he envisioned, so he immediately applied for a world-wide patent.

Vshake came to fruition out of Sagi's personal frustrations with the overhead and effort involved in reaching and connecting with key people and decision makers, finding business partners and investors, and especially penetrating inner circles that require unofficial membership in order to join and participate. The main idea was to create a platform to help facilitate and foster innovation and help people propel their careers and lives forward by easily reaching people outside their network of direct contacts.

Sagi relays: "In all my various job experiences I discovered how difficult it was to reach C-level executives. Upon moving to the United States, I had to build my network from zero, since I had great contacts with the VC community, academics, and various other professionals in Israel but not in the US. Using the internet, I recruited several MIT alumnae to my startup, as well as a CEO who successfully sold a cable company. I started participating in entrepreneurial events in Boston, New York and Silicon Valley. The cost associated with these conferences was high, $55–$300 per conference. I was thinking to myself—if I could reach these targeted people via other means than face to face, I could save a lot of time and money. The problem was that in order to reach VCs and high net worth individuals (some of whom receive an overwhelming two thousand business plans a year and therefore prefer to read only the ones that are provided by referral from a trusted source) you need to have a trusted source refer you to them. However, they are always on the look out for good deal flow, so I also realized the importance of building a strong advisory board that can open doors to these potential investors."

With a background in computer game development, system and security engineering, technical instruction, e-distance learning, pre-sale engineering and founding multiple startups, Richberg knows the value of making connections and networking power.

Sagi soon was joined by Sergey Gribov, who became Vshake's co-founder and CTO. Sergey brings over fifteen years of both management and hands on experience in software development, security, and IT operations across different industries, and he headed the creation of the site as well as all other technical aspects of the company.

We hope Vshake will help propel ideas, innovations, businesses, partnerships, joint ventures and people's lives in general, forward. Vshake is intended to bridge the gap between individuals, be it entrepreneurs looking to secure financing from investors; sales and marketing people hoping to generate high quality leads by reaching C-level executives in corporations; up and coming artists and performers trying to break into Hollywood; or people looking to connect with individuals in any industry which may be closed in inner circles.

Vshake is also a tool which will allow users to exchange information and share knowledge with one another, rewarding people monetarily for their hard earned contacts.

Simply stated, Vshake addresses basic human nature, which is incentive driven, i.e. 'what's in it for me?' And we believe that this type of social capital psychology will lead to customer loyalty, retention, and appreciation for our business.

Vshake can also help you to gather market intelligence, identify trends, and insights into the economy, increase referrals and find unadvertised jobs. Vshake assists with building your credibility and is the most cost efficient way to market yourself, your business and services, giving you the opportunity to become a trendsetter, brand ambassador and buzz generator.

Vshake's Fundamental Difference
Vshake is creating a trusted new market place and platform that facilitates and fosters collaboration and interaction between its users, helping propel their businesses and lives forward. The core idea behind Vshake's model, and what makes it novel and fundamentally different from other sites offering online social networking, is its ability to empower the users of its system with a tool-set. This tool-set enables users to set a different price for each method through which they can be contacted by other people looking for them, i.e. phone, chat, e-mail, IM. The toolset also produces an automatic filter against spam.

Hi An,

In regard to your questions, I will try and answer the best I can:

1. *Founders and Management: Sagi Richberg: Founder & CEO, Sergey Gribov CTO*
2. *Founding year: 2005*
3. *Address: 225 Algonquin Tr. Ashland, MA USA*
4. *Target Audience: C-level executives, Job Seekers, Recruiting Firms, Entertainment Industry*
5. *Top three countries using Vshake: US, Israel, Netherlands*
6. *Main Business + Technical Features:*
   A. *Visually search, pinpoint and connect with executives, decision makers, VIPs, celebrities and potentially any individual on this planet by using the unique and cutting edge graphical interface.*
   B. *Make money, generate revenue, supplement income and receive compensation by (optionally) charging for how people contact you, be it contact by e-mail, chat, phone or however you decide. You can also charge for services that you provide to others.*
   C. *Protect your privacy even after a contact has been established.*
   Future development: 3D GUI, Integration of SNS with Shopping, Family Tree.

support@vshake.com
sagi@vshake.com

Based in Boston, Massachusetts.

http://www.downtownwomensclub.com/
Founded as a networking organization in Boston by a group of energetic and enthusiastic young professionals in 1998, the Downtown Women's Club (DWC) has evolved into an online social network and in-person community designed for smart and sophisticated businesswomen on the

go. Our mission is to empower women through access to information and opportunities for collaboration. With our expanding club system and online services, no matter where you work, play, or live, you can join the DWC and interact with dynamic corporate executives and entrepreneurs from a variety of industries.

Diane K. Danielson
DWC Founder & CEO, Downtownwomensclub.com
DWC Services Inc.
P.O. Box 21
Cohasset, MA 02025

www.ryze.com (LS)
Ryze helps people make connections and grow their networks. You can network to grow your business, build your career and life, find a job and make sales, or just keep in touch with friends.
Members get a free networking-oriented home page and can send messages to other members. They can also join special Networks related to their industry, interests or location. More than one thousand organizations host Networks on Ryze to help their members interact with each other and grow their organizations.
Ryze members are around the world, with more than 250,000 members in more than two hundred countries.

Founded by Adrian Scott
press@ryze.com , or phone media relations at 415-462-1850.

www.zoodango.com
Zoodango is an online network of professionals, associations, companies, event planners, restaurants, entrepreneurs, and people who all believe networking is critical for higher success. Zoodango drives face-to-face meetings through our online platform.
When you join, you create a profile that summarizes your professional profile. Your profile helps you find and be found by people attending the same events you are attending. You can have your profile be open to the public or only to people attending the same events as you. By opening your profile, you open yourself to new opportunities.

Founded in December 2006 by James Sun.

900 Lenora Street Suite W305
Seattle, WA 98121
press@zoodango.com

http://www.jigsaw.com/
Jigsaw is an online directory of more than five million business cards. Every card on Jigsaw has an e-mail address and phone number, allowing members to bypass gatekeepers and get directly to decision makers and influencers. Jigsaw has become a required resource for sales people, recruiters, marketers, and small business owners.

Jigsaw's unique directory is built and maintained by over two hundred thousand members. Using a point system for credit, members trade business cards they have for business cards they need. Members also get point credits for updating incorrect contacts and get point penalties for adding bad contacts.

Jigsaw was founded by veteran sales executives Jim Fowler and Garth Moulton. The company is located in San Mateo, California and is funded by El Dorado Ventures, Norwest Venture Partners, and Austin Ventures.

http://hoovers.visiblepath.com/
Hoover's Connect, powered by Visible Path, enables you to expand your business network and connect to companies and the people who run them. Using unique social network algorithms, Hoover's Connect automatically rates relationship strength to help drive success, efficiency, and trust in your social network.
Launched on May 3, 2007.

www.linkedin.com (LS)
LinkedIn is an online network of more than 12 million experienced professionals from around the world, representing 130 industries.

When you join, you create a profile that summarizes your professional accomplishments. Your profile helps you find and be found by former colleagues, clients, and partners. You can add more connections by inviting trusted contacts to join LinkedIn and connect to you.

Your network consists of your connections, your connections' connections, and the people they know, linking you to thousands of qualified professionals.

Through your network you can:

- Find potential clients, service providers, subject experts, and partners who come recommended
- Be found for business opportunities
- Search for great jobs
- Discover inside connections that can help you land jobs and close deals
- Post and distribute job listings
- Find high-quality passive candidates
- Get introduced to other professionals through the people you know

LinkedIn is free to join. We also offer paid accounts that give you more tools for finding and reaching the right people, whether or not they are in your network.

LinkedIn participates in the EU Safe Harbor Privacy Framework and is certified to meet the strict privacy guidelines of the European Union. All relationships on LinkedIn are mutually confirmed, and no one appears in the LinkedIn Network without knowledge and explicit consent.

LinkedIn is located in Palo Alto, California, and is funded by Greylock and Sequoia Capital, the venture capital firms behind Google, Yahoo!, Cisco, and Apple. LinkedIn's CEO, Reid Hoffman, was formerly Executive Vice President of PayPal, the Internet's de-facto standard for secure, private financial transactions.

www.doostang.com (LS)

Doostang is a free invitation-only online career community that connects people through personal relationships and affiliations. Our members use Doostang to share relevant career opportunities and to interact with one another.

In order to join Doostang, you need to be invited by one of our members. If you have not yet received an invitation, please request one from one of your friends.

Founding team:
Mareza Larizadeh and Pavel Krapivin co-founded Doostang, Inc.

Contact information:
contact@doostang.com

Mailing address:
Doostang, Inc.
374 Palo Alto Avenue
Palo Alto, CA 94301
USA

Shared jobs

Our motto here at Doostang is "doo something great." We encourage our users to doo the same; share jobs with your friends by posting any interesting jobs you receive on Doostang. Collaborating will create more job opportunities than those that currently exist for all of us today.

Experts

Our experts work tirelessly to bring you the most sought after career opportunities.

Job Matcher

Enter keywords into the Job Matcher and see a list of the most relevant career opportunities.

Groups and Forums

Create groups to interact with members from your school, company, or with similar interests. Post questions, suggestions, and answers to our forums, and engage the community in meaningful discussion.

Unlimited resumes

Store an unlimited number of resumes for your future use. There's no catch, and like everything else on Doostang, it's free.

http://socialpicks.com/ (LS)
We looked around on the web and found that a lot of investment sites tell you that the way to become a good investor is to put in the hours and learn how to properly determine an investment's true worth. That hasn't changed, but we don't think that people are therefore destined to adopt a lone wolf approach to investing. We've learnt through experience that if you put sharp people together, they feed on each others' strengths and can pool together a broader set of resources and ideas. SocialPicks is our way of putting that into practice. We want to build an investment community that helps individual investors discover, analyze, and evaluate new investment opportunities together.

Our Team

We met during our time in Stanford's graduate programs in business, engineering, and finance and have joined Silicon Valley's entrepreneurial community.
press@socialpicks.com

http://www.lpn.org/index.php
The Latino Professional Network creates career, educational, and social opportunities for Latino professionals. We connect Latino professionals and college students with each other and with employers seeking to identify, retain, and develop Latino talent. L.P.N. fosters an environment for personal and professional growth for Latinos through monthly networking sessions hosted by area corporations, educational institutions and non-profit organizations.

http://www.startupnation.com (LS)
If you are looking for expert advice on all aspects of starting and growing a business and want to have fun along the way, you've come to the right place: StartupNation. You are joining a robust community of entrepreneurs and small business owners who are also "living the dream" every day. Yes, StartupNation is the destination where you can learn the important nuts

and bolts of business, such as how to patent your idea, build a business plan, or increase sales. While you're seeking that helpful information to build your business, StartupNation is also a resource for you to learn from peers, whether you're connecting with them directly or listening to them share all on StartupNation Radio!

Press contact: Melanie Rembrandt, melanie@startupnation.com

http://www.theworldbusinesscafe.com/
TheWorldBusinessCafe is a global project space for consultants. Founded by Tia Carr Williams.

Our primary goal is to create and implement a global, agile & dynamic vision of business. WBC members are entrepreneurs, accomplished professionals, and decision makers, who understand the value of the net in leveraging opportunities for peers in mutually positioned industries or services.

The Cafe creates 'Cooperative Collateral.' By providing serious 'value add' investment in each other's success, members forge chains of sustainable growth through continuous business referral and reciprocity.

Globally networked expertise, local knowledge and communication, we provide powerful search tools for finding business opportunities, the ultimate business intelligence resource. Streamline your network, do more business.

http://www.joinnetworkplus.com/ (LS)
The goal of Network PLUS is to create the best environment for networking while offering a range of "plus" services that will assist its members in growing their business through education, motivation, and inspiration.

Ted Fattoross experienced over one hundred other networking groups during a ten year period. Many of the groups he attended were too rigid and came with too many rules and regulations. He found people within some of these groups sharing leads that had no value because mandates and quotas were made by these organizations that required their members to comply with the demands of giving leads and bringing guests. Ted found it necessary to create something better.

Network PLUS, LLC
Suite 512
55 Riverwalk Place
West New York, NJ 07093
Phone: 201-933-5235

Ted Fattoross:
tedfattorossceo@joinnetworkplus.com

http://layoffspace.com/
Layoffspace.com is an independent social networking web site launched
in spring of 2007. It is owned and maintained by Spacemen Labs, a
Pennsylvania Limited Liability Company. We are not affiliated with any
career or jobs web site, nor are we related to any existing social network.
When we formed Layoffspace.com, we had one goal in mind: to create a
community where unemployed people could come together.
Layoffspace allows members to network, form groups, chat, share ideas,
find work, discuss career topics, schedule events, create blogs, access
career resources, and ask for advice and support from other members and
career coaches. Our members can also search for other members based on
their location, interests, career, and education. They can create valuable
connections that can last a lifetime with just a click of a button.

feedback@layoffspace.com

http://www.inmobile.org/ (LS)
Inmobile.org is a learning, sharing, and networking center for wireless industry
leaders. Community activities are on-line, via conference call and in-person
events. The private, invitation-only forum is fueled by a genuine and generous
exchange of ideas, observations, exciting new information, and analysis.

The forum was conceived in early 2005, as the wireless industry was feeling
the optimism of convergence, the increased flow of investments, and the re-
emergence of substantive innovation. This momentum, with the associated
opportunities and pitfalls, convinced the inmobile.org founders that the
leadership community could prosper from an online environment of private
discussions and perspectives.

Hi An,
Vanessa DiMauro encouraged me to participate — good luck with this project.

-Founders & management
INmobile.org is a private community for executives in the wireless and related industries. An executive search firm focused on wireless, IdealWave Solutions, founded the community in April 2006 and personally invited many of the founding members. Adam Zawel, former Director of Wireless research with the Yankee Group (Boston-based research and advisory company), is the community's "Chief Collaboration Officer."

-Founding year & address/nationality
2006,
INmobile.org
6 Lancaster County Road
Harvard, MA 01451

-Target audience & membership level (number of users):
No specific target number. The idea is to gather the influencers in the rapidly changing wireless marketplace. The community has members from the core wireless industry (e.g. Motorola, Vodafone), but also adjacentindustries (e.g. Facebook, Disney, Comcast, Yahoo). Currently we have 550 members. There are strict requirements for membership:
C-level (small companies)
VP-level and above (medium sized companies)
Director-level and above (large companies)
No Sales
No Journalists

-Top 3 countries in which the community is used
US, Canada, UK (members from 25 countries total)

-Main technical features and possible features in the near future
Message Boards and Member Profiles are the top two website features. The community also gathers in person at major industry events, host conference calls, and webinars.

-Languages in which the service is available
English

Adam Zawel
978-772-2622 x 231
azawel@inmobile.org

http://canyouconnect.com/ (LS)
After about a year of research, funding, and development, CanYouConnect. com launched in August of 2004. The site is completely free and very easy to use. Unlike the competitors, we have put a great deal of thought in the design of the user interface as well as features that people actually need and want. The most exciting feature of the site is the ability to login to one site to manage both your personal and professional networks seperately.
Can You Connect is an online community and service that helps individuals harness the power of their existing relationships and assist them in establishing new relationships. CanYouConnect.com allows you to tap the true power of your social networks to find friends, jobs, leads, and everything else in between. The potential is limitless. We're here to help you by offering a fun, easy to use, and powerful site with the tools you need to achieve your networking goals. Please let us know how we can improve our services by e-mailing us at feedback@CanYouConnect.com .

CanYouConnect.com is a service of Can You Connect, Inc., a privately held corporation founded in 2003 by a team of entrepreneurs and experts from a range of industries. The company is headquartered in Baltimore, Maryland.
david@canyouconnect.com

http://ysn.com/ (LS)
YSN is short for Your Success Network
YS Media Corp.
4712 Admiralty Way #530
Marina del Rey, CA 90292
(310) 822-0261
press@ysn.com
Launched on January 13th, 2007 by Jennifer Kushell and Scott M. Kaufman, co-authors the NY Times bestseller *Secrets of the Young & Successful: How To Get Everything You Want Without Waiting A Lifetime.*

http://www.christianpronetwork.org/
Why A Christian Professional Network?

~To reach the hearts of business people and community leaders with relevant leadership training.

~To connect Christian business owners and professionals for business & professional support, encouragement, education, and mentoring.

~To be a gathering place for Christians in the Marketplace both online and at networking meetings.

The cost of this is $199.00 (including set up and changes needed during the year) for the first year; $99.00 to renew each year. Your eProfile webpage will include a photo in .jpg form that you provide, a bio of yourself, your business or your church, and the contact information including a link to your own website. You will also be included in the "Featured Business of the Week" section on the front page. If you are local to the Mobile area (in order to attend the meetings), you will also be featured at the meetings (on the basis of first come first serve) by having ten minutes to tell of your business or church and have a display table.

Claudia Givens of Mobile, Alabama is the Founder of the Christian Professional Network (to connect Christians in the marketplace). mailto:cgivens2006@gmail.com

C G Enterprises, LLC
962B McCay Avenue
Mobile, AL 36609

http://www.lawbby.com/
Lawbby.com is the brain-child of Chris Rempel and Kevin Cross.

- Lawbby.com is a free online resource where legal professionals can create a profile, build up a network of "friends," publish blogs and create their own groups and forums.

- Lawbby.com users can use the site for business or pleasure, and it will serve as a great place to "relax" or take a "time out" online. (This is why it was named "lawbby" – just like a lobby.)
- Lawbby is a refreshing break for attorneys that are used to listserves and forums that use extremely dated technology.
- Lawyers and other legal professionals will be able to network easily and meet referral partners by navigating through the site, interacting on forums and building their list of friends.
- Lawbby.com launched on April 22, 2006.

Media Contacts:

Chris Rempel
Webmaster & Marketing Director
Lawbby.com: "Where Lawyers Mingle"
1-877-529-1390
Direct Line: +1-614-441-9608
E-mail: chris@jv-web.com

http://nurselinkup.com/
Niche network for nurses.

ItLinkz Corporation is a leading developer of social networking web sites for a wide variety of professional, community, and hobbyist groups in the United States. ItLinkz was launched to meet the growing demand for virtual communities interacting via the Internet. Our sophisticated, yet easy to use software allows our members to create dynamic online communities where they can connect on both a personal and professional level with people who share similar interests. Users are able to collaborate and share knowledge and openly exchange their opinions and experiences. For more information on itLinkz Corporation vist our corporate web site at www.itlinkz.com.

Jeremy P. Feakins
Founder & Chief Executive Officer

Press contact:
Kathryn O'Connor
Associate Vice President
Gregory FCA
27 West Athens Avenue
Ardmore, Pa. 19003
Main: 610-642-8253, ext. 154
Kathryn@GregoryFCA.com

Company contact:
Terry McDermott
Director of Marketing
itLinkz Corporation
1800 Fruitville Pike
Lancaster, Pa. 17601
Main: 717-390-3777, ext. 115
TMcDermott@itLinkz.com

http://www.mediabistro.com/ (LS)

Mediabistro.com is dedicated to anyone who creates or works with content or who is a non-creative professional working in a content/creative industry. That includes editors, writers, producers, graphic designers, book publishers, and others in industries including magazines, television, film, radio, newspapers, book publishing, online media, advertising, PR, and design. Our mission is to provide opportunities to meet, share resources, become informed of job opportunities and interesting projects and news, improve career skills, and showcase your work.

Laurel Touby, Founder, CEO, & Cyberhostess
laurelT@mediabistro.com

The original idea for mediabistro.com was cooked up in 1993 when Laurel—then a freelance business writer and Glamour magazine contributor—and a friend decided to host a mixer for media people. About twenty editors, writers, and other content creators came to that original cocktail party at Jules Bistro in the East Village. Attendees bought their own drinks and enjoyed casual after-work bonding in the company of like-minded people. The parties quickly grew, and soon Laurel had four thousand of New York's top media talent on her e-mail list. After creating a website in 1997 and adding features such as job listings, bulletin boards, classes, e-classes, media, and a freelance marketplace, Touby's business began to take off. Today, the site also includes news, events and "learn" e-mails, as well as media industry blogs. More than six hundred thousand media professionals have registered for various mediabistro.com services around the world.

http://nextcat.com (LS)
Nextcat, Inc. was founded in April, 2005 by longtime technology entrepreneurs/business partners Jeff Pucci and Richard Viard. The Nextcat. com web site caters to working entertainment professionals as an extension of the way their industry already functions – making it a natural application for a social networking site.

http://www.ilearnium.com
Social networking for E-learning professionals.
2945 Bell Rd #335, Auburn, CA 95603

http://aggreg8.net/
Aggreg8 is a social networking and collaboration space for the IT community. Inside you can keep track of your trusted network, find others through your network with similar interests or situations. Then you can collaborate with anyone in the community inside our working groups.

http://www.mywallst.net/ (LS)
Financial social network. Founded on January 16th 2007.
2355 Main St
Suite 120
Irvine, CA 92614
info@mywallst.net

http://microsoftdynamicslive.com/community.htm
Microsoft Dynamics Live 'Beta' Finance Community

Would you like to learn from and collaborate with individuals who work in the same way you do? Then join the Microsoft Dynamics Live Finance Community! This Finance Community offers a plethora of tools and resources to help foster community collaboration – all year round. Interact with other Finance Professionals via the Blogs, Forums, and Networking tools; learn more about the topics of most interest to you via the Featured Articles and Expert Columns; plus get into the minds of Microsoft Executives to help you understand how the future of technology will impact your business via the Executive Insight Blog.

What's in the Community?

Topics of Interest
The Microsoft Dynamics Live Finance Community includes Expert Columns featuring articles and columns from some of the industry's leading experts. Get into the minds of the Microsoft Executive team and understand how those within Microsoft deal with financial issues and the future of the industry. The community will also feature articles and tips to help you deal with some of the most common finance questions and problems!

Collaboration and Learning Opportunities
Take the experiences from Convergence online. Tools and resources in the collaboration and networking area allow you to continue the learning and sharing of Convergence and experience the benefits year around.
Networking will allow you to continue the learning and sharing of Convergence year round. You will be able to do this by participating in working groups. The Finance Working Groups will enable those individuals who have similar roles, responsibilities, and interests to communicate, collaborate, and work together to improve the way they work.
Once inside a working group, you can add content through postings that are rich text, upload files or videos or post events. As the owner of the working group you can add RSS feeds into the group, so it can aggregate data from existing sources. Of course, you can tag postings, reply to them, and rate them so you can find the most important information. And you don't even need to be in the working group to see the activity as each group provides RSS feeds as well as e-mail subscriptions.
Unable to find an existing working group? Or maybe you are looking for a more private group, no problem; you can create your own. You will be able to set up the working groups you create to be open to anyone, or you can mark them as private and send invitations to join.

Benefits:

- Experience the collaboration and sharing of Convergence year around.
- Public and Private work groups allow you to choose whether or not you want to have your workgroups open to the public.

- Find new tips and tricks to improve the way you work.
- Meet new individuals who have similar roles as you.
- Work together to solve difficult tasks.

Microsoft Corporation, One Microsoft Way, Redmond, Washington 98052-6399 U.S.A.

http://www.cafepharma.com (LS)
Cafe Pharma is a site for drug reps by drug reps. We hope you find a sense of community here – a place where you can meet with others in our industry and share your successes and struggles, etc. Here, you may learn which companies are hiring and firing, which companies you want to work for and which ones you don't. Often your fellow reps are a great source of "behind the scenes" information. We also provide links and services to help you become more effective in the field and make the most of your valuable time.

If you are not already in the industry, then Cafe Pharma is a great place to find out more about pharmaceutical sales and possibly find a position with a company that suits you.

Develop a network of pharma industry contacts
Powerful referral system to extend your reach in the industry
You decide how much information you want to share with others
Online Journals (blogs)
Shared bookmarks
Explore groups and events

Contact: webmaster@cafepharma.com

Cafepharma Inc.
1205 Johnson Ferry Rd., Suite 136 #183
Marietta, GA 30068

http://www.bizster.com/
Become a beta tester and your first year's membership is free!
Register today to network with other Entrepreneurs in our forums, download business documents from the library, read the latest small business news,

register for upcoming events, post your own blog, create your personal profile page, and much more.

Matt Stout
VP, General Counsel
100 West Road
Suite 300
Towson, MD 21204
Ph: 410-832-7470
Fx: 410-374-9039

http://adfemme.com/ (LS)
AdFemme.com was launched in February 2006 by Lindsay Mure, as an e-newsletter and news portal for women who work in advertising and marketing. Since then, Ad Femme has grown to include exclusive news, tips, trends, hot topics, the Ad Femme of the Month, memberships, web design services, events, job & resume postings, and special newsletter editions.
In 2007 Ad Femme Members will be able to build profiles with their contact info, bio, company info, picture, and favorite quotes/tips. Through the Member Profiles, Ad Femmes can message each other for easy networking and business building. Messaging can be direct to another member or posted in the Networking Room (due to launch in January 2007).

531 Main Street
New York
NY 10044
info@adfemme.com

http://sermo.com/ (LS)
Community created by physicians for physicians. Here, physicians aggregate observations from their daily practice and then – rapidly and in large numbers – challenge or corroborate each others opinions, accelerating the emergence of trends and new insights on medications, devices, and treatments. You can then apply the collective knowledge to achieve better outcomes for your patients.

215 First Street, Cambridge, MA 02142
gshenk@sermo.com

http://biznik.com/ (LS)

Hi An,

Sounds like a fun project. I'm happy to collaborate with you on that. Here're my responses to your questions:

-Founders & management

Biznik was co-founded by Lara Feltin and Dan McComb (husband and wife team). I'm a web developer, and she's a photographer — we couldn't find a business networking group that we liked in Seattle, so we decided to start our own!

-Founding year & address/nationality

2005, USA (Seattle)

-Target audience & membership level (number of users)

Indie business people — that is bootstrapping entrepreneurs and business owners, anyone thinking of starting a business, or looking to grow their existing one. Biznik currently has 2,300 members (Feb 2007), mostly in the Seattle area, and is growing at the rate of ten new members per day. It is being spread entirely through word of mouth — no advertising of any kind.

-Top three countries in which the community is used

Biznik currently has members in fifty-six countries, but, as you can see, it is mostly a Seattle, Washington, USA network at the moment.
United States (2,107 - 1,404 in Seattle area)
India (42)
Canada (41)
UK (26)

-Main technical features and possible features in the near future

Biznik is a business-building social network for indie professionals. It's event-based networking, and all of the events are hosted by members. Events include educational workshops as well as happy hours. Members can use the website to publish their events, and other members can RSVP, participate in discussions, and maintain a profile. We are working on a new version of the site that will support the formation of groups, and it will filter by location, so that Biznik will become a networking platform rather than a large Seattle community, which is what it is at the moment.

-Languages in which the service is available
Currently English only. We have no immediate plans to support other languages, but as membership grows, we'll take a look at that if it seems viable.

Phone: 206.228.0780
Biznik LLC
4318 5th Ave. NW
Seattle, WA 98107
E-mail: info@biznik.com

http://www.airtroductions.com (LS)
AirTroductions.com, the only online business networking and personal dating service that lets you make arrangements to meet your business or personal contacts while traveling.

This Service is provided by Airkarma, Ltd, a New York Corporation, with registered offices at 111 Broadway, 13th Floor, New York, NY 10006.

http://steamstreet.com/
Investor community founded by Jon Nichols. SteamStreet was born on December 1st, 2006. Private beta started in June 2007.

SteamStreet is based in the US, in Santa Cruz, California.
Contact: jnichols@steamstreet.com

FRIENDS & FAMILY

http://www.myspace.com
MySpace is an online community that lets you meet your friends' friends. Create a private community on MySpace, and you can share photos, journals, and interests with your growing network of mutual friends!
See who knows who or how you are connected. Find out if you really are six people away from Kevin Bacon.

MySpace is for everyone:

- Friends who want to talk online
- Single people who want to meet other Singles
- Matchmakers who want to connect their friends with other friends
- Families who want to keep in touch—map your Family Tree
- Business people and co-workers interested in networking
- Classmates and study partners
- Anyone looking for long lost friends!

Australia http://au.myspace.com, Canada (in English) http://ca.myspace.com, Canada (in French) http://cf.myspace.com, France http://fr.myspace.com, Germany http://de.myspace.com, Ireland http://ie.myspace.com, Italy http://it.myspace.com, Japan http://jp.myspace.com, Mexico http://mx.myspace.com, New Zealand http://nz.myspace.com, Spain http://es.myspace.com, U.K. http://uk.myspace.com

MySpace, Inc.
8391 Beverly Blvd. #349
Los Angeles, CA 90048
USA

www.tribe.net (LS)
At tribe.net, we believe in the power of connecting to other people to get things done. Since that can be surprisingly hard in a city, we founded tribe.net to make it easier. Whether it's for finding the right job, a killer apartment, a good restaurant, a gentle dentist, or a hiking buddy, we think those tasks are best done by connecting with other local people for advice and sharing. The people you connect to can be your friends, people who live in your neighborhood, or people who live in your city who share a common interest with you. Tribe.net makes finding those people easier. You can invite friends, search for people with similar interests, and join or create tribes (member-created online groups) dedicated to interests you might have. The more people you're connected to, the better tribe.net will work for you.

www.bebo.com (LS)

-Founders & management
Michael Birch
Co-founder and CEO
Bebo's CEO and founder Michael Birch has been the driving force and chief architect behind the development of six consumer web sites over the last decade. In 2001, he co-founded word-of-mouth marketing site BirthdayAlarm.com as a simple way to remember birthdays. The idea caught on, and today the site provides more than 45 million members an assortment of e-greeting cards and services. Following this, he started Ringo.com, one of the first social networking sites launched in 2003. The site was later sold to Tickle.com and is now owned by Monster.com. Birch has a BSc in Physics from Imperial College, London.

Xochi Birch
Co-founder and President
Xochi Birch has co-founded several Internet community web sites over the last five years, including BirthdayAlarm.com and Ringo.com, bringing a blend of technical and financial skills, as well as a strong entrepreneurial spirit to each role. Birch launched Bebo with husband Michael Birch in 2005 and is currently responsible for overseeing general operations and the day-to-day running of the company. She also oversees operations at BirthdayAlarm.com, a word-of-mouth marketing site with more than 45 million members. Xochi Birch has a BSc in Business Administration and Economics from St. Mary's College, California.

Other members of the team:

VP Business Development & Sales: Jim Scheinman
Communications Director: Sarah Gavin
Head of Corporate & Social Responsibility: Rachel O'Connell
Head of Sales UK & IE: Mark Charkin

-Founding year
Bebo was launched in July 2005

-Target audience & membership level (number of users) and top countries in which the community is used
Bebo is the next generation social networking site, focused on designing the cleanest, safest, and most fun multimedia user experience on the web. Since its official launch in July 2005,

the San Francisco-based site has grown to more than 30 million registered members turning more than 5 billion monthly page views. According to third party sources such as Nielsen, Hitwise and Media Metrix, Bebo is the largest social networking site in the UK, Ireland, and New Zealand.

Recent Comscore numbers rank Bebo as the third most popular social network in the US, based on uniques and pageviews, and show Bebo to have the highest engagement with 720 pageviews per unique in August (2006). Bebo is also considered the most 'sticky' social network as shown by data released in August by Media Metrix:

	Average Minutes per Usage Day	Average Minutes per Visitor
MySpace_US	21.8	188.9
Facebook_US	17.1	133.5
Bebo_US	38.4	230.1

Bebo continues to grow rapidly in its other core markets and is currently the second and third most popular social network in Australia and Canada respectively.

It also secured the coveted 'People's Voice' Award at the 10th Annual Webby Awards for 'Best Social Networking Web Site of 2006.'

NB. Teens are often the early adopters of new trends, and that's no different with Bebo. Our broad based demographic is 13 to 30 years, and our most active group of Beboers in the UK are aged 16 to 24 years. We launched Bebo in six countries—the US, Canada, UK, Ireland, Australia and New Zealand, and those countries make up 99% of our traffic today. We also launched around high schools and colleges, and that age demographic makes us about 70% our demographic today (13–24).

Our audiences are slightly different in each of our six core markets, and like us our audience is starting to age, especially in countries where we have fully penetrated the teen audience, like in Ireland, where we have more than 90% of Irish teens on Bebo. If you're an Irish teenager in Ireland and you're not on Bebo, you're missing out on a part of popular culture, part of life. Since our minimum age is 13, when we penetrate the market like this, the only place to go is older.

-Main technical features

- *BeboTV is now the 5th largest video sharing site on the web—we're bigger than Google Video!*

- *Bebo Bands — we have an average of 2.5 thousand new bands and artists uploaded to the site each day (Bebo Bands was launched in July 2006)*
- *Bebo Skins (Skins were launched on Bebo in early 2006 as a response to users' requests to be able to further customise their homepages. A user can upload a number of images of specified size to make a custom skin for their own homepage or have another Beboer make a skin for them. Brands can also develop what we refer to as Sponsored Skins)*
- *Personal profile features include: Bebo Mail (multimedia enabled), Bebo personal 'Home' page, Bebo Widgets, Whiteboard (patent-pending), Comments, Friends, Quizzes, Flash Box, Polls, Photos, Blog, Schools, and Colleges, Skins, Skype integration and Gold membership*

There are some broad based aspects that social networks could be considered to have in common, e.g. blogs, music, and the grouping around schools and colleges, but those who regularly use social networking sites will understand that each site is very different. For example, feedback from Beboers and other stakeholders has highlighted the view that Bebo has as a cleaner interface, less invasive advertising, and more intuitive navigation.

From the launch of Bebo in July 2005, Bebo's founders, Michael and Xochi Birch, sought to develop what they believe is the best social networking site. Using their knowledge and experience from their first SN site Ringo (which they sold to Tickle in 2004) and Jim Scheinman's experience at Friendster, they knew what features would work and what wouldn't. They knew how to develop the best framework for a social networking site, allowing for scaling and future innovation. These initial, but important, steps have provided Bebo with a robust platform upon which to build, allowing it to introduce new areas such as Bebo Bands and Bebo TV in a way that is unique and always intuitive to its users.

Experience also taught Bebo that attracting users is important, but keeping hold of them once you've got them is the aim — building the stickiness factor into the site. This is where the real value is and is one of the biggest differentiators between Bebo and other sites such as MySpace and Facebook (Cosmscore data below). Beboers spend more time on Bebo than any other SN site — we have the most engaged audience:

	Average Minutes per Usage Day	Average Minutes per Visitor
MySpace_US	21.8	188.9
Facebook_US	17.1	133.5
Bebo_US	38.4	230.1

Bebo is a much more immersive and engaging multimedia experience.

-Languages in which the service is available

We have focused our initial attention on the six core English speaking markets.

We are seeing more and more that individuals who succeed online are becoming influencers who then inspire and stimulate trends and fashions. Leading Brands are discovering the power of associating themselves with these cool people and are embracing user generated content as a great way for them to build, extend, and substantiate their brands.

We are seeing brands starting to leverage the trends in, for example, video with viral video advertising. For the first time television style advertising has become a reality online, but the differences are that we can target the commercials to the demos that the brand is seeking and the Beboer can click and take an immediate action in response to that commercial. This is hugely powerful when trying to communicate with today's teenage audiences who are spending more time online and tuning out traditional advertising. In order for Brands to reach Gen Y, they've got to engage them with great content, and if they do that, Beboers will engage with that content, make it their own (like by reskinning their Bebo homepage with a cool branded Nike or ipod skin) and spread the brands message virally through the word of mouth marketing tools that are available to them on Bebo. This is all opt-in, we never push any branding or advertising on Beboers. Again, if it's great content (funny, emotionally moving, cool, etc.), then Beboers will love it, even if it is a commercial ;-) This is our business model: we sell Bebo Engagement Marketing programs to companies like Coke & Disney and many more...

Sarah Gavin
Communications Director
T: + 44 (0) 20 7016 6816
M: +44 (0) 7894 640 790
E-mail: sarah@bebo.com
E-mail: sarah.gavin@o2e-mail.co.uk

Bebo, Inc.
142 Tenth Street
San Francisco
CA 94103
USA

http://www.bakotopia.com/ (LS)

Bakotopia is an online community for the young, hip, and young-and-hip-at-heart of Bakersfield, California. We're here to help you meet, hook up, sell stuff, buy stuff, vent and much more. We know that as Bakersfield has grown and changed; it's become harder to do all of these things – especially for young and hungry college students and people who are just starting out. While we can't make Bako smaller, we hope that in some small way we can make things a little easier.

Bakotopia is based in Bakersfield and is specifically for people in Bakersfield. Unlike many other Web sites that offer local services, we are not part of any large national or multinational company. And we think that's cool! If you have thoughts, feedback or questions about Bakotopia, we want to hear them. You can post them publicly in our feedback board (under Rants & Raves> Your Feedback).

Or you can contact us in the following ways:
Mailing Address: Bakotopia, P.O. Box 2454, Bakersfield, CA 93303
Phone: 661-395-7660
E-mail: spud@bakotopia.com

Bakotopia is a product of Mercado Nuevo, LLC.

http://www.metromojo.com/
Metromojo is building relationships and promoting culture via our unique network of online communities. Unlike many national sites, most of our members are local to one another – it's the best way to actually meet new people, not to just add someone to a generic "friends" list. Our sites are focused on specific groups – either by locale or sites built with a certain group in mind. We provide a massive amount of free services, including: personal profiles, open event calendars, private messaging, chat, interest groups, forums, classifieds.

MetroMojo LLC
History: Louisville firms Kanti Communications Inc. and eBrand Group LLC formed a joint venture in September 2003 to promote the concept locally and take it to other markets. In February 2004, the partners changed the corporate structure, forming a separate entity called MetroMojo LLC. Web site: www.metromojo.com

LouisvilleMojo.com
Launched: June 2003
Registered members: About 24,640
Growth rate: Site averages as many as 1,800 net new members each month
Site traffic: More than 547,700 visits in January

http://www.redtoucan.com (LS)
RedToucan is an online social network that helps people remain in touch with their many friends, family, and contacts in their own time and private space online. Members sign up for free to use the many of the site's features.

How it came about?

RedToucan was founded by a couple of Internet executives who felt that most Social Networks were too open for the typical Internet user to participate in – requiring you to share your world with all! RedToucan was conceived on the premise that most people have a need to better communicate with their existing social circles than trying to make new friends.
RedToucan's social network concept is grounded on a simple philosophy: to allow users to replicate their offline worlds online by having the site mimic the natural social behavior of relationships and their interactions.

Founded in 2004 by Willy Aenlle and Frank Balle, RedToucan, Inc. is a privately held company based in Altadena, CA.

RedToucan, Inc.
573 Alameda St.
Pasadena, CA 91001 USA
press@redtoucan.com

http://www.bobojam.com/
Bobojam.com, an online service for people to meet and make friends through a networks of friends.

http://esociallife.com/

I.Q. Webquest, Inc. announces that the beta version of its flagship networking site, esociallife.com, will be launched in early February. Esociallife.com is not your average web portal. This interactive social networking site promises to be the most innovative community on the web. By combining both social and business interactions, esociallife.com will be able to offer the most comprehensive networking community on the web. Not only will esociallife.com provide social networking through an array of interest based sites ranging from gender specific sites to those catering to alternative life styles, specific religious, and ethnic preferences, but it will also be a premier destination for the business community as well as providing such services as industry forums, password protected private conference areas, and employment information in a simple to use format.

ESocialLife is the premier outlet for uniting young professionals across the world. Our community provides everything a young professional could want for online interaction with others. Looking for a new job? No problem! Want to meet others in your industry? No problem! Searching for the happy hour hot spots around town? We provide that! Blogs? Vlogs? Instant messaging? Yes to all of the above and so very much more!

support@esociallife.com

CEO Arnie Fox

http://www.teenspot.com (LS)

TeenSpot.com was founded over seven years ago (Online since June, 2000) as a small and simple chat site with the aim of providing a fun and free community for all teenagers. Since then, TeenSpot.com has expanded its features and grown and is now the premiere entertainment and community hangout for teenagers online! TeenSpot.com offers a wide variety of interactive and daily updated features that make us the most popular and dynamic teen site on the web.

The new TeenSpot.com that you see today has been in the works for over a year and is the result of care and commitment of dedicated teenagers, who work hard to provide an even better interactive community for teenagers. TeenSpot.com is now completely integrated – a free, quick, easy, and one-time registration gives you access to all of the features of the website, including live moderated and unmoderated chat rooms, message boards, web blogs, music, and movie reviews, free music, web-based e-mail, a store, celebrity interviews, cool prize draws and your own custom user profile.

Press info: Mike Brede at info@netfxmedia.com

www.facebook.com (LS)
Facebook is a social utility that enables people to understand the world around them. Facebook develops technologies that facilitate the spread of relevant information through social networks, allowing people to share information online the same way they do in the real world. Facebook is made up of many networks — individual schools, companies or regions— each of which are independent and closed off to non-affiliated users. To join Facebook, people can authenticate into a school or work network, or they can join a regional network. They can then create profiles to connect with friends, share interests, join groups, send messages, write notes, and post photos.
Facebook gives people control over what information they share and with whom they share it. Using Facebook's privacy settings, people can limit the information visible to someone or block that person from seeing them completely. The ability to control their information means people can stay current with their friends and the people around them in a trusted environment.

Facebook launched in February of 2004, and the website now has over 30 million registered users across over 47,000 regional, work-related, collegiate, and high school networks.

According to comScore, Facebook is the seventh-most trafficked site in the United States and the number one photo-sharing site.

Mark Zuckerberg, Founder and CEO
Dustin Moskovitz, Co-founder and VP Engineering
Owen Van Natta, COO
Adam D'Angelo, CTO
Matt Cohler, VP Strategy and Business Operations
Chris Hughes, Co-founder
press@facebook.com

http://www.hoverspot.com/
HoverSpot.com is a free social networking website that facilitates online communication through an interactive network of photos, weblogs, personal web pages, and an internal e-mail system. HoverSpot enhances your interactive experiences with your Buddies and other HoverSpot members by providing features not available from other social networking sites. HoverSpot provides you with a wide variety of rich content templates with which to customize your Website. We also provide you with the HoverBuilder, a tool that allows our members to express themselves freely, customizing their Websites without knowing the inner workings of HTML and CSS.

http://www.ivillage.com
IVillage Connect is a new suite of tools that allows iVillage members to create and share their own personal online space within the iVillage community. When you create your profile, you have the ability to create a blog, upload your own photo, and video galleries, keep a personal calendar, create your own group and connect with others who share the same interests.

iVillage Inc.
500 Seventh Avenue, 14th Floor
New York, NY 10018
212.600.6000

Corporate Communications:
Jane Lehman
Director, Communications
212.600.7838
iVillage.PR@nbcuni.com

http://www.esidewalk.com/ (LS)
Online community that connects people through networks of friends for dating or making new friends.

Copyright Agent, eSideWALK, Inc.
Middletown, NJ 07748
dcolavito@esidewalk.com

http://www.neighborwork.com (LS)
Launched on December 20, 2004 in Atlanta, Austin, Boston, Chicago, Dallas, Denver, Houston, Los Angeles, Miami, Nashville, New York, Philadelphia, Portland, San Francisco, and Washington DC and has plans to expand to other major cities in the coming weeks. People outside of these major metropolitan areas are still able to register and use the site via a zip code lookup.

Neighborwork.com is the brain child of David Goldstein, Arnold Kovelman, and Aaron Levine. The three realized how little they knew about the people inhabiting their New York City buildings, let alone the surrounding neighborhood. Fueled by the idea that most city-dwellers had this same problem, they brainstormed how to bring the neighborhood together to meet, work, and play, and neighborwork.com was born.

"This model has proven successful for many purposes, as we've seen the rise of dating on the internet and sites based on the 'networking' mentality. However, none of those captured the idea of staying close to home and learning about your surroundings through the people that inhabit that immediate area with you, a feature that we thought was extremely desirable and worth creating," said neighborwork.com founder David Goldstein.

Neighborwork.com allows users to create a profile, upload photographs and send messages to other users, thus creating a network of members. A personal network consists of a user's neighbors as well as the extended group of people that a user is connected to via chains of mutual neighbors. Through this model, users are able to network for professional reasons, meet people nearby for friendships, and get to know other single people in the area for dating purposes. Other new and exciting features are currently in the works and will enhance the site's abilities even further. The user-friendly features already allow neighbors to communicate twenty-four hours a day, seven days a week.

info@neighborwork.com
Jessica@Neighborwork.com

http://www.yapperz.com (LS)
Yapperz.com joins the new generation of social networks that enables high school, college students, and everyday people a way to stay in touch with

their friends, find long lost friends, meet new people, and find romance partners. Officially launched in September 2005, in just seven months of development, the social network is now open to millions of prospective members. The privately-held company is operated by a thirty-one year old entrepreneur of Phoenix, Arizona. The CEO and Founder launched the first social networking site of its kind in Arizona. "Arizona is a rapidly growing state, and we are in need of a portal for everyday people to locally interact; that's why I came up with Yapperz, Inc.," says the entrepreneur. We are still in an early phase, having entered a public beta only last month. But the service so far looks promising!" Yapperz.com focuses on word of mouth advertising for its free memberships. In a nutshell, anyone can register for free and create a specialized profile to chat, write blogs, meet people, share photos, post ads, and much more.

Thai Doan
press@yapperz.com

http://www.mygoodfriends.com/
MyGoodFriends.com is the place to keep in touch with friends, family, and neighbors. MyGoodFriends.com is a trusted network, where you decide who is in your circle of friends. You can read and send messages, post photos, collaborate in group discussions, schedule calendar events, keep a personal journal (blog), post classified ads, chat in real-time, create a private family area, plus many other features! Content on MyGoodFriends.com is closely moderated, so you can be assured it is a safe place for all ages.

http://www.meetup.com/ (LS)
Meetup.com helps people find others who share their interest or cause and form lasting, influential, local community groups that regularly meet face-to-face. We believe that the world will be a better place when everyone has access to a people-powered local Meetup Group. That's our goal.

Meetup Groups help people:

- Find others who share their interests
- Get involved locally
- Learn, teach, and share things
- Make friends and have fun

- Rise up, stand up, unite, and make a difference
- Be a part of something bigger—both locally and globally

We're proud to give more power to the people, and we believe it's possible to make a profit *and* make a difference.

Scott Heiferman, Co-Founder, CEO
Peter Kamali, Co-Founder, CTO
Matt Meeker, Co-Founder, VP/Operations

Meetup Inc.
632 Broadway, 10th Floor
New York, NY 10012
E-mail: privacy@meetup.com

www.reunion.com
With a membership base of more than 25 million and growing by up to 40,000 new users every day, Reunion.com is the leader in keeping people in touch online. With its unique Who's Searching for You? and People Search features, Members can find and reconnect with friends, classmates, lost loves, family, and all their important relationships. To stay in touch with contacts in their social network members use the online My Contacts and patented 'Reunion.com for Outlook' software to share contact information and other important announcements as life changes. A privately held company, Reunion.com is based in Los Angeles, Calif.

Reunion.com
12100 Wilshire Blvd. Suite 150
Los Angeles, CA 90025

media@reunion.com

http://www.mycrib.net
MyCrib was released on Janurary 29, 2006 at 11:00 PM (PST). It is a social networking site.
MyCrib is for everyone:

Friends who want to talk online
Single people who want to meet other singles
Matchmakers who want to connect their friends with other friends
Families who want to keep in touch
People who look for long lost friends

http://fo.rtuito.us/
Called Friends4Days since October 2006. Upon registering, you're randomly introduced to another Fo.rtuito.us member—without the influence of factors such as age, sex, and race. You then have four days to get in contact with the member (hence the new name, Friends4Days), and after those four days, it's up to you to either stay friends with them, in which case they're added to your permanent friends list, or move on. Either way, the process is repeated.

http://consumating.com/ (LS)
Consumating is a new way to find people who don't suck. It's a social network, an online hang out, and a contest of wits all wrapped up in an addictive candy shell!
Consumating was created by Ben Brown and Adam Mathes. It began its life as a joke between friends about online dating.
The site was purchased by CNET Networks in 2005. Ben Brown continues to manage the site on a daily basis with the help of Josh Goldberg.

CNET Networks, Inc.
235 Second Street San Francisco, CA 94105
415/344.2000

benbrown@consumating.com

http://www.muvas.com/ (LS)
Hi An,

Info is below. If you need anything else, let me know, and I wish you much success with your book!

Long description:

Muvas aims to become the largest directory of Lifestylers online. It is a community of individuals who enjoy vastly different lifestyles. Muvas was formed as a way for people of similar lifestyles all over the world to find one another. Likewise, Muvas has been created in order to offer the opportunity for you to meet people who have a different lifestyle than you.

The differences are what make interacting with one another so interesting. Once you register your profile on Muvas, you can begin searching for people all over the world based on Lifestyles. Whether you have moved to a new city, want to make new friends or are just curious, you can do all that on Muvas.

By creating an online community based on different lifestyles we can learn more about one another and have a better appreciation and more tolerance for our differences. On Muvas you can share photos, ideas, and music with people from all over the world.

Description:

Muvas is a social networking site where people from all over the world can create a profile to share pics, blogs, and travel stories with people of similar or different lifestyles. Interact with people from all over the world and share your passions.

Muvas also offers a Marketplace section where small businesses or aspiring artists or musicians can create a profile to promote their product or service.

Muvas.com, 701 West Delavan Ave, Buffalo, NY 14222 or at ideas@muvas.com

http://www.socalspaces.com
If you live in San Diego or Los Angeles, SoCalSpaces is a great place to find people to hang out with for free. You can rate your favorite restaurants and write reviews of your San Diego and L.A. hot spots.

www.mychain.com (LS)
MyChain.com is a South Florida based start-up trying to bring the fun and the sun of Florida to online communities and social networks.

General Inquiries - mychain@mychain.com
Business Development and Advertising - bizdev@mychain.com
Employment at myChain.com - jobs@mychain.com

Mychain.com PO box 2345 Miramar, Fl 33321

http://mixermixer.com/
MixerMixer is about getting to know the people in your local community. Come here to form friendships the way you normally would – at local hangouts, while hiking, eating, exploring the city, whatever – basically doing the stuff you'd normally do with others like yourself who've realized that the best part of life is connecting with people and sharing new experiences. 100% free. We don't charge you to attend any activities or events. You use the site to put them together yourself. Not a dating site. We are about local community and hanging out with friends. Everyone is welcome. Most of us are in our 20s and 30s, but we welcome everyone. Married, single, in a relationship – it doesn't matter, as long as you're friendly and like to have fun!

www.wallop.com
Wallop, a spinout company from Microsoft, redefines the popular social networking space by introducing a new social experience that integrates self expression with exclusivity, a revolutionary new business model, and solutions to the problems nagging today's social networks. Wallop started as a Microsoft research project more than four years ago. Veteran entrepreneur, Karl Jacob, had been looking for a technology that would fulfill the vision he had around leapfrogging the current state of social computing with a marketplace business model. Karl found the research project at Microsoft and recruited Sean Kelly, the inventor of Wallop, as a founder. They immediately had a huge advantage in bringing Wallop to market a little over a year later.

www.multiply.com
Multiply, Inc., based in Boca Raton, Florida, was founded in December 2003. The company launched its flagship web site, Multiply (http://multiply.com), in March 2004, effectively defining the new field of social communications. While "social-networking" sites were gaining popularity as an easier way to meet new people, Multiply's founders believed that the most valuable use of having your network of friends and family

on-line is to enable communication on a broad scale with the people you already know, either directly or indirectly through mutual friends, family, and business relationships.

With Multiply's proprietary integration of web-publishing and network-based messaging, its users are actively sharing digital photo albums, videos, music, blogs, restaurant, and movie reviews, and calendar events. More importantly, their content generates lively discussion and active feedback from people they care about – something that is missing with other web-publishing tools. Additionally, with detailed relationship paths and its unique proximity index, Multiply is able to document the connection between the producers of content and the consumers. These explicitly defined relationships and their implicit trust make the content more relevant and entertaining, and provide a comfortable forum for discussion, feedback and solicitation of advice.

Multiply's usage has been steadily gaining traction as one of the most popular sites on the Web today. During 2006, Multiply saw a 500% growth in reach, page views and items posted, and in March 2007 the site surpassed 4 million registered users.

Peter Pezaris, President and Founder
Michael Gersh, Vice President of Sales and Marketing
David Hersh, Vice President of Business Development

http://buddystumbler.com/ (LS)
Buddystumbler allows you to search for new friends with similar interests. If you find someone you'd like to be friends with, and they in turn want to be friends with you, you exchange IM sign-on names. The rest is up to you!

An,

Here is information on buddystumbler.com:

There are millions of users on existing IM networks chatting with known friends, colleagues, and family members. Until buddystumbler.com there wasn't an easy way for these users to find other like-minded people to chat with on existing IM networks like AOL, MSN, Yahoo, Google, etc. Other social networking sites like Friendster, MySpace, etc. do not cater chatting on existing IM networks and/or are not focused on finding new buddies.

Buddystumbler.com is the only application on the web which allows the exchange of instant messenger (IM) addresses based on user profile, interest, and location, announces its launch. Buddystumbler.com caters to individuals who want to meet new people to chat with over existing IM networks (AOL, MSN, Yahoo, and Google/Jabber).

Buddystumbler.com provides users with a simple search like interface and is unique in that it requires both parties to acknowledge interest before IM addresses are exchanged. The buddystumbler.com interface leverages the Web 2.0 paradigm and is built using the Ruby on Rails development framework.

Though today the buddystumbler.com enables IM address exchange, our future includes tighter integration with IM networks (AOL, MSN, Yahoo, Google, etc.) and even with IM clients (AOL, Yahoo, MSN Messager, Google Talk, Trillian, etc.).

The site was launched earlier this year (2007), and the response has been very positive with hundreds of users already registered and meeting new friends. The future of the site looks very promising. Currently the site is only in English and supports US locations, but soon we are going to be supporting international countries.

The founders are Rajesh Bhatia, Han Yuan and Yim Lee. They are Americans and have a Chinese Asian ethnicity. The founders are Silicon Valley veterans. Between the founders and early team members, we have over twenty-five years of software industry experience.

Please let me know if there is other information I can provide. We would be excited to be included in your book.

Thank you again.
Rajesh

Buddystumbler.com, Inc.
979 Pinto Palm Terrace
Suite 15;
Sunnyvale, CA 94087
E-mail: buddystumbler@buddystumbler.com

http://www.tworl.com/ (LS)
Based in Los Angeles, California.

Tworl lets you randomly connect to another member of Tworl.com using AIM (and in the future, other chat programs too). After a connection is made, both participants are shown a chat details page containing the two member profiles, the option to rate each other, and a map showing where both people are located.

http://www.nexo.com/ (LS)

Nexo is a free and easy online service for groups that facilitates formal and informal group communication and collaboration. Nexo.com is the first and only solution to bring together all that groups need in one free, easy and secure service – a full-featured, collaborative website, e-mail integration, real-time communications, and social networking – to let groups interact naturally and cohesively.

Why should I join?

Nexo can help you and your peers communicate and collaborate better. Nexo brings communities of all types closer together, whether they are school groups, sports teams, families, project teams, event planners, neighborhood associations, religious communities, book clubs, alumni groups, or other communities.

Launch at Demo on February 1, 2007. Based in Palo Alto, California.

An,

Thank you for your interest, and we would love to be included. Here is some information about Nexo for your book. Please let me know how else we can help you.

Thank you
Gina Jorasch
VP Marketing
www.nexo.com

Founders & management:

Nexo was founded by Craig Jorasch, Tom McGannon, and Gina Jorasch. Craig and Tom have been friends since kindergarten and have collaborated on numerous start-ups previously, including Metropolis Software, which was sold to Clarify/Nortel, and Octopus Software, which was sold to Ask.com. More detailed information about the management team is below:

Craig Jorasch - Nexo CEO
Founder & Chairman, Octopus, acquired by Ask.com
VP of Business Development, Clarify
Founder & CEO, Metropolis Software, acquired by Clarify
Booz, Allen and Hamilton
B.S.E. Princeton University

Tom McGannon - Nexo VP Operations
Founder & VP Operations, Octopus, acquired by AskJeeves
Director of Services, Clarify
Founder & VP Services, Metropolis Software, acquired by Clarify
B.S. and B.A. Stanford University

Gina Jorasch - Nexo VP Marketing
VP Marketing, Recruitforce.com, acquired by Taleo
VP Product Marketing, Vocent, acquired by PassMark
Director of Marketing, VeriSign 1995-2000
Hewlett Packard, SGI, C-ATS Software, Booz Allen & Hamilton
M.B.A. Stanford University, B.S. Yale University

Founding year & address/nationality:
Nexo was founded in late 2005 and launched in January 2007.
Nexo is based in the United States.
Nexo Systems, Inc
419 Maple Street, Suite 200
Palo Alto, CA 94301

Target audience & membership level:
Nexo is for anyone who communicates and collaborates online with groups of any kind. Groups include families, friends, social clubs, religious groups, sports teams, event planners, school-based clubs, and classes, non-profits, neighborhood and other community groups, fan clubs and interest groups, professional associations, clients, project teams, and work groups, and more. With over 50 million U.S. youth sports organizations, 75 million U.S. families, and countless other groups around the world, the target market has many hundreds of millions of users.

Nexo has just launched its service and is rapidly growing its user base.

Top countries in which Nexo is used:
United States
Germany
United Kingdom
Austria
Canada

Main technical features now & in the future:
Nexo redefines online groups. It's free and easy service combines rich website creation, integrated e-mail communications, social networking, and real-time group collaboration in a secure environment to fundamentally change the way groups work together.

Groups communicate in many different ways: real-time alerts for fast-breaking news, chat for interactive discussions, invitations or polls for group input, websites for posted documents & multi-media, e-mail for group or individual communication, and collaboration products for shared files.

Up to now, groups had to rely on many different products to meet all their needs. Nexo is the first solution to provide group interaction in all the ways groups naturally communicate and collaborate online, securely, easily and at no cost.

Website Features
- Customization - personalized look and feel, custom content
- Widgets - Shared Bookmarks, Calendar, Comments, Dictionary, Feeds, Files, Images, Blogs, Lists, Maps, Rosters, Polls, Search, Tasks, Videos, Weather, Web pages, Yellow pages, Amazon, Q&A, Encyclopedia, Thesaurus, Text
- Social Networking

Group Features
- E-mail integration - Send group e-mails, invitations, polls, updates, requests for updates, Nexo pages, & more, reply directly from e-mail into the Nexo group
- Collaboration - simultaneous multi-user authoring and editing, version control, shared ownership
- Interactive comments - chat with other users
- Managed member lists

General Features
- Secure - multi-level access control, privacy settings, user-defined roles

- Easy - point and click
- Dynamic - real time updates, no need to refresh the page
- Open - add custom widgets and themes

Languages supported:
Nexo menus are in English, but user content can be in any language.

http://connect.tickle.com/ (LS)
Tickle is the leading interpersonal media company, providing self-discovery and social networking services to more than 14 million active members in its community worldwide. Formerly known as Emode.com, Tickle was founded on the belief that personal insight and connections to others could be both scientific and fun. Tickle was founded in 1999 as Emode.com by James Currier, who developed an early passion for Internet technology, new media, and social sciences. Currier envisioned how the Internet could be used to help people learn more about themselves and better connect with others in a mutually beneficial environment based on trust and respect. Today, the company employs more than fifty people and is headquartered in San Francisco, CA.

Tickle launched the Tickle Social Network in October 2003. Tickle Social Network is the first social networking product to deliver deep user profiles that go beyond basic demographic data to include group affiliations, career history, and personality traits.

By staying true to the vision of delivering a deep, rich, and meaningful way for people to connect with one another, the Tickle team has brought the company to the forefront of the market. Operating as a profitable company for seven consecutive quarters, Tickle was acquired by Monster Worldwide in May 2004 and is now part of the overall Monster network.

Tickle Inc.
222 Sutter Street
5th Floor
San Francisco, CA 94108
pr@tickle-inc.com

https://www.spacecatch.com/
SpaceCatch is an Internet service that connects people through network of friends for communicating, sharing, and making new friends. This service further allows people to create custom collections of tags, which can be used by other users to submit personal or non-personally-identifiable information.

SpaceCatch gives you a simplified view of your

- Global Profile
- Photos and Videos across networks
- Your Contacts

Once your space is linked, you can:

- Manage your profile collections
- Add unlimited number of photos and videos
- Instant message your contacts
- View your network of friends up to 3rd degree of separation
- Find cool spaces and people using *Space Tag Search*

info@spacecatch.com

Founded on July 25, 2006 in Las Vegas, Nevada.

http://network.inlist.com/
Social network.
Based in Massachusetts.

http://social.backwash.com/
Backwash.com, inc. is a Boston, Massachusetts based company that grew out of a personal project of founder David Ring, who received his education from the University of Chicago and NYU Graduate School of Film. It was originally founded August 1997, incorporated February 2000 and officially relaunched in its current format on October 1, 2000.

We are privately held and are not backed by Venture Capital nor any outside angel investors. We openly welcome inquiries for partnerships, development deals, and/or investment, particularly from individuals and companies in leadership positions in media and/or the Internet.

http://www.buddybridge.com/ (LS)
BuddyBridge is based out of Yorba Linda, California. BuddyBridge takes pride in maintaining a commitment to quality, service, support, and, most importantly, its users and affiliates.

Three internet companies teamed up to bring you buddyBridge. One hosting company, which provides secure, dedicated, state of the art equipment. A development and marketing company to build the web interface and market the website. Along with a database creation team which provides the backbone upon which buddyBridge is built. BuddyBridge is still very much in its growth stages. We welcome you to join us as we prove to be the largest online community on the internet!

Phone, Fax, and Address:
phone: 877-807-2239, fax: 877-807-2239 - press 2
address: 3900 H. Prospect Avenue, Yorba Linda, Ca, 92886, USA
staff@buddyBridge.com

http://renkoo.com/ (LS)
What is Renkoo?
Renkoo is about spending time with people you already know and care about – your real-life, off-line, non-virtual friends.
Renkoo is about giving you the Internet experience you want to have. Our service lets you use the Web, IM, text messages, and e-mail to communicate with your friends wherever you are and however you like.
Renkoo solves a problem we've all had: how does a group of friends decide on a place and time to get together (and maybe also an activity to enjoy)? Preferably without completely filling up your e-mail box or spending all day on the phone :-). We specialize in planning social events where you know whom you want to hang out with, but you don't know when and where.

About Us
Renkoo started out because our founders were spending all their time dealing with e-mail and IM to arrange everyday social events like lunches,

coffee dates, and movies. Joyce just doesn't like e-mail, and Adam gets 300+ a day…plus he hates to repeatedly paste in data like address, map, photo of himself for new acquaintances, etc. We thought there must be a better way, so we recruited a bunch of engineers who were experts at building social networking sites with PHP and Dojo and CSS, found a funder who took a chance on us – Bob Lisbonne of Matrix Partners – and started hacking away. Meet our team below:

The Team

- Adam Rifkin, CEO
- Joyce Park, CTO
- Anja, metrics engineer
- Bronwyn, QA engineer
- Jannis, engineering intern
- Jeff, sr software engineer
- Kevin, operations engineer
- Kirk, sr software engineer
- Wen-Wen, marketing director
- Yi, engineering intern

Renkoo
541 Jefferson Avenue, Suite 101
Redwood City, CA 94063

http://uboomeru.com/ (LS)
U boomer U is a social networking site niched to Boomers age 35–65, connecting people with friends and others who work and live around them. People use U boomer U to keep up with friends, learn more about the people they meet, including a place where they can also "Vlog, Blog, Post, Link and Buy."

UBoomerU.com's main office is in San Diego, California. If you need to contact us, simply use the appropriate E-Mail address:

Media Questions: tjohnson@uboomeru.com or sgreene@uboomeru.com

Phone: 310-226-7150
E-Mail: corporate@uboomeru.com

CEO Judy Myers
Alchemy Visions,
1626 North Wilcox Avenue
Hollywood , California 90028
Tel: (310) 226-7150
E-mail: corporate@alchemyvisions.com

http://popteenus.com/
Haruki Kadokawa Corporation (www.popteen.net and www.blenda.jp/
magazine), one of the largest publishers of teen magazines in Japan, is
shaking up the US teen interactive market with the launching of its cutting
edge fashion and style site www.popteen.us in February 2007. The site
provides an open forum where teen girls and young women can trade their
thoughts on fashion, style, what's hot and what's not, relationships, school,
and other experiences relevant to their lives. The site leverages a mix of
professional and member-generated content to ensure that the site is always
fresh and relevant.
About Digital Variant
Popteen.US and all Popteen.US operating initiatives in the United States
are managed by Digital Variant. Digital Variant is a full service Interactive
development, design, service, and consulting firm located in Poughkeepsie
NY. We specialize in the development of Community and Social
Networking site as well as custom development projects.

Popteen US, LLC
51 E. 42nd St. Suite 1506
New York, NY 10017

http://www.yuku.com/ (LS)
Yuku is profiles, image sharing, blogs and discussion boards all in one place.
Your Yuku account has up to five different profiles – because you don't
always want to use the same profile, but you do only want one account. Yuku
is a product from ezboard, Inc. who have been creating successful online
communities for over five years. comments@yukucorp.com

We're located at:
ezboard, Inc.
564 Market Street, 705
San Francisco, CA 94104
USA

http://ecrush.com/
ECRUSH.com, Inc. was founded in 1999 by Clark Benson and Karen DeMars Pillsbury. The Chicago-based business is privately held and has been profitable since early 2002. Revenues and EBITDA more than doubled from 2004 to 2005 and continues to grow. More than 1 million unique visitors hit the eCRUSH Network sites each month, and 90% are 13–19 years old.

eCRUSH.com, Inc.
2035 W Wabansia Ave
Second Floor
Chicago, Illinois 60647

Acquired by Hearst Magazines in January 2007. Users create a list of people they have crushes on, and the site e-mails all those people to ask them for a list of their crushes. If there's a match, eCRUSH connects them. In February, they plan to relaunch the websites for all these magazines with photos, video, podcasts – essentially, social networking, and sharing.

http://livedigital.com (LS)
Livedigital is a digital community that allows you to manage your entire digital lifestyle – from uploading photo and video albums, meeting friends, or just keeping a daily journal, all in one place! LiveDigital is a free community and always will be.

press@livedigital.com

(213) 408.0080
818 W. 7th Street
Suite 700
Los Angeles, CA 90017

http://www.talkcity.com (LS)
Chatting site
General inquiries:
Delphi Forums
25 Porter Road
Littleton, MA 01460
info@delphiforums.com

http://www.kuzoa.com/
Kuzoa is the world's first socially responsible, life-enhancing virtual living platform that features the Sentinel safety system and a vast array of activities that promote growth in the Seven Essential Life Foundations. Kuzoa is a truly unique environment full of curiosities that blur the line between virtual and real life and also offers the traditional social networking fare.

Press Inquiries: press@kuzoa.com

Kuzoa
15700 NE 15th Place
Vancouver, WA 98686

http://www.heycosmo.com/
Founded in November 2006, Arsenal Interactive, Inc. is a Web 2.0 social networking company. Arsenal Interactive next generation portal, HeyCosmo (Beta), is built upon its proven and scalable technologies by a team of experts with many years of experience in the fields of multimedia signal processing, and multimedia communications application, including advanced video/audio codecs, wireless multimedia, real time multimedia services application and multi-playable online games.

HeyCosmo allows friends, social communities and business people to simultaneously watch online content (YouTube, DailyMotion, Grouper, Revver, iFilm, MetaCafe, GoFish, BrightCove, Veoh and etc.), share high quality music (PodCast, MP3 and etc. from your favorite player such as iTunes, WinAmp, Windows Media Player, Real Player, and etc.), and interact through multi-way audio/video conferencing and desktop sharing. HeyCosmo gives people with common interests the freedom to easily find, engage, and participate in a broad range of live interactivity through its directory, IM, blog, and search engine.

James H. Im; Founder and CEO
Dr. K. Yang; CTO and VP, Engineering
Alvaro Saralegui; VP Sales and Business Development
Ricardo Gonzalez; VP Marketing and Product Management

mailto:webmaster@heycosmo.com

http://www.girlfriendscafe.com/
Founded by two best friends, Linda & Lee, in February 2007, the site is aimed at women in the United States and Canada.

GirlfriendsCafe.com
118 Flamingo Avenue
Daytona Beach, FL 32118
Telephone: 386-254-3425

E-Mail Contacts
Webmaster: webmaster@girlfriendscafe.com
Press and Media: press@girlfriendscafe.com
Advertising: admin@girlfriendscafe.com

http://www.herorbit.com/

HerOrbit.com is a women-centered social networking site connecting members to family, friends, businesses, and other people with similar interests world-wide. HerOrbit is owned and operated by HerOrbit, Inc.

The people at HerOrbit are committed to providing the best possible online social experience available today. That's why at HerOrbit we believe we are continually redefining online networking and creating lasting contributions to the members we serve.

HerOrbit is building a community for women to be used every day to connect, share, network, and stay informed, discussing topics that really matter to our members/users. Best of all, the service is free for all members.

Founded by Jennifer Bellofatto and Cherry Mendoza and based in Orange County, California

press@herorbit.com

http://teamsugar.com (LS)
TeamSugar is the place for you to meet friends, discuss the latest gossip, share online shopping finds, dish on fashion, learn beauty secrets, swap delicious recipes, blog about your day and much, much more.
Sugar Publishing Inc.,
One Sutter Street, 6th Floor,
San Francisco, California 94104.

support@sugarpublishing.com
Due to tight integration with the blogs PopSugar, DearSugar, TeamSugar, and FabSugar, users can quickly switch between the various sites and see the most recent content on each spin-off of the Sugar Network, a series of blogs that seem to target fashion-conscious women. The most popular is PopSugar, where celebrity gossip is the pressing issue of the day.

www.friendster.com
With more than 40 million members, Friendster is the best way to stay in touch with your friends, and it's the fastest way to discover the people and things that matter to you most.
Headquartered in the San Francisco Bay Area, Friendster aims to make the world a smaller place by bringing the power of social networking to every aspect of life, one friend at a time.
Entrepreneur Jonathan Abrams founded Friendster in 2002. The company is backed by Kleiner Perkins Caufield & Byers, Benchmark Capital, Battery Ventures, and individual investors.

Press contact:
Jeff Roberto
press@friendster.com

http://speecho.com (LS)
Speecho.com is an open, unrestricted online community that allows and encourages members to meet new friends and invite and reconnect with friends they invite into the service. Speecho.com members can talk for Free via VoIP (Voice Over Internet Protocol, i.e. a VoIP-enabled computer and headset) with anyone in a private chat session or totally public room,

party-line atmosphere. Florida-based. admin@speecho.com. Founder: Elliot Krasnow

http://shoutcentral.com/ (LS)
Based in Fairfax, Virginia and launched in late March 2006, Shoutcentral is a social networking site like MySpace but with AJAX messaging and real time chat built into your page, and you are provided with a list of your friends so you can instantly chat with whoever is online, simple, and easy.
In January 07, founder Brian Hoffman decides to sell due to his "lack of time to update and improve the site." Although the site is quite nice, it could use some improvements to bring it up to par with some of the larger social networks.

Brian Hoffman
brian@shoutcentral.com

http://matchactivity.com (LS)
MatchActivity.com is an activity — based site that connects people through I-on-I activities. It's for people who like to socialize, date, or simply meet new people for activities such as: bowling, concerts, movies, and sushi. MatchActivity uses shared interests to make finding a quality match much more fun, efficient, and honest. MatchActivity lets you immediately plan an activity; set the time and place; and find someone who shares your interests.

press@matchactivity.com

http://www.entertainmates.com/
Entertainmates.com provides a way for people of all ages and backgrounds to find people like themselves who enjoy the same hobbies and interests. We help people forge new friendships and provide expert advice on how to maintain them. Entertainmates.com was founded in January of 2002 and is owned and operated by Entertainmates Media Group, LLC. Based in New York City, we have a highly trained and professional staff of writers, programmers, and consultants that work hard to make your experience at our site fast, safe, and fun.

http://www.virb.com/
A place that lets you put all of the things that make you you – photos, videos, blogs – in one place. So you can find friends (and friends can find you). More specifically, VIRB° is our vision of a social community – done right. A website that combines you, your interests, your friends, and the things you like with music, art, fashion, film, and more. Stay connected with your friends. Find new music. View and upload good videos, photos and more.

Unborn Media, Inc.
119 Braintree Street, #605
Boston, MA 02134
Telephone: (617) 987-2324
Fax: (617) 987-2327
E-mail: legal@unbornmedia.com

http://tagged.com
Tagged.com is the premier social networking destination for the Millennial Generation and an ideal place for advertisers who are trying to reach the teen market. Greg Tseng co-founded Tagged in October 2004 and has served as Chief Executive Officer since its inception. He has been a driving force in creating Tagged.com with his partner, co-founder and long-time friend, Johann Schleier-Smith. On the board of directors (amongst others) Reid Hoffman is Founder & CEO of LinkedIn, an online professional networking service. Previously, Reid was EVP at PayPal, where he was in charge of all external relationships and payments infrastructure. In addition to Tagged, Reid serves on the Boards of Grassroots.com, Six Apart, and Vendio. Reid is an angel investor in Ironport Systems, Friendster, and Nanosolar.

http://360.yahoo.com/
Social networking for friends from Yahoo.

http://spaces.live.com/
Windows Live Spaces has a drag and drop profile page, so you can make your profile look the way you want it to and put the items on the profile page in the order you want. There are also different layouts and themes you can use for your Windows Live Spaces profile. There is a way for you to add music

and video you like to your profile page, but you need to host it elsewhere. There is even a photo album and blog on your Windows Live Spaces site.

http://www.piczo.com

Piczo has created a space that gives teens around the world the freedom and tools to express themselves and connect with friends in a safer social networking environment. Piczo allows its users to create fully customizable personal websites that do not require any understanding of html code. Users share their life stories with friends by designing their sites with multiple pages featuring photos, graphics, guest books, comment boards, music, and more. Each site can be linked to other friends' sites, and users can interact with them and their friends and meet new people online. Since its launch less than two years ago, Piczo has grown to over 10 million monthly unique visitors and 2.5 billion monthly page views solely through the viral efforts of its loyal members. Rave reviews from these users claim that Piczo is unmatched in the control it offers over their sites, ease-of-use, and 'walled-garden' approach with no searching for users.

http://www.friendsmix.net/

Friendsmix is a social networking site designed as a representation for the South. If you are from the South, then you will meet all types of friends here ranging from Texans to Georgians. But to join Friendsmix does not mean you have to be exclusively from the south. Fans of the South can join too. Membership is opened to everyone looking from a smaller community that puts the focus back into social community.

DATING

http://bigjock.com/ gay men

BigJock.com is an online community modeled for your life and style where you can connect with old friends, make new friends and meet their friends. Not just a social network, forum, meeting place, blog, photo album, diary or classified spot, BigJock.com aims to be the destination site for the Gay Community.

Based in San Francisco, California
Contact@BigJock.com

http://dlist.com/
Based in New York. Powered by KCT Partners LLC.

support@dlist.com

http://glee.com/site/glee.php
Community Connect, the largest niche social networking company and Wilderness Media & Entertainment (WME), the gay media and entertainment portfolio company owned by Logo founder Matt Farber, proudly announce their partnership to create the first social and professional networking site for the lesbian, gay, bisexual, and transgender (LGBT) community. The site, Glee.com, will be launched on CCI's technology platform that supports BlackPlanet.com, MiGente.com, and AsianAvenue.com and their sixteen million combined members. The focus of the brand will be Glee Groups—an outlet for networking around both social and professional interests. In the area of professional networking, members will be encouraged to create profiles, forums, and groups that will connect them with others in their chosen careers. Glee.com members will benefit from the already established relationship Community Connect has with Monster.com that delivers targeted job opportunities to its members.

Based in New York.

glhelp@mail.glee.com

http://www.connexion.org/ lesbians & gay men
Connexion is a social network with a twist. It not only allows you to meet new people and explore the connections among your friends, but it also allows you to be informed (in a non-obtrusive manner) about that most important of American institutions: Voting.Connexion contains a full range of searching and messaging systems. It is the place to meet people. But Connexion can do more. If you become an eActivist, it will inform you about upcoming votes and even tell you where you have to go to cast your ballot! Connexion is a not-for-profit enterprise.

webmaster@connexion.org
Connexion

419 Race St.
Denver CO 80206

http://lovetastic.com/ gay men
"Finally, gay personals that treat you like a person," the site says.
Lovetastic says its goal is to bring together husbands. It used to be
called Scene404. There are randomly generated interview questions
for profiles and nude or shirtless pictures are prohibited. The site is
ad free.
Founded by Ryan Norbauer & David Kooy.

http://www.ourchart.com/ (LS)
Showtime Networks and Ilene Chaiken, the creator and executive producer of
"The L Word," have formed a joint venture to launch a social networking site
for lesbians inspired by the pay cabler's series. The site, OurChart.com, will
feature content from the series and will launch next month along with Season
4 of "The L Word." With a title drawn from one of the series' central story
lines, OurChart is believed to be the first U.S.-based social networking site
launched around an entertainment property. It also is the first ad-supported
venture for the premium cable channel, which does not accept paid advertising
on its network.

launched: January 8, 2007

press@ourchartinc.com

http://www.socialbutter.com (LS)
This gay and lesbian social network is set to launch in mid-
January, providing a platform for "online socializing and real world
connections." It's the work of one developer and powered by Ruby on
Rails.

ann@socialbutter.com

http://fabfemme.com/
The premier online social network for gay and bisexual women passionate
about their lives and careers, FabFemme lets you create a lifestyle that's as

stylish and vibrant as you are. At FabFemme, you turn online connections into real-world fun. 30 Days free trial.

FabFemme Incorporated
590 Sixth Street, Suite 303
San Francisco, California 94103

E-mail: service@fabfemme.com

http://www.queercity.com (LS)
Tony Young co-founded QueerCity in April 2006 with former colleague Chris Bull and friend Oliver Kay.

QueerCity.com is the first truly interactive LGBT social networking and entertainment site. It provides users with a vibrant local experience—a single, comprehensive source for venue reviews, travel features and news—as well as entertainment, cultural, and community listings.
QueerCity.com is the ultimate insider's guide to what's hot, new, and undiscovered in major metropolitan areas. The city guides serve as a launching pad to a rich social networking experience based on shared interests and cultural activities.
In addition to user reviews, news stories, ratings, and commentary, QueerCity provides users with original expert reviews, syndicated content, and entertainment listings essential to gay life.

Last Call Media Inc.
PO Box 77002
San Francisco, CA 94107
Phone: 415-373-1881
Fax: 416-373-1886
General Information:
info@queercity.com

http://connect.olivia.com/
Lesbian community, founded in January 2007. Originally founded as a women's record label in 1973, Olivia has evolved over the years into the definitive leader in lesbian travel, offering a one-of-a-kind experience for women on our cruise and resort vacations.

http://crushspot.com/
CrushSpot.com is the premiere community website for meeting new people online, for platonic and/or romantic relationships. CrushSpot allows you to create a user profile where you can upload pictures and post a little or a lot about yourself. You can send members public messages on their message board or private messages in notes. CrushSpot users also receive a blog, or web log, short for online journal, where they can post their thoughts and opinions on things going on in their life or anything in general. There's also a forum for public discussion on a variety of topics. Photo albums, Chat Rooms, and a site Instant Mes senger are also in the works.

When was CrushSpot created?
CrushSpot.com was open for user registration as of March 7th, 2005. Design began late December 2004 and was continuously tested throughout the construction of the site.

http://sweetsecond.com/
Welcome to Sweet Second, a free online dating service for divorced singles. If you want to meet a new friend for fun, friendship, travelling, or love & romance, there's someone for everyone, and you'll find them at SweetSecond.com.

Tel: I-(800)-12345
Fax: I-(800)-12345
E-mail: info@sweetsecond.com
http://www.meetmoi.com (LS)

MeetMoi LLC developed the technology behind the MeetMoi website and dating service. The company intends to license its technology in other areas. The company has filed a provisional patent on the mapping technology it employs in its site. MeetMoi is based in New York City and is the brainchild of Andrew Weinreich. The inspiration for MeetMoi grew out of his frustration desperation with dating in New York. You can send Andrew an e-mail by writing to Andrew@meetmoi.com.

http://www.intellectconnect.com/
Intellect Connect offers an exclusive meeting place for thinkers, brainiacs and the intellectually curious. We know how hard it is to find these types of

people on regular online meeting sites, which is why we've brought them all together here. New York based.

http://www.muslimica.com
Muslimica is a Muslim matrimony site. The word 'Muslimica' is coined to mean 'Muslim continent'. The word 'Muslim' is suffixed with 'ica' to make it MUSLIMICA and sound like the continents Afr(ica), Amer(ica), Antart(ica), etc. We at Muslimica.com strive to provide our members a simple, easy to use, convenient, experience on a safe and secure website. Features include photo gallery, anonymous private mailbox, chat, privacy options, blogs, forum, polls, quizzes, rate photos, classifieds and much more.

SPECIAL INTEREST

Arts & Crafts

http://www.humblevoice.com
Humble Voice offers a variety of inspired features geared toward both local and widespread audiences to view and create artist profiles. Each profile offers ample views of photography, art, film, writing or music. By creating a profile, one can upload, maintain, and manage not only a community of friends and family, but also a vantage point to share your own artistic creations – in whichever form they may abound.

Each artist community homepage contains featured artists, each day's top listened to/viewed/read creations as well as a shout out to the newest members of each community. Members can manipulate their own profiles by uploading a profile photograph, their own art of any and all kinds, basic biographical information, messages and friends' profiles as well as unique-to-the-site features with bulletin boards, commentary, featured texts, blog space, and community actions and photos.

http://www.selfportrait.net/
Online community of artists (photography- music- film/video- writing- studio arts- acting- computer arts- fashion & dance). Artist's profiles are

ranked according to daily volume of their art views and art sales. Work exhibited on Selfportrait can be bought or sold.

Paris Ionescu, Chairman
Jonny Rooms, co-creator

Selfportrait.net and parent company SWIBcorp are located at 37 w. 28th st., New York, NY, 10001

http://designstolove.com/ (LS)
DesignsToLove is a free online gallery & community dedicated to craft. DesignsToLove receive approximately 200,000–300,000 views per month from craft enthusiasts from around the world.

jan@designstolove.com

http://lov.li/
Lov.li is a community of people who make art and crafts. Share your art, make friends, and buy things you love.
Portland, Oregon-based. Launched on January 12th, 2007.

http://www.artslant.com/ (LS)
Artslant is the brain child of three women – Catherine Ruggles, Amber Noland, and Georgia Fee. The concept for this site has been brewing since 2004, but the actual development began in May 2006.

Artslant is built on a ruby on rails platform with web 2.0 enhancements. It is designed to encourage and depend on input from our community. It is our fervent wish that this site becomes a reflection of our contempory art world: its faces, images, triumphs, and falls.

From our base in Los Angeles, we plan to spread the artslant spotlight throughout the art cities of the world.

Hi An:

We've looked at your website and read about your project. We will definitely write something for you and send it in the next couple of weeks. Let me know if you wish anything else.

Thanks for including us!

Georgia Fee

-Founders & management
Artslant was designed and built by Catherine Ruggles, Amber Noland, and Georgia Fee. After graduating from Yale University, Catherine Ruggles spent the next twenty-five years as a software developer and high tech executive, serving as the CTO for several start-ups in the Silicon Valley as well as heading up development teams for the Norton and Symantec products. Catherine built the artslant website over the course of about eight months, using Ruby on Rails software with web 2.0 enhancements to create a fluid and open community website. Amber Noland received her BFA from Otis College of Art and Design and her MFA from Claremont Graduate School. After graduating, Amber founded Art Collections Management, Inc., a full-service management company for the high-end art collector. She has worked with a select group of contemporary fine art collectors from around the world. Besides her expertise in the art market and art community, Amber designed the graphical interface of the artslant website, giving it that distinctive look and feel. Amber's intimate knowledge of the contemporary art scene underscores her development of the community focus found in Artslant. Georgia Fee received her MFA from California State University Los Angeles. After graduation, she became involved in numerous aspects of the professional art world: exhibiting, curating, and teaching. She spent five years working with the Armory Center for the Arts in developing and teaching arts curriculum as well as producing the projects room for their professional gallery. Georgia defined the basic idea for the website and developed its architecture along with Catherine Ruggles. Georgia's voice is heard throughout the site in her writing and vision. Together, the "artslant girls," as they loosely refer to themselves, manage and run the corporation.

-Founding year & address/nationality
Artslant inc. was formed in the US in November 2006 and is based in Los Angeles, CA. Their address is 8721 Santa Monica Blvd., Ste. 843, Los Angeles, CA 90069, USA.

-Target audience & membership level (number of users)
Artslant.com was launched in Los Angeles in February, 2007. Their target audience is comprised of the "arts inclined," including artists, art lovers and art professionals. The primary focus is on contemporary art, although historical museum shows are covered as well. The artslant target tends to be well-educated, affluent, and culturally astute, and ranges from the young, emerging artist and art goer to the mature art lover, collector and art professional. Their current user base is about three thousand per month, but the community is growing rapidly.

-The top three countries from which the artslant community comes
US, England and Germany

-Main technical features and possible features in the near future
A localized and comprehensive calendar of art exhibitions, openings and events that is city-specific; dynamic showcase of artists, arts organizations and art venues that has global reach; and community reviews and recommendations of exhibits and events.
Coming up: Expansion to other art cities in the US and Europe within the next year; flickr and You Tube mashups, video, and online messaging.

-Languages in which the service is available
English

Address:
8721 Santa Monica Boulevard, Ste. 843
Los Angeles, CA 90069
USA

Phone & fax: 310-882-5515
E-mail: artslant_info@artslant.com

http://makeoutclub.com/
Created from a small apartment in Cambridge, MA during the summer of 2000 by Gibby Miller.
Makeoutclub.com is an interactive online community for art and music oriented people interested in meeting one another. Indie rock kids, punks, hardcore kids, painters, photographers, writers, musicians, programmers, and record collectors are all part of our fold, and you are welcome here!

http://www.maccaca.com/ (LS)
The site to promote amateur artistic talent and provide a venue for the artists to showcase their talent. Bringing Aspirations One Step Closer to Your Dreams for artists. For consumers of artistic talent this site provides ample content to view artistic talent from around the world.

Launched on March 16th 2007. Florida based.
help@maccaca.com

Books

http://www.goodreads.com/ (LS)
Most book recommendation websites work by listing random people's reviews. On Goodreads, when a person adds a book to the site, all their friends can see what they thought of it. It's common sense. People are more likely to get excited about a book their friend recommends than a suggestion from a stranger. Since its launch in December 2006, Goodreads has grown exponentially, increasing its userbase nearly 4% a day. Users have reviewed seven thousand books this past month and show no signs of stopping.
Goodreads is a privately run website started in 2006 by software engineer and entrepreneur Otis Chandler. Prior to founding Goodreads, Otis was Product Manager of LoveHappens.com, a subsidiary of Tickle.com. Monster Worldwide purchased the company in 2004.
otis@goodreads.com

http://www.shelfari.com/
Seattle based network for book lovers.

http://www.gather.com (LS)
Writers, authors, photographers, and bloggers, Gather is the social networking site for you. Come together and meet like-minded people on Gather. Share your stories and write your articles on Gather and share them with other writers, authors, photographers and bloggers. Gather uses tags to help you find stories and articles you want to read. Earn Gather points by participating in Gather.

Public Relations
Kel Kelly
Kel & Partners
pr@gatherinc.com
Address
Gather Inc.
85 Devonshire St., 3rd Floor
Boston, MA 02109

http://www.revish.com/
An exciting new book review site launching on March 30th, 2007. Founded by Dan Champion.

http://bookmooch.com/ (LS)

BookMooch is a community for exchanging used books.

BookMooch lets you give away books you no longer need in exchange for books you really want.

- Give & receive: Every time you give someone a book, you earn a point and can get any book you want from anyone else at BookMooch. Once you've read a book, you can keep it forever or put it back into BookMooch for someone else, as you wish.
- No cost: there is no cost to join or use this web site: your only cost is mailing your books to others.
- Points for entering books: you receive a tenth-of-a-point for every book you type into our system, and one point each time you give a book away. In order to keep receiving books, you need to give away at least one book for every five you receive.
- Help charities: you can also give your points to charities we work with, such as children's hospitals (so sick kids can get a free book delivered to their beds), Library fund, African literacy, or to us to thank us for running this web site <grin>.
- World wide: You can request books from other countries, in other languages. You receive three points when you send a book out of your country, to help compensate you for the greater mailing cost, but it only costs the moocher two points to get the book. John Buckman, who runs BookMooch, has lived in California, England, France, and Germany, and he was frustrated by the vast number of books that were printed in just one country and not available in the other countries (for example, many books are published in Britain and never made available in America).
- Wishlist: you can keep a "book wish list" that will automatically arrive to you when you have the points and/or the book becomes available in our catalog.
- Feedback score: each time you receive a book, you can leave feedback with the sender, just like how eBay does it. If you keep your feedback score up, people are most likely to help you out when you ask for a book.

Founder is John Buckman. The company is California-based.

http://www.librarything.com
LibraryThing was created by Tim Spalding, a web developer and web publisher based in Portland, Maine. Tim also runs www.isidore-of-seville. com, www.ancientlibrary.com, www.bramblestory.com, and mothboard. com. Since becoming a "real" business in May, LibraryThing now employs a number of talented people. LibraryThing is a full-powered cataloging application, searching the Library of Congress, all five national Amazon sites, and more than sixty world libraries. You can edit your information, search and sort it, "tag" books with your own subjects, or use the Library of Congress and Dewey systems to organize your collection. If you want it, LibraryThing is also an amazing social space, often described as "MySpace for books" or "Facebook for books." You can check out other people's libraries, see who has the most similar library to yours, swap reading suggestions, and so forth. LibraryThing also makes book recommendations based on the collective intelligence of the other libraries.

http://www.mybloglog.com/ (LS)
MyBlogLog is launching this new Communities service to empower authors and readers to operate at the same level. For the first time, everyone who reads a web site or blog can learn about and engage with one another, and in the process take the conversation to a whole new level. Readers can become friends with other people who read your favorite blogs. See what else they're reading. Check out their MySpace and Friendster profiles and view their Flickr photostreams. Authors can learn more about their readers individually and as a group.
Bought by Yahoo in January 2007.

media@mybloglog.com

Cars

http://webridestv.com/
WebRidesTV was created by gearheads for gearheads.
We live for cars. We can't get enough of them. We breathe exhaust, drink gas, and eat donuts. Our cell phones don't ring, they rev. And our computers roll supercar screensavers. Our obsession has destroyed friendships, ruined relationships, and depleted bank accounts.

Our goal is to be the web's premier provider of original auto media. The videos you see here are original. We shoot the footage, we design the graphics, and we cut the content. We're out to prove that auto content can be informative without being boring. If you've got motor oil in your veins, this is the place to be.

http://www.infieldparking.com/ (LS)
Infield Parking leverages the power of social networking to bring together the millions of race fans eager to share their passion for the sport with fellow racing fans and also makes it easy for fans to connect directly with their favorite drivers, teams, and sponsors. Users can easily create their personal profile ("Infield Parking Space") and post photos, blogs, podcasts and video clips to share with their growing circle of friends in the community.

An,

Please see the information below. Thanks for you interest in our site.

-Ed

-Founders & management
Co-founders: Dale Earnhardt Jr, Ed Sullivan, Maz Nadjm;
Management: Ed Sullivan- CEO; Dale Earnhardt Jr- President; Kelley Elledge- Vice President; Thayer Lavielle- Vice President

-Founding year & address/nationality
Founded: Dec 2006
Address: Infield Parking, LLC; P.O. Box 209; Mooresville, NC 28115
Nationality: US

-Target audience & membership level (number of users)
Target Audience: NASCAR Race Fans
Membership Level: Under 1 Million

-Top 3 countries in which the community is used
United States
Canada

UK

-Main technical features and possible features in the near future
Full standard social network platform
Mobile platform- summer 2007

-Languages in which the service is available
Currently available in English
Spanish & French by end of 2007

Infield Parking's goal is to become the Ultimate On-Line Fan Experience for NASCAR's 75 Million race fans. Infield Parking features participation from all of the Top Nextel Cup drivers and is an enabling tool for the entire NASCAR racing ecosystem.

Infield Parking, LLC
P.O. Box 209
Mooresville, NC 28115
CEO & Co-Founder- Ed Sullivan
President & Co-Founder- Dale Earnhardt Jr.
CTO & Co-Founder- Maz Nadjm
feedback@infieldparking.com

Comics

http://www.comicspace.com/
ComicSpace is a place for comic fans and creators to connect with each other. Comic creators can host their comics for free.

http://www.hypercomics.com/
HyperComics is the interactive social network and industry resource where next-generation amateur and professional comic book creators can showcase their original comic books, discuss them with their peers and find an audience. Launched on January 2007.
Based in Orange County, CA, Planetwide Media is a provider of innovative software applications, proprietary online technology and online video games.

http://www.mytoons.com/
Video and image-sharing site for cartoons.
MyToons is the world's greatest online animation community. It's the place where people who really love animation "from seasoned industry pros to rabid animation fans" can upload and share their creations and animated favorites with the entire world for free.

http://www.animeonline.com/
Based in Texas. Launched in February 2007.

Welcome to animeOnline. And let us be the first to congratulate you. You're about to embark on a life-changing online experience. Not like moving to a new town life-changing, or even winning the lottery life-changing. It's going to be a bit more subtle than that. In fact, it'll probably mostly consist of you changing your homepage to animeOnline.

Oh sure, you love your Yahoos and your Googles, loading patiently whenever you open a browser, and we don't begrudge you that, what with their news and the e-mail and their double-o's. And many of you start each online experience with MySpace, checking up on friends, family, and stalking your ex-boyfriends and girlfriends. We're down with that too. And surely there are a few of you dedicated anime fans who open your browsers to anime news and fansites. We say right on.

But we also say: it could be easier, couldn't it? For instance, if there were a site that had news and a social network all in one, well, that would be pretty convenient. And if it had some additional entertainment and informational resources on it, that would be great. And if a site had all that, and then it was tailored specifically to fans of anime, manga and Japanese culture, well...then it would be animeOnline.

We're trying to do it all at once. Anime news and information, updated constantly, every day, an online community tailor-made for (and by) anime and manga fans, and entertainment in every way we and you can think of. It's kind of like one big, 24-hour, 7 days a week, 365 days a year anime convention, except it's free, and there's a smaller chance you'll see Man-Faye. But you don't have to take this small paragraph's word for it — we invite you to take a quick tour to find out everything that animeOnline offers, what we're trying to do and mainly how this site is yours as much as it is ours.

Fashion

http://www.nirvanawoman.net/
In 2004, a group of professional South Asian-American women broached the idea of launching a high-fashion magazine reflecting the ultimate in South Asian infused design, beauty, and lifestyle.

Ethnic magazines were one of the fastest growing segments of the publishing industry; however, for these creative and dynamic young women there remained a void. No single publication captured their lives – grounded in the grace and elegance of the East while moving at the trendsetting pace of the West. They also recognized that high-fashion and luxury brands were missing a platform from which to demonstrate their recognition of the value of today's South Asian-American woman.

Nirvana Woman strives to fill that void, celebrating the modern South Asian-American Woman – her sophisticated style, progressive outlook, and desire for the ultimate that life has to offer. Nirvana Woman's mission is to represent the glamorous, sophisticated, and confidant South Asian-American woman.

82 Pioneer Way, Suite 110
Mountain View, CA 94041 (U.S.A.)
Tel: 650-210-3788
Fax: 650-210-3601
info@nirvanamedia.com

http://www.fashmatch.com/ (LS)
FashMatch is an online community for anyone who shares a love for clothes, fashion and dressing stylishly.
FashMatch is based on two things: The first one is fun. Creating your own looks via the terrific brands, FashMatch not only provides you with an endless source of entertainment but also saves you time finding the look that is right for you. The second one is sharing the fun! Like a great friend, FashMatch

is the ideal companion, offering to the visitors an opportunity not to be only their own stylist but also an influence and inspiration to someone else.

Hi An,

Let's start with this info. Let me know if you need anything else!

What is FashMatch.com?
FashMatch.com provides a vertical social network where users can get or give fashion advice. What we do is leverage the good sense of style of our users to provide personalized, dynamic and virtually unlimited advice on 'what to wear' or 'how to dress.' At FashMatch.com people can look for a specific item (something they own perhaps) and see what other users think goes along nicely with it. Indeed, people hardly look for or buy complete outfits but rather look for a 'top that would go along nicely with these pants.' Alternatively, users can share their take on fashion by making matches and sharing them with the world. These matches are ranked by all users so that if someone is looking to match a specific item she finds first what everyone likes best. To this date we have over 4,400 matches made by our users, and we are growing exponentially.

-Founders
Jonathan Gheller — CEO

-Founding year & address/nationality
Nov, 2006. USA, Miami.

-Target audience & membership level (number of users)
Currently women of all ages. Plans to cater other demographics.

-Top 3 countries in which the community is used
USA, Italy and Japan

-Main technical features and possible features in the near future
An open, virtual closet where users can both build matches (outfits) and also see matches built by other users.

-Languages in which the service is available
Currently English.

jon@fashmatch.com
Miami-based, founded in 2006.

Film

Spout — www.spout.com
A community of film lovers, who earn their money by selling DVDs.
Spout LLC
80 Ottawa Avenue NW
Suite 310
Grand Rapids, MI 49503 (Michigan)

www.flixster.com
San Francisco
Flixster is community for movie fans of all shapes and sizes.

http://www.filmspot.com/
The sleekest, most in-depth online movie resource, FilmSpot features movie summaries, critical opinions, trailers, news, photos, actor and character guides, celebrity bios, theatrical and DVD release schedules, and box-office results.

Fans can easily add their names to the site's credits via movie reviews (both text and video), ratings, actor bios, blogs, forums, polls, trivia, and images.

A CNET Networks Entertainment property, FilmSpot seamlessly connects fans with related content in other entertainment zones, including television, music, and gaming.

http://www.jaman.com/ (LS)
Jaman is a global online community for people passionate about world cinema — a place to discover, enjoy, and connect with cinephiles. We provide a secure way for filmmakers to distribute films with unmatched cinematic fidelity over broadband. Launch at Demo on February 1, 2007.

Based in 607 Market Street, 3rd floor, San Francisco 94105, California.
Contact: Danielle Farrar
dfarrar@jaman.com

http://filmties.com/

FilmTies.com is the world's first Membership based, Social Network Interactive Film Financing Community. We provide the complete interactive tools to our members who visit the site to socialize, meet friends, classmates, and interact with the film and music industry. FilmTies.com is part of the AdFilmTies Film Finance Model; it empowers screenwriters, musicians, actors, directors, producers, sponsors, and most importantly the movie watching public.

FilmTies.com is a celebration of ideas, dreams, and visions. FilmTies.com launched with our screenplay and music competition that brings concepts to our members who will vote and decide. It is the goal of FilmTies.com by and through the AdFilmTies Patent Pending Film Finance model to fund $100,000,000 in independent film productions over the next three years by tapping into the 12 billion dollar a year internet advertising industry.

By forming a successful cooperative of advertisers, artists, and audience, the patent pending AdFilmTies Film Financing Model was conceived. Today, FilmTies.com is proud to provide both an opportunity and the necessary funding for dedicated artists, writers and composers hoping to find a large audience and financing for their inspiring works.

Based in New York.

Food & Beverage

http://bakespace.com/ (LS)

BakeSpace.com was created by media producer (and avid baker) Babette Pepaj as the first true social networking website devoted to bringing together people who enjoy cooking and baking. It's an online community where you can make new friends, exchange recipes, share ideas, find answers to your questions, download coupons and, in general, get inspired about one of life's great pleasures.

pr@BakeSpace.com

http://www.biteclub.com/

The Biteclub was formed by Sonny, Randy, and Mark, who are all in the restaurant and bar life.

The site is operated by SoRaMa, LLC. at 1403 28th Street, Sacramento, CA 95816. The phone number is (916) 452-3335. feedback@biteclub.com

http://www.friendseat.com/
A Web Social community focusing on the dining and culinary arts.

May 1, 2007 – FriendsEAT.com announced today the U.S. beta release of their food and dining Web community. FriendsEat.com is a social network, showcasing a plethora of user-generated content such as customizable blogs, personal pages, recipes, events, and restaurant reviews.

"FriendsEAT provides an important service for an audience that has not been properly engaged in social networks," said Antonio Evans, the site's Founder. "Our thousands of users are young professionals who see dining as a distinct culture and think of their personal homepage as their spokesperson."

http://www.grouprecipes.com/ (LS)
Group Recipes wants to be the world's neatest food site. From meeting other food lovers to nifty recipe predictions and taste compatibility, Group Recipes has your grub needs covered. The project's goal is to harness the tastebuds of the masses to create a really useful resource for food lovers.
Founded in October 2006 by Kristopher Lederer in San Diego, in California.
lab@grouprecipes.com

http://corkd.com/
Cork'd is a free service for wine aficionados. You can use Cork'd to catalog, rate, and review wines you've tasted. You can also keep track of wines you'd like to try and buy as well as subscribe to what your buddies have reviewed. Cork'd is a product of Tundro, a development agency building web applications. Founders: Dan Cederholm is a designer and author, specializing in web and interface design. Dan Benjamin is a programmer and writer specializing in web applications, database design, usability, and business development.

http://extratasty.com/ (LS)
Social network with coctail recipes.

Founded by Jacob DeHart and Jake Nickell

4043 N Ravenswood Avenue 106
Chicago, IL 60613
info@extratasty.com

http://www.coastr.com/ (LS)
Coastr is a simple and free service for people who love beer. Our goal is to allow you to connect with other passionate, like-minded people in order to discover new brews that you would have otherwise not known about.
To get started, sign up for an account and create a list of your favorite beers and places to drink beer. The more beers and places you add to your list, the more you'll start to become connected to our ever-growing network of beer fanatics. Coastr was started last year as an experiment in social networking. It was conceived, designed, programmed, and is maintained by Brian Eng of Luckymonk, and none of it was built while sober.

coastr@gmail.com

http://www.chugd.com/
The Web 2.0 social network for beer lovers. Founded by Chris Matthieu.

Gaming & 3D

www.Warcraft.com
World of Warcraft is a massively multiplayer online role-playing game (MMORPG). In World of Warcraft, thousands of players will have the opportunity to adventure together in an enormous, persistent game world, forming friendships, slaying monsters, and engaging in epic quests that can span days or weeks.

Managed by Blizzard Entertainment
P.O. Box 18979
Irvine, CA 92623

http://www.dotsoul.net/ (LS)
2247 Vineyard St

Wallaku, Maui HI 96793
lauramarle@dotsoul.net

http://myminilife.com/
MyMiniLife is located in sunny Los Angeles, California, USA. Please send
an e-mail to info@myminilife.com or feel free to talk to us on AOL Instant
Messenger.

http://www.there.com/
There is an online getaway where you can hang out with your friends and
meet new ones — all in a lush 3D environment that's yours to explore and
help build. Check it out here!

About Makena Technologies
Makena Technologies, Inc. is a privately held corporation, headquartered in
Silicon Valley, CA. Entrepreneur Michael Wilson founded the company in
2005.

Management Team
Michael Wilson
CEO

Steve Victorino
President and COO

Press:
press@thereinc.com

There — Silicon Valley
1855 South Grant Street
3rd Floor
San Mateo, CA 94402
Tel: (650) 433-4040
Fax: (650) 433-4060

There — Southern California
c/o Makena Technologies

1833 S. Coast Highway Suite 220
Laguna Beach, CA 92651

http://www.whyville.net/ (LS)
Whyville is a "Second Life'" for kids.
300 S Raymond Avenue #7, Pasadena, CA 91105
infoplease@whyville.net

http://www.imvu.com (LS)
IMVU is a consumer internet startup in downtown Palo Alto. IMVU makes the world's best 3D instant messenger, which is now in beta testing with more than 1 million customers around the world. The service lets users express themselves by creating and customizing a 3D avatar with a wide variety of clothes, accessories, pets, and scenes. The service has been live for over a year, and it is generating a rapidly growing revenue stream from the sale of virtual currency. IMVU's culture is maniacally focused on rapidly developing and testing features and business ideas to learn from our customers what will make a great business. IMVU has top tier venture investors and an extraordinarily talented team with deep experience in games and virtual worlds.

press@imvu.com
411 High Street
Palo Alto,
CA 94301

http://www.gamervision.com/
Gamervision LLC
P.O. Box 1806
Doylestown, PA (Pennsylvania) 18901
USA
(215) 297-8760
info@gamervision.com

http://www.kongregate.com/ (LS)
Founded in 2006 and currently in a state of heavy development, Kongregate seeks to create the leading online hub for players and game developers to

meet up, play games, and operate together as a community. By wrapping user-submitted Flash games with various community features, Kongregate's site serves as a unique way for users to play great web-based games alongside friends. Anyone can add their own games to Kongregate's library in a process that's fast and simple. Kongregate operates with an understanding of how difficult it can be for talented game developers – from the aspiring gamesmith to the independent studio – to get the recognition and compensation that they deserve. That's why Kongregate shares microtransaction and advertising revenue with contributing developers, who retain the full rights to their games.

430 Fillmore St. Suite A
San Francisco, CA 94117
inquiries@kongregate.com

www.activeworlds.com
Active Worlds, the web's most powerful Virtual Reality experience, lets you visit and chat in incredible 3D worlds that are built by other users. Think you have what it takes to build your own world or Virtual Reality game? Active Worlds is the place for you, where in minutes you can create fascinating 3D worlds that others can visit and chat in. The Active Worlds Universe is a community of hundreds of thousands of users that chat and build 3D virtual reality environments in millions of square kilometers of virtual territory.

Activeworlds Inc.
95 Parker Street
Newburyport, MA 01950
Telephone: (978) 499-0222
Facsimile: (978) 499-0221

http://www.sayswap.com/
The SaySwap network unites gamers with common interests to swap games, stories, and hints. We are the engine that powers a thriving community growing by up to thousands of users each day.

Our network of game swapping platforms enable Gamers to get video games for a combination of Purchase Points and Trading Tokens. Any games that you get are owned by you. You can keep them or at some point send them to another gamer for new Purchase Points so you can get another game.

Founded by Brad Greenspan, the founder of MySpace.

PO Box 2541
Maple Grove, MN 55311-9998

http://secondlife.com/
Second Life is one of several virtual worlds that have been inspired by the science fiction novel *Snow Crash* by Neal Stephenson and the cyberpunk literary movement. The stated goal of Linden Lab is to create a world like the Metaverse described in the novel *Snow Crash*, a user-defined world of general use in which people can interact, play, do business, and otherwise communicate. Despite its prominence, it has notable competitors, among them Active Worlds, considered by some to be the founding company of the 3D internet concept in 1997, There, and newcomers such as Entropia Universe and the Dotsoul Cyberpark.

http://www.vlb.mtv.com/
MTV Virtual Hills - Following up on the launch of Virtual Laguna Beach, MTV is launching MTV Virtual Hills — a 3D world based around the MTV show "The Hills." It's powered by the makers of There.com, a rival of Second Life that didn't get so much traction.

http://www.greatgamesexperiment.com/
Social network for gamers, developers, and publishers of games. By providing a free resource for developers to network and promote their own games, users have an opportunity to play games that cannot be found on other aggregation sites. Along with indie games, GGE hosts games ranging from free Flash games to old classics and mainstream commercial titles.

Ratings, recommendations, and popularity statistics for each game ensures that the cream of the digital crop rises to the top in dynamic fashion. Tags, friendships, and comments supply a more personalized means of distinguishing the exact types of game a user wants to play. The games themselves can be downloaded from their individual game pages, and many are even available to play instantly in your browser. Personalized gamer badges let others know what games users are playing and can be added to blogs, forums, and social networking sites by embedding the provided html code. All of these features add up to a centralized location for a large audience with a specific focus on the gaming industry.

GarageGames, Inc.
245 West 5th Ave
Eugene, OR 97401
USA

http://www.kaneva.com
Kaneva is the online "canvas" (Kaneva is canvass in Latin), where anyone can showcase and share their passions, interests and talents with the world. A truly innovative Social Entertainment Network, Kaneva fuses self expression through the creative sharing of media with the power of social networking and the imaginative forum of a 3D Virtual World to offer an interactive entertainment experience like never before. We are not about Internet TV or just shared video. Gone are the days when you just lean back and watch entertainment. Kaneva invites everyone to lean in, engage, and interact with the best in both amateur and professional content on the Web...online and in a Virtual World. Kaneva empowers anyone to create their own Profile or Channel for total self-expression. Whether it's creating their own easily customizable Profile all about them or a topically rich Channel, Kaneva provides the ability to share, comment, rave, tag, and search a wide range of media including videos, blogs, photos, music/audio, games, and even a 3D virtual world. Kaneva is closely connecting people through media – giving the community the ability to find, meet and socialize with one another around their passions and interests in a way that is exciting, fun, and rewarding.

Christopher W. Klaus - Founder / Chief Executive Officer
Greg Frame - Co-Founder / Chief Gaming Officer
Robert Frasca - Chief Operating Officer
Animesh Saha - Vice President of Engineering
Michael Dowdle - Vice President of Business Development

5901 C Peachtree-Dunwoody Rd. NE
Suite 300
Atlanta, Georgia 30328
USA

http://www.flowplay.com/
Online social-gaming site targeted at 13- to 17-year-olds. Participants create identities, choose their games and interact with others. They play on the same team and learn how to work together.

Team
Derrick Morton, CEO
Doug Pearson, CTO
Christian Oestlien, Co-founder

Contact
506 2nd avenue 4th floor
Seattle, wa 98027
Phone: 206-219-0537
Fax: 206-418-6683

http://www.areae.net/ (LS)
Areae, Inc. was founded in July of 2006. We're venture-backed now and run by our President, Raph Koster, and John Donham, veterans of the whole "massively multiplayer" scene. We're working on some new tech that will literally change how virtual worlds are made. Areae is an MMOG similar to Second Life.

Raph Koster, President
John Donham, VP of Production
Areae, Inc.
11770 Bernardo Plaza Court
Suite 101
San Diego, CA 92128
Press: pr@areae.net

Good Causes

http://www.zaadz.com/ (LS)
We're in the process of building the most inspired community of people in the world...social networking with a purpose, a community of seekers and conscious entrepreneurs circulating wisdom and inspiration and wealth and all that good stuff. We're passionate about inspiring and empowering people to bring their dreams to life, learning and growing and getting paid to do what they love, using their greatest gifts in the greatest service to the world. You can also contact the Zaadz Wizards or send any inquiries directly to Matthew via Zaadz mail, direct e-mail:
matthew@zaadz.com , or by phone at 1-888-MY-ZAADZ.

http://dianovo.com/
An online community for people interested in helping themselves and the planet.

Jedi Wright
Co-founder and COO
Dianovo, Inc.
1067 Summit Road
Watsonville, California 95076
phone: 831.274.2727

E-mail: jedi@dianovo.com

http://www.2people.org/
The mission of 2People is sustainability in one generation. To achieve this, we must make the connections between many issues, from pollution and poverty to women's rights and democracy. However, we have come to believe that the disruption of our climate threatens to make all other sustainability goals unachievable. Therefore, our immediate goal is to build an overwhelming public mandate for real solutions to the climate crisis. We are a non-profit organization, started by Phil Mitchell. You can contact us at info@2people.org.

http://www.riverwired.com/
Very quickly, green living has become everyday living, and RiverWired, the new eco-friendly online destination, is here for you.

RiverWired is the one place online for you and your friends to find more. More inspiration. More knowledge. More fun. Whether you want to find the perfect hybrid vehicle or simple, practical ideas for your greener lifestyle, we've got the best of the web information and community for you. Maybe you're curious to hear how other people make green choices in their daily lives, or you'd like to join the conversation and blog about your eco experiences. If it's friendship you're looking for, why not make a friend who shares your interest in getting more out of living a greener life?

Here are the basics: RiverWired is a content and social networking site dedicated to all things green. Our platform makes finding information, making friends and posting content easy, fun, and rewarding. We search article, blog, audio, and video material on sustainability and green living from all over the web and give you the most relevant items in easy-to-find format. We provide you with forums to post videos and pictures, join a blog discussion, invite friends and colleagues, and create a group or club. Our mission is to help make your life and our world greener and better.

Riverwired Team
Catherine Billon, Founder and CEO
Cris Popenoe, Executive VP Development
14 Fifth Avenue, Suite 2D
New York, NY 10011
press@riverwired.com

http://change.org/
Today as citizens of the world, we face a daunting array of social and environmental problems ranging from health care and civil rights to global warming and economic inequality. For each of these issues, whether local or global in scope, there are millions of people who care passionately about working toward a solution but have no way of connecting with each other to advance a common goal.

Change.org aims to transform social activism by serving as the central platform that connects likeminded people, whatever their interests, and enables them to exchange information, share ideas, and collectively act to address the issues they care about.

Change.org was conceived by Ben Rattray in the summer of 2005. With a friend from Stanford, Mark Dimas, and with the support of a founding team of Darren Haas, Rajiv Gupta, and Adam Cheyer, Change.org was finally launched in February 2007.

http://www.idealist.org/
On Idealist, you can imagine a better world, connect with people who want to help build it, take action in your community, reach out to others, post, and find nonprofit jobs, volunteer opportunities, events, and more, and donate to support all this.

Founded by Ami Dar, Executive Director (NYC).

New York City
Action Without Borders/Idealist.org
360 West 31st Street, Suite 1510
New York, NY 10001
United States
General inquiries, billing, and media: 212-843-3973
Questions about posting on Idealist.org: 646-290-7725
Fax: 212-564-3377
Hours: Monday to Friday, 7 – 4 EST

Portland, OR
Action Without Borders/Idealist.org
1220 SW Morrison, 10th Floor
Portland, OR 97205
United States
Please contact our Portland, OR office for questions and information regarding our nonprofit career fairs, graduate school fairs, nonprofit career and human resources programs, and partnerships.
Tel: 503-227-0803
Fax: 503-914-0344

Hours: Monday to Friday, 7 – 4 EST

Washington, DC
Action Without Borders/Idealist.org
1776 Massachusetts Avenue NW
Suite 450
Washington, DC 20036
United States

Buenos Aires
Acción Sin Fronteras/Idealistas.org
Viamonte 1181, Piso 6
(C1053 ABW), Buenos Aires
Argentina
Please contact our Buenos Aires office for questions about our Spanish-language website, Idealistas.org.
Tel: (54-11) 5238-2294 or (54-11) 5238-2295
Fax: (54-11) 5239-1980
Hours: Monday to Friday, 9:00a.m. – 5:30p.m.

Our English-language press liaison is:
Amelia Byers, Director of Community Outreach
She can be reached at our New York City office:
(1) 212-843-3973
Monday to Friday, 9:00a.m. – 5:30p.m. Eastern

Our Spanish-language press liaison is:
Rosario González Morón
She can be reached at our Buenos Aires office:
(54-11) 5238-2294 or/o
(54-11) 5238-2295
Monday to Friday, 9:00a.m. – 5:30p.m.

Our French-language press liaison is
Pabló Tiscornia, Coordinator
He can be reached at our Buenos Aires office:
(54-11) 5238-2294 or (54-11) 5238-2295
Monday to Friday, 9:00a.m. – 5:30p.m.

http://www.begreennow.com/
BeGreen Carbon Offsets is the latest innovative product offered by
Green Mountain Energy Company, one of the leading providers of
renewable energy in the nation. Green Mountain began in 1997 with a
simple idea: "to change the way power is made." The company began in
the renewable electricity market with the belief that if given a choice,
consumers will choose a cleaner electricity product over polluting fossil
fuels.

Green Mountain Energy Company
P.O. Box 689008
Austin, TX 78768

http://www.stepitup2007.org/
This is our organizing hub for a National Day of Climate Action – April
14th, 2007. On this one spring day, there will be hundreds and hundreds
of rallies all across the country. We hope to have gatherings in every state,
and in many of America's most iconic places: on the levees in New Orleans,
on top of the melting glaciers on Mt. Rainier, even underwater on the
endangered coral reefs off Key West.

We also need rallies outside churches, along the tide lines in our coastal
cities, in cornfields and forests and on statehouse steps. Every group
will be saying the same thing: "Step it up, Congress! Cut Carbon
80% by 2050." As people gather, we'll link pictures of the protests
together electronically via the web – before the weekend is out, we'll
have the largest protest the country has ever seen, not in numbers but
in extent. From every corner of the nation we'll start to shake things
up.

stepitup2007@gmail.com

(802) 735-1270
(866) 289-7010 (Toll Free)

12 North Street
Burlington, VT (Vermont)
05401

http://www.care2.com
Over two thousand interest groups including Cat Lovers, Human Rights activists, Healthy Cooking, Spirituality and more!
Free photo album service—unlimited storage
Express yourself through network messaging.
Meet new friends/reconnect with old.
Birthday reminders.
Share. Debate. Have fun. Make a difference!
All 100% free.

Care2.com, Inc.
275 Shoreline Drive, Suite 150
Redwood City, CA 94065
Phone: 650-622-0860
Fax: 650-622-0870

Health

http://www.patientslikeme.com/ (LS)
PatientsLikeMe is more than a company. We're building a worldwide community of patients, doctors, researchers, organizations, and companies working together to create a new system of medical care by patients for patients. We're here to give patients the power to control their disease and to share what they learn with others. PatientsLikeMe Inc. is a privately funded (external funding received in Feb 2007) for-profit company tasked with making the PatientsLikeMe vision a reality. Our goal is to enable people to share information that can improve the lives of patients diagnosed with life-changing diseases. To make this happen, we've created a platform for collecting and sharing real world, outcome-based patient data (patientslikeme.com) and are establishing data-sharing partnerships with doctors, pharmaceuticals, medical device companies and non-profits. Contact us if you're interested in working together to achieve our goals.

Founded in 2004 by three MIT engineers whose collective experience spans from running the world's only non-profit biotechnology laboratory to large-scale online commerce applications.

E-mail: support@patientslikeme.com
postal mail:
PatientsLikeMe Inc.
222 Third Street, Suite 0200
Cambridge, MA 02142

http://www.dailystrength.org
Social networking and support for patients.
DailyStrength was created by Doug Hirsch, Josh DeFord, and Lars Nilsen.
We are three internet veterans with more than twenty years of experience
conceiving, building, and running the largest communities on the web,
including Yahoo Mail, Yahoo Photos, Yahoo Personals, Yahoo Groups,
GeoCities, Facebook, My Yahoo, Yahoo Message Boards, and more.

http://www.activevibe.com/
ActiveVibe brings you the best in fitness and health. We are launching the
online resource for all your active lifestyle needs. We bring you the best
coaches, the best events, and the best workout programs. We are also
bringing you the online fitness and health community for you to meet and
get moving other active people just like yourself. Launch in Summer 2007.

http://taumed.com/
TauMed is a virtual health community for people to ask, share, interactively
navigate, and search the most relevant personalized consumer health
information available on the web. Instead of shuffling through countless web
pages of irrelevant information, we have created a user-experience whereby
consumers can connect quickly with the most relevant health information.

Our mission is two-fold: to create virtual health communities where people
may ask and share health information with other community members and
to offer a search engine with the most relevant and credible consumer health
information available on the web. Founded in December 2006.

Our Investors

We are a privately held company. We are funded by private individual
investors:

Tauseef Bashir
President and CEO

Ewald Pretner, M.D.
V.P. and Chief Medical Officer (C.M.O.)

Sung Yong Chun
V.P. of Engineering

For press inquiries e-mail pr@taumed.com.

http://www.revolutionhealth.com/community
Portal and social network about health(care).

Revolution Health's objective is to give consumers more choice and control over their health care, enabling all of us to live healthier, better lives.

We're doing that in three ways.

We're creating a resource you can rely on. A place you can go to learn about all of the aspects of your health, from sources you can trust. Of course, we want to be the place you turn to when you have a symptom you are concerned about. But RevolutionHealth.com shouldn't just be a place you visit when you're sick — we want it to be a place you visit regularly to stay healthy. Indeed, we think there has been too much focus on treating ailments and not enough focus on prevention and wellness. So you'll find more than one hundred fun, easy to use tools to help you and your family get and stay healthy.

But perhaps more than anything else, RevolutionHealth.com is a community, where you'll find support and insight from people who have been where you are. For example, if you or someone in your family is battling cancer, you can connect with others who are living through that experience. You'll learn what worked—or didn't work—for them. Or you can set personal healthy living goals, and we'll connect you with people like you, who have set similar goals. It's a unique, dynamic community we'll all build together.

Additionally, we've created Revolution Ratings to help people when they are looking for a doctor or hospital or evaluating treatment options. Isn't it crazy that we have ratings to help us pick movies, restaurants, and hotels but no comparable tools to help evaluate doctors, hospitals, and treatments? We aim to change that — and with your help, we will.

On our own, we can each do a little. Working together, we can do a lot. That's the "people powered health" philosophy that underlies RevolutionHealth.com.

Although we are striving to use the power of the Internet to empower people and ignite a revolution in health, we realize that health is complex, and that not every problem — not every challenge — not every question can be dealt with online. Sometimes, you just need somebody to talk to, to help walk you through your diagnosis or navigate the complex health care system.

So we've created a membership program, as an optional adjunct to our RevolutionHealth.com free site. And we've worked hard to add as many benefits as we can while keeping the price as affordable as possible. You can call us and speak with someone who can help. Whether it's a question about a diagnosis, difficulty finding a doctor or issues with your insurance company, we'll intervene and handle it on your behalf. We stand ready to help. And to thank the pioneers who join us during this preview period and help us build RevolutionHealth.com, we're pleased to waive the membership fee during 2007.

More than 40 million Americans don't have insurance, and many of them don't really know where to turn. And a growing number of Americans are being offered new kinds of health plans by their employers, and the choices can be confusing. We want to help there too.

When it comes to health insurance, we don't believe that one size fits all. We think it has to be personalized to meet your needs. That's why we've created a marketplace that will bring you a wide variety of insurance options along with the tools and information you need to make the right choice for you and your family.

Steve Case
Chairman
Revolution Health & ex AOL

Our Parent Company

To learn more about our parent company, Revolution LLC, please visit: www.revolution.com .

Mailing Address
If you'd like to write to us, please send your correspondence to our mailing address:
Revolution Health
P.O. Box 58174
Charleston, WV 25358-0174

Corporate Office
Our headquarters address is:
Revolution Health Group
Ste. 600
1250 Connecticut Avenue, NW
Washington, DC 20036-2651

media@revolutionhealth.com

https://spinal-cord-injury.clinicahealth.com/
Welcome to the Christopher and Dana Reeve Foundation paralysis community!

While paralysis can occur from trauma, disease or birth condition, many of the day to day medical and lifestyle issues are the same for all, regardless of diagnosis. This is the place on the Internet to connect with experts, ask questions, meet friends, and share stories – all within a reliable, safe and secure environment.

ClinicaHealth
2200 Wilson Blvd.
Arlington, VA 22201
703.243.0303

spinalcordinjury@clinicahealth.com
www.clinicahealth.com

http://hivconnect.net/
HIVConnect is committed to making a difference in the daily lives of HIV-positive people.

Our membership is composed of HIV-positive people and their loved ones all integrated with the healthcare community in a safe, private environment.

HIVConnect provides information in a unique way with a library of current articles from medical journals, as well as published and personal articles contributed to the library by healthcare providers, HIVConnect writers, and the members. We encourage members to post comments on articles giving them the opportunity to share their experience on any topic.

A community for the 'long term survivor.'

HIV and the medications used to treat it are both evolving. Those who have lived with HIV for a long period of time have stories and experiences that must be shared. These stories must be made available to other long term survivors, the newly diagnosed, and healthcare providers.

Healthcare providers often struggle for answers to new questions as the combination of HIV and the medications used to treat the virus create health challenges in many individuals. As answers are found for individuals, they must be shared with the community for us to continue to learn how the virus adapts, how the medications and HIV interact in individuals, and how we can overcome these seemly unique challenges.

A resource for the newly diagnosed.

Being diagnosed HIV-positive today is an experience that is much different than the experience of being diagnosed HIV-positive twenty years ago. The history and the experiences of 'long term survivors' must be shared with the new generation of HIV-positive people and the health care community.

We all know we have come a very long way. We have learned from experience how to manage this infection, how to live with the daily struggles, and how to overcome new challenges as they arise. Now, through HIVConnect we can all learn from each other's experience.

We welcome you to join our community and share your experience. Whether you are HIV-positive, an organization that supports HIV-positive people or a supportive friend or family member of an HIV-positive person, you will find friendship, support and community with HIV Connect.

mailto:support@hivconnect.net

http://www.organizedwisdom.com/
OrganizedWisdom is a health-focused, social-networking site that enables consumers, physicians, healthcare professionals, and health organizations to collaborate on more than 6,500 health topics.

We help people make more informed health decisions by giving them free access to the doctor-reviewed health information enhanced by user-generated health wisdom.

We hope you'll participate in OrganizedWisdom by sharing at least one piece of health wisdom and sending us your feedback as we make improvements and launch new features.

We're a privately-held New York City-based company that has successfully worked together since 1998, and we love what we do. OrganizedWisdom was founed on October 3, 2006.

Steven H. Krein, Chairman & CEO
Unity Stoakes, President
Howard Krein, MD, PhD
Gregg Alwine, CTO
Adam Ingberman, Vice President, Product Development

Latino

http://mimun2.com/
Latino community. Founded by twelve math and science professors at a Massachusetts Institute of Technology think-tank on December 2005. Bought by IDT, a telecoms company, in January 2007.

http://redvida.com
Edgar Veytía. CEO, RedVida—Founder of RedVida. Edgar Veytía, born in the United States of Cuban and Honduran parents, raised in Cuba until six years of age, then Miami and Honduras after fleeing Castro's ascendancy to power. Edgar's fluency in American and Latin cultures was enriched through his many years in business throughout the southern hemisphere. From family-owned lumber and tobacco operations, Edgar went on to partner with Carlos Devis to co-found Comunicación y Desarrollo Integral, S.A., a management consulting and training organization with offices in Chile, Colombia, Venezuela, Mexico, and the United States. Together they co-designed the Target Training program, which propelled the company's success for years.
In English and Spanish.

RedVida.com is a division of RedVida, Inc., based in Nevada, USA

www.elhood.com (LS)
Hoodiny was formed to create the leading "digital escapist" of the Hispanic entertainment market. What is Hispanic entertainment? It is not easy to generalize, but to us, it represents entertainment that is conceptualized, influenced, and developed for the millions of Spanish speakers and/or persons whose ancestry hails from Spain and Latin America. But if you like Shakira, Carlos Mencia, and Daddy Yankee, you like Hispanic entertainment. We believe that the digital age is upon us and allows all—artists, consumers, and fans—to escape the limitations of the traditional media world and interact in ways never before possible. We dig digital. We will develop technological platforms and content for this new medium, so it can be accessed in a ubiquitous, personal and interactive manner. You will be able to find us in your TV, radio, computer and mobile device. At Hoodiny, we celebrate artistic inspiration and embrace technological innovation; it is

this powerful combination that we believe will change the dynamics of the Hispanic media world.

Hoodiny's team is composed of bi-cultural (or, as we define ourselves, "multi-cultural") and successful artists, geeks and business visionaries:

Demian Bellumio, President
Ariel Bellumio, VP online Entertainment
Andres Dalmastro, VP Music entertainment
Scott Brogi, COO
Fabian E. Schonholz, CTO

US | Miami
4970 S.W. 72nd Ave.
suite 100
miami, fl 33155

Spain | Madrid
c/albasanz, 55
28037 madrid
3er piso

info@hoodiny.com

http://www.migente.com/
MiGente.com is a registered trademark of Community Connect Inc.

http://latinosconnected.com/
San Francisco-based LatinosConnected launched in December 2006 to help Hispanics, ages 16 to 35, connect with peers to share their Latino experience, be it good or bad, said founder Veronica Alvarez.

http://latinosenel.com/
Latinosenel.com is a social networking web site in which members can stay in contact with their friends, share photos, music, videos, and connect with your colleagues. Here you can discover new things and explore the Latin-American culture. This site is designed by and for Latinos for the advantage

of all Americans and other cultures interested in Latinos. Our main goal is to unite our people with one another in one location, where our member can enjoy a community free of charge, while providing a top of the line quality service. The people who work with Latinosenel.com have noticed that what makes social networking so exciting is the fact that you never know who is online and their connection to you.

Henry Vásquez
webmaster@latinosenel.com
New York, USA

http://quepasa.com
Headquartered in Scottsdale, Arizona, Quepasa maintains sales offices in New York, New York and Miami, Florida and technical operations in Hermosillo, Mexico.
Quepasa Corporation, owner of Quepasa.com, is the world's largest, bicultural Hispanic online community. The Company is committed to providing entertaining, enriching, and empowering products and services to millions of Hispanic users throughout the U.S. and certain areas of Latin America. English & Spanish version available.

http://www.barrio305.com/
A premier broadband and social media destination for the latino youth audience. Platform Includes: Viral Widgets, Broadband Video, Social Networking, Photo & Video Share, Slideshow Generator, Profile Resources, Tagging.

http://vostu.com/
Vostu is an online social network, aiming to join the whole Latin America in a channel of free, open and fun dialogue.

Vostu was designed by Latin-Americans for Latin-Americans to cut down the distance between our people and stimulate dialogue in our region. Having been in contact with other social networks in Europe, as well as North America, and aware of the vertiginous growth of the access to the internet in Latin America, Vostu's team decided to create a tailored social network, adapting its features and services to the cultural idiosyncrasy we grew up in.

Given that the needs in Latin America are different from the ones in other parts of the world, there is Vostu: your parties and friends, your photos and stories, your city, your football team... your best moments. Fully in Spanish, with a young and fun interface and the latest internet technology, Vostu promotes the free flow of information online within Latin America.

Founded by three Harvard students: Daniel Kafie, Joshua Kushner and Mario Schlosser. Based in Cambridge and founded in February 2007.

Contact: dkafie@vostu.com

http://www.lazona.com/
Founded by MTV Networks Latin America, Inc. and focused on the Latin-American community. Spanish only.

http://hispanito.com/
Hipanic social network, in Spanish only. Founded by Juan and Sami.

juanito@hispanito.com

http://visionjoven.com/
VisionJoven is an online community that allows you to meet the friends of your friends.

Once you register in VisionJoven, you will be able to share photos, blogs, and hobbies in an expanding network of friends in common. In addition, you will be able to see who knows whom or how people are linked. Find out if your friend knows a friend who is, at the same time, friends with some famous Christian singer.

VisionJoven is for everyone:
Friends willing to talk online.
Classmates who need to do a project together.
Professional writers who want to write a blog.
Teachers or youth leaders who want their group of children or youngsters to be connected through a virtual group.

- Single Christians willing to get in touch with other single Christians (why not? God may surprise you!).
- Relatives wanting to keep in touch with their loved ones and share the pictures of the new member of the family with the granny.
- Businessmen and partners interested in working online.
- Anyone looking for old friends.

VisionJoven was founded in Argentina in 1989 and is considered the first magazine exclusively for young Christians. Eighteen years later, technology allowed us to create the first online social community in Spanish for young Christians. We would like to be a medium of communication, a tool, and not a product in itself. We promise to create new features as soon as possible and make this website a meeting point where your dreams may come true. Communication is the first step to success!

How do I use VisionJoven?

- First, register and fill in your profile (your profile is your space on the web, your own page, where you can describe yourself, your hobbies and pastimes. You can also upload photos, write blogs, create groups, talk online, etc.).
- Invite your friends to join your personal network or search for your friends who are already registered in VisionJoven.
- Take a look at the links you create between your friends and theirs. Thousands of people are included in some people's networks. Meet your friends' friends and request them to add you. You can get in touch with any person in your personal network.

All in all, the aim of this site is to help you have fun, meet new people, strengthen your faith and develop socially.

http://www.batanga.com/
Batanga is a media and entertainment company reaching Hispanics across multiple platforms, including the cool online entertainment destination you are on right now, nationwide events as well as targeted magazines for the New Generation Latino.

Batanga headquarters are in Miami, Florida and maintain offices in New York, Los Angeles and Greensboro, North Carolina where it all started! Twenty-six Free Online Radio Stations, 2000+ Music Videos, User generated Radio Stations: "My Radio", Latin Music Blogs, Music download store and exclusive content on sports, autos, lifestyle, and even greeting cards.

http://www.fotolog.com/

One of the world's largest social networking sites, Fotolog is an ever-evolving global network where members communicate and connect through photographs. A simple and fun way for anyone to express themselves on a daily basis, Fotolog allows members to easily publish an online photo diary, or photo blog, and share it worldwide. What makes Fotolog special is not just the ability to post photos, but the ability to connect with people. While many people use Fotolog to stay in better touch with their friends and family, others use it to explore the wider Fotolog universe, discover the photos of new people from around the world, participate in group projects and, perhaps most importantly, receive personal feedback on their photos. Launched in May 2002, Fotolog has grown from a small community project of two hundred friends into a global cultural phenomenon, where more than 5 million members from over two hundred countries have shared more than 160 million photos. Each month the Fotolog site generates over 2.5 billion page views and receives over 10 million unique visitors. Based in New York.

Music

http://www.splicemusic.com/ (LS)
Music remixing community

212 N Canal, Ste. 300
Chicago, IL 60606-7407

http://www.gruuve.com

Gruuve is a music social network. Gruuve's mission is to "Connect Everything Music"– that means music, fans, events and more. Thousands of users are already connecting with their favorite music, bands, and events using Gruuve.

Team
Daya Baran
Chief Gruuve

Wayne Radinsky
Chief Technology Guru

Gruuve Inc
333 Cobalt Way
Suite 107
Sunnyvale, CA 94086
USA

http://www.fuzz.com/
Fuzz is a music company providing a one-stop solution that connects artists and fans. Artists can promote, stream, sell music and merch, and efficiently manage every aspect of their careers. The Fuzz community enables fans to discover, share, review, interact, influence, hear, and buy music in a user-friendly forum that encourages participation.

Fuzz Artists, Inc.
602 20th Street
San Francisco, CA 94107
Telephone: (415) 449-6947
Fax: (415) 449-6947
E-mail: copyright@fuzz.com

http://www.music.com/
Music.com is here because music is central and essential to our lives. Today, music.com is served to you in pre-release phase while we continue to add functionality enabling you to find people through music and music through people. We appreciate your patience and amazing feedback during this stage of our growth. You are the voice of music.com. We're busy adding the features you are requesting, which will empower you with more ways to connect and discover. Your voice breathes life into music.com.

Music.com helps you make the most of an online community that is passionate and opinionated about music; your music, your friend's music, all music. You know how a great song inspires you to share it...learn more about it...find more like it? Music.com is a catalyst for exploring, expressing and connecting through music.

As a member, you can build your own personal profile page and create favorites lists. This presents other users with a musical mosaic of who you are. From there, you can begin making connections, exchanging ideas and adopting new influences. The music.com affinity engine uses your ratings and lists to determine who and what you might like. Your activity within music.com directly serves to shape your experience with the community.

Anything you'd ever want to know about every song, genre and artist, we've got it. While we can boast about having millions of pages of music information, we are by no means complete. This site is a work in progress — a sort of collective effort. If you stumble upon something missing or lacking, we welcome your contributions. Or if you know something we don't, please share it with us and everyone else. Users can submit information to us regarding inaccurate or incomplete credits. This information is reviewed and added to enhance the accuracy and personality of the site. Ultimately, music.com is a reflection of you and the collective passion and knowledge of our users.

Each and every word and rating you contribute affects the identity of the site. Simply put, your voice is heard (or at least read). In this way, the site is a continually evolving reflection of you and all other users, presenting a launch pad for everyone and anyone to sound off.

Finding music is enabled all through the site. Clicking the "shop for" link (found on nearly every page) will bring up related items provided through our affiliate partners. Our marketplace page provides a similar service and enables you to search for just about anything. Soon you will also begin seeing community input. It will serve as a quick pipeline to music downloads, instruments, books, electronics, t-shirts and more. Think all things music, and you've got the picture.

Music.com: an amazing network of people, ideas, and...of course, music.

Music.com
6767 Sunset Drive
Suite 333
Hollywood, CA 90028

PR@mdc.music.com

http://www.hiphopcrack.com/
Hip hop social network.

Triumph Media Holdings, Inc.
8033 West Sunset Boulevard
Suite 1038
Hollywood, California 90046

crackspace@crackspace.net

http://www.buzznet.com (LS)
Buzznet is the web's best destination for music and pop-culture content
and community. Highly passionate members of Buzznet are continuously
programming content on thousands of music and pop-culture topics.
Buzznet members publish their thoughts using photos, videos, and blogs,
creating authentic and credible multimedia communities. These communities
not only attract the fans but also the top bands and pop-culture icons are
leading this multimedia conversation. By having the best and most up-to-
date media on these topics, Buzznet is able to maintain active communities
for millions to enjoy. Buzznet is transforming traditional media models of
top-down programming by giving tools to everyone and creating a bottomup media community programming paradigm. Buzznet enables members to
collect, create, and share multiple media types and formats to community
blog, but more importantly it gives members and viewers methods to
communicate with each other. This combination of media programming,
viewing, and communicating is the evolution of web entertainment. Buzznet
is confident that the future of media will have elements of user generated
and programmed content within web community environment. Buzznet is
committed to making this happen.

Buzznet.com
2404 Wilshire Blvd. #11b
Los Angeles, CA 90057
(213) 252-8999 phone
(213) 252-8955 fax

Anthony Batt - CEO & Founder
Marc Brown - VP Partner Marketing & Founder
Steve Haldane - Director Application Engineering & Founder
Chris Tragos - VP Advertising and Marketing

http://www.mystrands.com/ (LS)
Barcelona (Spain), June 16th, 2005

MyStrands announces today the launch of the company. MyStrands helps people discover and enjoy music, and provides music recommendations based exclusively on the listening behaviors of individuals and social networks.

MyStrands offers two music recommendation flavors:

- MyStrands, the personal DJ that gives real-time recommendations based on what people are actually playing (a plug in for your media player, now available for iTunes).
- Universal access to personalized recommendations, through MyStrands.com.

The Founder and CEO of MyStrands is Francisco J. Martin (34), a PhD in Artificial Intelligence. MyStrands has offices both in USA and Europe, with a team of 35 individuals coming from countries such as Spain, USA, Korea, and Switzerland.

Gabriel Aldamiz-echevarria
VP Communications
MyStrands

http://blog.MyStrands.com
Cell: +1 541 829 00 97
AIM/Skype: aldamiz

aldamiz@MyStrands.com

MediaStrands, Inc.
Attn: General Counsel
760 SW Madison Ave., Suite 106
Corvallis, Oregon 97333

dmca@MyStrands.com

http://mog.com/ (LS)

Hi An,

Thank you for your interest in MOG. Below, please find an outline of the company and service, including the specific information you requested. Let me know if you need anything further from me.
Best,

Dana

MOG (www.mog.com) *is the web's most raging music scene created by a passionate community of music lovers and powered by cutting edge filters that make it ridiculously easy to find the music, videos, news and reviews that match your musical taste. Completely free, MOG was started by David Hyman, former CEO of Gracenote, former SVP-Marketing at MTV Interactive, and self-proclaimed music freak. MOG was founded in June 2005 and is headquartered in Berkeley, CA. MOG launched its public beta July 2006 and launched out of beta March 2007.*

When you download the MOG-O-MATIC application, MOG tracks everything you're listening to on your computer and iPod and automatically posts it to your MOG page. With that information MOG is able to connect you with others who are most like you musically.

MOG's most talked about feature is MOG TV, a personalized music video channel, streaming music videos and live concert footage twenty-four hours a day. MOG TV is the ultimate mash-up leveraging YouTube content. Push the "Magic Button," and MOG computes everything we know about your musical taste to drive instant recommendations of all MOG content, including music, videos, news, and reviews.

Location: *Berkeley, CA USA*
Target audience: *Music lovers/people interested in discovering new music*
Language: *English*

Dana Smith
Dadascope Communications
510.524.2066
M. 510.682.3141

dana@dadascope.com
Reporters, please direct media inquiries to pr@mog.com

http://zooped.com/
Zooped.com is a new Business Music and Personal Social Network.
Connect with old friends, make new friends and connect with local businesses.
Build your own play list up to fifteen songs for your profile page.
Musicians can share up to ten songs with their fans.
Zooped.com is compatible with any MSRS, customize your profiles easily.

Based in New York

admin@zooped.com

http://www.haystack.com/ (LS)
Music and social networking

Haystack wants to be an extension to your life as a musician, music seeker or music recommender. We launched into "Public Preview" on 11:54 PM on October 25th and are open for the world to see. Why are we different? Haystack is here to help you collect your life on and off the web and put it in context with artists and music. Music is meant to be shared. We hope that Haystack can someday become the legal and free alternative to file sharing.

Haystack gives you several tools to make finding and promoting music just a bit easier:

* Play directly from a search result

* "Stack" links to artists to share reviews and experiences

* Receive automatic notifications of new uploads by users and artists

* Drill-down search results to find exactly what you're looking for

* Play music from page to page and keep the player on the page

Who are we?

We're all musicians ourselves (as well as web 2.0 geeks!) and are on a mission to find a way for artists, labels, publishers, peddlers, and freaks to reach their fan bases in a real way. Same goes with music fans. When's the last time your ran into one? Yeah, exactly.

We're music lovers too – big ones. It's sad that many of our old stomping grounds like record stores (and street corners) are no longer the places that people share their music recommendations with each other but thats life in the iPod age. Haystack is going to bring the p back into people and help you to find something real for once.

press@haystack.com

http://www.indiepad.com/

Unlike other digital music services, indiepad does not have the strict requirements, long delays and excessive fees associated with adding a new artists; any artist may purchase an account, upload their music, set prices for downloads and display band information and photographs using any web browser. Artists on indiepad can expect to pay $20 for a lifetime membership, which includes an allotment to upload twenty songs, four albums with artwork, band contact information, and a photo. After an account is created, each artist has a specific page dedicated to them which contains all of their music and information where visitors can easily purchase an artist's entire catalogue. Artists can link directly from their website to their artist page on indiepad, so that visitors to the artist website can easily view, hear streaming samples, and purchase all the digital music that artist has for sale. Artists can login and view how well their items are selling, update their account information, upload music, and request payment for music sold. Unauthorized downloads are prevented by a proprietary three layer file protection for maximum file security.

Visitors to indiepad can browse the entire music catalogue by genre or using a keyword search to find a specific artist, song or album. Visitors who have purchased an item are able to download that item a maximum of three times and leave a review for that item which will be displayed to other visitors as a guide to the best content on the site.

About Connected Industries, Inc.:
Based in Carson City, Nevada, with additional offices in Anaheim, California, Connected Industries Inc. has become an innovator in niche e-commerce solutions and has developed enterprise web-based software for higher education, travel, and consumer-to-consumer commerce.
Launched in January 2007.

http://www.justrhymes.com/ (LS)
Music social network, launched January 2007.

Sorry for the delay in getting back with you, we've been swamped over here! I've attached the word document as well as copy and pasted in below this text. Please fill me in on where/when/link to get to the book and/or internet text. Thank you again and best wishes!
JustRHYMES is an online music-community that promotes rising, underground and mainstream artists, exclusive to hip-hop its rap-rooted genres some of which include: Crunk, Reggae, R&B, Underground, Soul, and many more. It is both free to listen and free to setup an artist account. Reaching over twenty-six countries and within launch of the beta version merely six months ago, already reaching well over 2.3 million hits.

As a key vehicle for music discovery, JustRHYMES connects artists directly with listeners and music industry execs through individual artist profiles consisting of streaming media (downloadable if permitted by artist) as well as news, tours, photo gallery, upcoming shows, contact information, biographical information, and music videos.
Founded by David Grau, a recent Chapman University graduate in Orange, CA www.justrhymes.com started the beta version in Sept of 2006 with plans of releasing the official 2.0 version this month. The target audience ranging from 18–34+ makes up both the visitors as well as artists and talent already attached. With the ability to listen, download for free, along with (some future plans not yet able to be disclosed) the technicalities are boundless. The streaming content, biographies, and photo galleries reaching nationwide the main viewing language English, the justRHYMES teams have their sights locked and is full speed ahead for the future of their music community.

www.justrhymes.com | Connect to the street.

David Grau

Founder | *justRHYMES.com*
david@justrhymes.com
www.justrhymes.com

http://www.reverbnation.com/ (LS)
ReverbNation.com is a "music-only" community where artists, fans, and venues interact to share information, create realtionships, and discover music. At the epicenter of our community is the Artist. We serve them, their fans, the venues that host them, and other members of the music community.

ReverbNation.com
1123 Broadway
Suite 317
New York, NY 10010
Ph: 212.367-0826
jedcarlson@reverbnation.com

ReverbNation is owned and operated by eMinor Inc. - a company founded with the goal of "Serving Music 2.0." ReverbNation is not owned, operated, or in any way beholden to anyone inside or outside of the music industry. We are here to serve the interests of all members of the music community. Suggestions are always appreciated at comments@reverbnation .com.

http://www.mp3.com/ (LS)
A CNET Networks Entertainment property, MP3.com is a slick, all-inclusive music site that caters to both artists looking to promote their material and connect with listeners and to fans who thrive on discovering new music and expressing their opinions. MP3.com's active community fuels the site with user-generated content, ranging from independent and major-label artist pages with songs, videos, similar-artist lists, photos, and news to fan ratings, reviews, blogs, and forums. The site also offers robust

artist information like discographies, bios, and song clips, plus thousands of free music tracks, daily news, live sessions, exclusive interviews, weekly podcasts, charts, a tech guide, and more.

Press: Jean.Levandowsky@cnet.com

http://www.midomi.com (LS)
Midomi is the ultimate music search tool because it is powered by your voice. Sing, hum, or whistle to instantly find your favorite music and connect with a community that shares your musical interests.

Our mission is to build the most comprehensive database of searchable music. You can contribute to the database by singing in midomi's online recording studio in any language or genre. The next time anyone searches for that song, your performance might be the top result!

At midomi you can create your own profile, sing your favorite songs and share them with your friends and get discovered by other midomi users. You can listen to and rate others' musical performances, see their pictures, send them messages, buy original music, and more.

Media and Press Inquiries
Marcy Simon
marcy@midomi.com
I (917) 833-3392

http://www.projectplaylist.com/
Project playlist is a free music playlist site and free music search engine. We help you find music throughout the web the same way that Google or Yahoo helps you find webpages, images, and other media but with a social/community twist.
Once you find music tracks that you like through our music search engine (or on another user's playlist), you can add them to your personal playlist and then share your playlist with others. You can post your playlist on myspace, friendster, xanga or any other website or e-mail them to friends!

Parents

http://www.connectingmoms.com/
ConnectingMoms.com is a hip, new social-networking website designed specifically for expecting, new, & savvy moms in mind. Our site allows members to set up unique, personal profiles describing their individual interests allowing them to build and establish bonds with other mothers. Members can view each others' profiles, share photos, write movie and TV reviews, join interest groups, post diaries (blogs), engage in discussions, shop online, and post classifieds. Imagine giving and receiving real everyday know-how on the many stages of motherhood.

ConnectingMoms, LLC.
36 E 23 St, Suite 5R
New York, NY 10010

http://www.momjunction.com/
MomJunction is a full featured online life tool that simplifies daily life coordination and information gathering for busy moms. MomJunction allows moms to connect select elements of their lives with other moms that they know and trust creating a powerful stream of personalized knowledge.

MomJunction does this in three ways: MJ offers the only full featured tool set and personal mini site for moms to coordinate their busy lives, including calendaring, organization and sharing of photos and videos; MJ allows moms to communicate through personal and public groups, so that information, ideas, and knowledge can be shared safely and easily; MJ has created a unique process called Ripple that connects moms across groups to her extended network—friends of friends and so on. Through Ripple, moms can seek out or share information comfortably with people they know and trust, but also benefit from the knowledge of potentially millions of moms.
Founder: Sang Kim (male)
Launched November 1st 2006.

http://opmom.com/
OperationMom is founded by Carrie Pacini, CEO of TriTaur LLC in Texas.

http://www.mayasmom.com/
The Palo Alto-based company has received a modest $1 million (approx) angel round from the likes of True Ventures. Launched 26 October 2006. Maya's Mom is a community project designed to encourage parents to share information with each other.

Address: 235 Alma, Palo Alto, CA

http://www.mothersclick.com/
Andra Davidson, Co-Founder. Content driven: most of the activity revolves around answering questions, joining groups and sharing your experience through blogs. Launched October 17, 2006.

http://www.mommybuzz.com/
MommyBuzz is the perfect solution for busy moms who want to connect with other moms, stay in touch with friends and acquaintances, and get involved with groups of moms who share a common interest. MommyBuzz allows moms to connect whenever they have time: naptime, late night, at the office or whenever. You can create and share your personal profile webpage, send and receive messages, post photos, collaborate in group discussions, keep a personal journal (blog), post classified ads, chat in real time, and much more!

Plus, MommyBuzz is an opt-in network where you decide who is in your circle of friends and who can see your personal information. Find many acquaintances or just a few very close friends…you decide.

And if you are a member of Moxie Moms (www.moxie-moms.com), you are already a member in MommyBuzz! Just log into MommyBuzz (using your Moxie Moms ID & password), build your profile, and then connect with your Moxie Moms friends and invite your other friends to join you for free!

Launched June 2006.

http://www.clubmom.com/
ClubMom is the premier online destination where thousands of moms connect and share with each other. Whether helping each other meet daily challenges in MomAnswers, sharing photos with friends and family in the ClubMom Scrapbook, or winning great prizes in ClubMom's Sweepstakes and contests, members come to ClubMom.com to connect, share, and have fun every day. And through the ClubMom Rewards program, moms earn ClubMom Points they can redeem for rewards just for them.

Established in 1999, ClubMom was co-founded by Meredith Vieira; Andrew Shue, actor and social activist; and Michael Sanchez, ClubMom CEO and entrepreneur. Prominent investors include Highland Capital Partners and Draper Fisher Jurvetson.

ClubMom
303 Park Avenue South, #1046
New York, NY 10010
Telephone: 646-435-6500
Fax: 646-435-6600

http://www.cafemom.com/
CafeMom was started by the same company that runs ClubMom, another leading mom's website

303 Park Avenue South, #1046
New York, NY 10010

http://www.myfamily.com/
Since 1998, myfamily.com has provided private family web sites to help millions of people stay connected with those who matter most. Continuing that tradition, myfamily.com 2.0 beta introduces a new generation of free family web sites for sharing photos, stories, news, and more.

CEO: Tim Sullivan
Phone: (212) 221-1616 ext. 122

The Generations Network
Attn: Customer Solutions
360 West 4800 North
Provo, UT 84604

http://www.parentsconnect.com/
ParentsConnect is dedicated to providing you with the guidance of the real parenting experts – other parents. The content you'll find here is 100 percent parent-created. It is led by a team of specially trained Host Parents, who also share their own experiences in raising kids. Backed by MTV. Launched August 2006.

http://kincafe.com/
Kincafe is all about connecting, bonding and cherishing loved ones – the ones you grew up with, the ones you care for at the center of your heart. We bring you latest updates from your family and friends to you. You can build and link family trees together, remember birthdays and anniversaries, share your photo Albums, blogs and other family treasures such as scrapbooks, interests, and family news with all who care most.

Our Family tree-based navigation technology allows you to easily reach anyone within your core and extended families. You no longer have to remember sooooo many different website or home page URLs just to reach family – at Kincafe you can go to your own family tree and navigate to anyone connected to you. Even better, Kincafe finds the latest updates of albums, blogs, announcements within your network and gives you all this information right on login.

We use state of the art Security Technologies. You have complete control over who can see your family's content. You decide whether to allow your friends and relatives, friends of friends and relatives, everyone, or no one outside your family to see your family's content.

Kincafe is growing rapidly into a global service for families worldwide to stay in touch and share special moments.

Launched in March 2007. Based in California.

http://www.geni.com/
Geni is a unique approach to solving the problem of genealogy, which is the question of how everyone is related.

Geni lets you create a family tree through our fun simple interface. When you add a relative's e-mail address, he or she will be invited to join your tree. That relative can then add other relatives, and so on. Your tree will continue to grow as relatives invite other relatives.

Each family member has a profile which can be viewed by clicking their name in the tree. This helps family members learn more about each other and stay in touch. Family members can also share information and work together to build profiles for common ancestors.

Geni is a private network. Only the people in your tree can see your tree and your profile. Geni will not share your personal information with third parties.

Geni was founded by former executives and early employees of PayPal, Yahoo! Groups, Ebay, and Tribe. It is backed by venture capital firm Founders Fund.

Based in Los Angeles, California.

http://www.parentography.com/
Social network for family-friendly excursions. Launched by Tim and Noelle Ludwig on January 23rd 2007.
Parentography is a totally free, vibrant online community for parents who want honest tools, advice, and ideas for family-friendly excursions, whether they plan to travel around town or around the country. It is shifting local conversations that routinely take place in parks, playgroups, and on the phone to a national hub for parents and helping to take a lot of the guesswork out of trying new places. Parentography is always up-to-date, presents unfiltered advice and opinions from parents everywhere, and covers the entire United States (we will add international coverage as soon as we are able).

http://www.cingo.com/

Cingo was created by Fingertip Marketing, LLC, a privately held, Virginia based internet marketing company. We believe that consumers and particularly families are really struggling with the trash, clutter, adware, and spyware they must sift through to get the information they want on the internet. With Cingo, it doesn't have to be that way. We built Cingo to help families make the internet work for them, not against them.

http://caresquare.com/ (LS)

CareSquare is dedicated to connecting parents and caregivers in their local communities. CareSquare was created by parents of young children, who understand the personal and complex process of finding trusted babysitting and nanny care. We're here to help families and caregivers easily contact, schedule, and book childcare.

Hi there An — We would be happy to participate. Thanks so much for thinking of us. . Here's the info you requested:

-Founders & management
Ariel Kleckner Ford and Alex Kaplinsky

-Founding year & address/nationality
We founded CareSquare.com in April, 2006 and launched our beta product in the San Francisco Bay Area in October of 2007. Full US and Canada release is slated for April 2007.

-Target audience & membership level (number of users)
CareSquare.com services parents, babysitters and nannies. We currently have about two thousand beta users. That number grows daily.

-Top three countries in which the community is used
United States, Canada, South America

-Main technical features and possible features in the near future
Our current beta product connects parents and babysitters/nannies in a basic social networking environment, allowing for peer-review, feedback, and real-time booking of care. Our full release comes out in April of this year and will offer greatly enhanced social

networking features, including job boards, share care boards, discussion boards, messaging, and blogging. Later in the year, we plan to expand our recommendations into products and other household services.

-Languages in which the service is available
Beta product in English, Spanish scheduled for release in April 2007.

Hope this is enough — let me know if you would like more. Best, Ariel

E-mail: info@caresquare.com
Phone: 650-328-8568 Address: CareSquare
131 Lytton Ave.
Palo Alto, CA 94301

http://famster.com
Family-oriented social site.

http://www.daddaily.com/
Social network exclusively for dads. Founded by tax attorney and dad of two, Art Giacosa.

Pets

http://www.dogster.com/ (LS)
Dogster.com is a website for sharing dog facts and photos with other dog lovers. It is operated by Dogster, Inc., a privately held company in San Francisco, CA, USA. Launched January 2004.

Ted Rheingold founded Dogster & Catster as a way for pet lovers to unite around their common passions.

http://www.catster.com
Launched in August 2004.

http://www.pikapet.com
Pikapet is an online playground for pet owners who want to have fun with their cute pets. Pet owners upload cute pictures of their pets, and they get

to participate in online contests, attracting users to browse and vote for the cutest ones. This interaction makes Pikapet a fun place to hang out, participate and explore hundreds of pets of all kinds and from all over the world.

http://www.animalbuds.com/
Animal Buds is a social network that connects your pet with other pets from around the world. Why should you have all the fun on your favorite social networking sites while your best animal friend is left out? Animal Buds gives your best friend the social network site they've been waiting for. Create an Animal Bud account for your pet and "unleash" their social powers. You can create a customized webpage just for your pet, make some friends, and even upload pictures of your loveable animal friend.

http://pugspot.com/
PugSpot started as an idea in late 2006 and came to fruition in early 2007. We are the proud parents of pugs and starting a pug community seemed like a natural extension of our love for pugs!

We want this place to be a wonderful community of other pug lovers who freely share their pug lives with photos, videos, and community!

PO Box 630726
Littleton, CO 80163

We can be reached via e-mail at info@pugspot.com , or you can reach us by telephone at 1-877-387-6127.

http://pawspot.com
Based in Washington

Let's face it—we all love our pets to pieces. But sometimes caring for our furry family members can be a daunting responsibility, especially when we have to be away from home. Finding someone to care for our pet is usually a frustrating experience, with an expensive solution. If you are a pet owner who travels on occasion, you are most likely familiar with the calls to family and friends, begging for their pet sitting services. And then of course, there's always the dreaded last resort: the kennel.

Not any more! PawSpot has the solution to your pet sitting needs. At PawSpot you can exchange pet sitting for free with pet loving friends who you know and trust. All you have to do is register yourself and your pet at www.pawspot.com, invite your closest pet loving friends to join your network, and PawSpot will take care of the rest!

Next time you are planning to go away, PawSpot will send a pet sitting request out to your network of pet people and find a close friend to care for your pet. The best part is you will get the piece of mind knowing that you are leaving your pet in the competent hands of a fellow friend and pet owner. Plus, you and your friends can easily reciprocate pet sitting for each other, so there is no guilt, no begging, and no expensive kennel bills involved. It's easy, it's safe, and it's free!

In addition, PawSpot is a great place to post and share photos of your pet, exchange advice on pet health care and happiness, and learn about local pet services in your community.

PawSpot is yours for the making. We hope that you enjoy partnering with us to create a vibrant online pet community for your neighborhood. Register now or log on now to explore our beta site and let us know what you think. If you are already a member, for pet's sake, invite your friends to help PawSpot become a vibrant community for pets and their owners.

Thanks,
The PawSpot team

support@pawspot.com

Politics

http://www.hotsoup.com/ (LS)
Hotsoup.com
3299 K Street, NW , Suite 500
Washington, D.C. 20007

info@hotsoup.com

Hotsoup.com is the first online community that joins Opinion Drivers from across the spectrum. The community connects well-known influencers from the worlds of politics, business, religion, and popular culture with influencers who drive opinion at the grassroots and community levels. Harnessing the power of social networking technology, Hotsoup.com levels the playing field by giving anyone and everyone a voice in how America's institutions can work better. Carter, Chip, Joe and Mike, prominent Democratic strategists, and Mark and Matthew, Republican heavyweights, had successful private sector practices that specialized in helping corporate clients find Opinion Drivers. It was frustrating; the rise of the Internet and other societal trends made Opinion Drivers both more important and harder to reach. At the same time, Internet veterans Allie, Bart, and John were consulting on better ways to reach and engage Opinion Drivers online while simultaneously launching a new social networking site called Sisterwoman.com. And Ron, one of the country's most respected journalists, was observing his readers' behavior change and co-authoring a book, *Applebee's America*, about this audience and the community-building potential of the Internet.

http://network.baconsrebellion.com/
Bacon's Rebellion is owned and published by James A. Bacon Jr., who left his job as publisher and editor in chief of Virginia Business magazine to pursue a dream of starting his own publication. After the smartest business minds in the country lost billions of dollars in dot.com bombs, Mr. Bacon figured, hey, why shouldn't he squander his life savings, too? Bacon's Rebellion commenced publication in July 2002.

Bacon's Rebellion reaches Virginia's political and legislative decision makers. We target the following groups:

- Members of the General Assembly and their staffs
- City councilmen and county supervisors
- State and local government officials
- Lawyers and registered lobbyists
- Trade association staffs and board members
- Advocacy groups and citizen activists

- Political party activists
- Economic developers
- Virginia citizens seeking an alternative editorial voice

As of July 2005, circulation exceeded 2,400.

http://my.barackobama.com/ (LS)
Social network site of presidential candidate Barack Obama, where his supporters can connect through blogs, the creation of fundraisers, build a network of friends etc – mostly the features you find on 'ordinary' social networks but with a political agenda.

Obama for America
P.O. Box 8102
Chicago, IL 60680

You can call us at:
(866) 675-2008
For press inquiries, please contact media@barackobama.com

http://www.essembly.com
Essembly is a free, non-partisan social networking site that provides tools for politically interested individuals to connect with one another, engage in constructive discussion, and organize to take action.

Our Mission Statement
Essembly was created by a group of college students frustrated with the increasing dominance of money and special interests in the political process. At the same time, labels like "liberal" and "conservative," "Democrat" and "Republican," had deeply divided and polarized Americans, limiting the potential for constructive political discussion. We felt that our voices were falling on deaf ears, drowned out by deep pockets and uncompromising ideologues. Essembly emerged as an attempt to use online social networking technology to stimulate bipartisan discussion and provide tools for individuals to connect with one another for the purpose of political collaboration, organization and action. Our objective is to make the tools of the political elite available to all Americans and increase individual participation in the democratic process at every level.

http://www.gop.com/MyGop/
MyGOP is the next generation of political organizing. It's an online gathering place for Republicans and a personal Campaign HQ all rolled into one. Here's how it works. You set up your own personal website on GOP.com with your message and your photos. You set the goals. You build a team. It's your own version of GOP.com – built just for you.

http://www.democrats.org/page/user/login?uu=/page/dashboard/ private
PartyBuilder includes...

- A user dashboard that pulls data from all tools into one easy-to-manage interface.
- A social networking tool that allows for people to connect with one another.
- A search tool, allowing users to find each other or to find established groups based on name or zip code.
- A groups tool, allowing users to join together for an issue, cause, or candidate. Users then share a common blog, events management system, and listserv.
- An events tool that allows users to create real-world events of any kind.
- A personal fundraising system that allows users to take control of the financial future of the party.
- A petitions section, allowing users to add their voice to a host of important issue statements.
- A letters tool that easily connects users with the editors of their local papers. Talking points are conveniently provided for a range of issues.
- A blog for every user, complete with full management control and commenting functionality. The blogs have an integrated, shared tagging system for system-wide categorization.

Religion

www.Koolanoo.com (LS)

The Jewish people are the world's most tightly knit social, cultural, and economic network. Jews were networking long before the Internet ever existed and will be doing so for centuries to come. That's the beauty of Koolanoo – membership is a given, all you have to do is sign up.

Koolanoo gives you the platform to network your way around the globe, reaching Jewish people everywhere.

Connect, Share, and Invite.
Koolanoo offers Jewish people everywhere an opportunity to come together and share trusted, select and relevant information about anything and everything. Link-in, exchange information, share access, build up or maintain relationships with people whose friendships could bring invaluable advantages.

All content on the Koolanoo is produced and posted by our members. The site offers an array of networking tools created to enable the most convenient information sharing and communication. So make sure you enjoy the full scope of activity when building your personal profile – live forums, chats, blogs, photos, messaging, video conferencing, advanced screening mechanisms and more and more...

info@koolanoo.com

http://www.b-linked.org/
Jewish teens, international

http://www.chosennet.com/ (LS)
ChosenNetTM, owned and operated by Who New LLC, offers the Jewish community a dynamic online community network where members can search for, meet, and communicate with other members through their friends and friends of friends. ChosenNet's purpose is to enhance the power of each member's personal network and to increase the connectivity of the entire Jewish community. Founded by Jed Dempsey. Who NewTM LLC is the leading operator of community networking websites that serve specific cultural communities.

Who New LLC
3450 Sacramento Street, #300
San Francisco, CA 94118
media@ChosenNet.com

http://jsonlive.com/ (LS)
The site is meant to be used as a resource as well as a social networking tool
for alumni of Jewish service programs affiliated with the Jewish Coalition
for Service, listed as affiliates on this page: www.jewishservice.org/aboutus.
JSoN, the Jewish Service Online Network provides a virtual "town square"
for participants in Jewish service programs and for anyone from the Jewish
community who cares about societal problems and issues. JSoN enables our
community to be more engaged in and have an impact on social issues and
Jewish life.

An Online Community Customized for Participants in Jewish Service
Programs: Alumni of Jewish service programs can create a free profile and
access an ever-evolving menu of collaborative features, including social and
career networking, job postings, blogs, chats, wikis, scrapbooks, interest
groups, and bulletin boards – providing a platform and tools to make a
difference.

Navit Robkin
Program Associate
Jewish Coalition for Service
475 Riverside Drive, Suite 1367
New York, NY 10115
Ph: 212-870-2450 ext. 4
Fax: 212-870-2455
navit@jewishservice.org

The Jewish Coalition for Service, 475 Riverside Dr. Suite 1367, New York,
NY 10115, e-mail us at info@jewishservice.org

http://shoutlife.com/ (LS)
ShoutLife.com officially launched in December of 2006. ShoutLife.com
is a free Christian owned and operated public blog website, complete with

full access to unlimited photo uploads, categorical groups, private messages, instant messaging, and more... This website is completely open to the public, and it is presented as a fun, clean and enjoyable blogging experience for everyone involved. ShoutLife is founded by Paul Mc Lellan, Steve Mc Lellan, Steve Shletty and Hauns Froehlingsdorf.
info@shoutlife.com

http://www.oaktreeidea.com/
Oaktreeidea.com provides our unique website and online services in accordance with our Christian statement of faith. We understand that denominations adhere to different teachings, and as a result, we also provide our own statement of faith as a guideline for Christians and others visiting / joining the site. Oaktreeidea.com welcomes members of all denominations, as well as those seeking to learn more about the Christian faith. Members posting information contrary to the basic principles of Christianity do so at the risk of their Oaktreeidea.com membership.

www.myPraize.com (LS)
2428 Collins Rd
Collins, Ohio 44826
webmaster@mypraize.com

http://www.xianz.com/
MySpace for Christians. Xianz is a place where friends help friends do everything like locate a new church, exchange prayer requests, share their favorite worship song and more. Founded by Robbie Davidson on May 25, 2006.

US Office:
Phone: 615-550-2305
Street Address:
Xianz Inc.
317 Main Street
Suite 205
Franklin, TN 37064

Or

CAN Office: 780-410-0848
Street Address:
Xianz Inc.
870 Birch Ave
Sherwood Park, AB
T8A1X3

www.christianster.com (LS)
Christianster is a site made by simple Christians for the benefit of fellow Christians. Christianster is about people, not about doctrines, agendas or denominations. We feel it is important as Christians that we surround ourselves with Christian friends who can help us walk the narrow path that leads to Life. By keeping in touch with each other, receiving mutual support and encouragement, praying for and caring for one another's burdens, we hope to be sanctified from worldly influences that grieve our spirits. As the saying goes, "Tell me who your friends are, and I'll tell you who you are." There are a lot of sites on the web for making new friends, but very few, if any, that facilitate the forming of friendships rooted and grounded on the foundation of Christan faith and love. This site is not about individual popularity or about how many friends one has. The focus here is only the popularity of one person – Jesus Christ. He is the center of all our relationships. Through Christianster, we hope to nurture a place on the web where Christ's Name is exalted, Christ's message is propagated and Christ's love is put into action.

Based in California.

http://www.4marks.com/ (LS)
4marks.com is an Internet platform which helps people meet and exchange information, enabling them to connect in the physical world and strengthen Christian culture.

4marks, LLC
P.O. Box 154
Zelienople, PA 16063

http://www.mychurch.org
MyChurch.org is a free online tool for churches to outreach and build community by networking their congregation. Amongst some of its features

are a library for sermons and media, a social network, a classifieds board, a collaborative blog, a photo sharing app, and an event calendar for you and your church. There are premium subscriptions available for a monthly fee for churches who wish to have extra disk space, support, and services. Founded by Joe Suh.

http://www.sermoncloud.com/
Online sermons from preachers
For the Community: Sermon Cloud is a website for a community to interact with sermons. What are the powerful sermons people are listening to? Who are the up-and-coming preachers of the day? Where are the messages about themes that you need to hear? How can you find a great preacher in your home town? Sermon Cloud was designed to help you with all of these questions.

Sermon Cloud users help let each other know which sermons they amen. An 'amen' is a recommendation of the sermon. Users can post comments about their interaction with these sermons (even the comments can be designated as helpful or unhelpful).

Sermon Cloud was created by Monk Development and is powered by Ekklesia 360 CMS.

Monk Development
2802 Mimika Place
San Diego, CA 92111
(877) 452-0015 Toll-Free
(877) 452-0015 Fax
info@monkdevelopment.com

http://www.buddhistconnect.com/site/
BuddhistConnect is the first online network for the Buddhist community that provides a truly trustworthy network for meeting friends, finding romantic partners, and making business contacts. You don't need to be religious to join—it's a network of friends with similar interests and values.
BuddhistConnect is an independent company truly dedicated to the ideal of sound business practice and encouraging positive values in today's world. BuddhistConnect is not affiliated with any other group or organization,

religious or otherwise. BuddhistConnect is wholly owned by Simpatico Networks Inc., the company that created the largest network of multi-faith spiritual content on the Web, Faith.com. Simpatico Networks Inc. is also the owner of BuddhistConnect's sister site: Buddhist Gateway.

On Buddhist Gateway, you can find information on Buddhist holidays and rituals, Buddhist sacred texts, thousands of links to Buddhist Resources, carefully selected Buddhist articles, audio clips, and video clips as well as a directory of Buddhist centers. The editors of Buddhist Gateway and of this site, BuddhistConnect, are Harvard-educated specialists in religion, who have worked for many years to bring only the most captivating and relevant Buddhist material to these carefully curated websites.

BuddhistConnect is a trademark of Simpatico networks.

Simpatico Networks
Planetarium Station
P.O. Box 269
New York, NY 10024

Sports

http://sportsvite.com/
Sportsvite is a privately-held company based in New York City and Northern Virginia. Our main office address is 72 Madison Avenue, 5th Floor, New York, NY 10016.

Vinodh V. (Vin) Bhat, Co-founder and President
Steve Parker, Co-founder and CTO
Neal Shenoy, Co-founder and VP, Corporate Development
Bob Daly, Director of Engineering
Clint Balcom, Creative Director
Brian Litvack, Director of Business Development
Keith Emmer, Communications Director
Nirav Patel, Key Engineer

Sportsvite was started for everyone who loves sports but finds it frustrating to actually organize games or find people who want to play them. To help, we've built the premier Web service for organizing active sports and connecting with other players for league teams, pick-up games, and sports/ activity groups.

Sportsvite combines sports-specific targeted search and member profiles with user-friendly invitation and game management tools. Members can also keep track of stats and future games, send out e-mail invitations, and maintain their schedule for their teams in leagues or casual pick-up games. Sportsvite is and always will be a free service for our members.

http://urbantailgate.com/
Site for sports fans. Founded by Stroker and Chris. Based in New York.

http://takkle.com/ (LS)
Mostly aimed at high school foot/basket/baseballers mostly in the U.S. Takkle is the social network for high school sports. Join today, and you can post photos and videos, share stats and schedules, and a whole lot more with others throughout the Takkle community. Takkle is a place where students, athletes, coaches, and fans can share their passion for sports.

press@takkle.com

http://crickem.com (LS)
CrickeM is a place to meet other cricket fans and players, share your own experiences and enjoy photos and videos from around the world. Mr. Sashi Chimala, co-founder.

PayPod Incorporated
2275 East Bayshore Road, Suite 115
Palo Alto, CA 94303-3224
info@paypod.com

http://goruneasy.com/
Promotional social network for runners by Reebok.

Reebok Customer Service at 781-401-5000 or write to us: Reebok International Ltd., Attn: Customer Service-RunEasy, 1895 JW Foster Boulevard, Canton, Massachusetts, 02021 USA.

http://www.macexperience.com/

MAC Experience (MAC) is the premier, global martial arts inspired multi-channel broadband video, digital marketplace, and social network destination. This family-friendly lifestyle brand celebrates the influence of martial arts inspired entertainment and personal development. Based in New Jersey, MAC Experience is part of Breakthrough Interactive Group, Inc. (BIG)

http://outdoorzy.com/ (LS)

Hi An,

I have prepared a brief overview of our company in the format you requested (attached). Please feel free to ask any questions you would like and also to use our logo in the book if you want. I would love a copy of the book when it gets published. Your subject should make for a very interesting read!

Please keep us updated on your progress!
Thanks,
Wade

-Founders & management
Wade Heflin — Marketing, Advertising, Business Development, Member Development
Emile Webb — Financials, Design, Marketing, Business Development, Member Development
Lynn Miller — Design, Site Development, Technical Development, Business Development

-Founding year & address/nationality
In January of 2006 Wade and Emile were talking about the lack of a good online community to discuss outdoor related topics. There were several good message boards, review sites, gear sellers, and blogs. But there wasn't a good way to actually network and interact with other "outdoorzy" people. So in response we began designing Outdoorzy.com. Not long after this, Lynn came onboard. This rounded out our skill sets, and we got the site built and began beta testing in November of 2006. The site combines a blog, message board, reviews, and ties them all together with a robust community.
Now, working from a bedroom in a little house in Kentucky, we are building a community of amazing outdoor adventurers. Every day new members join who blow us away with their stories. We are truly humbled by the company we are in on Outdoorzy.com.

Address: *739 Fern Hill Bowling Green, KY 42101* Nationality – *U.S.*

-Target audience & membership level (number of users)
Avid outdoor sports enthusiasts are our target market. We are focused on the hardcore outdoor athletes who spend their spare time pushing themselves through their adventures. Currently (February 2007) we have over three hundred members. Feel free to contact me with a more updated membership count closer to publishing time, we are growing rapidly.

-Top three countries in which the community is used
US, Canada, Spain (UK closely trails Spain)

-Main technical features and possible features in the near future
Main features - Trip Reports, Gear Reviews, Gear Lists, Event Calendar, Personal Messaging, Comment Capability (for Profile, Trip Reports, Gear Reviews, and Gear Lists)

Features being developed or planned - Life Goals are where members create a checklist of life goals pertaining to their outdoor pursuits, Business Profiles designed to help outdoor oriented businesses promote themselves, Video Upload Capability, Mapping Software for members to map their own adventures, Business Mini-Stores to assist small outdoor oriented businesses in selling their products online, Member Blogs (an abbreviated version with more simplistic features than Wordpress, etc.)

-Languages in which the service is available
English. We have plans to provide a Spanish option as well.

http://golferlinkup.com/
Welcome to Golfer Linkup!
Connect with Golfers all over the world.
Share your knowledge and learn from others.
Golfer LinkUp is the premier online golfing community for golfing enthusiasts.

This site is made up of tools and functionalities designed specifically for your needs. They allow you to create a profile and connect with others. Learn from the community and from syndicated content and contribute your own content as well.

Profiles – Create your online identity. Post pictures and information about yourself, so others can get to know you. Easily create your very own blog. Manage all of your Golfer Linkup activity and postings from one convenient place.

Linkup – Connect with your community. Find people with the same goals and interests as you. Share your experiences and connect with people who are involved with the golfing community. Send messages, meet new people and add new friends to your personal community.

News & Articles – Read exclusive content from top industry sources. Expert authors provide insights into the issues that affect you. Read & post comments about current topics that impact your hobby.

Forums – You have an opinion... share it with your community. Use forums, commenting and community centric messaging to make your voice heard. Participate in discussions, share information and learn from the interactions that take place.

Founded in April 2007.

http://ultrafan.com (LS)

An,

Below you will find a one-page description of UltraFan.com, which addresses the questions you had listed in your original e-mail. If you need additional information please don't hesitate to contact me. I hope this helps with your book and please send us a copy when it is published! By the way, when do you anticipate it will hit stores?

Best regards,

Anna Marie Neri

Community Overview:

UltraFan.com is a sports-specific online community developed by XOS Technologies in late 2006. Still in beta mode, UltraFan inspires team fervor among its more than 100,000 member account users while simultaneously bridging the communication gap between worldwide sports fans. The social networking site has formed a steadily growing community of sports fanatics who foster friendly rivalry and encourage a whole new generation of cyber sports fans to extend spirit into their personal online realms. Fans can create a free profile by visiting www.UltraFan.com

Founders and Management:

UltraFan was established by XOS Network, a business unit of XOS Technologies (www. xostech.com). The company is headquartered in Orlando, Fla. and offers comprehensive, cutting-edge technology solutions geared to help professional and collegiate sports teams, conferences, leagues, and athletic administrators win on and off the field. XOS serves more than 480 clients representing more than 900 teams in the NFL, AFL, CFL, NBA, WNBA, NHL, MLB, MLS, NAIA, NCAA, and in NASCAR.

Nada Usina serves as XOS Network president and oversees the entire business unit. Usina plays an integral role in the development of new business and emerging technologies. Under her leadership, the concept of UltraFan became a reality.

Jeff Abele serves as XOS Network's director of product marketing and initially developed the product plan for UltraFan and XOS' community initiatives.

Kim Matlock serves as XOS Network's vice president of Community. Matlock provides strategic direction for the development, growth, and marketing of UltraFan and leads her team in the pursuit of new opportunities to strengthen the brand through strategic partnerships.

UltraFan Stats:

Established in beta form in November 2006
Developed and marketed within the United States (uses the English language)
Currently has more than 100,000 member accounts
Target audience is sports fanatics of professional and collegiate sports — any team, any league.
Current Features include posting video files, posting pictures, blogging, posting comments to friends, sending messages/e-mails, rating other fans' profiles.

XOS plans to offer UltraFan capabilities to its more than 150 Network partners to provide greater content and sharing opportunities for UltraFan users and to boost brand awareness for its partners. In addition, XOS will continue to expand interactive functionality during beta phase.

UltraFan is a community and social networking site designed especially for sports fans like you. Each UltraFan will be able to create a full profile page with the ability to post their own video, photos, and blogs. In addition, each UltraFan will be able to mark and share favorite video and photos and actively participate in message boards and adding comments to profile pages.

601 Codisco Way
Sanford, FL 32771
Main Line: 407-936-0800

Media Contact
Anna Marie Neri
Public Relations Manager
Office: 407-936-2593
Cell: 321-262-6325
aneri@xostech.com

http://www.freethefan.com/
We set out to create a place for fans to take control of sports talk. We want to give you the platform to voice your opinions, passions, and predictions.

We know you don't want to be left on the outside, being told what to think. So we have created an arena for you to debate the hottest sports headlines, win prizes, and watch the best sports video online.

Sharing your videos and opinions is easy. Choose between Recording with your Webcam, Uploading Video from your computer or Embedding video from other sites like Youtube and Revver.

You can make a statement about last night's game or share that amazing clip that you found first.

It's your site. We give you the tools and get out of the way.

Contact

Free The Fan is a privately held company with offices in Jersey City, NJ and Denver, CO.

Free The Fan
30 Montgomery St
Suite 1502
Jersey City, NJ 07302

http://www.bikespace.net/
We are two graduate students who made a website.
BikeSpace.net is an online social network for cyclists. We have recently just released an alpha version of our site; it is free to all and offers some serious tools. Some of our current features:

-User profiles with bio, photographs, and a section to show off your gear
-Map, store, and share your favorite riding routes with other cyclists
-Create a friend list and send out invitations for rides. You can make your rides public (all riders in your area) or private (only people you specifically invite)
-Form groups of riders, post news and pics, and send ride invitations to your group

BikeSpace.net is just getting started, and we are asking cyclists to check it out and let us know what you think. Your feedback is greatly appreciated. We are hoping to have an official beta release by the end of the year and look forward to meeting you online, as well as on the road.

http://www.fasthockey.com/
FASTHockey

The FASTHockey community is designed to help hockey players advance their playing careers. Players have the ability to showcase their resumes to coaches, scouts, and family. FASTHockey also gives coaches an easy-to-use site where they find, interact with, and recruit players.

FASTPlayers

Hockey players joining the FASTHockey community are all ages, all skill levels and from the United States, Canada, and Europe. Each player creates and updates their own FASTHockey profile for coaches, scouts, family advisors, and others to view. They also have access to forums, chat rooms, an on-line store, and other team members or hockey friends.

Coaches, Scouts & Family Advisors

Coaches, Scouts & Family Advisors joining the FASTHockey community have access to all of the same features that players have with the addition of Recruiting Management, Calendaring, and Contacts. They search the FASTHockey community to find players that they might want to talk to while, at the same time, adding their own players to their "FASTRecruits" page—a page that only they and their coaching staff see.

Coaches, Scouts & Family Advisors in the FASTHockey community are quickly realizing that FASTHockey is the one place to keep all of their player recruiting information in a safe, secure, and valuable Web based environment.

Massachusets-based. Launched in March 2007.

http://www.yogamates.com/ (LS)
Looking for a place where yoga is the common ground? Want to talk asanas or find a yoga-minded roommate? Yogamates.com is the Web's premiere online yoga community, bringing yoga off the mat and onto the internet.

A forum for the likeminded, yogamates.com brings yogis together to meet, exchange ideas, share services, buy yoga products and find studios, or take their practice on the road with yoga travel and retreat escapes.

Looking for enlightenment? Yogamates.com is also a worldwide yoga community bulletin board, broadcasting the latest in healthy living, conscious careers, yoga and meditation practices, healing and interactive media.

6464 W Sunset Blvd.
Ste 1080
Los Angeles, CA 90028
323 464 8848
877 YOGAMTS
info@yogamates.com

http://www.ruggerspace.com/ (LS)
For rugby enthusiasts.
RuggerSpace.com is an International Online Rugby Community. RuggerSpace was started in an effort to connect rugby players and fans all over the world. Rugby being one of the most popular sports in the world is played or watched by millions of people. RuggerSpace was founded by Danny Graves, Jason Brink, and Nav Ghildyal. We continue to provide our members with the most cutting edge technology available today.

Contact us at info@ruggerspace.com

http://faniq.com/ (LS)
What is FanIQ?
FanIQ is a new type of sports site that empowers sports fans to be sports experts. For the first time, sports fans can accumulate a wide variety of statistics to prove their sports knowledge. Individually, fans compete to provide the most accurate predictions, submit the best news articles and write the best blogs. Collectively, this competition results in the best sports content from across the Web and proprietary "Wisdom of Crowds" data.

Why does the world need another sports site?
FanIQ is challenging the traditional sources of sports expertise by bringing accountability to the world of sports. FanIQ has developed a proprietary peer to peer poll system and a wiki-like system to let fans submit predictions on behalf of their favorite sports "experts." For the first time, it's easy to pull together opinions from a wide variety of sources as evidenced by the eight million sports opinions and predictions that have been collected so far. How do fans do vs. the experts? The FanIQ Consensus beat the expert average from sites like ESPN, SI.com, and Sportingnews during the 2006–2007 NFL season.

Who?

FanIQ was founded by a frustrated sports fan who was tired of hearing friends complain about sports experts. FanIQ is located in San Francisco and is angel-funded by a group of successful entrepreneurs.

www.joga.com

The community for soccer players dedicated to keeping the game beautiful. Joga is a place to meet other soccer players, share your own soccer experiences and enjoy photos and videos from around the world. Joint venture between Google and Nike.

http://golf.sossoon.net/

Founded by Tia Carr Williams.

The Fairway is a premier online golfing community serving golfers worldwide. Here you can grow your golfing connections, find friends, create golf outings, share tips, vacation and play the world's best courses.

Specialised event planners can create Business Golfing Experiences for your corporate outings. Join today and enjoy three months free membership.

http://go211.com/

Go211.com is the premier community hub created by and for action sports athletes and enthusiasts. It's the place to hang with the Pros and friends to:

- Watch exclusive content of the top athletes in the world
- Vote on videos
- Upload your own videos to share with your friends
- Listen to music tracks & create your own playlists
- Express your individuality by creating your personal profile

Go211.com is taking action sports to the next level.

Founded in March 2007.

Ceo Sean M. Aruda

http://www.iamatrailblazersfan.com
Trail Blazers and Hands on Greater Portland Launch First Social Networking
Site for Fans in Partnership with Affinity Circles.

The iamatrailblazersfan site is the first official social network for professional
basketball fans, providing a unique opportunity for fans to connect with
one another, the team, and the community in new and innovative ways.

http://sportsmates.com/ (LS)
SportsMates, Inc. is a privately-held firm based in Marin County,
California. It operates SportsMates, the first global social networking and
next-generation community service for sports fans. SportsMates is designed
to enable sports fans to connect and communicate using a robust social
networking platform.

SportsMates originally began in 2004 when its founders recognized that
niche social networks focused on topics that people are passionate about
and that play a role in people's daily lives would provide the most value to
users and would have long-term staying power. Having been deeply involved
in the online sports media business, the founders knew that sports was the
perfect niche for social networking and that a viable business model could
be built around the sports social networking concept.

SportsMates is a global sports social network founded by a group of
passionate sports fans, who have created and managed some of the largest
sports communities on the Internet over the last eight years. SportsMates
creates an environment where fans and athletes from all cultures and
geographical locations can share their passion for sports with likeminded
fans. SportsMates combines:

- Thousands of communities ("clubs") for international pro sports
  leagues, teams and players
- Full-featured message boards
- Feeds from over a thousand of the Internet's best sports blogs
- Fan directories
- An online event posting, RSVP and alert system
- Fan-created link directories

- Advanced search tools that enable you to locate and connect with fans who share your sporting interests
- The ability to create your own public or private online club complete with message boards, events and fan and link directories

Upcoming features include photo galleries, video and live 24/7 chat, including hosted chats with professional sports personalities.

SportsMates is the only sports social network that is building a program that rewards its users for their active participation! When you contribute to the community and recruit your friends, you're building points that will soon be redeemable for sports-related products and services, as well as eligible to receive special offers and promotions from sponsors!

CEO Blair Cummins

SportsMates, Inc.
448 Ignacio Blvd. PMB 349
Novato, CA 94949
Phone: (415) 884-9645
press@sportsmates.com

Students

http://mycollegedaily.com/ (LS)
Why MyCollegeDaily?
MyCollegeDaily: Music network? Video network? or Social network? All of the above.
What's Different?

Social Networking 2.0! The first of its kind to actually combine verything you want in one location. Nowhere else can you share uninterrupted music, watch exclusive videos, view photos from last night's kickin party and simply represent all that is college.

Who's Here?

The students. You govern this site. So join now and invite your friends. (Remember, in order to be part of this exclusively college student network you will need an .edu account.)

The MyCollegeDaily.com Web site is provided by CO-ED Media Group, Llc.

CO-ED Media Group, LLC
c/o Muchnick, Golieb & Golieb, P.C.
200 Park Avenue South, Suite 1700
New York, NY 10003

http://carmun.com/

Carmun was born out of my own frustrations during graduate school. After many years of working as a senior executive at AOL, I went back to school to get a Ph.D. in business. Collaboration is necessary and expected, but I failed to find that same camaraderie when I began my program in medieval Celtic and Insular literature. Graduate school was lonely. I struggled to find anyone willing to burn the midnight oil discussing Beowulf, and there were even fewer who would listen to me read it aloud in Old English. I figured that there had to be fellow travelers out there, but I just didn't know how to find them.

Through this experience came the idea for Carmun. It connects students who share academic passions. It easily organizes academic research, and it is expanding the boundaries of universities by creating a database of rated and reviewed source material. Imagine an academic community where you can tap into the intellectual horsepower of students around the country or even the world. We hope you will help us build this at Carmun.

By the way, there is a story behind the site's name, but to find out you will have to join, search for my group on Celtic studies, and read about it on my blog!

Jonathan Edson
Founder and CEO

Contact us at help@carmun.com
809 Massachusetts Avenue, Lexington, MA 02420.

http://schoolster.com/

Schoolster helps people connect and stay in contact with high school and college friends within an online community.

Schoolster is owned and operated by Trancos, Inc., a privately held, Internet media company, that was founded in 1999, with headquarters based in Redwood City, California.

http://www.myyearbook.com (LS)

MyYearbook.com is an online yearbook for the digital age where more than 1,700,000 young people around the world — from teens to college students to young professionals — gather to socialize. The youngest internet site for social networking, myYearbook.com was founded by Catherine Cook, a high school senior, and her older brother Dave Cook, who graduated from high school in June 2006 and is now a freshman at the University of Colorado, Boulder. Their first investor was their older brother, Geoff, a veteran Internet entrepreneur, who founded and sold a set of online writing and editing services, EssayEdge.com and ResumeEdge.com, while a Harvard undergrad. The company is headquartered in New Hope, PA.

david@myyearbook.com , catherine@myyearbook.com

http://www.sconex.com/

Sconex is the unofficial website for your high school — a place where you can read about your classmates, share stuff with your friends, and communicate with people from your school and nearby ones.

Here are some of the things you can do once you're a member of Sconex:

1. Set up a profile, share photos, post a mini-blog.
2. Learn about classmates and checkout who they know.
3. Post and read messages for your school, clubs and classes.
4. Search for other high school students.
5. Secretly test if someone likes you.
6. See what's popular in your school and nationwide.
7. Make and Take Fun Quizzes.

Based in New York. Founded by Josh Schanker.

https://www.ripl.com/
Located in Seattle's Belltown, RIPL is changing the way people interact online with a personalized, dynamic experience that makes it easier and safer for you to exchange ideas, interests, pictures, and music only with people you know.

RIPL was founded by it's current CEO, Bill Messing. Membership is free, but by invitation only. The site is aimed at students (18-24-year-olds).

Patrick Barthe
Customer Relations
RIPL Corp.
2226 Third Avenue
Seattle, Washington 98121

patrick.barthe@ripl.com
Cell: 206-351-8664

http://www.b4class.com/
High school network with free tutoring, founded in March 2007 by Sofia Loginova, 17y, of Quincy (Boston), Massachusets.

I have created B4Class.com as a way to communicate with your friends in a real time manner. Where else can you web cam to web cam and also be updated on what's hot or not?

My goal is to provide a fun and interactive online community that is user-friendly and allows members to freely and safely meet other great people. We're unique. We are offering something nobody is offering – how about free online tutoring for your GMATS, LSAT, and SATs. We will have one of the country's best tutors giving you free tips on how to score higher on your tests. Each week we will also allow you to interact with Super Dan in real time. Imagine being able to increase your scores and not have to pay thousands of dollars for a few hours of tutoring.

Members enjoy free use of all site services and features, including detailed online profiles, photos, group chat, one-to-one video chat, onsite e-mail, event planning and detailed member searches.

Our secure online server makes talking with friends anonymous and safe. Feel free to meet new people from the comfort of your own room.

http://localschools.com/
LocalSchools.com is an interactive education web portal that connects prospective students to accredited colleges and universities in the US with the mapping and communication technologies of web 2.0. LocalSchools.com provides students, parents, educational institutions, guidance counselors, faculty members, and professionals a one-source medium of communication among each other and insightful information about the education market. LocalSchools.com is the place for prospective and current students, Alumni, and educational institutions to meet each other and interact on a variety of platforms.
The LocalSchools Website Features:

- A complete directory of over 3,400 accredited campus-based colleges and universities in the US
- Up-to-date information about each school including
    o   enrollment numbers
    o   programs offered
    o   application fees
    o   information about surrounding cities and towns
    o   applicant test score averages
- Easy to use searches that allow you to find a school by
    o   geography
    o   degree programs
    o   school size
- Saved searches
- Side by side school comparison charts that allow you to narrow down your search
- A helpful resource section with recent articles on
    o   trends in education

- o   financing your education
- o   local & national scholarship information
- o   pre-tests to help prepare you for the college entrance exams
- Create your own secure home page that links you to
  - o   career placement websites
  - o   RSS feeds
  - o   chat rooms
  - o   instant messaging
  - o   prospective, current, and former students
  - o   educational institutions

LocalSchools is owned and operated by EduCatalyst, Inc.

EduCatalyst, Inc.
340 Central Avenue
Suite 302
Dover, NH 03820
Phone: 800.379.6147
Fax: 603.749.4280

http://www.zinch.com/
(...)And that is why I founded Zinch: to level the playing field and to provide a means by which individuality and greatness can be extracted from everyone during the college admissions process. Zinch turns the tables of college admissions, putting the control back in the hands of the student. Every student will now have an equal opportunity to basically say, "This is me. Love me, hate me, recruit me, or trash me. This is who I am."

Mick Hagen
Princeton University, '09
President/Founder of Zinch

Phone: 801.830.2048
Fax: 801.356.0293
E-mail: info@zinch.com

42 N. University Ave. Suite #210
Provo, Utah 84601
USA

http://thecollegelife.com/
Welcome to TheCollegeLife.com, the next generation in social networking for college students. Our goal is to create an online community for students by students. We offer a centralized forum that allows students to interact with peers on their campus as well as others across the country. We focus on a philosophy of listening to our users and providing them the opportunity to voice their opinions in the growth and development of the site. We welcome all suggestions and criticisms as our objective is to give you what you truly desire from a social networking destination. College is in our name and at the core of our vision, and we intend to keep it that way. We are not looking to take over the world with social networking, and we recognize that college students need a place to call their own without worrying that high school students and their parents are going to access their profiles.

If we are not open at your school and you would like us to consider adding it, please let us know and help spread the word at your campus. If we get enough interest generated, we will expand to include your school.

Founded in Illinois in March 2007.

http://collegeclub.com/
The top online destination for college students, CollegeClub, gives students access to a vibrant community of their peers and content specifically focused on college life, delivering an authentic voice to college students.
Target: 18 – 24 year olds.Monthly Uniques : 313,000.

http://www.connectu.com/ (LS)
ConnectU is an online meeting place for students by students. ConnectU tears down the walls that separate you from so many people in your hectic life. Tired of slim-pickings? Can't find anyone who shares your same interests? Now you can instantly search and view profiles of students at over 500 universities. And as if we didn't make it easy enough for you already, you can instantly chat with any user online.

The idea of ConnectU was spawned in the winter of 2002 after it became obvious that the social and dating scene at Harvard needed some work. Initially we may have used the site as a springboard for hitting on Boston's finest, but we eventually decided to deliver on our claims to improve our campus social scene by creating an online, university-wide friends and dating network.

Based in Boston, Massachusets
admin@connectu.com

http://campusbug.com/ (LS)
Campusbug is the leading provider of internet services for today's students. Members can access a wide range of services to meet their needs. These services include online educational assistance, social networking, an online marketplace, and much more. Our goal is to provide a global distributed information network that brings people together for an inexpensive and easy to use learning environment.
Vak Sambath founded Medmania, Inc. in 2004. The corporate office is headquartered in Orange County, Ca. The flagship website is Campusbug. Campusbug delivers a first class service that integrates quality, volume, and reliability through a variety of services.

Campusbug.com
1643 W. Chapman Ave.
Orange, Ca 92868

campusbughelp@yahoo.com

http://www.collegetonight.com/ (LS)
College Tonight is the premiere nightlife and social networking site on the internet.
Catering to college students, graduate students and alumni, it focuses on the local nightlife that surrounds each college, and acts as your general, social sidekick.

Zach Suchin
President & CEO

Daniel Weisman
Director of Media

College Tonight LLC
dweisman@collegetonight.com

http://campusrank.com/
CampusRank is a social network that lets you find and rate your friends in yearbook style categories. (based on Facebook)

Press, privacy, business, bugs, kudos, complaints: info@campusrank.com

CampusRank
617.308.5395
Cambridge, MA

www.classmates.com
Classmates Online, Inc., founded in 1995 and based in Renton, WA, is a leader in online social networking. The company operates Classmates. com (www.classmates.com), connecting millions of members throughout the U.S. and Canada with friends and acquaintances from school, work and the military. Its Classmates International subsidiary also operates leading community-based networking sites in Sweden, through Klassträffen Sweden AB (www.stayfriends.se), and in Germany, through StayFriends GmbH (www.stayfriends.de). Classmates Online is a wholly owned subsidiary of United Online, Inc. (Nasdaq: UNTD). For more information about United Online and its Internet subscription services, please visit www.untd.com

Management Team:
Sanjay Anand, Senior Vice President of Operations
Michel Lindenberg, Senior Vice President, Europe
Brian Pane, Senior Vice President, Chief Technology Officer
Lisa Sharples, Senior Vice President of Marketing
Drew Atherton, Vice President of Finance
Shawn Davis, Vice President of Direct Marketing
Abani Heller, Vice President of Analytics & Reporting
Bob O'Keefe, Vice President of Creative Services

Brett Thompson, Vice President of Human Resources
Brad Toney, Vice President, Corporate Counsel
John Uppendahl, Vice President of Public Relations & Community Affairs

Our address:
Classmates Online, Inc.
2001 Lind Ave. SW
Suite 500
Renton, WA, USA 98055

http://www.lifeatcollege.com/ (LS)
LifeAtCollege.com is privately owed. LifeAtCollege.com specializes in the college market and has been in operation since 2002.

Wesley Killian
CEO

860 Boardman Canfield Rd. Suite 205
Boardman, OH
USA 44512
Voice: 330-965-0739
Fax: 330-965-3859
E-Mail: wes@lifeatcollege.com

http://www.campusgrind.com/
Gregory Rzeczko, Campusgrind creator, said his main reason for creating the site is to give students the opportunity to make money off of their used books. A friend from his high school, Wojciech Pirog, who was studying computer science in Poland, joined him. Ever since, the two have been the only ones working on the site.
The site was officially launched on June 21, 2004.

http://www.biglicku.com/
Big Lick U is a social web site that seeks to bring together college students in Southwest Virginia through news and information, entertainment and advertising. Though most of the site is public, only registered users with

valid .edu e-mail addresses can take full advantage of our site because we recognize that college students want and need their own place on the Web (and other sites have decided to take that away).

Registered users, or Big Lick U students, can set up their Planners and DormRooms, connect with current friends in the area or make new ones, seek out the hottest things going on in the region, rate and review businesses from Pulaski to Roanoke, manage the clubs and organizations they belong to, follow their favorite college sports teams (from intercollegiate to club to intramural), listen and download music from local bands and keep up-to-date with news and information that they won't find anywhere else. Launched in the spring of 2007, Big Lick U is a property of the Times-World Corp., a subsidiary of Landmark Communications, a privately-held Virginia-based company.

http://www.student.com/ (LS)

The Student Center is a community site for college students, high school students, and teens. We reach a 13–24 year old audience of students. Our company, The Student Center, Inc., also owns and operates Campus Hook. The Student Center was founded in 1995 by Jeff Edelman. Back then, the site was very, very small with not much content. There were a few helping hands here and there, keeping the content fresh and interesting. At that time, there was no logging in, no points, no profiles – we just had the discussion boards and forums!

In March 2000 Matt Hollander joins up with Jeff to start developing the site. His brother, Mike, joined up to help create the login system, the points system, and the fortune wheel. Slowly but surely, the Student Center was on its way

The Student Center, Inc.
9A Main Street
Irvington, NY 10533
USA
jeff@student.com

http://www.campushook.com/
Social networking site specifically for college students ages 18–24. Operated by The Student Center.

Travel

http://pairup.com (LS)
Esteban Sardera is the founder of PairUp, a combination of travel planning with social networking. Started in May 2006.

PairUp, Inc.
3700 Divisadero Street Suite 303
San Francisco, CA 94123

Press: info@pairup.com

Esteban Sardera
CEO
PairUp
Mobile 888 ESTEBAN (888 378 3226)
esteban@pairup.com

http://matadortravel.com/
Matador is a meeting place. It's a place for you to express yourself, tell others about your adventures, get meaningful travel advice, and take inspiration from the beautiful and remarkable things others like you have discovered all across the globe.

We started Matador because we love to travel. When we travel, we are constantly amazed and inspired by the people we meet, the cultures we're exposed to, and the adventures we have. We want to share our discoveries with you and allow you to share yours with us. The result will be a community of travelers, adventurers, and vacationers connected by their thirst for the unknown.

Travel is a vehicle for uniting individual voices, minds and ideas. As travelers, we are, in a sense, freelance ambassadors; not only do we return with stories of other cultures and ways of life, but we also share our own culture and ways of life with the people we meet along the way. We at Matador believe this exchange is essential to bringing about positive development in our rapidly changing world.

Founded by Ben & Ross.

info@matadortravel.com

Based in San Francisco, California

http://tripup.com/

Founded August 2006. Sam Rogoway and Emily Dahlberg recently left behind exciting entertainment industry careers in the heart of Hollywood to realize their dream of running a successful internet start-up. Are they crazy? Maybe.... but they love to travel and wanted to create the coolest interactive travel community on the web.

Sam Rogoway (CEO, Founder) graduated summa cum laude from Loyola Marymount University in Los Angeles with a B.A. in Political Science and obtained his law degree from Boalt Hall School of Law, at the University of California, Berkeley. After passing the action-packed bar exam, Sam practiced entertainment law at a prestigious Santa Monica law firm. However, a career as a lawyer to the stars did not allow Sam the time he needed to pursue his internet endeavors. So he left the legal world and started TripUp, Inc. Originally from Portland, Oregon, Sam has lived in London, England and Florence, Italy, and has traveled all over the world, including stops in Japan, Turkey, and throughout Europe.

Emily Dahlberg (V.P., Marketing & Public Relations) graduated from Pepperdine University in Malibu with a B.A. in Public Relations. Upon graduation, she began working her way up in the entertainment industry, one desk at a time. Eventually she became a personal publicist for celebrities at a well-respected boutique PR firm in Beverly Hills. While red carpet life in the PR fast lane was a glamorous one, she wanted to explore her inner entrepreneur and left the biz to join Sam on the TripUp journey. Originally from Wayzata, Minnesota, Emily has lived in Florence, Italy, and has traveled to France, Switzerland, Israel, Costa Rica, and Australia.

The idea for TripUp originated with a group of friends vacationing in the Caribbean who became frustrated when out-of-date and out-of-touch guide books led them to deserted clubs, stuffy hotels, and horrible restaurants. Sitting in an empty bar (described in one guide book as "the place to party"), they imagined a website where you could ask locals and fellow travelers (the real travel experts) for candid advice about your upcoming trip and also meet cool people to hang out with or even travel with while away. Upon their return, they developed TripUp to improve their future trips, as well as everyone else's. Additionally, they added a bunch of exciting features, so you can plan and share your fantastic travels with your friends.

Whether you are interested in meeting locals or fellow travelers during a trip or finding a "trip buddy" so you don't have to travel alone, TripUp gets you connected before you depart. Plus, as a TripUp member, you can create Trip Flicks, Trip Blogs and Trip Albums to share your travel videos, journals and photos, find current and candid information about your destination from our member-created travel reviews and Trip Forum, ask a "trip guru" for insider advice about your destination, organize group trips with Tripvite, and explore all of the fun places your tripmates have discovered.

TripUp is based in Los Angeles, California

Miscellaneous

http://www.seatsnapper.com/ (LS)
SeatSnapper.com is a search platform for sports, concerts, theater, and other live event tickets. At its core, SeatSnapper.com features an interactive seating map system which makes it easy to compare the seat positions of available tickets for any given event.

The SeatSnapper Social Network is an extension of SeatSnapper Memberships, which enables members to create profiles and Wish Lists that can be used for business networking or online dating. Once signed up for this free service, members complete a profile, upload a photo, and indicate which events they wish to attend. They can now also invite friends to join their social network and can choose to use the Plaxo Address Book Access Widget to easily invite people from their address book.

SeatSnapper is owned and operated by Strongtooth, Inc.
Strongtooth, Inc.
386 Park Avenue South
13th Floor
New York, NY 10016

Tel: +1-212-481-1326
Fax: +1-212-504-2755

Seatsnapper was launched on September 20, 2006.

Media Contact:
Evan Kaye, Founder & CEO
Strongtooth, Inc.
evan@strongtooth.com

(212)-481-1326

http://www.respectance.com/
Respectance is a social network where you can honor the deceased by
creating a profile for them on the Web.

220 Montgomery Street, Suite 1105, San Francisco, CA 94109
support@respectance.com

http://copconnection.net
Online, invitation-only community for cops and law-enforcement officers.
Features include:

- Collaboration Tools
- Discussion Area (access through profiles)
- Phone/Conferencing (through profiles)
- Wiki Pages (password available – profiles)

The community is based in Nashville, Tennessee.

http://www.themulch.com/
Online community for gardeners, created by Mitch Shirts. Based in South-
California.

http://www.naseeb.com/
Naseeb ("destiny") is an online community that connects young, educated,
professional Muslims through networks of friends. The site provides a safe,

discreet, and trusted environment for meeting other people with similar backgrounds.

Naseeb.com is for people who are single, people who are married, and anyone who wants to make new friends or help their friends meet new people. The site can be used for personal, social, and business networking.

Naseeb.com is a service of Naseeb Networks, Inc., a Silicon Valley new media company which also operates EidMubarak.com. Naseeb Networks was founded by Internet entrepreneur, Monis Rahman. The site is venture-backed.

1299 Del Mar Avenue
Suite 110
San Jose, CA 95128
USA

http://www.mecca.com/
Ibrahim Al-Husseini and Sami Al-Taher have founded mecca.com. The site is being developed and hosted in partnership with a major, respected web portal in the Middle East. The mecca.com site will be initially launched in Arabic and English to the Middle East, USA, and Great Britain. In the second phase of deployment, strategic partners in Asian and European markets will translate and promote the site to online Muslims in their regions.

http://www.ravelry.com/
Ravelry is a place for knitters, crocheters, designers, spinners, and dyers to keep track of their yarn, tools, and pattern information, and look to others for ideas and inspiration.

Founded by Jessica and Casey.

http://aquariphiles.com/
Aquariphiles is an online gathering place for aquarists. We are an online community providing blogs, social networking opportunities, photo galleries and more to aquarists, fish clubs, and aquatic retailers.

Founded by Don Albrecht, a web developer from Rochester NY
Contact: Donald.albrecht@gmail.com

http://www.curbly.com/
Curbly is a Web community for people who love where they live. Curbly
is the best place to share pictures of your home, find design ideas, and get
expert home-improvement advice.

Team:
Bruno Bornsztein & Ben Moore

Address:
Curbly, LLC
1550 Fulham Street
Saint Paul, MN 55108 (Minneapolis)

http://kuler.adobe.com
Kuler is a color collaboration service. It offers space for those who visit the
site to view colors and information related to colors, and it allows registered
users to additionally create, share, and store color swatches, to discuss color
and to download color swatches.

Founded by Adobe.
Adobe Systems Incorporated
345 Park Avenue,
San Jose,
CA 95110
USA

http://www.tapatap.com
Tapatap is "Your Contest Community" offering infinite contests for fun
and prizes. Create your own contests to share and enter your photos to win.
Explore the community and see how your votes stack up. Tap enough points
and take home some goodies!

Who is Tapatap for?
Tapatap is for anyone who wants to join a community where they
can play in contests, enter contests, or create contests. You may want

to create a contest to get noticed, settle an opinion between friends, promote your band, promote your new products, or just to show off your creative genius. Tapatap is only for people over 13 years old.

Our mission is to create social entertainment networks where you and the community are the fun. You create it, share it, and play it wherever you are across both the web and mobile devices.

Tapatap was founded by three entrepreneurs, Isaac Babbs, Andy Riedel, and Ken Scott, who wanted to create a fun and rewarding community that could be accessed from your PC or on the go.

Mailing Address & Phone
Tapatap, Inc.
2 Fifth Avenue, #301
San Mateo, CA 94402
Tel: +1(650) 344 94 88
Fax: + 1(650) 344-9508

General Inquiries
info@tapatap.com
Launched on June 15, 2007.

http://www.mypicklist.com (LS)
Online shopping has now established itself as a rapidly growing channel for consumers and merchants to buy and sell goods and services. The Internet is a powerful medium for buying and selling goods and services. Consumers benefit from the convenience, selection, and savings available from shopping online; however, they need help in sorting through the large volume of information and choices. MyPickList.com helps consumers make informed purchase decisions. In English terms – MyPickList.com drives word-of-mouth commerce "which retailers love." MyPickList.com integrates a user profile and users' favorite product recommendations into a portable widget (what we call a PickList). Once a user creates a pick list, it can be shared with family, friends or the public by adding the widget to any site that accepts it, including popular sites like MySpace, LiveJournal, Xanga, Friendster, Tagworld, Typepad, Blogger, and his.

MyPickList.com
1117 Sawgrass Corporate Parkway
Sunrise, FL 33323
Phone: (954) 579-6181
Fax: (954) 838-9588

If you have press inquiries, please write to us at press@mypicklist.com

http://www.fanlib.com/
FanLib.com is a free, online service for people who want to write, share, and review fan fiction stories. From time to time, FanLib.com users can also participate in fun fan events.

Headquarters:
FanLib, Inc.
445 S. Beverly Dr.
Beverly Hills, CA 90212

http://www.naturallycurly.com/
Site for curlyheads. Founded by Michelle Breyer & Gretchen Heber in 1998.

For media inquiries, please contact MKlein Communications.
Their phone number is (203) 938-2553

NaturalyCurly.com's snail mail address is
NaturallyCurly.com, Inc.
3415 Greystone Drive #300
Austin, TX 78731

NaturalyCurly.com's phone numbers:
512-371-7545
888-249-9250
512-241-0259 (fax)

http://homeandtell.com/
HomeAndTell is the friendliest place to see real homes and real projects created by real people. From college dorm rooms to apartments in the city,

lofts in the warehouse districts, and craftsmen in the suburbs, homes come in many shapes and sizes and mean something special to each one of us. Each home represents different moments in our lives and is the place where we raise our families, settle our roots, and grow with our community. Capturing the spirit of what home means to each of us is what HomeAndTell is all about! We want you to tell your home story.

While magazines showcase houses built by professional designers and filled with expensive furniture, HomeAndTell brings it down-to-earth and creates a special and relaxed virtual neighborhood for real people to showcase their real homes. Like show-and-tell, the site allows you to proudly share your experiences by displaying photos of your home, projects you have worked on (or are working on), events and parties you're planning, and really letting others get to know you and your own story. And unlike magazines, at HomeAndTell, you can ask questions, share your thoughts, and freely contribute to your community.
At HomeAndTell you can:

- Share your experiences. Do you remember how good it felt to walk into your first home – be it a college dorm room, your first apartment, or the first home you owned? Life is about the experiences we live each day. Write it down and share it, and others will feel as good as you.
- Browse homes or projects. Check out other homes, and you just might find your next home improvement idea.
- Share your thoughts. It's always good to hear what others think, so we've created a way for you to speak your mind through ratings, comments, or compliments.
- Create your own neighborhood. This world doesn't have to feel so big, so go ahead and connect with your neighbors in another city, state, country, or right down the street.
- Collaborate with others. Join a forum and discuss all things home-related. If you've got a question, go ahead and ask and your neighbors as well as our experts will help you out.
- Keep up with the news. Thanks to your neighbors at HomeAndTell who submit and rate new stories, the articles section will keep you up to date with all the latest buzz. You can be part of the news by submitting an original article!

Created by Christine and Jay Nath. In the spring of 2006, they were ready to take the plunge and buy their very first home. Based in San Francisco, California.

Media Inquiries
media@homeandtell.com

HomeAndTell Headquarters
Phone: 510-898-2984

http://ratemyroom.hgtv.com/
Launched in February 2007 by a media concern.

Do you think you've got a flair for decorating? Share your photos with the world and show off your favorite rooms. Just sign in and name your rooms and you're ready to upload photos! Share with friends, rate your favorites and browse other users' rooms for inspiration.

Headquartered in Knoxville, Tenn., with offices in Atlanta, Chicago, Dallas, Detroit, Los Angeles, Nashville and New York, HGTV is wholly owned by The E.W. Scripps Company (NYSE:SSP), which also operates Food Network, DIY Network, Fine Living TV Network and Great American Country.

http://hummingboard.com/ (LS)
Welcome to the HummingBoard — the place where anyone who has been scammed by a business can share their stories and warn their friends.

Operated by Genuosity
E-mail: info@genuosity.com

Genuosity is a private company registered in California with offices in Vancouver and San Diego. Our company is dedicated to the development of word of mouth marketing tools that benefit both consumers and merchants.

http://yacht6.com/user/login
Yacht 6 is an exclusive online community based upon the understanding
that the affluent share a unique lifestyle and social world, one that is better
enjoyed with the advice and company of its peers. Membership is by
invitation only.

Joseph Kumph
josephkumph@gmail.com
10 Startups, Inc.
481 Willow Rd
Menlo Park, CA 94025

http://www.skyspace.biz/
SkySpace is the brainchild of Argentina-born Pablo Bertorello, who affirms
"skySpace is the first social network for Skype, christening new business
models around user-generated content: artistic personalization, original
products, and third-party add-ons like printing, fax, and backup."
SkySpace, the only media-centric social networking software, launched on December
21, 2006. SkySpace will multiply the volume and quality of information shared
among Skype's 136 million users, creating a new market category.

To contact us please call CEO Pablo Bertorello at 1.877.660.6400, Skype:
pmrbertorello.

http://www.well.com/
Stewart Brand and Larry Brilliant founded the Whole Earth 'Lectronic Link
in 1985, starting with a dialog between the fiercely independent writers and
readers of the Whole Earth Review. Salon.com bought The Well in 1999 and
upgraded its servers to greet the century. You don't need an invitation from
a member in order to become part of The Well. The service is distinguished
by our non-anonymous participants and by uncommon policies.

The Well is registered in the U.S. Patent and Trademark Office as a trademark
of Salon Media Group Inc.
101 Spear Street, Suite 203
San Francisco, CA 94105
Telephone: 415 645-9300
Fax: 415 645-9309

http://www.yelp.com/
Yelp is a website that allows users to write and share reviews of local (especially San Francisco) businesses. It also has social networking features (adding friends, groups, etc.) to share reviews with a trust network. The idea is that people generally trust their friends' recommendations. Since July 2004, co-founders Jeremy Stoppelman (CEO) and Russel Simmons (CTO) and their Yelp crew have been striving to make life better for people who love to patronize great local businesses.

http://www.asianavenue.com (LS)

http://www.blackplanet.com/
BlackPlanet.com is a registered trademark of Community Connect Inc.

http://www.net4mac.com/ (LS)
Networking platform for Mac users worldwide. Net4mac offers friends an opportunity to meet friends-of-friends in a known, trusted environment and save valuable time in connecting with the best people, leads, and information. Whether you're looking for a job, a roommate, or a babysitter, your Network of net4mac is the best place to find what you're looking for and to connect with people who share your interests.
press@net4mac.com

USA
net4mac
5126 Stevens Creek Blvd Ste 136
San Jose, CA 95129

France
net4mac
47, rue Maurice Flandin
69003 Lyon
France

Italy
Coming soon

http://militaryspot.com/

With the tremendous success of our postal site – PostalMag.com, we received suggestions that we also design a military site to help American military people find and share military information. We were reluctant at first. The military category is huge, with five services, thousands of different jobs, and bases and operations around the world. We researched other sites and found several that tried to cover everything, but only had a little about a whole lot. But we also found many interesting sites that expertly covered certain segments/categories of military information. Overall, we found that the sum of these many sites were greater than any one site could ever hope to offer. So instead of being redundant and wasting our time and yours by duplicating this info on one site, we decided to offer a military portal. For example, instead of developing our own Army equipment facts files, we have a direct link to the U.S. Army's online facts files. Instead of trying to post all of the day's diverse military news, we've included links (including up-to-the-minute Google news links) to a number of military news sources. That way, you get all of the news, instead of just the top headlines. We've applied this idea across our entire Web site to give you immediate access to all military information, not just some of it!

Chief executive Tom Wakefield
Contact
Mailing Address:
MilitarySpot.com LLC
317 Hunters Creek
Mesquite, TX 75150
Phone: 469-360-9134
E-Mail: contact@militaryspot.com

http://thehuntzone.com/ (LS)

TheHuntZone.com is a social networking service that allows Members to create unique personal profile and web pages dedicated to hunting and outdoor recreational activities online. TheHuntZone.com provides hunters and non-hunters the opportunities to share hunting experiences by providing a service that allows members to share photos, post journals and comments describing their outdoor and hunting activities. The intent of TheHuntZone.com is to become the online campfire where stories are exchanged and friendships develop.

TheHuntZone.com Corporation
406 Tailfeather Ct. NW Bondurant
IA 50035
U.S.A

http://prisonerlife.com/ (LS)
Please contact the WebMaster if you have any problems
P.O. Box 1664 Voorhees, New Jersey 08043
webmaster@prisonerlife.com

http://schoolleadersnetwork.org/
Eduardo Briceño
Co-Founder, School Leaders Network
MBA & M.A. in Ed. Candidate, 2007 | Stanford University
(650) 219-8827
ed@schoolleadersnetwork.org

http://www.yourville.com/ (LS)
Website designed exclusively for expats, their friends, and families. Inside, you'll enjoy a wide array of really cool features that'll enable you to build your own expat community and share your own expat experiences. Want to share the inside scoop on great, fun places to enjoy in Costa Rica? YourVille makes it easy for expats to share all sorts of information while you make new friends.
Texas based.

http://dayzloop.com/
Dear An:

Finally a follow-up about DayZLoop: I have included a short description of our mission, link to our Jan 2007 press release, and an interview questionnaire we were asked to complete for a reporter at 606tech — it seems that you are looking for similar background information. I have also included my short bio and attached my photo along with the DayZLoop logo.

I hope this provides you with sufficient information about DayZLoop, the founder, and our mission.

Wishing you the best of luck and much success with your new book!

Warmest Regards,

Ceca

About DayZLoop ~ DayZLoop.com is the first online infotainment video network that touches on all facets of teen girls' lives. Through channels titled Deco, Subciety, Life-Mode, Shine, E-topia, and Cash-Flow, the site provides meaningful, relevant content for 13- to 17-year-old girls. DayZ Loop is a virtual environment where teens can watch video content, as well as socialize and participate in spiritual, practical, artistic, cultural and fun online activities. The mission of dayZloop.com is to positively impact female youth development and growth, resulting in a change of the fabric of our society for future generations. Our six channels inspire and assist girls to develop and build their self-esteem and the programming provides an essential foundation for living a fulfilling and meaningful life within the context of today's society.

About Ceca Mijatovic — Ceca has over thirteen years of Information Technology experience in successful delivery of profit-driven technologies and professional services. She has worked on numerous large scale, cross-organizational, multi-vendor, global IT implementations; she has also managed and led initiatives and organizations in executive roles in fortune 20 companies and in the startup working environments. She holds a BA in Applied Mathematics.

1000 Connecticut Ave NW
Suite 1000
Washington, DC 20005

http://www.wiredberries.com (LS)
WiredBerries, a subsidiary of Realtimepublishers.com, is a Web 2.0-based social network for women dedicated to pursuing a healthy lifestyle. Created for women, WiredBerries wraps weekly and daily written and audio editorial content of the highest quality around a core of user-generated blogs, photos, recipes, music playlists, outdoor adventures, health and household tips, meditations, fitness advice, and more. Late summer of 2006, WiredBerries

will introduce a revolutionary advance in social-networking functionality and user experience. Chief Executive Officer & Founder: Bailey Sory editor@wiredberries.com

By postal mail or courier:
WiredBerries Editor
Realtimepublishers.com
300 Montgomery Street., Suite 1121
San Francisco, CA

http://www.imbee.com
Imbee is the "first secure social networking and blogging destination for kids." Users can't just connect with each other by browsing profiles. They need to know the e-mail addresses and/or imbee user names of other imbee members.

Kids cannot join the site without a credit card being on file (and not necessarily charged), meaning that someone – probably a parent – is going to have to be involved from the start. Parents can also control the way their kids interact on the site. New messages, connections, and other profile changes get put into a queue for parents to approve – depending on the approval rules put in place.

http://www.eons.com
Eons is a media company scheduled to launch on 31 July 2006. Jeff Taylor, founder of monster.com has raised $10 million in venture capital from several firms to support this project. Eons will focus on the 50-100 year-old age group, which is growing rapidly as the baby boomer generation matures. According to their website, "Eons celebrates life that begins at 50, inspiring a generation of boomers and seniors to do more, see more, learn more, be more on their way to the reachable goal of living to be 100.

http://www.friendsover50.com/
Friendsover50 is an interactive online community for mature adults who want a new way to connect, communicate, and share information with people with similar interests, issues, and challenges.

http://www.vois.com/
Social networking community for users age 30 to 50.

VOIS Inc. (OTC Bulletin Board: VOIS, VOISW) is one of the first publicly traded companies dedicated to uniting social networking and online commerce into social commerce (sCommerce). Led by former AOL senior executives, the company is using advanced technology to merge the power of social networking with online commerce in a single, multi-interest online community. VOIS members will conduct peer-to-peer, business-to-consumer, and business-to-business interactions and commerce transactions with other members inside their multiple communities of interest. VOIS, headquartered in Delray Beach, FL, was founded in June 2007.

http://mytimehero.com
MyTimeHero.com is a community that is designed from the ground up to serve a more mature demographic with relevant content, features, and capabilities that reduce the amount of "tweaking" and configuration that similar sites require.

The true mission of myTimeHero.com is to provide a community that allows simple, quick, and proud usage of the Internet to extend gratitude and respect to those who have become heroes in time. Our TimeHeroes are those who have experienced and endured significant social and technological change in their lifetime. TimeHeroes have contributed to their families, their communities, their culture, and humanity. Now they can be recognized and share their contributions and opinions, their likes and dislikes, their passion and their cynicism with other TimeHeroes.

When you join, you will be able to use all of the following primary features.

- Personal customizable profiles
- Create and join interest groups
- Write articles in your blog
- Search for other TimeHeroes
- Send and receive on-site messages
- A safe all-around experience free of "spam" and "phishing"

Contact: mthsupport@mytimehero.com

Founded by two students at the Rochester Institute of Technology, Ian Peterson & Josh Olin.

http://www.yfly.com

YFly is an entertainment-based social network. Our mission is to provide Gen Y with an excellent social platform and the most entertaining experience online. Who is behind YFly? YFly was conceived by young entrepreneurs Drew Levin and Daniel Perkins while attending the University of Florida. Their vision to create the ultimate social network was accelerated when they met Nick Lachey through common friends and joined forces to bring YFly. com to life. Early stage funding was provided by Tom Petters (Petters Group Worldwide) and later AJ Discala (Brax Capital Group). Media@YFly.com

http://www.mythings.com/

Here at MyThings, we think it's time everyone got more value and enjoyment from our stuff. We all have things—consumer electronics, valuable furniture, collections, or collectibles. Whether you have a household of stuff, a collection of great art, wines, comic books, or sports memorabilia—you name it, MyThings provides a safe, easy-to-use place for you to catalog it and track it online.

Why catalog your things online? For many reasons! Perhaps you want one safe place to house all those details—you know, the random receipts and warranties you've stuffed in a shoebox or in that famous junk drawer. Or maybe you want to better manage your things—like when you need to upgrade or replace certain items, see what's missing in your favorite collection, or time which wines to drink within the year. Or perhaps you want to know how much your cache of valuables is really worth. It can be any of these things, but the point is with MyThings you can have peace of mind because it is safe and secure and can be accessed anytime from anywhere.

That's what MyThings is, an online service that helps keep track of belongings, when and where they were bought, for how much, the services provided with them, and their value. We offer useful services and deals, such as valuations, accessories, warranties, lost and found, and product updates and information.

Once you're a member (free of course), you can keep private portfolios for your own records or insurance-related purposes, or choose to make your items public and share them with others. It's all up to you. If you want to show a friend the cool new bicycle you just bought or share your enthusiasm for your antique card collection with someone else who collects them, the options of meeting others with similar interests are endless.

So what's in it for us? We think that as consumers we're bombarded with product and services information. But we also know manufacturers, retailers, and other sellers want to offer a better way to provide their services to you. With MyThings we provide that option based on your preferences. We can all appreciate when the right offer or information comes to us at the right time—such as rebate information when you trade in your old MP3 player for the latest model. Or how about when an auction house has an interesting sale coming up of 1960s comic books? Even when someone is ready to sell their porcelain pug dog collection. You get the idea.

MyThings is an infomediary, a trusted third-party between buyers and sellers. We're not here to buy and sell—eBay, Craig's List and lots of other sites do that really well already. We're here to simply allow consumers to have one central place to manage their things and to allow businesses, whether big manufacturers or individual sellers, to have a much better idea of the consumers who will truly care about what they have to sell.

We got our start with a service called Trace (www.trace.com), the world's first online database of used and stolen valuables. Primarily for the fine arts community—auction houses, dealers, insurance companies and law enforcement—Trace is a service which allows these sellers to check if items are registered as lost or stolen, so they aren't selling stolen goods.

We realized we could expand this idea for everyone. We can all better manage our things—not just if something is lost or stolen. Catalog it, photograph it, share it, value it. In short, feel better about being a bit more organized. And to do it all in one easy-to-use, friendly environment where you can get useful, related services that pertain to what you really care about. That's what matters to us.

Founded in 2004 by retail, insurance, and technology executives, MyThings is a global business with offices in Menlo Park, California; London, England;

and Tel Aviv, Israel. Now go on, catalog the things that matter to you so you can spend less time worrying about them and more time enjoying them.

mailto:media@mythings.com

MyThings, Inc.
855 Oak Grove Avenue, Suite 105
Menlo Park, CA 94025
U.S.A.

MyThings (UK) Limited
162-164 Finchley Road
London NW3 5HE
United Kingdom

MyThings, Ltd
32B, Ha'Barzel St.
Tel-Aviv 69710
Israel

http://www.fanpop.com
It's a one-stop destination for fans of anything and everything and the place to find fellow devoted fans (TV shows, music). San Francisco based.

http://www.globalpauhana.org/
Global Pau Hana is a world-wide grassroots community that helps people with an affinity to Hawaii.

http://www.tagdeaf.com/ (LS)
TagDeaf.com aims to serve as a bridge to connect deaf and hard of hearing people, as well as any interested parties, and enable them to share photos, stories, advice and make new friends.
webmaster@tagdeaf.com

http://www.panjea.com/ (LS)
Panjea is the first social media network to share the wealth by providing a marketplace and economy to its members.
Panjea is where the world's creative people come together to make a living from their dreams.

Panjea empowers you to easily express yourself online in words, music, photos, and videos, while earning rewards for your participation and cash for your creative contributions.

You bring the creativity, we deliver the sponsors.

You earn a percentage of the advertising revenue when others visit your page on Panjea, and you make money when people download your music and videos.

Launched at Demo on February 1, 2007.

Panjea
4712 Admiralty Way #121
Marina Del Rey, CA 90292
Main Number: 646.452.8842
Fax: 212.898.1133
Press Inquiries: press@panjea.com

http://www.fastcompany.com/cof/
Company of Friends is the name of FastCompany's readers network.
Fast Company, 375 Lexington Avenue, New York, NY 10017

http://modelmayhem.com
We are only accepting members who fall into one of the following five categories: model, photographer, makeup artist, hair stylist or wardrobe stylist.

Model Mayhem
334 East Lake Rd #144
Palm Harbor, FL 34685

http://www.gaiaonline.com
Founded in 2003 by a few comic book fans in a garage, Gaia Online has become the fastest-growing hangout on the web. Millions of teens come to Gaia every month to play games, make friends, and participate in the world's most active online community.

Gaia provides a fun, social environment that inspires individuality and creativity. With everything from art contests and poetry forums to fully customizable profiles and digital characters, Gaia is a place where teens can create their own space and express their individual style.

Fabulous Features:

- Online Hangout: Millions of teens spend hours a day on Gaia, exploring, chatting and just hanging out. Whether they're posting on our forums, participating in special events, or playing our multiplayer mini-games, there's always something fun to do.
- Endless Customization: Gaia revolves around creative customization. Every member can create their own virtual character and dress it up with over five thousand items: clothes, accessories, pets, masks and just about anything else imaginable.
- Thriving Community: Gaia Online boasts one of the most active forum communities in the world with over one billion posts to date. Members can chat in our online games, post messages on our forums, or send each other private messages.
- Gaia Gold Marketplace: Gaia Online is free to join, and members earn free Gaia Gold for everything they do on the site- posting, playing games, or just hanging out. Members can buy thousands of items in our virtual stores, or they can set up their own shops. Our virtual auction house lets members buy, sell and trade their items— over 50,000 auctions are completed every day!
- Fun and Games: Members can interact, have fun, and earn Gaia Gold with our quick and casual online games. They can also go head-to-head in our Avatar Arena to see who can make the coolest virtual outfit, or test their talents in the Art Arena, where thousands of members vote on the best original artwork.

Some fun facts!

- More than three hundred thousand members log in to Gaia every day, and the average user spends two hours on the site daily. That means that over seventy years are spent browsing Gaia every single day! Since there are only 24 hours in a day, this will probably break the space-time continuum and destroy the universe.
- Nearly two million unique visitors log in to Gaia every month. If we assume that each of those visitors were a quarter of a mile tall, they would stretch to the moon and back! While many of our members are well under a quarter of a mile tall, we must entertain

the possibility that some members may be many, many miles tall, significantly raising the average.

Gaia Interactive, Inc., located at: PMB 414, 105 Serra Way, Milpitas, CA 95035 and E-mail: service@gaiaonline.com.
mailto:pr@gaiaonline.com

http://zoji.com/
Founded by Dan Shen and Kevin Tao.
Based in Washington.

http://amodus.org.uk/ (LS)
Amodus is a private community, designed to provide a stimulating and provocative environment for a diverse and intelligent membership.
Composed in the main of business leaders, innovators and creatives, the amodus membership seeks to avoid the stridency of standard networking sites by nurturing trusted and sustainable professional and personal relationships.
The core values of the amodus community comprise creativity, innovation, intelligence, discernment and diversity. Informing and considered debate are very much the order of the day, with no room for the bland, the trivial, or the unquestioning adherence to the status quo.
To complement its online presence, amodus runs an ongoing series of events in major cities across the world. These events offer an enjoyable place to relax and meet with other members.
Membership is primarily by invitation; most new members are introduced to amodus by existing members. Membership is not automatic but subject to the approval of the Board.

E-mail: info@amodus.org.uk
COO is Tia Carr Williams
tia@amodus.org.uk

Amodus Inc.
58 West 58th Street
Suite 10D
New York 10019
Tel: (001) 937 644 2436

http://netparty.com/
Netparty functions as the entry point for a network of parties held in seventeen U.S. cities, aimed at professionals in their 20s and 30s. The events, held at stylish clubs, are designed to combine business networking with social fun.

155 E 77th St
New York, NY 10021

http://www.trustedopinion.com/
Intelligent online platform for sharing ratings and recommendations between trusted individuals, which serve up commercially untainted and personally tailored recommendations.

Shahar Smirin, Founder
Tom Schulz, Co-founder, VP Business Development
Todd Greene, VP Marketing
Melinda Roberts, Community Manager
Ilya Axelrod, Mathematics and Algorithms
Ronny Kohavi, Ph.D., Scientific Advisor
Jeff Black, Advisor

Trusted Opinion, Inc
228 Hamilton Ave., 3rd Floor
Palo Alto, CA 94301

Press inquiries: press@trustedopinion.com

http://faqqly.com/ (LS)
Social network based around questions and answers
dave@faqq.com

http://slifeshare.com/
Slifeshare is an online space that lets you share your digital life activities such as browsing the web and listening to music as a way to keep in touch with your friends, family or anyone you care about. It's about social connectedness and awareness.

Slifeshare is produced by Slife Labs, the guys behind Slife.

Slife Labs is a small software company located in Somerville, MA (Davis Square to be exact).

Slife is an awareness browser that observes your computer activities such as web sites you visit, music you listen to and e-mails you read, and it displays them as graphical visualizations at multiple level of granularity. The software lets you tag, group, search and filter your activites. It's currently available for the Mac OS X.

Slifeshare is an experiment in social-connectedness. It is an online space where you share your digital life activities as a way to keep in touch with people you care about – your friends, family or anyone else. You can share what you are doing in your computer in real-time, such as web sites you are browsing at this exact moment, or just highlights such as the top RSS feeds that you read in the past month.

Slife Labs is led by Edison Thomaz, who founded the company in 2006, together with a group of collaborators, some local, some half-way around the world. We are small at the moment, but our ideas are quite big. We can't do everything at once, but over time we will release some new apps that we think are pretty cool, so stay tuned.

Slife is a new application for the Mac OS X that lets you visualize and organize your computer activities like never before. Slife observes your every interaction with applications such as Safari, Mail and iChat and keeps tracks of all web pages you visit, e-mails you read, documents you write and much more.

www.xanga.com
Xanga is a community of online diaries and journals. You can easily start your own free journal, share thoughts with your friends and meet new friends, too.
Based in New York, the site is available in English and Chinese.

http://www.family.com
Social network made by Disney.

WDIG
500 S. Buena Vista Street
Mail Code 7716
Burbank, CA 91521-7663
family@family.com

http://www.agester.com/
Agester is a new community where you can guess people's age, find out how old you look, and meet new people.

Founded on March 19th, 2007 in California.

contact@agester.com

http://www.celebralike.com/
Celebralike.com is a site geared toward the teenage crowd. The site allows users to upload their photos and vote on who looks the most like celebrities. The site also allows users to find their "twin" among the other members of the site. Additionally, the site includes the following features:

* celebrity news aggregation
* celebrity RSS feeds
* tagging and tag clouds of celebrities and users
* favorites list
* friends lists
* messaging between users
* user sharing of photos they've taken of or with celebrities
* discussion forums for each celebrity

Founded in March 2007 in New York.

http://famesource.com/
Founded in Los Angeles in February 2007, Famesource is a media and networking company whose aim is to provide up-and-coming talent with a world-wide stage to share their abilities across the web.

Everyone can share their talent on Famesource—and if you don't have a talent, you become the critic! Talent categories include Music, Acting,

Sports, Comedy, Modeling, Dance, or anything else we didn't think of. As more and more people upload videos and vote, FameSource becomes the premier avenue for people to gain exposure and "claim their fame!"

How does it work?

This free service allows users to create descriptive profiles and to upload videos, images, and audio for the general viewing public to vote on. Voters choose to "Fame" or "Shame" a talent and can add themselves as a "Fan" of talent they like. Users with the highest number of votes in each category then make it to the front page of the website, where they gain an enormous amount of exposure and judgment. The talent with a combination of the most votes and fans in all of the categories will be considered the "Featured Talent" and will be highlighted in its own section on the main page. Every visitor to Famesource.com will notice them as the current "web celeb"...

For users who do not have the exposure they think they deserve, we have our "Wall of Fame," which grants users the opportunity to "buy" their fame. Users bid for the limited number of spots on this page, with outbid users being bumped down to lower spots.

Famesource is building a community that is highly motivated to watch, judge, and vote on talent. The service is free for everyone and will always be free for everyone.

http://www.sowesay.com/
We created SoWeSay to provide you with a place to share your voice and opinions about anyone, including friends, family, peers, all the new people you are meeting online and anyone else who just plain matters to you.
We also provide you with a powerful tool to gain insightful feedback from the people you know with SayWhat? customizable polling.

SoWeSay is a community of empowered voices — your voices! The greater the collaboration, the greater the fun!

SoWeSay was founded in the fall of 2006 by two ex-Yahoos.

http://www.paltalk.com/
Paltalk is the largest video chat community on the Internet with over four million active members participating in live voice- and video-enabled chat rooms. We allow thousands of simultaneous users to communicate using video and voice all in the same chat room. The Paltalk Messenger is also compatible with leading instant messaging (IM) services.

World's largest video chat community – over 4 million active members!

- Thousands of chat rooms to choose from
- Topics include – politics, friendship, dating, finance, trivia/games, current events, plus many more!
- Build your own Profile and meet new people
- Create your own room – it's FREE
- Instant Message with AIM, Yahoo! & ICQ

www.imeem.com
Imeem is headquartered in Palo Alto, California and is backed by Morgenthaler Ventures.

Imeem is a new online service that combines the best of instant messaging and social networking. Check it out! The imeem service is available through our website and also through a more powerful software download version – and it's 100% free.

With the imeem software download you can:

- Use any and all of your IM services from one application
- See full profiles with photos, music, videos and blogs from your buddy list
- Get automatic notifications when friends post new content into photos, music, videos and blogs
- Create a profile and share your own digital media with friends
- Create a rich custom blog, photo blog or video blog with your own URL
- Find new friends and create/join online groups (we call them "meems")

Joel Smernoff, President
P.O. Box 2412
JAF Station
New York, NY 10116-2412

http://www.splashvision.com/
SplashVision is the Only Social Network in the world targeted towards Scientists, Water Enthusiasts, Seafarers, Beach Lovers, and Hobbyists. It is a community site which has to do with anything related to bodies of water, including: Oceans, Lakes, Ponds, Canals, Fjords, and the like. Also included are Beaches and Vacation destinations along their shores and the People, Organisms and Creatures who survive, navigate, search and scour them. Sign up today and see what you have been missing.

Based in Fort Lauderdale, Florida.

Launched and backed by Chief Executive, real estate investor and acclaimed mega yacht captain, Todd Weider, in 2006, SplashVision.com is now stocked with thousands of Videos and Photos in its beta release.

http://vertagio.com/
Founded by Eonix in April 2007.

Eonix Corporation of America
Attn: Vertagio Media N.A.
3155 E Patrick Lane Suite 1
Las Vegas NV 89120

Eonix Corporation Canada
Attn: Vertagio Media CA
4798 - Station Main
Vancouver BC V6B 4A4

Media & Investor questions may be directed to:

Jordan Mazereeuw
evite@vertagio.com

http://www.wellsphere.com/ (LS)

Wellsphere is...a refreshing wellness community that brings together people, places, things and information to help members live healthier, happier lives.

Ron Gutman,Co-Founder & CEO
Dave Kashen, Co-founder and Chief Financial Officer
Geoffrey Rutledge, MD, PhD and Chief Medical Information Officer

380 Brannan St., San Francisco,
CA 94107
Phone: (415) 512-8000
WeCare@wellsphere.com

http://mixd.yahoo.com

Mixd is about going out. Coordinate last-minute meetups, share pictures and videos from your phone, and remember last night on a website we create for you automatically.

How? Mixd is group texting and photo & video sharing. No downloads or installs required. Just text 445566 and you're off and running. Owned by Yahoo.

http://popist.com (LS)
mailto:press@Popist.com

http://twitter.com/ (LS)

A global community of friends and strangers answering one simple question: What are you doing? Answer on your phone, IM, or right here on the web! Twitter was born as an interesting side project within the offices of Odeo in March of 2006. We are a part of Obvious Corporation in the beautiful South Park neighborhood of San Francisco, California.

help@twitter.com

http://www.goingon.com (LS)
Hi An,

Here is the information you've asked for.

GoingOn Networks, Inc. will become the first provider of an integrated blog publishing and social networking platform designed for business and professional use. The platform will host various networks of private-labeled communities. End-user membership profiles will seamlessly interoperate throughout each community within the GO universe. In this way, GoingOn simplifies the management of an individual's digital lifestyle by aggregating services and data into one single, centralized location.

Companies will use the GoingOn platform to easily and inexpensively create highly interactive communication networks which encourage dialogue and collaboration within communities that are critical to their success, including customers and prospects, user and developer groups, management teams and employees.

Key Platform Features of the GoingOn Networks Platform:

- *Private and public communities*
- *Integrated ad serving, management, and revenue sharing*
- *Advanced backend and editorial management*
- *Hosted confederation of networks and individual members**
- *Support of all open standards and micro-content publishing**
- *Membership profiles interoperate across all GO networks and groups**
- *Personal navigation toolbar available at all times**
- *Support of integration of existing blogs, forums, message boards**
- *One-time content posting to multiple networks, external blogs, and web services**
- *Comment tracking across all networks**
- *Automatically generated "About this Network" page with advanced traffic, content, and member data analytics**
- *Customized cross-network advertising packages and revenue sharing**
- Unique to GoingOn compared to competitors, such Six Apart and WordPress

Company & Media Brand Benefits	End-User Benefits
• Build community around brand and expertise • Improve communications with customers and employees • Increase brand loyalty and trust • Full transparency of members • Increase site "stickiness" • Increase prospects and connections • Ability to react to market in real time • Gain valuable feedback and product ideas • Identify external and internal resources with robust search engine • Gain instant visibility and traffic from other GO networks and GO members	• Can join a network of built-in communities with just one click • Find and make connections based on shared interests and context • Aggregates web services such as Skype, Flickr, del.icio. us, BrightCove, and external blogs in one place • Broader exposure of content with built-in network syndication • Free multi-media gallery for storage of audio, video, and picture files

Members will be able to join any public network with a single click of the button. No more filling out a new profile for each disparate online community. For example, a member of the Skype network can join the McDonald's network with a simple click within the GoingOn universe. More importantly, the GoingOn network will be a highly active, current media window into all communities on GO that highlights the most read content, tracks the most popular communities, provides positive and negative sentiment on a company or its brands in the blogosphere, and more.

Tony Perkins, Co-Founder & CEO
Chris Dobbrow, President & COO
Carl Wescott, CTO

Bernard Moon, Co-Founder & Vice President of Business Development
VP of Business Development
GoingOn Networks, Inc.
(c) 415.314.0082
(f) 847.919.3479
Skype: moocowhog
MSN: bernardbmoon@hotmail.com
http://goingon.com/user/bernard
http://bernardmoon.blogspot.com

Feature Chart on June 2006. *Please note that these data are courtesy of GoingOn, and do not necessarily represent the author's opinion.*

	GoingOn	I Upload	Five Across	Pluck	Six Apart
Platform					
Network of Networks	•				
Integrated Multiple Networks/ Communities	•				
Open Third-Party Technology Integration	•	x			x
Based on Open Source	•				

Publishing					
Dynamic Content Publishing Tools	•				
One-to-Many Publishing	•	x			
Publish to External Blogging Platforms	•				
RSS Syndication	•	x	x	x	x
Granular RSS Syndication	•				
Video Upload Tools	✯				
Mobile Blogging Support	✯	x			x
Community					
Network or Group Functions	•		x	x	
Easy Setup. Build a community within minutes.	•				
Design Variety	✯	x	x	x	x
Rating System	•		x	x	
Voting/Polling Tool	•	x			

Wiki	*		x		
Message Board	*				
Community Media Gallery	•				
Tagging/Categories	•		x	x	x
File Upload/ Sharing	•		x		
Community Calendar	•				x
Robust Content Search	•			x	x
Robust People Search	•				

• Existing GoingOn feature
* Launching within 3 months
x Existing competitor feature

	GoingOn	I Upload	Five Across	Pluck	Six Apart
Individual					
User Profile ("Member Page")	•	x	x	x	
Personal Media Gallery	•				
Personal Calendar	•	x			
Personal Blog	•	x			
Personal RSS Reader	•				
Online Reputation Aggregator	✫				
Security					
Abuse Management	•		x	x	
Language Filter			x		
IP Address Blocking	•				
Access Controls	•		x		
Privacy of Specific Content	✫				
Identity Verification	✫				

Academic Verification	*				
Job Verification	*				
Other					
Ecommerce	•				
Multi-lingual Support		x			x
Traffic & User Reporting	*	x	x	x	
Demographic Data	*		x		
Text Ad Management	•				x
RSS Ad Management	*	x			x
Podcast Ad Mt	*				
Open APIs	*			x	x

• Existing GoingOn feature
* Launching within three months
x Existing competitor feature

GoingOn Networks, Inc. PO Box 620100 Woodside, CA 94062
E-mail: feedback@goingon.com

http://www.rateitall.com/ (LS)

RateItAll is an online community and social network built upon one of the most extensive and diverse online databases of opinions, ratings, and reviews in the world. Participating members of RateItAll can earn cash for various activities on the site. RateItAll is a pioneer in the area of consumer-shared content. The site was launched in 1999 to enable the free and unfettered exchange of ideas and opinions. You can use this web site to connect with people who share similar interests, build trusted networks of reviewers, and find, share, or solicit opinions on virtually anything — for example, consumer products, celebrities, politics, travel destinations, sports, local businesses, and much more.

San Francisco, CA
E-mail: lawrence@rateitall.com (Lawrence Coburn)

http://nextcat.com/

Online networking community for all things relating to the entertainment industry.

We're 100% independent and not beholden to any large corporation. With Nextcat.com, we hope to provide a marketplace of ideas and opportunities for both established and emerging talent, as well as a forum and meeting place for fans and enthusiasts. Nextcat's founders recognize that the traditional way the entertainment industry has operated for the last half-century is getting turned upside-down — at light speed. We firmly believe that from all of this disruption can come refreshing new opportunities — and we'd like to become a catalyst in this process, by providing artists and musicians (like ourselves) with a broad platform to freely exchange ideas, job opportunities, and much more.

Founded by Jeff Pucci and Richard Viard.

http://shuzak.com/ (LS)

Shuzak strives to nurture and network the combined intellect of the individual members. A social network for geeks is an idea wherein the community is internally networked through seamless communication among like minded intellectuals rather than through friends. This is not a MySpace for geeks. MySpace, Bebo, Friendster, Orkut,

Facebook, and most other social networks are peer-to-peer, while Shuzak is intensely focused on networking peer-to-group.

Founder, Jawad Shuaib
jawad@shuzak.com
1-416-879-4659

http://www1.zebo.com
The platform that gets shoppers together to access the best-selling products at the best price.
Zedo Inc., located at 215 Second Street, San Francisco, CA 94105.

http://usuggest.com
USuggest provides a helpful community allowing you to discuss, suggest, and purchase the best products online.
Join our thriving community of shoppers, suggestors, and bloggers. It's free to suggest, so start today! Shop, Suggest, and Start Earning Money Now!

http://www.loowa.com
Social network where your profile revolves around your e-mail address. People can visit your profile by typing: http://www.loowa.com/your e-mail.
Loowa is based in Los Angeles, California.
help@loowa.com

http://www.socializr.com (LS)
Socializr is a free web service for sharing event and party information with your friends. By the founder of Friendster.

Socializr, Inc.
660 4th Street, Suite 240
San Francisco, California 94107
press@socializr.com

http://www.helloworld.com/
Helloworld will "Make your digital life simple." They are coming out with their new 5.0 version in the Fall. You can upload all of your pictures, videos,

and music on to one site. Other features include video e-mails with branding capabilities. Video IM. You can launch a live broadcast over the web in a few seconds right from your computer. You will be able to update your personal or business blog with pictures from your cell phones. Podcast events and manage all of your content online.

DigitalFX Networks
3035 E. Patrick Ln.
Las Vegas, NV 89120
retailsupport@digitalvm.com

http://info.placesite.com/ (LS)
Mososo.
Contact : sean@placesite.com

http://start.aimpages.com/
An AIM Page is your face and space on the Web. AIM Pages' features and tools help you easily express yourself, connect with friends, family, and others like you. When you create an AIM Page; you can include photos, videos, news, music, and more. With our publishing tools, your can "skin" your page with different themes and choose modules that allow you to be as creative as you want. An indicator on your AIM Buddy List will notify you when your buddies update their AIM Pages.

http://blubrry.com/ (LS)
Blubrry is a social podcasting community that connects podcast producers, advertisers and everyone looking for great independently produced content.

Todd Cochrane
ceo@rawvoice.com

http://www.vox.com/
Blogging platform from the company Six Apart.

Six Apart U.S.A.
548 4th Street, San Francisco, CA 94107
Tel: 415 344 0056 - Fax: 415 344 0829

Six Apart Europe
Six Apart Sa, 48 rue de la Bienfaisance 75008 Paris
Tel: +33 1 45 61 20 85 - Fax: + 33 1 44 14 15 15

Six Apart Japan
5-2-39 Akasaka, Entsuji-Gadelius Bldg.
7F, Minato-ku, Tokyo, 107-0052, Japan
Fax: + 81 3-5549-2081

http://www.oomph.net/
Oomph.Net was founded on the idea that women should have a safe space to meet online, to blog and chat about the issues that concern them, and to form communities around their interests. So many social networks that exist today serve as virtual water-coolers for the young, hip crowd — but equivalent resources for more mature, intelligent women are much harder to find. At Oomph we believe that women have a lot to say, and we give them a place to say it, an online haven for strong women to find and give emotional support with other women around the world. As we like to say, Oomph is "Self-help for women who don't really need it."

Oxygen Media LLC, Attention: Rights and Clearances Department, 75 9th Ave., 7th Floor, New York, NY 10011

http://www.ialmond.com
IAlmond is a social networking site that lets you add lots of photos and even has a complete photo album that you can use to upload and organize your photos. Use the iAlmond journal to tell your profile's readers about you and what you like to do. If you want to keep your profile, photo album or journal private, you can set your privacy settings to private. If you share your profile, you can use mood settings and see how many people visit your profile each day.

TESTIMONIAL
Online Social Networking by Shally Steckerl

Online social networking provides you with a venue to connect with people who you already know, grow your relationships, and find new people who are already connected to you by a common contact. Effective utilization of your personal network is no longer a competitive advantage; it is a survival tool.

Although the hackneyed phrase "it's who you know" has been abused by companies touting their latest and greatest flavor of Social Networking software, it's not far off the mark. The truth is that in today's over-informed digital business world where bloated data moves at the speed of thought, it is not who you know that really counts, but who knows you. Professional online social networking tools are invaluable in creating personal brand equity and raising awareness about who you are.

There is a significant business need for these tools as aids to help us expand our professional influence beyond the Dunbar number. According to theories evolving from Social Networking Architecture research, British Anthropologist Robin Dunbar (http://en.wikipedia.org/wiki/Dunbar's_number) estimates that humans can only maintain stable relationships with around 150 people. That number refers to significant relationships like those in a family or tribe and other purposeful groups. However, in The Tipping Point, Malcolm Gladwell explores the Dunbar number's effects on the dynamics of social groups and those theories have been popularized and given rise to many business related applications. Interestingly, systems for managing and sharing relationships have been around for a long time. From the original contact management systems like ever popular ACT! and GoldMine to the very first networking sites like sixdegrees.com, they all walk a fine line between sharing too much information and not enough to be of use, but they have all tried to multiply our ability to maintain business relationships with hundreds or even thousands of people.

There is one important weakness in this new generation of collaborative social networking. If users do not trust the system to protect their relationships, then they will not use the application effectively and gain very little incremental advantage from their connections. On the other hand, too much protection limits the effective range or depth of penetration achievable within a user's extended "friend of a friend" network, thus also limiting the effectiveness of such a network. Somewhere between those two extremes lies the advantage of a well-utilized and semi-trusted professional social network. Let's explore some of the pros and cons offered by constructs such as LinkedIn.

The Hype

This is not a new concept. Because the media has been giving it much attention lately. These online networks are beginning to grow in popularity and are becoming increasingly useful. Before social networking software, we would gather at meetings, conferences, symposiums, and trade shows to share leads and make new connections. Online, people meet in discussion forums and discover each other by reading profiles. Online social networking software adds another set of tools to our network building tool bag by allowing us to find out who our friends already know.

Meeting in person, we can only make connections one by one. Some of the best business deals are forged with a casual meeting where someone you already know introduces you to someone they think you should meet. Online, these connections can occur much faster, and there is the added value of being able to search through our friends' connections to help us achieve specific networking objectives.

How does this relate to recruiting? Networking is something all good recruiters do. Like with face-to-face meetings, we find common areas of interest with potential candidates and interact with them to build relationships. This can result in new placements or new business.

Why does it work? Talented people have two things in common:

1. *They easily relate with people they already know and*
2. *They love to talk about themselves.*

But why invest time in an online social network and not just continue our business as usual?

Major Benefits

Online social networking software enables you to find quality people who may not be familiar with you, or with your organization, and creates an opportunity to connect with them and sell them on your opportunities. They may be unfamiliar with your company or business or may not have even been looking for something.

Because you already know someone who knows them, you can feel more comfortable that they are a quality prospect or at least can do some checking around. Also, because of that mutual connection, you can more easily overcome cumbersome barriers and begin a relationship with a little more trust and warmth than with a total stranger. Like "six degrees of Kevin Bacon," social networking sheds light on the contacts you never knew you had. Here are some advantages:

1. *You can contact people in your network to:*

   - *Rekindle old connections*
   - *Maximize value in your weak connections*
   - *Build business relationships with clients or hiring managers*
   - *Find and meet prospective jobseekers*

- *Grow a referral network*
- *Heighten your corporate and personal brand*
- *Make new connections and grow your sphere of influence*
- *Open doors to future career opportunities, increased pay or promotions*
- *Increase visibility which improves influence and effectiveness internally with your organization as well as externally*

2. *Find new leads for networking into companies to:*

- *Educate yourself and ask questions about other organizations*
- *Conduct competitive intelligence on companies, industries or individuals*
- *Make fewer cold calls and better prepare for them*
- *Leverage contacts you already have*

Major Players

With most services the initial sign up is free. We begin by filling out a form with personal data and then invite our friends. With some networks we can upload our current contacts, but with others we need to invite our contacts directly through the application's interface. Our connections then invite their own contacts, and that's how our network grows.

There are hundreds of online social networking sites. Most of the applications competing for your attention offer a combination of professional and personal networking. Some are better suited to find a date, while others are more serious, oriented to business. After joining and reviewing the top twenty players, three of them stand out:

1. *LinkedIn.com*

- *Profiles look very much like a resume, excellent mix of people from different levels in the organization, and many industries.*
- *Endorsements set trusted people apart.*
- *Search for: industry experts, potential employees, hiring managers, deal- makers, people from specific geographies, or people with particular keywords in their profiles.*
- *Particular focus on business networking. Over 8.5 Million members.*

2. *Plaxo.com*

- *Keeps all of your current contacts' information updated automatically, thus it's extremely useful in rekindling old relationships and staying in touch.*
- *Not a tool to build your network, yet, though it does have a very useful "mini blog" feature to help you keep friends informed. About 15 million people use Plaxo.*

3. *Spoke.com*

- *Focused on providing sales prospects. Large database but not very "recruiter friendly."*
- *Deeply integrated, extracts contact data from enterprise applications (e.g. Outlook, Notes, etc.) to establish and leverage connections. About 30 million contacts.*

Other Networks you Should Explore

While there is a long list of social networking sites with a business focus, there are only a few with large enough populations to be of use in recruitment. In fact, there are so many social networks that they are too numerous to list in this article. A majority of them, like friendster. com, flickr.com and orkut.com among hundreds of others tend to revolve around strictly social categories like dating, common interests, finding friends, and photo sharing. Arguably, community web logging sites like MySpace.com, Windows Live Spaces, LiveJournal.com and Blogger.com are also networking sites. Here are some other notable networks with a decidedly business or professional purpose, ranked by size:

1. *Hi5.com — 50 million users. General social networking and business.*
2. *Passado.com — 4.7 million users. Europe's largest business network.*
3. *Xing.com — 1 million users. Was OpenBC. Business networking.*
4. *Ryze.com — 250,000 users. Business networking.*
5. *Ecademy.com — 100,000 users. Business networking.*

Major Concerns

1. *Privacy*

- *Online networking is safe. The major players are mindful of your privacy. Thatsaid, each network has its own privacy policy — so read it, and if you don't like it, don't join!*

- *Uploading your contacts doesn't mean they get to keep them or use them in any way. They use your contacts only to tell you who is already registered, or to help you with your connections. Be careful, however, because if you invite someone who wasn't already a member and they join now that person will be available to others who may want to connect directly with them.*
- *If someone gains access to your passwords, they could log in and export all your contacts. Use good judgment protecting your account.*
- *Remember, the more you share the more you are exposed. But you will increase your benefit from the network with more exposure.*
- *The basic concept involves a little trust. I scratch your back, you scratch mine. For the network to be most useful to you there needs to be a little reciprocity. People who are very guarded about their privacy may not get great results from using these networks.*

2. *Barriers of Entry*

- *Getting started means investing time to enter your information into the application. This can take anywhere from a few minutes to a few hours, depending on how much you want to get out of using the network. The more you share about yourself, the easier it will be to make connections.*
- *If you only upload a few contacts, you get very little benefit since these systems only search for connections through people you already know.*
- *You need to know at least one person with a large network or else you are very limited with whom you can reach. Search for people you know who may already be in the network and ask them for a connection, particularly if they are well connected themselves.*
- *The most challenging barrier is getting people from your "in person" real life network to sign up. You know they have lots of connections, and they would be willing to help you, but they are not already signed up. If you get them to sign up, you can both benefit from each other's connections, but then you become their mentor and may feel obligated to help them more than you would otherwise.*

3. *Maintenance*

- *If you have a large network, you could get to a point where you are getting barraged with requests. The good news is you can turn on or off e-mails about your accounts* or from your network, and with some networks you can even hange your settings to accept requests from specific levels. The other side of turning off the communication is that you lose out on reminders that help you to remember to groom your network.

- Evaluating new "friends" is difficult. You may get requests from people you don't know or don't remember, and it can be awkward to write back telling them you don't remember them. Just like meeting someone in person, you may have to bite the bullet and confront them with a "have we met?" or you may need to just ignore them.

- Don't add everyone indiscriminately. Be just a little picky in adding new friends you don't know. Remember, you are a reflection of your networks. People know you not only by who you are but also by those with whom you choose to associate.

4. Integration with software and between networks

- With Plaxo you can export your data in a flat file format making it easy to transfer your contacts to a new application.
- Some networks like LinkedIn have useful Toolbars that integrate with Outlook and make it easier to keep your network fresh.
- With most of the networks you can export your contacts. Do this regularly so that if for some reason your account is lost you can still retain your connection's contact information. You can also take it with you to import it into another network.
- Note that it's impossible to synchronize across networks. You may find some of the same people in several networks, but the best strategy is to choose your favorite three or five and stick to them or else you will be spending all your time maintaining several networks.

5. Losing touch with the "Real"

- E-mail is very cold and unemotional. Relying on e-mail and similar messaging to connect with people can wash out the emotional side of building relationships.
- Remember to pick up the phone and call your contacts every once and a while. This way they are more likely to forward your requests and ask you for requests, making your network stronger.

6.   *Free now, pay later?*

   • *Many of these services are not currently charging fees to get started in them, but they may begin to impose membership fees for even the basic accounts or activities.*

Conclusion

Social Networking is getting involved and getting your name out every chance you get. Like meeting people in person, it can be hit or miss. The single most powerful advantage of online networking is finding new connections you didn't know you already had. It takes time and energy to build a network, either in person or online. With the Internet we have the ability to reach more people. Don't be afraid to connect, stay connected, share, participate, be vulnerable, open yourself to the world. Being connected in this way is an incredible leverage that will prove invaluable in your business development. Connections can have many unexpected positive results.

Shally is a talent acquisition consultant, strategist, and speaker originally from Colombia, South America, now residing in Atlanta, Georgia. Mr. Steckerl is the Founder and Chief CyberSleuth of JobMachine, Inc. (www.jobmachine.net), the premier provider of Sourcing Consulting Services and Research Training. During his time with Microsoft he managed the research arm of their global centralized sourcing team. He is the author of Electronic Recruiting 101 and the award winning blog Cybersleuthing! (http://www.ere.net/blogs/CyberSleuthing).

TESTIMONIAL
Social Networking; not just for teens anymore
By Vanessa DiMauro
Principal, Leader NetworksBoston, MA

What do executives and teenagers have in common? While this may seem like a trick question, the answer is the ability and desire to use online communities to make decisions. Research has proven that executives make strategic business decisions based upon peer information, much like their teenage counterparts.

However, there are relatively few opportunities for executives to connect with each other online, other than via e-mail. They often need to wait for a conference or in-person event to learn who is doing what with whom in business. Conversely, throughout the web, teenagers have a myriad of forums where they are talking about themselves and their experiences. They are sharing information and collaborating with each other in powerful ways. Armed with their peers' perspectives, they are using new tools to make decisions about what they buy, where they go, and what they do. In essence, they are changing the global economy through their online collaborative behaviors.

The potential for this opportunity exists for executives as well, as this constituent is also very driven by leveraging peer referral and experiences to shape future decisions. So, while teens are discussing which music to download or party to attend, executives need a means to discuss industry changes and trends, management issues, which product or service to buy for their company or how to best leverage their organization.

Accordingly, professional social networks are becoming the new strategic business mandate — especially in the business to business space. Effective customer relationships are the core to any successful company and the strength of any organization is largely dependent upon the company's ability to deliver the right products and services to its customers in a timely way. Knowing what the customer wants and understanding their current and future needs is paramount to increasing revenue and exceeding customer expectations. Professional social networks provide a prime opportunity for companies to get to know their customers more intimately and keep the finger on the pulse of their needs and behaviors. There are a few powerful examples of social networks being used by business successfully.

While LinkedIn is the premiere example of a professional social network, there are many different permutations of professional social networks that are thriving online. One example of a professional social network is INmobile.org (http://www.inmobile.org). This group is an executive community of the top wireless leaders worldwide. It is an exclusive social network, where affiliation and thought leadership are the ways in which the executives connect to each other and gain value from participation. This community is open to any wireless or mobile executive (except sales), and hundreds of companies are represented within its membership.

More frequently, professional social networks occur within an organization as a customer service offering to its clients. These are most frequently private communities where admittance is dependent, not on seniority, like the example of INmobile listed above, but on affiliation with the organization. Notable companies like EMC, SUN and others are establishing professional social networks for their top tier customers as a way of getting closer to the top buyers and to establish and sustain relationships with them online. These are different than technical support groups, and instead cater to the senior buyer level to help them lever the product or service from a strategic level, grapple with ROI metrics, access best practices and other activities that impact executives who are making or have made significant enterprise purchases. Internal professional social networks such as these can give key clients access to people and information they need to help support them in useful ways.

The time is now for companies to embrace social networks to help them serve their clients better, faster, and in more cost-efficient ways. Through the use of professional social networks, companies now have an opportunity to forge a dialogue with their customers actively throughout the lifecycle — not just at the point of sale — to learn what they like and don't like about a product or service.

There is nothing more dangerous to an organization's lifeblood than a group of dissatisfied customers. Yet, often times, an organization may not even be aware of clients' issues until they have incurred reputation damage or a trending loss in revenue. By cultivating meaningful relationships online, product development leaders can work with clients to share roadmaps and plans — and to get early input from the people who would be their buyers at a later stage. Marketing can learn what messages are most effective with their constituents and have greater opportunities to educate and inform the customer, not just with shiny whitepapers and marketing newsletters but by bringing them into the discussion and process of product and content co-creation. Professional social networks also offer opportunities to make heroes out of users, enabling them to share best practice stories and to connect with other clients. This is especially effective with enterprise level support when the key buyer is a C-level executive: information sharing could result in strategic growth opportunities for all involved.

So, although teenagers and executives do have their differences — and it is unlikely that many C-level executives will be submitting YouTube videos any time soon — professional social networks are well within reach. And they are an extremely viable medium that can be harnessed for substantial gain.

Vanessa DiMauro is Principal of Leader Networks whose extensive client list includes EMC, TowerGroup, DCI, SAP, Patricia Seybold Group and others. Vanessa DiMauro is a pioneer in online community and interactive marketing. She has been a virtual social network builder for more than fifteen years. Working for forward-thinking organizations such as Cambridge Technology Partners and TERC, Vanessa DiMauro has helped shape the role of virtual communities play on the Web.

Vanessa DiMauro was the vice president of strategy and research for CXO Systems, where she also founded the Peer Visibility Network (PVN). She was the Executive Director of the ComputerWorld Executive Suite and ran Computerworld's public communities. In the mid to late 1990's, she spearheaded virtual community strategy for Cambridge Technology

Partners. She was the Director of Online Communities for Cambridge Information Network (CIN) — a division of Cambridge Technology Partners.

She frequently gives talks on the reality of building and sustaining online communities, serves as a social network judge for the Global Information Infrastructure awards, and has authored numerous academic research and general articles on social network building. Women in Technology International (WITI) named her one of Boston's Most Influential Women in Technology. She has taught Executive Education at UCLA — Anderson School, University of Miami and University of Chicago.

E-mail: vdimauro@leadernetworks.com

VIDEO/PHOTO

www.youtube.com (now owned by Google)
Chad Hurley, Steve Chen, and Jawed Karim founded YouTube, Inc. on February 14, 2005. Jawed Karim left the company to pursue an advanced degree at Stanford. YouTube received funding from Sequoia Capital in November 2005, and the service was officially launched in December 2005. Chad Hurley and Steve Chen proceeded to become the first members of the YouTube management team and currently serve as Chief Executive Officer and Chief Technology Officer respectively.

YouTube is a place for people to engage in new ways with video by sharing, commenting on, and viewing videos. YouTube originally started as a personal video sharing service, and has grown into an entertainment destination with people watching more than 70 million videos on the site daily.

www.bolt.com
With all the excitement about file sharing, blogging, camera phones, social networks, video ipods, 'Really Simple Syndication,' and 'bigger pipes,' we started daydreaming about an online portfolio— a place where you could store, organize and share all the media you create in the course of your digital life. A place where home movies can attain cult status, where snapshots from your last vacation might inspire a stranger to make the same trip, where the most timid voice can find a listener, and the most obscure subject, an audience. We built it and called it Bolt.

http://eyespot.com/
Eyespot allows users to mix video, photos, and music into a single, edited video that can then be distributed to mobile phones, websites, portable devices or e-mail since its beta launch in April of 2006. Jim Kaskade, the company's co-founder and CEO. The company was founded in 2005 by digital media and technology industry veterans and is based in San Diego, California.

Press Inquiries
Contact: Anna Vrechek
anna.vrechek@edelman.com

http://soapbox.msn.com/
YouTube from Microsoft.

http://www.godtube.com/
Christian online video social networking site that connects Christians into a network of believers. GodTube.com allows users to view posted video clips. Registered users can take advantage of many other features offered on GodTube.com, including the ability to create unique video personal profiles online. GodTube.com is owned and operated by Big Jump Media, Inc.

http://worldwidefido.com/
Video network for dogs.

Our mailing address is
Worldwide Fido
Legal Department
1633 Broadway
Fourth Floor
New York, NY 10024

We can be reached via e-mail at fido@worldwidefido.com

http://www.ebaumsworld.com
eBaum's World
P.O. Box 18091

Rochester, NY 14618
press@ebaumsworld.com

http://www.gofish.com
GoFish Corporation, headquartered in San Francisco, is a leading consumer online video destination which in two years has grown to deliver millions of videos per month to a rapidly growing audience of enthusiasts. GoFish is a place on the web where millions of people come to upload, share, and watch their favorite videos.

Press Contact
Amy Bonetti Price
Principal
Big Mouth Communications
415-384-0900
amy@bigmouthpr.com

http://www.myheavy.com/
MyHeavy is a free social networking site where members can view, upload, and share their videos with others. MyHeavy is brought to you by the same folks who created heavy.com and contains features and functionality that few sites in the space can match.

Ari Feldman
Executive Producer

Heavy
330 W. 38th Street
11th floor
New York, NY 10018
support@heavy.com

http://www.wewin.com/
WeWin is an online video sharing community that rewards it members with prizes. Whether by viewing the WeWin.com extensive database of videos or referring friends to the site, WeWin.com members have daily opportunities to win valuable prizes and connect with people who share their interests.

WeWin members can view each others' photos, videos, profiles, communicate with old friends and meet new friends on the service, post comments and describe their interests.
Founded in January 2006 by Brian Carrozzi.

Media Contact
Carla Vicens
blast! PR for WeWin.com
(919) 833-9975 x 10

4900 Hopyard Road
Pleasanton
California 94588

http://www.ziddio.com/
Ziddio – a new online and on demand channel from Comcast featuring user-generated content. Ziddio.com is a place where you can create, watch, and share videos.

Comcast Interactive Media, LLC
1500 Market Street
Philadelphia, PA 19102 U.S.A
press@ziddio.com

http://www.liberatedfilms.com/
Liberated Films is an online film community that is San Francisco-based. Founders Tobias Batton and Marcus Hogue wanted to create a place where filmmakers could get exposure for their work. Liberated Films started in November 2006.
feedback@liberatedfilms.com

http://www.vmix.com
Greg Kostello, CEO, vMix Media Inc.

http://umundo.com/

Umundo is an innovative service provided by Hexlet LLC, a web 2.0 technology company based in Fremont California and founded by experts of both web and mobile technologies. The company leverages its know-how in content syndication technologies (RSS feed parsing, tagging, optimization and management) the delivery of personal video content to bring a patent pending solution, enabling the delivery of personal video content to public sites.

Umundo aims at providing consumers a unique service, subscription-free with their cell phones: instantly send video clips direct from the phone to popular sites such as MySpace, my Yahoo, Google, iTunes for easy viewing and sharing by family members and friends of the sender.

http://www.flixya.com/
Founded in July 2006 by Adam Oliver and Ivan Wong, Flixya is an online video sharing community with rewards. With the growing number of video sharing sites online, Flixya differentiates itself by giving back to its users through rewards and ad revenue sharing. We also offer a charity program that gives back to the community. contact@flixya.com

http://grouper.com/
Grouper Networks enables its members to watch, share and create video on the Web, desktop and connected devices and continues to be the leading innovator in the user-generated video space. Members can browse videos on Grouper.com and post them to a wide variety of third party Web sites directly from Grouper. With one-click members can add video to their personal pages on MySpace, Facebook, Y!360, Friendster, Blogger, and any webpage. Grouper Networks is located in Sausalito, California.

Josh Felser,President: Josh co-founded Grouper in 2004 and serves as its President. Dave Samuel, President: Dave is a co-founder & currently President.

Aviv Eyal, VP, Technology and CTO: Aviv co-founded Grouper in 2004 and serves as its VP, technology and CTO.

http://www.heywtf.com/
Funny videos.
videosupport@heywtf.com

http://www.jumpcut.com
Jumpcut.com is a product of MiraVida Media, Inc., based in San Francisco, California. MiraVida Media, Inc. was founded in June of 2005.

http://www.blogcheese.com/
Based in San Jose. Founders Charlie Good and Dave Stubenvoll met at Adobe and launched the service to do one trick, video blogging, very well.

http://vume.com/ (ex http://eefoof.com)
Vume.com is a community driven website built around one principal rule: the authors of Internet content should be paid for their work and not have it exploited for others' gain. With other sites, signing a sponsorship contract means you lose the ownership of your content. Not here. We will send you a percentage of our site revenue via an electronic transfer each month, depending on how well your content has performed. For every unique view your work gets, you will earn money. Vume will never redistribute your work for profit. We're also artists, and we want what's best for our users. Vume (Eefoof.com) was started in California in May 2006 by Kevin Flynn, Matt Farley, a seasoned web developer and Alex Annese, a Computer Science student at Northeastern University in Boston.

http://evideoshare.com
Online video sharing portal that provides a complete, simple, easy-to-useservice for uploading, managing, and sharing videos. Users can upload their videos from a Web browser or directly from their PCs via the eVideo Share smart client. These videos can be shared publicly on the eVideoShare community, as well as linked to from blogs, online user groups, websites, and auction entries, amongst others. Video cell phone users can also e-mail video clips directly to their eVideoShare accounts.
Users can post comments to the videos and browse for videos in different groupings such as Most Popular/Recent/Viewed/. Videos can be easily searched by publisher, title, description, and comments. Private sharing allows users the ease and control over sharing of specific videos only with specific people.

Founded by Ajit Parab.

http://www.ourmedia.org

What's the big idea here? The idea is pretty simple: People who create video, music, photos, audio clips, and other personal media can store their stuff for free on Ourmedia's servers forever, as long as they're willing to share their works with a global audience. Ourmedia's goal is to expose, advance, and preserve digital creativity at the grassroots level. The site serves as a central gathering spot where professionals and amateurs come together to share works, offer tips, and tutorials, and interact in a combination community space and virtual library that will preserve these works for future generations. We want to enable people anywhere in the world to tap into this rich repository of media and create image albums, movie and music jukeboxes and more.

Who is behind Ourmedia? Members of the creative community, technologists, educators, librarians, and others interested in spreading digital culture are behind Ourmedia. Leading the effort are J.D. Lasica, author of "Darknet," editor with the Online Journalism Review, and evangelist for participatory media, and Marc Canter, a well-known technologist and open standards advocate who co-founded the company that became software giant Macromedia. This is an open-source, volunteer effort with a small team of paid developers.

http://one.revver.com/

Founded in November 2005 by Steven Starr, the founder and CEO. Revver is the first online service that allows digital video creators to share and monetize their content across multiple distribution channels: broadband, mobile, and broadcast. When submitting videos to Revver.com, users can automatically share them online and also opt into mobile and broadcast distribution. On the Internet, Revver matches each video with relevant advertising, encourages video sharing and then uses its proprietary technology to track videos as they are viewed. Regardless of the distribution channel, Revver always rewards users with a percentage of the revenue generated, creating a virtual marketplace for digital video. Revver also vigorously upholds creators' rights by individually screening each video submitted and not accepting copyright-infringing content.

press@revver.com

http://www.videoegg.com/
Founded in 2005 by David Lerman, Matt Sanchez, and Kevin Sladek. The VideoEgg publisher is a small website plug-in that makes it simple for end-users to capture, edit, encode, and post digital video online. A "universal adapter" that captures directly from hundreds of devices and reads dozens of formats, the VideoEgg Publisher allows users to painlessly publish videos that anyone can watch without worrying about player compatibilities, encoding settings, or extra software.

180 Townsend Street, Floor 3
San Francisco, CA 94107

http://vimeo.com
Vimeo began as a side-project in November 2004, and now there are over 75,000 registered users. The Vimeo staff is Jakob Lodwick, Zach Klein, Kunal Shah, and Andrew Pile. The current version of the site — Version 4 — was launched in April, 2006.
Vimeo is developed at Connected Ventures in New York City.
Contact : Vimeo.feedback@gmail.com

http://shycast.com/
Shycast is a community of people and brands, working together to make great new things happen in the world of social marketing. At Shycast we see the future: brands opening up to their customers, and people becoming more able, interested in, and open to a real relationship with their favorite brands.
Our first feature that brings brands and people closer is an automated video contest engine. We encourage brands to use Shycast to engage their fans and to contribute to the community with contest, prizes, and more: we want to see brands go a step further and work with the Shycast community to come up with great promotional concepts, and new and innovative rewards.
To support the flow of ideas, Shycast will run continual challenge that asks community members to come up with their own contest ideas. In the background we will solicit brands to embrace the community's thinking and launch contests created by, and starring, their real life customers.

Shycast
30 Murray Place
Princeton, NJ 08540
feedback@Shycast.com

http://www.ifilm.com

Leading online video network, serving user-uploaded and professional content to over ten million viewers monthly. IFILM's extensive library includes movie clips, music videos, short films, TV clips, video game trailers, action sports, and its popular 'viral videos' collection. IFILM is one of the leading streaming media networks on the internet. Through its broad network of distribution partners, including portals, search engines, social networks, video blogs, mobile operators and consumer electronics companies, IFILM reaches tens of millions of visitors per month. The network offers unique brand-building programs for cutting edge advertising partners, including News Corp, Sony, Time Warner, Walt Disney, Microsoft, HP, Dell, Intel, Activision, SBC, T-Mobile, Verizon, Toyota, Honda, Unilever, and P&G. In October 2005, IFILM was acquired by Viacom International, Inc. and is now part of the MTV Networks family of brands that includes MTV, VH1, Nickelodeon, Comedy Central, TV Land, CMT, Spike TV, and Logo. As one of the largest global television networks, MTV Networks reaches over 1 billion people worldwide. In addition, MTV Networks operates MTV Films in association with sister firm Paramount Pictures, licenses consumer products based on its brands, produces video games, and operates over one hundred web properties.

http://photobucket.com/

Alex Welch, CEO and founder. Darren Crystal, CTO and co-founder. Founded in 2003, Photobucket is based in downtown Denver, Colorado with an additional office in Palo Alto, California.

Photobucket essentially serves as a central "hub" for storing, sharing, and publishing visual digital media. In just the last twelve months, Photobucket has accelerated its organic growth to welcome more than 10 million unique visitors per month. This growth has been purely driven by word of mouth. Most of our users publish their visual digital content, such as video, images, graphic art to two or more sites: saving time by uploading once to

Photobucket and then publishing over and over again to many community sites.

http://clipshack.com/
ClipShack is a community for videophiles, a destination where people can post their video for general public viewing and comment, share clips with friends and family, post video to blogs, share information and feedback with other videophiles and wireless media aficionados and gain industry information relevant to digital video creation.
The company was founded in 2003 and ClipShack launched in June 2005.

Reality Digital, Inc.
600 Townsend St., Suite 170e
San Francisco, CA 94103
Fax: (415) 503-3959
E-mail: copyright@realitydigital.com

www.blip.tv
Blip.tv is a free videoblogging, podcasting, and video sharing service. If you don't have a blog, we'll give you one, and if you have one already, we'll make it a show. Start-up in New York City that's grown out of the videoblogging community Media inquiries should be sent to Todd Barrish at Dukas Public Relations. He may be reached via e-mail at todd@dukaspr.com or by phone at 1-212-704-7387.

http://www.phanfare.com/
Permanent, polished, ad-free online photo and video albums.
Andrew Erlichson, CEO, member of the Board, Mark Heinrich, CTO, member of the Board.

Phanfare, Inc.
402 Main Street
Suite 100-304
Metuchen, NJ 08840
bizdev@phanfare.com

http://meefedia.com/

http://www.castpost.com
Founded in 2005, Castpost is an online consumer video service operated by Broad Holdings.

Contact: press@broadholdings.com

www.viddler.com
Viddler, Inc.
115 Research Dr.
Bethlehem, PA 18015

By E-mail:
info@viddler.com

www.Nelsok.com
Video sharing site based in Massachusets, WA.
No Registration Required / Anonymous Video Uploads.
Large file size limit—200 mb video file uploads.
All Services are free.

http://www.livevideo.com
LiveUniverse,Inc
840 Apollo Street Suite 251
El Segundo, CA 90245
violations@liveuniverse.com

www.vidilife.com
Based in 840 Apollo Street, Suite 251
El Segundo, CA 90245

http://video.google.com/
The Google Video index is the most comprehensive on the Web, containing millions of videos indexed and available for viewing. Using Google Video, you can search for and watch an ever-growing collection of TV shows, movie clips, music videos, documentaries, personal productions and more from all over the Web. The Video index is comprised of videos that people

have added using Google's services (YouTube, Google Video) as well as videos from other third-party sites.

http://vids.myspace.com/
The video place for MySpace users.

http://video.stumbleupon.com/
Stumble Video automatically finds and plays videos that match your interests. All you have to do is press Stumble! and rate the videos you watch. Stumble Video recommends great videos based on your ratings, and the ratings from other like-minded users. From the makers of StumbleUpon.

http://www.motionbox.com
Video sharing with editing. Motionbox also has some business applications for third parties.

Chris O'Brien is Chief Executive Officer & Co-Founder.

http://www.stupidvideos.com/
StupidVideos.com, is a viral video website dedicated to humorous, off-the-wall videos, including wild stunts, wacky animals, sports bloopers, funny commercials, song and dance parodies, and more. Our videos are submitted to us by users like you, licensed from our partners, or produced by the StupidVideos staff.
StupidVideos is located in El Segundo, CA and is part of PureVideo Networks (www.purevideonetworks.com).

http://www.veoh.com/
Veoh is a Web site that's headed for your TV. It's also the name for a suite of applications for collecting, publishing, and watching a vast selection of HD-quality video programming. Veoh is a diverse, virtual community of indie publishers coming together with their new audiences. And it's also a few offices in Southern California full of entertainment industry insiders, outsiders, and technologists.

7220 Trade Street
Suite 115
San Diego, CA 92121

Media and press inquiries: pr@veoh.com

http://www.gotuitmedia.com/
Gotuit is a software company delivering next generation video technology which enables advanced video discovery and monetization across broadband, mobile and cable. Founded in 2000, Gotuit is privately held and funded by Highland Capital Partners, Atlas Venture, Motorola, and private investors.

Gotuit Media Corp.
15 Constitution Way
Woburn, MA 01801

http://www.videosift.com/
VideoSift is an online community, passionate about Web video. Members submit video from around the net to be voted on by other Sifter and "sifted" to the front page.
Brian (Dag) Houston created VideoSift in February 2006 as a little summer project. He was born and raised in Anchorage, Alaska but currently lives on the Gold Coast of Australia. Dag is a refugee from the Pay TV industry and besides VideoSift, works as a consultant on various web and video projects.

http://uberchannel.com/
California based.
wattup@uberchannel.com

http://www.glance.tv/
Glance.TV's office is located at 22 E Gay St Suite 301 Columbus, OH 43215.

http://www.grindtv.com
At GrindTV we love action sports video and pride ourselves in producing the best original action sports content for all media.

GrindTV.com
841 Apollo St. Suite 310
El Segundo, CA 90245
feedback@grindtv.com

http://www.vsocial.com
V:social is a pioneer in the online video space, having launched the initial version of its service way back in 2002.

Team:
Mark Sigal Chief Executive Officer + Co-founder
Brent Oesterblad Chief Operations Officer + Co-founder
Brad Webb Chief Technology Officer + Co-founder

Tel: (480) 967-6555
Fax: (480) 967-9575

51 West 3rd street
Suite 101
Tempe, az 85281
info@vsocial.com

http://video.aol.com
AOL Video has millions of free, high quality videos including music videos, news clips, movie trailers, viral videos, and full-length TV shows.

http://stage6.divx.com/
DivX, the video company well known for its coding and compression technology, quietly launched a YouTube-style online video sharing community in 2006.

DivX, Inc., 4780 Eastgate Mall, San Diego, CA 92121
stage6support@divx.com

http://vidshadow.com
Vidshadow is the first video posting site that offers rewards just for participating. You make our site successful by posting your videos, bringing your friends, and commenting on videos, so let us return the favor. Seriously, you can start earning Shadowcash Points right away! VidShadow offers great social networking tools to help people stay connected. You can e-mail, create your own profile, start your own blog and see which of your friends are online. Vidshadow is California based.

http://snowvision.com/
Snowvision is a broadband channel for the snowboard community.
Launched in February 2007.

Created by:
Diversion Media, LLC
900 Broadway, Suite 900
New York, NY 10003

http://travelistic.com/
Travelistic is a site that lets you explore the world through video. We host
all kinds of travel videos, including user uploads, professional content, and
tourist board videos.
Launched in October 2006.
suggestions@travelistic.com

Created by:
Diversion Media, LLC
900 Broadway, Suite 900
New York, NY 10003

http://www.wiitube.com/
Niche video site for Wii videos.
ajvchuk@gmail.com

http://one.revver.com/revver
Revver is a video platform that shares revenues.

How it works ?

1. Upload your video.
2. We pair your video with a targeted advertisement.
3. Share your video across the web. The more people see it, the more
   money you can make.

We split the ad revenue with you 50/50.

Sharers earn money too! Help spread Revver videos and earn 20% of the ad revenue. The remaining money is split 50/50 between the creator of the video and Revver.

http://www.metacafe.com
Metacafe is one of the world's largest online video broadcasters with a global audience of 17 million unique visitors (comScore Media Metrix), watching over 400 million videos each month. We are a top 10 online entertainment destination for males ages 18 - 34 (Nielsen NetRatings) and one of the top 60 largest English language sites in the world (Alexa).
Using our VideoRank technology, Metacafe is the only site that mines the collective wisdom of its audience to filter and surface the most entertaining videos, making it the best place to both watch and distribute high quality video content. At Metacafe, we are completely committed to:
1. Helping viewers quickly discover the best short videos online
2. Empowering the creators of these videos to get exposure, earn money and receive acclaim
Metacafe has offices in Palo Alto, California and Tel-Aviv, Israel. The company is privately held with funding from Accel Partners and Benchmark Capital.

www.blinkx.com
Blinkx is the world's largest and most advanced video search engine. Fed by automatic spiders that crawl the web for audio video content and content partnerships with over one hundred leading content and media companies, blinkx uses visual analysis and speech recognition to better understand rich media content. Users can search for content, create personal TV channels that automatically splice relevant content together and even use our download feature to automatically download content to mobile devices. Blinkx is a privately-held firm, based in San Francisco and London and was founded in early 2004 by Suranga Chandratillake.

www.videobomb.com
Video Bomb is a project of the Participatory Culture Foundation (PCF), a non-profit organization based in Worcester, MA. Our mission is to build software and websites to create an independent, creative, engaging, and meritocratic TV system for millions of people around the world. Video

Bomb is part of the complete Democracy Internet TV Platform. Video Bomb was created to help people discover and share interesting videos and to integrate with Democracy Player. When you install Democracy Player, you can star video right inside the application.
Contact PCF by e-mailing: hello@videobomb.com

www.videoegg.com
VideoEgg was born, well, hatched really, in early 2005 when David Lerman, Matt Sanchez and Kevin Sladek were trying to crack the code on all things video (codecs, drivers and devices oh my!). At the time, the three Yale grads were involved in a social venture that was matching non-profit organizations who needed public service announcements (PSAs) with a nationwide network of filmmakers who were itching to make video with their cool new digital cameras and desktop NLEs.

www.veeker.com
Veeker was founded in September 2005 to lead the evolution of mobile communication from audio and text to video. According to IDC, during the period between 2005 and 2009, 2.4 billion mobile phones equipped with video cameras will enter the global marketplace. Veeker believes that mobile video communication will become pervasive and intends to help the Veeker Generation discover and define this exciting new form of communication. Veeker is headquartered in San Francisco, CA, and operates a wholly owned subsidiary in Beijing, China. The company's team includes executives, technologists, and artists from the entertainment, internet, mobile, and advertising industries.

http://www.smugmug.com
A digital photo sharing website, founded by a father (Chris Mc Askill) and son (Don) team in 2002.

Smugmug, inc.
Mountain View, CA 94040

http://www.faces.com/default.aspx
Started in 2004 and relaunched with additional features in 2006.
Photo Sharing Made Easy

At faces.com we make online photo sharing a snap. Upload and share your favorite photos and start taking advantage of our multitude of photo sharing services, including quality digital photo printing, customizable photo galleries, online scrapbooking, and much more! Invite friends and family to view animated online slideshows and personalized scrapbooks of the special events and occasions in your life. What's more, with our secure servers and free lifetime backup, you can rest assured that your uploaded photos will always be right where you left them.

Faces.com offers more than just photo sharing; we offer community. From blogging and free chat to online dating, our services help you to make new friends and keep in touch with the ones you already have. With online services from faces.com, staying connected has never been easier.

Based in Santa Clara County, California

http://orfay.com/
Previously called Yafro. Orfay is a website for sharing pictures.
California based.
team@orfay.com

http://www.theblackstripe.com (LS)
Upload & share photos securely.
info@theblackstripe.com

Los Angeles, CA.

http://radar.net/
Share what you do, while you do it. Shoot cameraphone pictures and immediately share them with your friends. Show them what you're doing and what's on your mind. It's easy, and it works with any cameraphone.

It's about you and your friends. When you share your pictures on Radar, your invited friends can immediately browse and comment from their phone or PC. And you can see their pictures, quickly and easily, wherever you are.

A conversation in pictures. It's not just picture sharing, it's a conversation with your friends. It's staying in touch and seeing what's up. It's why you have a cameraphone.

Contact us:
Tiny Pictures, Inc.
417 14th Street
San Francisco, CA 94103

http://myphotoalbum.com/
MyPhotoAlbum is a creation of FortuneCity.com Inc., a company founded in 1997 and headquartered in New York City. FortuneCity has grown to become one of the world's largest independent web service providers, hosting 10 million web sites that created the 11th most visited web property on the planet by early 2000.

http://www.ringo.com
Ringo is photo sharing made easy. Add friends, add photos, and we do the rest. Every week you get your friends' newest photos and comments delivered to you. Adding all your friends is just a few clicks. Adding photos is fast and simple from the web or using powerful tools. Best of all, it's all free! We pay for bandwidth using the ads you see on the site.

We are constantly trying to improve Ringo. We add features that we and our customers are excited about and tweak each experience to make it as easy as possible. We all use Ringo to share photos with our friends and the world, so we want it to be the best experience it can be. Just click on any of our pictures below for a snapshot of the people who help you get snapshots of your friends.

Part of the Monster group.

Ringo
222 Sutter Street, 5th Floor
San Francisco, CA 94108

MOBILE

MoSoSo, or mobile social software, is software – generally on a mobile phone or on a laptop computer – that facilitates social encounters, or mobile social networking by associating geographical location and time with one's own social network.

TESTIMONIAL

Mobile Social Networks – Idan Gafni

Mobile social networks seem to be the most logical approach towards social networks. The mobile phone is perceived as a personal / private device much more than the computer. The creation of a mobile social network can be done automatically based on phone records and contacts. Modern devices present rich functionality that is most suitable for social networks and social interaction: calls, text, internet connectivity, media creation / consumption capabilities, presence (availability status indication), location, and more. In the mobile medium we can have ad hoc media rich networks with contextual awareness, content creation, content consumption, and social interaction. But the most significant advantage over every other medium is its availability and mobility, we carry it everywhere. The mobile device is the little notepad in our pocket where we can write things while they happen where the computer is the diary we have in the drawer where we write the things we remember at the end of the day. The notepad (just like the mobile device) is small and less comfortable but it is available in the moments we have something we want to document. There are many reasons to why mobile social networks should flourish but some inherent disadvantages influence the current state of such networks.

An online mobile social network requires connected devices where the majority of mobile users does not have or does not use internet connectivity with their device. The mobile device has a small screen and a reduced keyboard. The small screen makes it less enjoyable to view text and graphics and the reduced keyboard makes it more difficult to browse through content and to write text. The biggest obstacle the mobile social networks have to deal with is the existing networks. Users tend to join networks that already have many members, where they can find friends, interesting content, and people they would like to connect with. Pure mobile networks, just like new web based social networks, need to get a critical mass of users in order to attract new users.

The barrier of the critical mass created mobile social networks that rely on existing web based social networks and function as a mobile extension to networks such as MySpace and facebook. This is demonstrated in statistics of the top visited mobile social networks in the US and Western Europe which are MySpace, facebook, and Bebo. While these are the dominant social networks used via mobile devices, these are not the networks that demonstrate the pure mobile social experience.

The pure mobile social networks take advantage of mobility and use the mobile device capabilities. Location and context are used in mobile social networks such as Dodgeball and loopt to provide the ability to search for friends near you. loopt lets you post directly from your device any type of content that is tagged to your current location. Your friends are able to browse through your content in the context of the location so they can read recommendations on restaurants in the area or watch pictures you took in that location. Content centric networks such as Mosh, myMTV, and PeerBox provide the ability to create and share content. Nokia's mosh acts as a backup and sharing service for mobile content. mosh lets you share pictures, audio, video, mobile applications, mobile games, documents, and even content stored in your home computer with fellow members.

Mobile social networks will have a key role in future social interaction. It is a slow process that will take some time but with more connected mobile users, these networks will grow dramatically. The form of mobile extensions to existing web based networks will be gradually replaced by pure mobile social networks that are made for the mobile experience. Future mobile social networks will provide us with an augmented experience of our surrounding and our social interaction.

Idan Gafni – Serial Entrepreneur, Connecting the dots between Users, Content, and Technology.
www.CellXpert.com

Examples

http://www.dodgeball.com/
Focuses on merging location-based services with social networks to help people connect with the people and places around them. NY based. Dennis Crowley is the founder of dodgeball.com but left the company in May 2007.
press@dodgeball.com

http://www.mozeo.com/
Mozeo is a new group text messaging service.

Through Mozeo's Go Service, anyone can reply to everyone. When a message is sent, everyone receives it. When someone responds, everyone receives it. People are free to communicate together using simple text messaging.

Founded in December 2005 by Nicholas Fruscello and Greg Lisnyczyj, cofounders.

Our Address:
Mozeo, LLC.
4465 E. Genesee St.
PMB #164
Dewitt, NY 13214

info@mozeo.com

Our Address:
Mozeo, LLC.
4465 E. Genesee S
http://zemble.com (LS)
Zemble.com is the social networking website that helps you interact with your friends through the power of text messaging.

453 S. Spring Street
Suite 1036
Los Angeles, CA 90013
contact@zemble.com

http://www.txtms.com/
Txtms, Inc. is dedicated to the mobile exchange and management of information. It boasts powerful features that can support the needs of any businessperson while still remaining simple enough for anyone to use. Txtms provides a free service that gives you the ability to exchange information using a mobile phone and manage it by mobile phone, e-mail, and/or Txtms.com. Our easy to use service has taken social networking to the next level by allowing people to connect in real-time. It is a practical and accessible service that will forever revolutionize old-fashioned business card as we know it; Txtms is the ultimate way to exchange and manage information.

Txtms, Inc. is a privately held company based in Los Angeles, California.

Vram Ismailyan is co-Founder and Vice-President.

http://expressitmobile.com/
Mobile social network made by Mobileplay.

Mobileplay
487 Third Street
San Francisco, CA 94107
Tel: 415-896-6600
Fax: 415-896-6601

http://web.ccube.com/ (LS)
Ccube.com is a social network with a twist. It's a way of finding and connecting to like-minded people over the phone – any phone, any carrier, no downloads. You can search for people with similar interests, listen to their voice profile before making contact, have ccube.com automatically call them, or decide when you want to be contacted. Ccube.com allows you to do all this from your phone while protecting your phone number and personal privacy.

Mahesh Lalwani
Founder & CEO, Ccube.com

19925 Stevens Creek Blvd
Cupertino, CA 95014
press.relations@ccube.com

http://www.moblabber.com/ (LS)
Moblabber's mission is to provide users with a venue where they can discuss their common interests online and mobile.
Moblabber will allow any user to create and manage groups. Group moderator can invite members by sending them an e-mail or by using the e-mail invite function of Moblabber. They can also post topics for their members to receive in their mobile phone. Members on the other hand can reply to messages being sent by the group moderator or by other members. Moblabber is a service developed and operated by San Francisco, California

based Feedtext Inc. Feedtext Inc. is a web and mobile entertainment company that develops consumer and business applications for media companies and wireless carriers in North America. The company also offers other services such as chat, community applications, interactive TV application and mobile entertainment storefronts. Feedtext Inc. is located in Bush Street, San Francisco, California 94104-3503, United States. We can be reached through info@moblabber.com

http://mocospace.com (LS)
MOffY and JNJ Mobile jointly announce the new cooperation to launch the MocoSpace – the brand new mobile communication application in the Asia Pacific Region. Today, MocoSpace puts the power of social networking onto mobile phones! MocoSpace offers everyone the opportunity to find friends, build a network and socialize all from their fingertips wherever they may be.
MocoSpace's main features include mobile blog, public and private chat rooms, forums, searchable profiles, photos, ratings, private messages, buddy lists status, private message box. As said by the founder of JNJ mobile, Justin Siegel, more existing features are coming soon, and we will not disappoint mobile users in Asia.

support@mocospace.com

http://imthere.com
Mobile social network created by student Benjamin Roodman in Saint-Louis, Missouri.

http://enpresence.com/
Enpresence is a mobile social networking service that uses Bluetooth to identify and communicate with the mobile phones of people within one hundred meters of you. So if you are walking down the street, sitting in your office, or dining in a restaurant or alone in a club or bar, Enpresence will automatically detect and notify you when some 'right' one is nearby. Then it's up to you to decide – meet face to face, ignore them, even block them so you'll never get a connection again. Unlike other mobile solutions, Enpresence does not share your location – instead it shares your proximity

to others, and it's up to you to choose whether you want to share your location.

At Enpresence we recognize that people are inherently social and belong to many communities. To help you connect with people from your online communities and your social networks, we bring them together on your mobile phone. Then we enhance them with automatic alerts when members of your network(s), or people you'd like to connect with, are nearby. It's like radar — automatically scanning your surroundings and notifying you when you are near someone you'd like to meet. Just turn on Enpresence, and we'll notify you and make the introduction.

Team:
Ben Taylor, President
Dave Cowing, CTO/COO

For media inquiries contact Richard Fouts
Comunicado
richard.fouts@comunicado.us
(212) 593-2291

www.flagr.com
Flagr, the US mobile location based tagging service has now gone live with a pretty slick beta. Flagr uses SMS to allow people to create a "tag" on a google map to share the places they go and the things they are doing in the real world. First impressions are pretty impressive — it's obviously early days, but the integration with Google maps works really well, and there's a lot of potential to build on the social networking and community aspects of the service.

www.phling.com
Oxy Systems is the company that brings you phling! We are an early stage software company focused on connecting you to your personal media and to your friends. Oxy has its headquarters in Cambridge, Massachusetts, one of the nation's high tech hot spots! Our goal is to enhance your mobile lifestyle to keep you entertained and to help you share your mobile experiences with your friends. We have pulled together a bunch of advanced technologies to

enable all this. We're talking real time IP networks, multimedia phones, and P2P communications.

http://rabble.com
Rabble is a location based social networking application you download to your mobile device. With Rabble, you can combine all the things you love doing on the web into an easy to use application for your phone.

http://www.jambo.net/
Technology has made great strides to automate and simulate the face-to-face experience of meeting up with someone who shares your personal or business interests. Innovative offerings abound in social software, location-based technologies, online meetings, and, of course, the old mainstays of e-mail, IM and SMS. Each has value, but none matches the experience of looking someone in the eye and talking live. It's ironic. We've become a world of mobile people, bringing along WiFi-enabled communications devices. Yet every day, as we enter places of work and study, sip coffee in public cafes, cool our heels in airport lounges, there are people nearby who could make a difference to us, people who share our common interests. Maybe the person at the next table went to your school or wants to buy what you sell or to hire someone with your qualifications. But you are both just faces in a crowded room, remaining strangers, both missing these invisible opportunities.

Jambo Networks is the first company to design technology to let you see these invisible opportunities, letting people who share something in common to directly find each other and network face-to-face, when they want to. You don't even need to be on the Internet to use it. You just need Jambo, a WiFi device and a common interest. You join Jambo through an affiliation you already have – your school, alumni association, a conference you attend, an online social network – any trusted network based on a common interest, and Jambo's mobile social software will find people from your network when they are nearby.

Public Relations pubrel@jambo.net
Team:
Charles Ribaudo, co-founder and co-CEO
214-450-1153
charles@jambo.net

Jim Young, co-founder and co-CEO
214-325-5186
jyoung@jambo.net

Founded in April, 2003, the company is privately held. Based in Dallas, TX

http://www.radiusim.com/
RadiusIM is Social IM. It's the only website that shows you where your friends are hanging out and lets you surf for other people based on location. It supports all the major networks: MSN, AIM/ICQ, Yahoo, and GTalk/ Jabber. And you can use radiusIM from anywhere because there are no downloads.

RadiusIM was founded by John Londono and Zohar Yardeni. The site is available in English, Spanish, and Portuguese.

158 Ludlow Street, 5th Floor
New York, NY 10002
info@radiusIM.com

http://www.mymososo.com/
My MoSoSo is Mobile Social Software that links you to a powerful, real-world, Digital Community.
With My MoSoSo installed, your portable Windows PC can introduce you to like-minded people located within range of your WiFi signal (up to 300 feet, outdoors).
My MoSoSo is a peer-to-peer Community. "Peer-to-peer" means all Members' PCs communicate directly — with or without an Internet connection. Using My MoSoSo is like having a sixth sense that tells you when those who share your interests or goals are nearby.

My MoSoSo can quickly help you discover whether anyone within the surrounding a six-acre area might...
...know information you need,
...need information you know,
...make a good collaboration partner,
...make a good friend,

...make a good date,
...wish to buy something that you want to sell,
...have an item for sale that you would want to buy.

Thus informed, you can use My MoSoSo's built-in private text-chat feature to arrange an immediate face-to-face meeting.

Founded by Steve.
He is a Technologist, who has been using, programming and modifying various types of computers since 1981. He believes one of Information Technology's greatest strengths is its ability to unite strangers who are unaware they have anything in common. To put this theory into practice, he created My MoSoSo.

Contact: info@mysmososo.com

http://info.placesite.com/
PlaceSite, Inc. grew out of Project PlaceSite, a final Masters project undertaken by two of the founders at U.C. Berkeley.

PlaceSite allows everyone using wi-fi in a given venue, block or neighborhood to meet and interact with the other people in that place. Users don't have to download, install or activate any new software. Tied to the place rather than the user.

Team :
Sean Savage, CEO
sean@placesite.com

Damon McCormick, Security specialist
damon@placesite.com

Parker Thompson
parker@placesite.com

Based in San Franciso, California.

http://www.sakimobile.com/

Launched in February 2006, Saki Mobile is quickly redefining the communication and entertainment landscape. Designed for today's ever-mobile consumer, Saki provides a unified set of easy-to-use services that allow people to access the best entertainment, information, and communication services from anywhere in the world!

Saki offers you more features and better choices in mobile!

- You Pick and Choose
- Exclusive Content from your Favorite Brands
- 100% Spam-Free and No Annoying Ads

Saki offers an entirely new approach for brand-to-consumer interaction. One hundred percent free from marketing spam and annoying ads, Saki is the only community truly devoted to allowing both brands and consumers to engage in a more meaningful, social experience with one another.

Saki Mobile is owned and operated by Digital Standard, Inc., a privately-held company located in Plano, Texas.

Saki is a new way to share and access exclusive content such as photos, videos, music, movies, news, weather, sports, E-mail, IM, and more – all in one place! Use Saki to manage your social network, find old friends, map favorite locations, create party invitations, express your opinions or even chat via Avatar IM.

With Saki, people can:

Browse: Search member profiles, find old friends or meet new people.
Themes: Customize your profile with cool themes, interactive widgets, and more.
GPS: Map yourself and your friends. See who's closest and furthest from you.
IM & E-MAIL: Chat using animated Avatars. Add your existing e-mail accounts.
Invites: Create party invitations for your latest shindig, meeting or event.

RSS: Plug-in your favorite news, weather, sports, gossip, and more!

Here is a list of just a few places where you can use Saki:

MySpace, Google, Windows Live, Yahoo!, TagWorld, PageFlakes

Saki works over a wide array of networks and devices around the world, including phones, PDAs, laptops and ultra mobile PCs. Available on all WAP-enabled phones – Spring 2007.

http://vixo.com/
Vixo is social networking system that uses text messaging.

Vixo puts SMS messaging back in your hands. The concept is simple: if you trust someone about a topic, you will recieve messages they send about that topic. You will also pass along the message to anyone who trusts you about that topic.

Become a member today and enjoy these benefits:

- Organize and advertise, from a night out with friends to notifying customers about promotions and events
- Receive alerts about anything in the world, from gigs in your area to the latest sport scores
- Save money on sending messages to all your friends

Launched in 2006.
Contact: vixo@vixo.com

http://www.zingku.com/
Zingku's mission is to enable individuals and businesses to "mobilize their passion" by leveraging their personal network.

We started in 2005 when we noticed that teenage/twenty something's and their friends were engaging in rich media conversations drawing upon the full reach of mobile text messaging, the immediacy and speed of instant messaging, and thoroughness of web browser interface. A single conversation would take place amidst all these communication channels... often leading to plans for the evening, a purchase down the road, or simply a series of chuckles that passed time.

Concurrently, we saw the arrival of inexpensive "next generation" mobile phones, providing a means to capture and play pictures, words, music, and video. These phones are full fledged production devices sitting in our pockets, allowing us to distribute our "creations" to friends who in turn can distribute to their friends. As we saw folks constantly bouncing media back and forth between their phones, IM, and web browser, it became clear that this manner of dialogue forms a distinct new medium.

Our Zingku service amplifies the capabilities of this new medium, enhancing our collective capacity to promote and share.

Our service is designed from the mobile phone, outward, allowing you to create and exchange things of interest ranging from invitations to "mobile flyers" with friends in a trusted manner. On the mobile phone, Zingku uses standard text messaging and picture messaging features that come with every phone. On the web, our service uses your standard web browser and instant messenger. There is nothing to install.

With Zingku, things you wish to promote or share can easily be created and fetched via mobile, instant messenger, and web browser. Our service integrates your mobile phone with a personalized web site so that you can easily move (zing) things back and forth between the web and and your mobile as well as powerfully connect with friends and optionally their friends.

Our service helps you swiftly reach your friends and, when desired, their friends. We have designed the service so that you can selectively make it easy for your friends to pass things along to their friends. We've provided a simple way of managing your inner circles of friends, expecting that you may wish to keep some things private, yet other things you may want to make available to different groups of friends or to the whole world.

Zingku services are also being made available to "merchants" who wish to reach an audience. Merchants create "mobile flyers" and then publish/e-mail a "zing-code" to their customers who opt to pull the flyer to their mobile phone. The customer can then zing it to those friends who they think may be interested. Our mobile flyers are interactive, can take a recipient through a mobile text and picture messaging journey. As such, 18 - 28 year olds, who have tuned out of e-mail and are tuned in into their mobile, respond far more actively than traditional marketing media.

It's quite polite and quite effective. Our view of a "merchant" is anyone who has something to promote, whether it be a retailer, a theater promoting a production, a band who has just produced a new EP, a humorist producing snack-size entertainment, or an event organizer of any kind!
Only available in the US. Massachusets based.

http://en.wikipedia.org/wiki/MoSoSo

https://www.loopt.com/ (LS)
Loopt is a Palo Alto-based startup that has built a revolutionary "social mapping" service to change the way people use mobile phones to keep in touch with their friends. Loopt uses GPS (and other location technology) to show you where your friends are by automatically updating maps on your mobile handset. Loopt also lets you send messages to nearby friends or receive automatic alerts when they're nearby so that you never miss an opportunity to meet. With loopt, mobile subscribers put themselves on the map.

Press inquiries?
Write to us at press@loopt.com

Loopt founder Sam Altman is a 21-year-old who left Stanford University's computer sciences program last year to start the company.

http://frengo.com/
Frengo is a new social play network that enhances the mobile experience. With Frengo, engaging with friends on a social network no longer means sitting in front of a computer. Equipped with a wide range of games, contests, and messaging features, Frengo members take their social network with them everywhere they go – interacting, planning, and competing with friends through their mobile phones.

Mahi de Silva Co-founder & CEO
Dan Mosher Senior VP of Operations & Business Development
Steve Manning Co-founder & Chief Product Officer
Sameer Merchant Co-founder & CTO

Frengo
460 Seaport Court
Suite 210
Redwood City, CA
94043

Mainline: 650 364 4456
feedback@frengo.com

http://hobnobster.com/
Hobnobster, operated by Feedtext Inc., is a web and mobile social networking and bookmarking service where individuals get to message, mix and mingle with individuals of their choice by making use of the advanced profile search engine and the easy browse feature for fast navigation through the member profiles found in the network. In addition, since it can help you hook up with members within your vicinity, you can actually meet online contacts in person.

http://friendstribe.com/ (LS)
Friendstribe.com is a mobile social network. It's similar to other social networking sites except every aspect of it was designed to be used from your cell phone through text messaging.

You can e-mail us at contact@friendstribe.com
Write to us at:
Luxinteract-Friendstribe
417 E 57th St. Suite 26B
New York, NY 10022

http://www.zannel.com
Zannel Inc. is a new mobile entertainment network that provides the easiest way to create, experience, and share content on any mobile device. Founded

by the team that built the largest mobile media platform in North America, Zannel has developed the first large-scale, multimodal distribution system, which allows users to seamlessly share entertaining videos, photos and social contests on mobile phones and the web. Zannel stands for Zillions of Channels, where every user can create a channel and broadcast to the world. Zannel has signed up more than 1,500 content partners, including top comedians, filmmakers, anime distributors, and extreme sports producers. Product features include:

- Upload – Consumers can upload videos or photos from their hard drive directly into their channel for instant interaction. Users can also upload content from their mobile phones into their channels by sending their video or photo to a designated Zannel e-mail address.
- Pass-It-On – Share videos or photos with anyone who has a mobile phone by simply typing in a phone number or e-mail address.
- Favorites – Bookmark all favorite channels or pieces of content in one place for easy access to view later or share with others.
- Edit Profile – Personalize any channel by setting a channel name, including a personal motto, and providing a description about yourself or your channel.
- Edit Content – Modify titles, tags, descriptions or designate a specific photo or video as your main channel picture.
- Browse – Search the Zillions of Channels on Zannel to discover fun, contagious content. Users can select to browse videos, photos, channels or all content.
- Collections – Store all photos, video, and channels in respective folders for easy retrieval and viewing.
- Rate Content – Rate your own or others' content based on a five-star user rating as another way to interact with the community.
- Comments – Post comments on your own channel, on others' channels or on pieces of content that catch your eye.
- Search – Discover content by searching for channels or content by username or descriptive keywords.
- Community Channels – Create community channels where fans can upload and share videos and photos, representing a new way to engage fans and host contests and promotions.

Zannel is backed by U.S. Venture Partners and Palomar Ventures.

For media inquiries please contact Allison Vano with Concept Commnunications: allison@conceptpr.net

Adam Zbar, chief executive officer

Zannel, Inc.
2735 Sand Hill Road
Menlo Park, CA 94025
USA

By phone:
(650) 292-7250

By e-mail:
biz@zannel.com

http://gotzapp.com/
What is GotZapp?
GotZapp is a new mobile social networking site that lets you send and receive Zapps to mobile phones.

What are Zapps?
Zapps are mobile photo galleries, blogs, stories, music, and media clips that you can send to most color mobile phones with internet access.

GotZapp.com
Customer Care – Privacy Policy Issues
311 Elm Street, Suite 200
Cincinnati, Ohio 45202

privacy@GotZapp.com

http://mobloco.com/(LS)

Mobloco.com is a mobile-enabled social community that gives consumers the ability to RSVP, tag and post events that are also viewable on any internet-enabled mobile device. The site connects consumers by allowing them to also create and send text messages to approved friends, create alerts, view profiles, and search for people or happenings based on their geographical location or user specified search criteria.

Sonja Williams
Chief Sales and Marketing Officer
(404) 931-0686
sonja.williams@mobloco.com
Atlanta-based.

CANADA

BUSINESS

http://salespider.com/
"Other social networks make you friends; SaleSpider makes you money"

The mission of Sales Spider is to provide a free sales portal, creating an interactive sales community which encompasses all the needs of sales professionals and empowers them with the tools they need to excel.

Our portal is designed to fit the needs of large enterprise accounts which have hundreds of sales representatives, small and medium size businesses which have multiple sales representatives and individual sales people or sales agents. We provide for all types of salespeople, like direct field representatives, commissioned sales agents, distributors, and inside sales representatives. We also cater to our members' specific needs by both industry a nd region.

Management Team:
Russell Rothstein – Chief Executive Officer & Director
rrothstein@salespider.com

Jeffrey Schwartz – Board of Directors
Arthur Yallen – Board of Directors

HeadQuarters Address
Sales Spider Inc.
101 Duncan Mill Rd
Suite 405
Toronto, Ontario
M3B 1Z3
Fax: 416-913-3966
Phone: 416-221-0447

General Inquires – info@salespider.com

http://westerncanadabusiness.com/
WCB (Western Canada Business) Network is the first of its kind in Canada!
Our mission is to level the playing field for every business in Western Canada by improving communication and increasing access to knowledge.
The two essentials for business are who you know and what you know.
Western Canada Business Network helps you with both.

With Western Canada Business Network you can:

- build your own network of contacts
- use our built-in communication services
- create classified ads and get responses
- create your own event
- attend other members' events
- join groups of similar minded people
- access our library of business resources

Powered by Zedbiz Ltd.
#17 - 4041 74th Avenue SE
Calgary, Alberta T2C 2H9
Phone: (403) 201-4444
Fax: (403) 206-7297

http://www.trybeta.com/
Our Mission
Help software developers improve the quality of their products by providing a platform for developers to find and locate reliable beta testers.

Facilitate feedback between beta testers and software developers.

Ensure software developers provide adequate compensation for beta testers who actively submit feedback and help improve the quality of the products they test.

About

Trybeta was the idea of a software developer frustrated by the fact that beta testers were so hard to find and that end users were becoming the real beta testers. When bugs and features surfaced after publically releasing an application, negative reviews were close to follow. Software developers should not be afraid to release new products or updates for fear of finding a hidden bug. Software users should not have to worry about an application crashing within three seconds of launching.

Paul Levine – President

Since 1999, Paul has been developing web development and file management products for the Mac through his software company, RAGE Software. Paul grew frustrated that from a list of almost two hundred beta testers, it was getting difficult to get proper feedback with each beta version sent out to these users. Managing each beta program was difficult due to the lack of structure and communication between beta testers. Paul saw this frustration in many other microISVs and decided he had to do something to help.

Mike Levine – Programmer

For almost ten years Mike has been developing web sites and providing web hosting to clients from around the world. As an avid software user, and an avid complainer, Mike grew frustrated each time he used an application that did not do exactly what he wanted it to do. This made it extremely easy for Paul to convince Mike to start working on TryBeta.

1054 Centre St. Suite #262,
Thornhill,
Ontario, L4J 8E5
Canada

support@trybeta.com

FRIENDS

http://capazoo.com
Capazoo.com is a web community that thrives on user-generated content. It's easy to get started, easy to use, and easy to share. Users can create a place for themselves, or a place to meet friends.
Capazoo will redistribute 7% of its profits directly back to all our members. We also support the greater community by donating 1% of our profits to charity – a charity that you choose.

http://www.espacecanoe.com/
Based in Quebec.

http://www.udugu.com/
Udugu is a Social Network service for adults (25+) to meet each other online, operated by Karen Koski (The Den Group). She is an artist, as well as a writer with a published book of Poetry. She works in finance, but her dream is to work with computers or something related. Udugu means "friendship" in Swahili. The site was launched in June 2006.

Contact: admin@udugu.com
Phone: 705-983-0388

http://www.webmate.com/(LS)
WebMate.com is an online community for you to build your social network, share your ideas, date someone and enjoy other online services. WebMate. com is a good friend and assistant to you.

Create a private community on WebMate.com, and you can share photos, blogs and interests with your growing network of mutual friends!

See who has already been in WebMate.com. Find old friends or classmates or colleagues with whom you have lost touch.

WebMate.com is for everyone:

Friends who want to talk Online
Single people who want to meet other Singles
Matchmakers who want to connect their friends with other friends
Families who want to keep in touch – map your Family Tree
Business people and co-workers interested in networking
Classmates and study partners
Anyone looking for long lost friends!
People who love other online services.

5334 Yonge Street,Suite 141 Toronto,
Ontario M2N 6V1 Canada
pr@WebMate.com

DATING

www.GaySingles.ca
Free Canadian Social Network

www.plentyoffish.com
PlentyofFish is strongest in Canada and the USA and growing fast in the UK. It's well represented in most English speaking countries.

www.TeenDate.ca
Free Canadian Teen Networking

www.Universitysingles.ca
Social networking for college and university students in Canada.

SPECIAL INTEREST

Gaming & 3D

http://clubpenguin.com/

In March of 2005, one of New Horizon's owners proposed using the company's talents, along with his own, to create an online world where young children could safely play games, have fun and interact.

As a parent and an Internet expert, he wanted a place he'd be comfortable letting his own kids visit. His two business partners – also parents – jumped on board.

The Club Penguin team got to work, consulting with educators, law enforcement representatives and other parents, doing extensive research into online safety, and conducting widespread testing. Eight whirlwind months later, in October 2005, Club Penguin opened to the public with about 25,000 users.

Word quickly spread, mainly due to great reviews from users and parents impressed by the quality of the games, activities and security functions. In March 2006, Club Penguin was showcased on Miniclip, the world's largest online game site. Since then, Club Penguin has become the number one game on Miniclip with an audience of more than four million active players.

In light of Club Penguin's incredible success, its founders continue to focus on the three key areas of fun, safety, and service. Club Penguin is updated every week, and most of the company's resources go into making Club Penguin safer than ever. Eighty per cent of Club Penguin's staff is made up of safety personnel and moderators, many of whom are parents.

Club Penguin is completely funded by subscriptions. There is no advertising or marketing of any kind, which is a further testament to Club Penguin's ongoing commitment to protecting its young users.

mailto:media@clubpenguin.com

Club Penguin: Attention Media Department
410-1620 Dickson Avenue
Kelowna, British Columbia, V1Y-9Y2
Canada

http://www.falconbeach.ca/
Created by A51Integrated, the Virtual Cottage Community is a virtual and interactive world based on the popular canadian tv show, Falcon Beach.
The community members can explore the many locations of the world, interact with each other, chat, and create their own cottage. Also there's a credit system that allows each user to buy their cottage or new furniture. Players can even share a place if it's too expensive to buy.

Music

http://rapspace.tv (LS)
RapSpace.tv is the world's first and only broadband hangout for the global hiphop community. Whether you have rhymes to record, beats to drop, lyrics to blog or just want to check out the latest hot indie rapper, RapSpace.tv is the digital voice for all things hiphop.
E-mail: questions@rapspace.tv

RapSpace
PO Box 2256
Vancouver, BC
V6B 3W2

Parents

http://mommyclub.ca/
Founders: Michelle Davies & Tanis Borbridge. Started on January 12th 2007.
MommyClub is your comprehensive lifestyle portal just for Canadian Moms, giving you access to events, resources, product reviews, friendship, community, and more.

Religion

http://www.muslimsocial.com/(LS)
Create a private community on MuslimSocial.com, and you can share
photos, blogs and interests with your growing network of mutual friends!

5334 Yonge Street,Suite 141 Toronto,
Ontario M2N 6V1 Canada
pr@MuslimSocial.com

Sports

http://fanpage.com/
Fanpage is a sports networking site, and we are committed to providing
our members with the ultimate arena to share their passion for sports with
others from around the world. Fanpage allows for its members to create
their own profiles, showcase their favorite teams and players, share photos
and keep a blog.

Fantasy Sports are the rage when it comes to sports fans, and Fanpage
offers a variety of fantasy games and office pools within the site. You can
also get in depth coverage of the latest sports news on the site, which makes
Fanpage your one stop shop when it comes to everything sports.

Based in Toronto, Ontario.

http://www.ilovetoplay.com/
ILovetoPlay.com is a sports community with a place to connect with one
another. This service is a little bit like the bulletin board that you would
find at your local gym or sports center, where people post messages with
descriptions of who they are and what they are looking for, but infinitely
more powerful, with much wider reach and exposure, extensive sports
coverage and searching capabilities, and the full force of the web behind
it. Just about everyone and every activity in sports can use and benefit from
iLovetoPlay.com: players, teams, coaches, instructors, schools, camps, clinics,
facility providers (such as gyms, courts, fields, and swimming pools), games,
tournaments, leagues, practice and training sessions, and more. In a nutshell,

iLovetoPlay.com is a global database of sports profiles and needs. This service is easy to use with features similar to those of traditional social networking sites.

Team:
Marc Chriqui
Founder/CEO/CTO

Sandy Dahan
Marketing/Business Development
Tel: 514-582-2266
E-mail: sandy@ilovetoplay.com

Founded in January 2007 and based in Montreal.

Students

http://graduates.com/ (LS)
Founded in 2003 by Jason Classon.

1238 Seymour St
Vancouver, BC
V6B 6J3
Canada
+1 604 222 5555, Fax: +1 571 434 4620
gradfinder@yahoo.com

http://www.campusbeaver.com
CampusBeaver.com is an organization created for the benefit of students. We provide information, community and resources to students free of charge. Our goal is to create a virtual eco-system which provides everything a student could need as an informal support system, free of charge.

923 Bellagio Dr Windsor
ON N8p Ij9
Canada

Travel

http://www.travelpod.com

TravelPod.com was released in 1997 when it was introduced as the Web's first site to enable its members to create online travelogues (travel blogs), which revolutionized the way people travel and share their adventures with the world. TravelPod.com remains, as always, a "for the travel community" service.

TravelPod Corporation
Box 13637
Kanata, Ontario, K2K 1X6
Canada

Miscellaneous

http://www.sneakerplay.com/

Toronto based

Robleh Jama, Mohamed Hashi and Rob Chia aim to connect the style conscious sneaker community. Since its inception in June 2006, Sneakerplay has established an influential and active community of avid sneaker enthusiasts, collectors, artists, designers, boutique owners, and photographers. Sneakerplay is an innovative invite-only social network designed specifically for our generation—a place where style conscious individuals can connect with friends, meet likeminded individuals and express their unique styles.

http://www.kidzworld.com/

Kidzworld.com is the leading safe, secure, content-driven community for Tweens, kids ages nine to fourteen. Established in July 1999, Kidzworld leverages contemporary technology to allow users to express themselves through the creation of original content, interact with each other in the chatrooms, on the boards and in their KW Zone profile, and explore the digital world.

Kidzworld Media
Suite 612, 475 Howe Street,
Vancouver, British Columbia
Canada, V6C 2B3

Tel: (604) 688-2010
Fax: (604) 688-2015
1-800-668-0071
info@kidzworld.com

Management

Allen Achilles
President and CEO
allen@kidzworld.com

Donovan Pagtakhan
Vice President - Director of Web Operations
donovan@kidzworld.com

Kyle Fletcher
Vice President of Sales
kyle@kidzworld.com

Melissa Wood
Editor-in-Chief

http://crackberry.com/cb-connect
CrackBerry.com is the # 1 place for BlackBerry Users and Abusers and the perfect place to meet people on the same wave length.

CB Connect is the social network and meeting place for all BlackBerry users – CrackBerry Addicts and Newbies. It's a place where you can find people to talk to, exchange info or just have some fun.

Create a profile, upload your picture if you wish, and share your thoughts with the BlackBerry community. Let others find you, and based on your interests, hobbies, or opinions they can contact you via the Berry.

Here's how it works. You load up your profile. You can put as much or as little information in your profile as you wish. People can surf the profiles, and if they see something they like or find interesting, they can request your PIN to contact you. You can accept or decline their request. It is all up to you. You have control. If you accept, you can begin chatting with a new friend.

Contact: info@CrackBerry.com

http://www.militarynetworking.com/
Create a private community on MilitaryNetworking.com and you can share photos, blogs and interests with your growing network of mutual friends!

VIDEO/ PHOTO

http://www.blogtv.ca
Blogtv is a video sharing service from Alliance Atlantis.

http://tontuyau.com
TonTuyau.com is the Quebec (French canadian) version of YouTube.

http://www.pixilis.com/ (LS)
1002 Sherbrooke Street West, suite 2020, Montréal (Québec) H3A 3L6, Canada.
feedback@pixilis.com

MOBILE

http://peekamo.com/
Peekamo is the next generation of combined mobile and online social networking. Peekamo's superior tools enable people to discover other people from around the world using either their PC or their mobile devices. Peekamo provides the vehicle to help people share their information and expand their reach through a social network they can take with them anywhere they go. Peekamo users have shown to be more responsive to their friends, family and extended networks because of their ability to communicate with no boundaries any time, anywhere, using their mobile device the same way they do online and in real life.

Peekamo is about the people's network and managed by the people. Networks are divided by regions from around the world, independently. To join Peekamo, people authenticate their mobile device/phone by means a unique first to market live "Text Back" authentication powered by the latest secure AJAX technology and your mobile phone. They can then send no cost text messages to anyone inside or outside the Peekamo Network, create their personal profile, and identity to connect with friends, share interests, join social groups, participate in programs such as Peekrtm, write notes, and post photos.

Peekamo's most prevalent feature is the ability to mask your phone number when you send text messages while still maintaining the ability to receive responses back. Peekamo gives people control over what information they share and with whom they share it. Using Peekamo's privacy settings, people can limit the information visible to someone or block that person from seeing them or sending them Peekamo messages completely (inside and outside the Peekamo Network). The ability to control their information means people can stay current with their friends and the people around them in a trusted and secure environment using their "Peekamo ID".

Peekamo launched in January of 2007 in beta 1 form and re-launched in April 2007 in beta 2 form after an overwhelming response from it's users to expand the features and services. Mobile users from all around North America have already discovered the benefits of securing their phone number, gaining access to no-cost text messaging, and more recently, mobilizing their social network.

Based in Toronto, founded November 2006.
Co-founder Al Sajoo.

http://kakiloc.com/
The Kakiloc service allows you the ability to associate your geographical location with your network contact list in order to better manage communication with those contacts and also discover new contacts within your proximity. You can:

- Create and maintain a list of Kakiloc members with which you want to share your geographical position and any other information related to it.
- Send you location information using your web browser, your mobile phone or any other mechanism made available to you by the Kakiloc service.
- Configure Kakiloc to send notifications when you reach a certain location or when members of your contact list reach a certain location.
- Directly send various types of messages to your contact list.
- Use the Instant Messaging service to communication with members of your contact list.
- Browse geographical location and associated information created the members of your contact list.

Founded in 2006 and headquartered in Montreal, Canada.

kakiloc@kakiloc.com

2 B What about Latin-America?

For a continent that is directly connected to the worldwide number one in social networking— the United States— Latin-America is surprisingly lagging behind on the Web 2.0 and social networking scene. Even with the linguistic hegemony of the Spanish language (nineteen of the twenty countries in Latin-America use Spanish as their national language, the exception being Brazil which uses Portuguese), local networks are far and few between. This is even more surprising when taking into account the large minority of Mexicans who are living in the United States.

There are quite a few social networks which are aimed at the Latino community and which are usually accessible in Spanish and English. Over the past year, we have even seen an upsurge of these networks, as corporations have picked up on a growing demographic with money to spend. However, these networks, more often than not, are created by North Americans in North America, as opposed to Latinos in Central or South America.

Of all the countries, Brazil seems to have taken the lead where social networks are concerned, and this both for professional networks as well as purely social networks.
It should be interesting to see which of the other Latin American countries will follow in its footsteps.

ARGENTINA

FRIENDS

http://www.tribufrizze.com/
Social network for Argentina, created by the brand Frizzé.

TESTIMONIAL *Hugo Antonio Reyes*

Since the end of 2004, Argentina has seen a massive surge of social networks. One of those is OpenBC (German network, now called Xing) and— more recently— Neurona

(Spanish). Nevertheless, it is Neurona which is more popular, mainly thanks to its origin and free access.

Both networks enjoy popularity in Argentina because they allow the management of professional contacts, the search of contacts which lead to new sales opportunities, colleagues from work, meeting managers and experts, and opening the doors of thousands of companies by knowing their managers.

In my case, social networking has allowed me to enter into many relationships, both professional and social. I have met people with whom I have struck a friendship, whether they came from faraway countries or cultures or whether they lived in Argentina: in both cases the costs of getting in touch face to face or by phone would have proved too expensive if it weren't for social networking.

My networking experience so far with these two networks (which are most widespread in Argentina) has been most rewarding, allowing me to connect with other specialists in my field of expertise. I have been able to exchange ideas and experience, which allowed me to grow in my job. It has even led to new business and future work opportunities.

Another rewarding experience for my family and myself is that we got in touch with a Spanish lady from Barcelona, who manages a company specialized in Prevention of Workrelated Risks. This has always been one of the areas of my work I have been interested in: how to take care of our workforce, how to make sure they work in a safe environment, how to diminish labor-related risks...

Hugo Antonio Reyes holds a Bachelor in Human Ressources Administration. Former Secretary of Labour in the Province of Entre Ríos (1999–2002). Former Secretary of the Federal Council of Labour in Argentina, an institution that coordinates all the Labour Administrations of the country (2001–2002), where he would also be the Secretary and President of the MERCOSUR Commission later on. He was the HR Director of the Province State-owned Company for System of Roads (Empresa Estatal Provincial de Vialidad) (2002–2005). At the same time, he works as a Professor in College education. He is the Director of the Degree in Human Resources of the Association of Company Managers of Paraná, HQ of the National University of San Martín (UNSAM), Province of Entre Ríos (Argentina). He is founding partner of Cadena de Valor, a HR consulting company.

BRAZIL

BUSINESS

http://www.via6.com/
Networking for professionals in Brazil. The site is in Portuguese only.

http://www.topexecutivenet.com
TEN – Top Executives Net is the first trusted worldwide, online, business community whose focus is to bridge and to accelerate business between Latin America and the international community. TEN offer the unique combination of membership and corporate sponsorship programs besides online advertising. It´s currently available in English and Portuguese. Spanish will be added within Q2 2007.

Our total target market is estimated in 60 million professionals composed of top executives so called "Made-in-Latin America," who are professionals with international ambition, qualification, and skills to compete and offer their products and services abroad and of foreign executives who have firm interest in representing Latin American products and/or services in their respective countries, set up strategic alliances and/or joint-ventures with Latin American companies, invest in projects in Latin America and/or with Latin American partners, recruit Latin American workforce for their global ventures and, even, look for representatives for their products and/or services in Latin America.

TEN will become the trusted central point of contact between Latin Americans and foreign professionals stimulating members to share their knowledge, to increase trust, to generate win-win business with increasing volume and frequency and, consequently to create wealth among all active members. The key differentiation points are:

1. Our members: composed of high caliber executives representing some of the leading corporations in the world.
2. First class Advisory Board formed of top-notch professionals with distinguished experience in business networks management.

3. Clear presence of CNO – Chief Networking Officer who will run the business community in a customized way. TEN has a personal face to attend its members.
4. The combination of the traditional membership program with the special and sophisticated corporate sponsorship program besides online advertisement.
5. "Glocal": combination of global presence and local approach in Latin America
6. User-friendly website offering a number of functionalities such as videos, wikis, blogs, articles, events, and polls.
7. Multi-lingual: English, Portuguese, and Spanish are our official languages. Members can post in anyone of them indistinctly.
8. Very high return of investment: very generous relation "how much you get" versus "how little you pay". In addition, there are a couple of group packages which incentivating members to invite their business partners and co-workers.

-Founders & management
Octavio Pitaluga – CNO – Chief Networking Officer

-Founding year & address/nationality
TEN was officially launched in February 2007, and it´s currently based in Brazil.

-Target audience & membership level (number of users)
Unique audience composed primarily of two very specific groups of top executives:

a) Foreigners interested in doing business primarily with Latin American companies and professionals.
b) Latin American companies and professionals interested in rolling out their operations abroad.
   We have around one thousand members as of today, but we are forming some strategic alliances in order to grow viral very soon.

-Top three countries in which the community is used
Brazil, the United States and the United Kingdom for the time being.

-Main technical features and possible features in the near future
One can post videos, wikis, blogs, articles, events, and polls.

-Languages in which the service is available
English and Portuguese for the time being. Spanish will come within Q2.

FRIENDS

www.orkut.com
People in Brazil are most crazed about Orkut 62.10%, next comes United States 14.28%, India 11.90%, Pakistan 1.73%, Iran 1.12%, and United Kingdom 0.70%

www.gazzag.com
The principal services offered by Gazzag include the following:

a) (Exchange of messages) Mural
b) Blog
c) Photo albums
d) Discussion groups (Communities)
e) Chat tool
f) Dating

http://peepow.com/
In Portuguese, English, and French
The only social network site with messenger and private communities.

http://uolk.uol.com.br/
Portuguese only

Beltrano.com.br (LS)
Portuguese only.
marketing@beltrano.com.br

SPECIAL INTEREST

Students

http://www.descolando.com.br/
Feedback from college students to other college students on teachers.

Operated by Neoconn Tecnologia da Informação Ltda.

VIDEO/ PHOTO

http://www.flogao.com/ (LS)
In English and Portuguese.

http://www.8p.com.br/
Fotolog with communities

http://www.vibeflog.com/

COLOMBIA

FRIENDS

http://www.colombia4you.com (LS)
Colombia4you started as a project between Germán Coy and the cooperation from Los Andes University (Bogotá). It began as a scheme of showing the country of Colombia as it really is. Rebuild the country's reputation. Start showing what Colombia has and gives to the people and even more to the people who travel around it and find out how it is for real, beyond the media's opinion. Like this, the project was updated as a thesis from Industrial Engineering, as it was performing the research of how to build an Online Social Network, in this case related to Alternative tourism and

backpacking (in the beginning). After the planning project was ended, its construction started as the builder Germán Coy got together with Andrés Umaña and Camilo Montenegro put efforts together and with the purpose of changing the image of the country "worldwide," Colombia4you set off on a real task and project. Today, Colombia4you has become real, and while its necessary work has started, the expectation about the future is positive. Many backpackers from the five continents are part of the network and have been taking and donating pictures, opinions and comments about our work and most of the country visited by them. In English, Spanish, and French.

MEXICO

FRIENDS

http://migoos.net/
Migoos is a virtual community that helps you making friends and keeping in touch with you friends.
Migoos is the first social network made by and for Mexicans.
Our aim is to give a great service to our users and keeping developing our new characteristics.
Suggestions and criticisms are welcomed. We will thank it to you.

How can I use Migoos?

1. Register
2. Log in and fill you profile and add some pictures
3. Invite your friends to be part of your space
4. Surf and see if any friends or people you know are part of Migoos
5. Look for people with same interests as like in a specific area
6. Make new friends and dare meeting them personally

SPECIAL INTEREST

http://www.yosilevoy.com/
YoSiLeVoy.como is the Community where thousands of Mexican Football fans share their passion. Meet friends and share your experiences: create your website, blogs and enjoy the best pictures, videos, and football news.

http://sexyono.com/
Get started and weigh up your sex appeal, meet people and make friends through the "Meet Me" section. Rate people based on their picture.

NICARAGUA

FRIENDS

http://www.puropinolero.com/
This site is dedicated to connecting the Nicaraguan Community through social networking and user supplied live content (Web 2.0).

Use PuroPinolero.com to:

- Create and Publish a Blog
- Create Interest Groups (both Public and Private)
- Build Wiki Pages, Create Polls, and much more

VENEZUELA

FRIENDS

http://amigoseninternet.com/
AmigosEnInternet is a service specialized in personal profile search systems that has created a virtual community that allows its users to interact with one another with advanced contact and tracking features. Our community's

goal is to break the paradigm and unpopularity of personal relationships through the web, as many statistics have proven that thousands of people have actually found love and friendship online.
Friendship & dating.

Based in Venezuela : also a sistercompany in Mexico.

VIDEO/PHOTO

http://metroflog.com/
MetroFLOG gives you the possibility of creating a personal space to share with whomever you want. This space is completely personalisable (you can include a personal description, favorite links and change the background colors). You can submit a daily photo to your metroFLOG and add a description or brief comment on it, giving your friends the possibility of posting their own comments and being automatically notified. You can also create albums with many photos (about travelling, birthdays, parties, events, and gatherings).

Unlike other photo albums, metroFLOG allows you to upload an unlimited amount of photos and organize them in different folders or albums. It also gives you the possibility of sharing a commented daily photo for your friends to post on it, notifying them automatically.

3 What about Africa?

With only 3.6% of the population having access to the Internet (according to http://www.internetworldstats.com/stats1.htm), Africa still has a long way to go in terms of social networking. Many will argue – and not without reason—that Africans have other issues to tackle before they should worry about mundane issues such as social networks; however, some applications could be quite useful in the area of knowledge sharing (education), politics and business to name just a few.

As with the Latino community, most social networks that cater to Blacks are operated by corporations in the United States with a predominantly white population. Also these communities seem to focus on American ("Afro-Americans") or European Blacks, leaving a cultural and economic divide.

GHANA

BUSINESS

http://www.obaahema.com
Obaahema's mission is to celebrate the achievements of Enterprising Ghanaian Women to inspire others to emulate their success and reach their fullest potential. Obaahema aims at achieving her goal of empowering the Ghanaian by: Celebrating the achievements of Ghanaian women who are making a difference both in Ghana and the world over. Obaahema hopes that they will serve as role models for other aspiring Ghanaian Women to follow, building of future business leaders and executives by educating and encouraging them to reach their fullest potential.

FRIENDS

http://www.clubgh.com
Started as spideronline.net, a website primarily focused on providing entertainment and news for Ghanaians everywhere, Spideronline.net became

clubgh.com in July, 2002. The main aim of clubGh is re-uniting old friends and helping them stay in touch. ClubGh has an average of four thousand visitors and three hundred thousand hits every day. About ten new members are added to the Club every day.

MySpaceAfrica.com: Powered by ForchuTeck Consulting Group Inc.

KENIA

BUSINESS

http://www.nairobist.com/tujuane/
Tujuane is an exclusive online social network, which is open to 25 - 50 year old professionals.

SOUTH-AFRICA

BUSINESS

http://www.mygenius.co.za/
The My Genius™ service, including the website at www.mygenius.co.za, offers a place for individuals over the age of eighteen to meet on-line, use the My Genius tools to identify and promote themselves, meet other members online, build relationships, share ideas, and join offline meetings and contribute to events. The Service is organised locally, with support of well known franchised brands, to help you connect with your community, grow your business opportunities or widen your social circle.

Team:
John Raath: Director: Partner Interface
Doug Timberlake: Director: Online Community
Raldo Loots: Director: Technology
Andrew Timberlake: Director: Innovation
Scott MacDonald: Director: Research & Development

My Genius corporate contacts: info@mygenius.co.za
Telephone: +27 (11) 326 2589

DATING

http://www.datingbuzz.co.za/s/
Dating site

http://www.sparkleroad.com/
South African dating site: blogging, photo sharing, video sharing, and the ability to include videos.

VIDEOS/ PHOTOS

http://www.zoopy.com/
To the world at large, we're South Africa's first video and photo sharing social network. And flipping proud of it too!

To you, we're the easiest way to connect and share videos and photos with friends, family, colleagues, and (some very nice) complete strangers. The process is unbelievably simple.

1. Take a picture or shoot a video
    No professional equipment required – if all you have is your mobile phone, that's all you need! If you don't have a camera phone or digital camera, just scan in your printed photos.
2. Upload your photo or video to your Zoopy profile
    Write a description, choose a channel to publish to and watch your masterpiece come to life in minutes.
3. Share it with someone
    Once your stuff is live, you'll soon have eyes from around the country (and the world) clicking through to see your latest photo and video creations. And for those special uploads, you'll always be able to invite other Zoopy members, friends, and loved ones to take a look.

At Zoopy HQ it's just the four of us, for now. And a few carefully selected contributors.

Our combined backgrounds in the world of online marketing date back to 95 (Beltel, anyone?) and bring Zoopy a solid business foundation, a reliable and secure IT infrastructure, some seriously smart strategies, endless years of online reading / posting / commenting / uploading / downloading, hardcore ROI focus and a good bottle of Tassies when all is said and done on a Friday evening. Oh and just in case it matters, three of us are under 30.

Zoopy is privately owned by Full House Technologies, an online and mobile social media company that's in business to make the world a smaller place that's far more fun to live in.

Contact: info@zoopy.com

ZAMBIA

http://www.bwanji.com/
Bwanji is a social network dedicated to connecting Zambians. They have about three thousand users. You have a photo album, the ability to gather friends, a blog engine and forums.

GENERAL

http://www.afriville.com/
Afriville.com started out as a social network, a place to meet friends, look at photos, give comments, look for events happening in and around you. In the past few months I have had the chance to watch it grow on a daily basis and question my motive behind the whole social networking site.

Afriville is a place designed to stimulate the African man or woman through the tools of social communication whether its meeting people, sharing opinions on the forum, starting groups on issues important to you, or the soon to be released blogging platform within the site which I am currently writing on.

I have a dream, a wish to live to see, a dream of a continent saving itself through the minds and hardwork of its youth. War, poverty and socio-economic conditions have dispersed Africans all around the world. Afriville is the place to reunite all Africans and rebuild our beloved continent.

admin@Afriville.com
Based in Los Angeles, California, USA

http://www.myspaceafrica.com/
MySpace Africa is an online community that lets you meet your friends' friends in the African diaspora. Our goal is to create an environment that will foster togetherness, networking, and communication among members. Africans are placed all over the globe, and MySpace Africa will bridge that gap, bringing Africans together for community and dialogue. Ultimately MySpace Africa intends to establish and support organizations working in Africa to end genocide, poverty, disease, and promoting education and international solidarity.

MySpaceAfrica.com: Powered by ForchuTeck Consulting Group Inc based in Los Angeles, California, USA.

http://www.afriqueka.com/vI/login.php

http://www.myafricasite.com/
This site is owned by Kendall Conglomerate Inc. and was set up so Africans worldwide can find each other and communicate effectively. Kendall Conglomerate, Inc., 1694 Pear Street, Victoria, British Colombia.

customercare@myafricasite.com

4 What about Oceania?

In Australia, broadband —the backbone for the Internet—is scarce, due to its prohibitive installation cost. Australia has about 20 million inhabitants who are spread over a surface of 7,617,930 square kilometres, and to make matters worse it is an island! This results in a relatively small amount of Australians who are involved in social networking or blogging. However, Australian Prime Minister, John Howard, announced a major investment plan in June 2007 that should deliver to ninety-nine percent of the Australian population very fast and affordable broadband in just two years' time. For rural Australia wireless Internet will be installed. It should be interesting to see in 2010 how the situation has changed.

BUSINESS

http://www.linkme.com.au
Online resource, which serves as your own personal career manager and PR agent. LinkMe allows you to upload your resume into the system and present your experience to thousands of recruiters and employers who are looking for staff solutions.

By having your resume on LinkMe, you're available for opportunities that you were not aware of. LinkMe gives you the chance to review opportunities as they come along, whether you're employed or not. LinkMe manages your career details and makes it easy to send your resume to anyone for review. Once your information is in LinkMe, you need only keep it up to date.

LinkMe also has a growing job board. When a person posts a job ad and you have your resume on LinkMe, you will automatically be suggested.
LinkMe also offers blogs for users, which work in combination with your resume to assist recruiters and employers wanting to make a placement. Your LinkMe blog should be used by you as a form of career diary or as way to present employment reviews or written references. In this way LinkMe assists you to present your experience more fully to prospective employers. Over the next few months, LinkMe will also be enhancing its networking

functionality so that you can use the LinkMe service to interact with other users, recruiters, and employers on the system. Creating links that result in a face to face meeting will always have value.

LinkMe Pty Ltd,
Ground Floor, 615 Dandenong Road
Armadale VIC 3143

FRIENDS

http://www.babbello.com
Babbello is a social networking and blogging website for Australian teenagers and young adults. It was launched in August 2005. The site is inhabited primarily by teenagers, and a majority of its members are female. The site has received exposure due to magazine ads, reviews and cross-promotions in Australia. The site currently has over thirty thousand members, making it Australia's largest social network.

http://getalife.com.au/
Getalife (also trading as Activityfriends.com.au and Jamani.com.au) is Australia's first activity based social networking site. All our events in Sydney, Melbourne, Perth and Brisbane are created by members themselves! The contemporary alternative to social clubs and dating services to meet people and form friendships by joining hundreds of local groups and activities, anything from bush walking, to theatre visits, to Friday drinks to dinner dates! Over twenty-nine thousand members. Free trial for two weeks.

DATING

http://websingles.at/

SPECIAL INTEREST

Arts & Crafts

http://www.redbubble.com.au/ (LS)

RedBubble is the online destination for creativity. With RedBubble, you can:

Display your creative work and raise your profile
Connect with a vibrant community of creative people
Turn your designs into physical products like t-shirts, framed prints, and more
Offer your creative work for sale in a hassle-free way
Founded in February 2006.
media@redbubble.com.au

Hi An,

As mentioned earlier, RedBubble would be happy to participate in your book on social networks. I've attached a 1-page overview of the company that should cover the points you were interested in. Let me know if there's anything else you need.

Good luck with the book, and we look forward to seeing the final outcome!

Best regards
Xavier
RedBubble.com.au

Xavier Russo-RedBubble Pty Ltd
Unit 2, 192 Argyle Street Fitzroy VIC 3065 Australia
PO Box 1024, Carlton VIC 3053

Tel: 1300 66 77 01 | Fax: 61 3 8415 0681
Mob: 61 414 545 171

RedBubble Submission for An De Jonghe's book on Social Networks

RedBubble is a creative community that helps artists display their work, offer it for sale online, and turn it into physical products such as framed and mounted prints.
Key features of RedBubble include:

- *A diverse creative community — photography, illustration, digital art, writing, poetry, etc*
- *Easy and friendly to use — free membership, keep your copyright, set your own prices*
- *Business model based on turning digital art into high quality physical products*

By combining the power of social networks with the rewards of e-commerce, RedBubble intends to help people everywhere make the most of their creativity. "Everyone has a creative spark. For most it is a labour of love. But wouldn't it be great if more people earned money doing what they love?" said co-founder Paul Vanzella.

RedBubble was born from the belief that creative people were not well-served online, despite the rise of various other social networks. "As a designer myself, I believe it is important to have a beautiful, well-designed website. Artwork needs to be presented in the right way," said Paul. "But it's about function, too, not just aesthetics. It really should be easy to display and sell your creative work online."

A free RedBubble membership allows people to customize their profile, share their thoughts in a journal, and exhibit and sell their portfolio of digital work. Members are in full control of what is for sale and how it is priced. RedBubble handles the customer orders and payment processing, manufactures and delivers the physical products, and pays the artist. "We take away the hassles, so you have more time for creativity," said Paul.

Paul teamed up with two entrepreneurial friends, Martin Hosking (ex-Looksmart) and Peter Styles, to develop the business concept. They discovered that plenty of other creative people wanted an online home, as well as a simple way to display and sell their work.

RedBubble was founded in April 2006 and launched publicly in February 2007, after being lovingly handcrafted in Ruby on Rails and MySql on Apple hardware.
Since launch, RedBubble has enjoyed a rapid uptake among photographers, graphic designers, illustrators and other artists. With a growth rate exceeding 100% per month, RedBubble is making a great start towards a potential audience of millions of people.

RedBubble has evolved into a strong community, with 20+ page views per user, high levels of interactivity between members, and an inclusive and supportive tone. Importantly, members have also proven quite willing to purchase products from artists on RedBubble.

Fashion

http://www.rogueconnect.com/
Fashion-focused social networking website, which provides special membership for socialites, men-about-town, fashion designers, labels, and models. The website was created by friends Daniel P Dykes (23), Tania Braukamper (22), Renata Braukamper (24), and Allan Barger (21) in May 2006.
Being an exclusive community, people must be voted in or invited by other members.

GPO Box 4462
Melbourne
Victoria
Australia
3001

Gaming & 3D

http://mycybertwin.com/
MyCyberTwin was launched in 2007 and is a wholly owned subsidiary of RelevanceNow!. Its invention was the result of the fusion of a number of creative and innovative ideas by RelevanceNow! co-founders, Dr John Zakos and Liesl Capper

MyCyberTwin can be used for fun or for business reasons such as answering frequently asked questions on a corporate website. MyCyberTwin can chat on your behalf through social networks such as MySpace, blogs, dating sites and MSN instant messaging. The more time you spend training it, the more it is able to take on your personality to interact with friends – talking on your behalf even when you are offline.

Liesl Capper
MyCyberTwin.com
0403 622 659
l.capper@mycybertwin.com

Parents

http://www.minti.com/

Minti is a virtual place where parents can visit anytime to share and gain valuable advice on parenting. The content is created by members in the form of articles. The articles are tagged, rated and commented on by the community to encourage the integrity and relevancy of the information created. Topics range from pre-pregnancy, pregnancy, babies, early childhood, schooling, tweens, teenage years and beyond. Consider Minti as your global parent support group and expect lots of new features to be constantly added to the site, so we can all be better at the most important job in the world: parenting. Minti.com Pty Ltd is a wholly owned subsidiary of Vibe Capital Pty Ltd which is a privately held Australian company.

The management team includes: Clay Cook - CEO & Co-Founder, Matthew Macfarlane – CFO & Co-Founder

History of Minti

Idea and initial research by Rachel Cook early in 2005. Saw a need for a "parent to parent advice-opedia". Saw benefits of Wikipedia. Wrote the first business plan Clay Cook appointed as CEO and Matthew Macfarlane joined to further develop the business plan for Angel and Round I fund-raising. Completed Round I capital raising. Capital raising including Angel round total AUD\$1.6M (USD\$1.19M) as of February 2006.

http://famiva.com

Welcome to the premier social network for families, a secure and password-protected place for you and your relatives to connect and collaborate. Work together to build the family tree, visualize the extended family network, share photos and stories, stay current with family events and reminders, explore family maps, and much more.

Based in Victoria, Australia.

Sports

http://3eep.com/ (LS)
3eep is for everyone who loves and plays sports – the players, fans, coaches, and administrators who make sport their lifestyle.

3eep is a sports-oriented online community (a social network) for sports team players, fans, and administrators to:

- create and share your own stories – through blogs and forums, group discussion, and by sharing audio, photos, and video;
- share team information in team zones; and to
- express allegiances to local, regional and global sport teams.

feedback@3eep.com

Founded by Nick Gonios and Rob Antulov, both seasoned entrepreneurs with a passion for sport, who believed that passionate sports fans and players wanted to extend their existing sports communities from their "on-field" world to an online one.

Team sports are played and supported weekly by millions of people globally. In all parts of our society, we actively play, and attentively watch, in our backyards, at the local oval, at the community centre courts, at the school cricket pitch. 3eep enables the extension of this passion into an online world.

Students

http://www.snog.orac.net.au/ (LS)
The Social Network of Graduates (SNoG) is a non-profit organisation, run by graduates for graduates, established over ten years ago.

SNoG aims to connect graduates of Public Service Institutions in Canberra through various activities and events. It is designed to help Graduates, especially those from outside of Canberra, to meet new people and familiarise themselves with the ACT.

Throughout the year, SNoG organises loads of activities and events for its members. Whether your interest lies in sport, arts and culture or sampling Canberra's nightlife – SNoG provides something for everyone.

The Social Network of Graduates is run solely by new graduates. Events are organised by the following committees:

Executive
Arts and Culture
Sports and Recreation
Social and Nightlife
SNoG Ball
Ski Trip
Trivia Night

PO Box 1096 Canberra ACT 2601
President Nicole Bilinsky
Nicole.Bilinsky@finance.gov.au

http://www.studentface.com.au/auth
Membership in StudentFace is exclusive to students who are enrolled in an Australian university and have a valid university (.au or .edu) e-mail address. The site was launched in 2006.

Miscellaneous

http://moob.com/ (LS)
Moob is a dedicated website for people into the party scene to share their ideas, build a network of friends and be in the know for the coolest events around town. Blending the best of social networking and event information with a new dimension of calendar and invitation planning, moob is the party catalyst. Behind the moob network is a team of committed people, designing, building and developing the moob world. We're interested in evolving with the moob community, so our work will always involve listening to moob users and making moob better as we go along. Let us know what you think: info@moob.com

Moob is a part of the Gravity Ventures group of companies.
Based in Sydney, Australia, Moob launched in beta back in September
2006: a hip-hop social network focused on Australia and New Zealand.

http://6park.com/
Chinese community outside mainland China.

VIDEO/ PHOTO

http://www.infectiousvideos.com
Infectious Videos is a free video sharing project. Some of the newest
technological innovations have been employed to ensure that each user is
greatly empowered with a set of tools for uploading and manipulating
their digital media files at a server level. Some other interesting features are
Automatic DNS inserts for new customers, meaning they will automatically
have their own subdomains (user.infectiousvideos.com), the ability to accept
MMS data and automatically add it to the senders account and settings for
live webcam feeds so that other users can watch you on your members page.
From http://www.infectiousconcepts.com.au

NEW ZEALAND

http://www.iyomu.com
IYomu ("I, you, me and us") is a social networking site for grown-ups(18+).
It provides an original way to present yourself so you make better matches
with people for sharing interests, doing business or just living.
The site was founded by David Wolf-Rooney in 2007.

iYomu Corporate Office
PO Box 106 366
Auckland City 1143
New Zealand

media@iyomu.com

5 What about Asia?

It has been very difficult to map Asia's social network communities, not in the least because many of these communities are only available in Chinese, Japanese, Korean or any other local language, thus effectively catering to their respective local markets but shutting out much interaction with the rest of the world. However, despite the fact that Asia counts less than 11% of its population with access to the Internet, those Asians who do have access are interested in social networking if the number of Asian online communities is anything to go by. It should also be noted that while Internet penetration in the general population might still be low, the potential of the Asian market is huge: almost 36% of the world's population with access to the Net is Asian.

CHINA

BUSINESS

www.appiir.com
The World's Leading Chinese Business Network.

http://www.tianji.com/
The Chinese characters "Tianji" literally mean heaven and connections and can be generally translated to mean "worldly connections". We are China's leading social networking service dedicated to business networking for professionals. The site does not have cute girls and cool dudes flashing in your face; it does not cater to the youth dating market. It is designed exclusively for the needs of career professionals to help them more efficiently build, manage and leverage their network of relationships – one of the most valuable assets in career-building.

CEO – Derek Ling
CTO – Guo Yingshou

Beijing Office:
Room 3208, Building 5, SOHO New Town,
88 jianguo Road,
Chaoyang District , Beijing 100022
China

Tel: (86) 10 8589 6500
Fax: (86) 10 8589 1918

http://www.agloco.com/
Based in Hong Kong

Dan Jorgensen
Agloco Member Coordinator

mailto:aglocoinfo@agloco.com
Also check Agloco under the Netherlands

FRIENDS

www.zorpia.cn
Zorpia was founded in 2003 with a goal of bringing people together from
all over the world and allowing them to share their ideas and interests.
Since then the Zorpia Team has worked ceaselessly to reach people's hearts
and provide the best features in order to maximize our users' satisfaction.
Our primary features are photo album, online journal, social networking,
customized homepage, comment system and discussion forum. The
headquarters are located in Hong Kong, China. However, we are planning
to open new branches in mainland China, US, UK, Australia and many
other countries as we grow bigger.

http://www.zhanzou.com
Facebook lookalike that acquired Yoolin in 2007, a social networking site
which was targeted at Chinese students abroad.

http://www.gbq.cn/
Cyber Century operates www.gbq.cn – for "girl, boy and Q (for question)." GBQ, established in 2000, currently has 2 million registered users, mainly 18 to 35 years of age, and mostly college students. Industry research provided through Cyber Century shows that the average user page view at GBQ is twice that of other social networking sites in China, and that GBQ has on-line dialogue between 10,000-plus members at any time. GBQ sponsors various off-line activities for members to meet in major cities, such as Beijing and Shanghai.

http://www.heiyou.com/
Social networking for friends in China.

http://i.yahoo.com.cn
Yahoo Space is a blogging & social networking tool for Chinese Yahoo users. Started in April 2007.

DATING

http://www.uume.com
The largest online dating community in China.

http://www.yeeyoo.com/ (LS)
EFriendsNet is the largest and fastest growing online dating platform in greater China. We provide serious dating, casual dating and matchmaking services on social networks. By integrating Internet and Mobile technology, our users can manage their dating activities and personal networks anytime, anywhere.

EFriendsNet was originated from the founders' business plan. It was the winner in 2003 Carrot Challenge, the largest business plan competition in US sponsored by Forbes and HSBC.

In September 2005, eFriendsNet was awarded as the Winner of "RedHerring 100 Asia Private Companies". RedHerring, founded in 1993, is a media company whose mission is to cover innovation, technology, financing, and entrepreneurial activity.

In December 2005, eFriendsNet was awarded as the One of "50 Most Innovative Chinese Internet Companies" in the "2005–2006 China Internet Industry Report".

Marine Ma
Co-founder & CEO

Yong Liu
Co-founder & COO

service@efriendsnet.com

kefu_inter@efriendsnet.com

SPECIAL INTEREST

Books

http://www.douban.net/ (LS)
Douban was conceived in fall of 2004 by Bo Yang, a bilingual book worm, partly out of frustration that he could not find anyone in Beijing to talk about his new English books with. It was decided that a pilot version should be made in Chinese. Douban.com (alpha of course) went live on March 6, 2005, from an $800 home-made server hosted in the cheapest datacenter in Shanghai. By December douban.com had attracted over sixty thousand registrations from Chinese speakers all over the world, over a million collections and ratings, and over thirteen thousand full-length reviews. The almost identical English version, douban.net, the one you're looking at, went on public testing on December 6, 2005.

webmaster@douban.net

Gaming & 3D

http://www.hipihi.com/
HiPiHi World is a 3D digital world as rich and complex as the real world and is created, inhabited and owned by its residents. The residents are

the Gods of this virtual world; it is a world of limitless possibilities for creativity and self-expression, within a complex social structure and a full functioning economy.

HiPiHi's founders are Hui Xu (CEO), Rao XueWei, and Xinhua Liu.

HiPiHi was founded in Beijing in October 2005 as a privately held company funded by GCIG. HiPiHi is the only Chinese virtual world. Available in Chinese and in English.
For more about HiPiHi, please call (8610) 58731100-810; or e-mail to info@hipihi.com

http://www.frenzoo.net/
Frenzoo is an exciting Internet company developing a new wave of online social networking for the global female youth market. By focusing on a market niche and offering a tailored, compelling experience, Frenzoo offers advertisers an active audience and viral network to promote a range of consumer products in an immersive manner.

Based in Hong Kong, the team is led by executives from the Internet and 3D gaming field including companies such as DoubleClick Media and THQ, with a prior track record including the hit PC game Jurassic Park. The development team comprises both 3D modeling and animation, 2D artists as well as client and server side programmers.

In Chinese and English.

Contact: info@frenzoo.com

http://coobico.com/
Coobico is a mix between an MMO and a social network. Developed by Linking People, a Hong Kong-based company, it was established in 2006 by three veteran web designers from Germany. Their audience are 30 and 40-year-olds.

Parenting

http://babytree.com/

Social networking for parents. The site was launched in March 2007 and is funded by Matrix partners.

CEO: Allen Wang
Location: Beijing, China

Students

http://www.xiaonei.com/
Oak Pacific Interactive (OPI), a Chinese Internet consortium, has acquired Beijing-based Xiaonei.com, China's leading collegiate social-networking site in October 2006. The one-year-old startup was founded by Tsinghua university graduate Wang Xing, who will head the newly merged business unit.

Xiaonei, which means "on campus," will merge with OPI's own collegiate social network site, 5Q. The combined entity will take its place beside other OPI properties, including the entertainment portal Mop.com, news site DoNews.com, YouTube clone UUMe.com, and classified ads provider RenRen.com, soft-launching in October 2005 and formally opening for business in December.

Xiaonei has about 6 million accounts.

VIDEO/ PHOTO

http://360Quan.com (LS)
Social network and video network. In Chinese only.

JAPAN

BUSINESS

http://www.ea-tokyo.com/ (LS)
The Entrepreneur Association of Tokyo was founded to promote and support entrepreneurship in Japan. EA-Tokyo creates an 'Entrepreneurial

Environment' in which members can learn from Japan's top entrepreneurs, network with like-minded individuals, and develop their own business pursuits.

Since June of 2003, EA-Tokyo has been holding monthly seminars featuring presentations by top entrepreneurs in Japan. Our seminars allow participants to learn from the experiences and insights of Japan's top entrepreneurs and network with like-minded individuals in a comfortable setting. The seminars are attended by a mix of Japanese and non-Japanese participants with diverse backgrounds, from established entrepreneurs, to aspiring entrepreneurs, professionals, and students. EA-Tokyo membership is open to those who have an interest in developing or enhancing their own businesses. We encourage people of all ages, backgrounds and nationalities to join.

Dave Mori – Founder & President
Marc Beardsley – Founder & Director
Hideyuki Yamakawa – Director

Entrepreneur Association of Tokyo (Mailing Address)
2-19-10 3F Bikou Biru
Nishiogi-Minami, Suginami-ku
Tokyo 167-0053

Tel: 81-3-5336-9236
Fax: 81-3-5336-9237
mailto:info@ea-tokyo.com

http://powerlink.jp
Business network for recruitment, to find business partners, customer development...

Address
101-0025 Tokyo Chiyoda Ku Kanda Sakuma Cho 3-20-5-4F

Phone: 03-5822-1095
Contact : Info@powerlink.jp

CEO: Hiroshi Nakagawa

Founded on July 1st 2005

http://www.carareer.net/
Business network for recruitment/job board.

FRIENDS

http://www.piqniq.jp (LS)
Piqniq is a new social networking site for foreigners in Japan. Their target audience is families that are English speakers, who are looking to help meet and socialize with others people and families in the same situation.

Piqniq.jp is a Fusion Gol service.

http://mixi.jp
Mixi is Japan's largest community. Their focus is "community entertainment", that is, meeting new people by way of common interests. Users can send and receive messages, write in a diary, read and comment on others' diaries, organize and join communities and invite their friends. Started in February 2004, there are 10 million members. The company went public in September 2006.

www.myany.jp
Founded on March 15th 2006

Address:
The Tokyo Shibuya Ku God south 1-20-9 according to of ABC-Mart park building 3F
Tel: 03-5459-4821
Fax: 03-5459-4824

http://gree.jp/
Gree lets you create a profile with your picture, blog, reviews, photo album, etc. There is also a mobile version available. They have 1.3 million members.

Founded on December 7th 2004.
President : Yoshikazu Tanaka
Address: The Tokyo Minato-ku Roppongi 3-5-27 the Roppongi Yamada building 6F

http://asoboo.com/
Asoboo means "let's have fun" in Japanese. This is the network for creative, internationally-minded people.

Meet creative, internationally-minded people.
Create groups with people who have similar interests.
Share info on the cool places to go and things to do.
Easily find out what's new in your network.
Keep a super-simple blog (or import your existing blog) that automatically alerts people in your network when you write something new.
Publish your blog so that the non-Asoboo world can also view it at http://[my name].asoboo.com.

SPECIAL INTEREST

Gaming & 3D

http://ncsquad.com/
Nunchuk (nuhn-chuhk) is the name of nintendo Wii controller attachment for WII remote (Wiimote); some people also call it Wii nunchak, Wii nunchaku, Wii nunchuks, Wii numchuks and remote Wii. All Nintendo Wii units come with one Nunchuk and one Wiimote.

Hello, my Wii friends! My name is Sergi and among many things, I am a geek... an entrepreneur... a Gamer and an Internet addict. I am Spanish, and I live and work in Japan, the home of addicted Gamers and Big Sumo Guys. I am fluent in Japanese, and in between games, I look outside my window and see the beautiful Mount Fuji, sip on a cup of tea and remember fond memories of my home town.

Last December, I decided I wanted a Wii to play, and after waiting for six hours to buy my Nintendo Wii, I ran back to my place and after connecting the console, to my surprise, I found that I had no wii friends to add on my Wii, and this is how I started my crusade to find Wii friends on the Internet.

Because of this, I decided to create my own website for international wii friends/players.
I have fun making new Mii's and get a lot of enjoyment from receiving Mii's from wii friends.
On this site you can swap Mii's, Wii game codes, DS Game Codes, Wi-fi codes, save games, share links of your favorite videos, exchange information and much more. Please have fun and make new wii friends from all over the world.

All members can contact me and give me feedback about the site.
We can't improve without your comments.

mailto:ncsquad@gmail.com
SKYPE # ncsquad

http://www.mbga.jp
Mobagetown ("Mobile Game Town") is a mobile-only site combining free games, SNS functionalities and avatars/virtual items that can be purchased with a virtual currency called "Moba Gold" and mobile commerce (mobile shopping, auctions and affiliate advertising). It is operated by parent company DeNa Co. Ltd.
The service, which is open to anyone without an invitation, has seen explosive user growth since its launch in February 2006. It has gathered more than 5 million members in a little over twelve months, and is currently generating about 400 million page views per day.
Mobagetown is especially popular with teenagers, but more recently, the twenties and thirties user segments are the demographic growth segments. While in early November 2006, 69% of all users were in their teens, 25% in their twenties and 6% in their thirties, these figures have changed to 53%, 34%, and 15%, respectively.
The Mobagetown model is to draw users with free games, get them to use the SNS functionalities as a result of playing games, which in turn motivates

them to become involved in the avatar features — which is the key part of the service that Mobagetown's revenue model is based on, as everything the users have to do to gather virtual currency to outfit their avatars will directly or indirectly generate revenues for DeNA by driving mobile commerce and advertising.

CEO: Tomoko Namba

The company has released a detailed report on its users, business model, marketing etc on June 18th, 2007. It can be consulted at: http://www. infinita.co.jp/Mobagetown%20Report%20Overview.pdf

Music

http://recommuni.jp/
Site for music downloads & recommendations to other community members.

Sports

http://spolym.jp/
General sports network.

http://89sns.jp/
Social network about baseball.

Students

http://faceren.com/
FaceRen is a social networking website intended for Chinese students/ scholars across the globe. Originally started by two Chinese Harvard students, FaceRen is becoming very popular among Chinese students in China and abroad now, especially with the launching of its entirely member-run online radio station.

service@faceren.com

Miscellaneous

For those of you who speak Japanese, please find an index site of social
networks based in Japan (and predominantly in Japanese):
http://www.sns-navi.com/index.html

http://www.popteen.jp
Japanese magazine for girls.

www.filn.jp
Started in November 2005.
Filn executive office 101-0021 Tokyo Chiyoda Ku 3-6-1
first harmony building 5 floor
Ph: 03-5294-8077

http://otaba.jp
info@otaba.jp

http://days.yahoo.co.jp/

http://www.qq.com

http://www.wealink.com/

http://www.yeskee.com/ (LS)
webmaster@yeskee.com

TESTIMONIAL

Daisuke Kano

Hello An,
OK, let me give you a short overview of the SNS market in Japan.
Before I answer, I should let you know that I also have been creating Social networking sites
(only for Japanese).

The facts:
- *The amount of SNS users: 8,000,000 in Japan.*
The most famouse site is "mixi" http://mixi.jp :it is about 5,000,000 users.

- *Japanese do not care much for social networking sites in English.*
The average would be about: Japanese-only sites 90% of all users, English spoken sites 10% of all users in Japan. Probably, the language is the problem.

- *I think the user's age average is about 15y-25y: 70%, 26y-35y: 20%, 35over: 10% University students are the main users. Business people don't use SNS, they are fully occupied with their work. In the weekends they enjoy playing sports or spending time with their family rather than doing SNS.*

My own thoughts on this:

I felt Social networking seemed to be getting unpopular because last year so many sites were created. We started trying being specialized in one field (e.g. music, education, soccer...). But, as we set up more and more sites, people became bored with trying to find the right site for themselves. That was the common thought of the beginning of this year.

Later this year, we launched a business SNS site. It became very popular, against my expectations.
What was different?
In my opinion, the timing was very good.
- *People got accustomed to using SNS sites.*
- *Japanese people still want to use Japanese sites, because they feel that it is immediately relevant to their business.*
- *Recently there are many employees who want to change jobs.*

In summary:

Social networking sites still have a lot of potential but will need to change.
How they connect to the real world will be very important in the next stage.

Best wishes
Daisuke

Daisuke Kano
Team Lab inc
http://www.team-lab.com
Japan

KOREA

FRIENDS

http://www.cyworld.com/
Cyworld started in 1999 and has 20 million members, making it by far the largest social network in Korea. It is in Korean only. Cyworld has sister sites in the US, China, Japan, and Taiwan as well.

http://www.uberme.com/ (LS)
Uberme is the ubercool place to hang out, and it's all about you!
It's where you can share your uberific moments through Blogs and showcase your Photos and Videos. It's where you can form interest Groups with like-minded folks to debate the latest topics and gossip. It's where you can make uberfun new Friends and connect instantly with all your buddies via Instant Message Chats and Personal Messages. It's where you can have your own personal Mobile Portal wherever you go via your mobile phone.

Operated by Samsung.

feedback@uberme.com

http://www.weppy.com/
Weppy is one of Korea's major portal web sites with over five million subscribers. Services offered include web-mail, instant messaging, messenger service, UMS, personal homepage services, SIGs, bulletin boards, shopping, and entertainment.

Owned by Unitel Networks.

http://www.lifeinkorea.com/
Life in Korea, Inc. forms a unique E-marketplace for foreigners, specializing in Korean tourism and culture. We present information about Korean travel, culture, language, food, shopping, sports, activities, history, and a wealth of other subjects. In addition to writings, the site shows Korea through thousands of pictures, going beyond mere words.

Seoul
Tel: (02) 6422-1714
Fax: (02) 2648-2942

USA
Tel: (661) 254-0893
Fax: (661) 259-4108
25129 The Old Road, Ste. 210
Newhall, CA 91381

MYANMAR (Burma)

FRIENDS

http://www.guanxi.com/ (LS)
GuanXi.com is a service mark of FriendFinder Network, Inc.

The Purpose
In 1996, Andrew Conru had a vision — to create a one-stop solution for seeking, finding, and managing all types of online relationships.
Today, the FriendFinder Network's twenty-five web communities have over 100 million registered members. It continues to grow with thousands of new members each and every day. Finally, people have a relaxed and safe environment to meet others all over the globe. Best of all, FriendFinder is open twenty-four hours a day offering a social life that fits anyone's schedule.

The Difference

GuanXi.com offers more than a static directory of people looking to connect with others. People join for a sense of community – the ability to be amongst other people with similar mindsets and desires. Without the limitations of geography, our members can develop relationships and enjoy all types of encounters with members from around the world!

GuanXi.com not only gives our members the opportunity to meet friends and partners, we also enhance the member experience with daily horoscopes, photo ratings, free e-greeting cards, and the interactive GuanXi.com Magazine written by and for our members. The Magazine includes member-submitted articles and poetry, as well as a question and answer advice forum.

The Evolution

GuanXi.com is constantly evolving to meet the wants and needs of its members. Our team is constantly exploring and developing new features according to the results of member polls and e-mail feedback. To help members make quality connections, we've created extended profile questions that delve further into personalities, likes and dislikes as well as lifestyles. Our team has also added a personalized, interactive Workshop to help members hone their skills most relevant to the relationships they're seeking.

The Company

The FriendFinder Network is the leading global online relationship network, allowing over 100 million registered members to meet people with similar interests and mindsets in a fun environment. Founded in 1996 and privately owned, The FriendFinder Network operates with a staff of more than two hundred from its corporate headquarters in sunny Palo Alto, California.

The GuanXi.com Management Team
Rob Brackett – Interim President
Natalie Cedeno – Director of Human Resources
Jay Sweeney – Controller

FriendFinder Inc.
445 Sherman Ave., Suite C
Palo Alto, CA 94306, USA

PHILIPPINES

BUSINESS

http://www.prnster.com/
It stands for "Pinoy Registered Nurses and Students Center". PRN also means "As needed" on medical terms. PRNster.com is an active online community-based website tailored with one-of-a-kind features to suit the needs of Filipino Nurses and Nursing students anywhere in the globe, 24-hours a day, 7-days a week. PRNster is initiated by a group of Filipino nurses working in New York and New Jersey, USA with the aim of bringing Pinoy Nurses and caregivers from around the world together.

FRIENDS

http://halohalo.com/
HaloHalo is an online community for Filipinos and people who have ties to the Philippines. It is named after the sweet and creamy traditional Filipino dessert made up of layers of interesting ingredients, which really come alive when combined and mixed together. The synergy of Halo-Halo, the dessert, is what HaloHalo, the community, strives to achieve. By mixing people socially and professionally, the Filipino community can experience some of the same magic.

http://filipinocommunity.multiply.com
One of the biggest and fast growing networks in Multiply's "culture and community groups" is called "Pinoy Kami" (http://filipinocommunity. multiply.com), an online community of Filipinos and their friends all over the world. The group's sites features discussions on Filipino culture, current events, and topics on how Filipinos could "improve ourselves as a people." The site has often become a sounding board on issues that help Pinoys worldwide define their "Filipino identity" in the age of globalization and the continuing diaspora.
http://davidllorito.blogspot.com/2006/05/rediscovering-connectivity-through.html

http://www.kababayan.ph/

Welcome to Kababayan.ph, the site for Filipinos to help find other Filipino "countrymen." That's right – long lost friends and family! Have you ever wondered whatever happened to your childhood friend or classmate? What about the teacher you always admired? What if you or someone you know has an inheritance coming, but nobody knows how to reach you? Just launched in September 2006, Kababayan.ph wants to connect and reconnect Filipinos wherever they may be! Send this link and encourage friends and family to sign up. The more, the merrier! Soon you will have a Filipino connection all over the world! Mabuhay ang Filipino! Find your kababayans!

http://www.fwendz.com/

FwendZ is an online social community website that allows its members to properly organize their relationships with each other. FwendZ members can view each others' profiles, communicate with old friends and meet new friends on the service, share photos, post journals and comments, and describe their interests. To enrich our members' experience, we request and display some personal information to other members and visitors, which allows our users to identify each other and expand their network of friends. FwendZ members can change their profile information at any time and can control how other members and the service communicates with them.

Suite 402 Central Plaza I
J. P. Laurel Avenue
8000 Davao City Philippines
phone: +63 (82) 3051266
web: www.fwendz.com

DATING

http://www.itzamatch.com/en/index.jsp (LS)

Itzamatch.com aims to provide an enjoyable and comfortable avenue for people to meet people over the Internet. It is itzamatch's mission to serve the needs of singles, whether in or outside of the Philippines, be it through matching them with their ideal partners, or hooking them up with other singles of common interests and likes. It is itzamatch's aim to help people meet and build long lasting bonds of friendship, intimate or otherwise.

Bigfoot Match
Bigfoot Center, F. Ramos Street
Cebu City, Cebu, Phils. 6000
E-mail: csfeedback@itzamatch.com

SPECIAL INTEREST

Gaming & 3D

http://www.mobiuskids.net/
Digital Media Exchange, Inc., an online game distributor and digital entertainment provider based in the Philippines, has just released its family-oriented website mobiuskids in the Philippines, Singapore, and Malaysia. The site offers educational games and activities centered on child learning and family interaction. Upon launch, it introduced two popular casual online games – Disney's massively multiplayer online game Toontown Online and virtual pet game GoPets. The site also has a child-centered social networking feature, arcade game downloads, piggybank, task scheduler, and goal tracker.

SINGAPORE

BUSINESS

http://iconnecte.com/
IconnectE.com is the primary offering of IconnectE Pte Ltd, a Singapore-based company.

IconnectE.com is an interactive portal that enables small businesses, entrepreneurs, and professionals to generate more opportunities by building meaningful business relationships in a marketing-oriented community. This is achieved by providing members a power professional profile that more succinctly conveys who they are and reasons to interact through relevant marketing content and events.

IconnectE.com was founded in 2006 and launched officially in March 2007. The service is currently in Beta and in the process of building its member base and making improvements based on user feedback.

IconnectE.com is the brainchild of entrepreneur Jesse Ting and is supported by the Economic Development Board of Singapore under the Innovation Commercialization Scheme. The portal is also part of Microsoft's Early Adopters Initiative Program for implementing Net 3.0 Technology. Muu Consulting and yolk design have played a key role in the programming and design of the portal.

IconnectE Pte Ltd is open to discussing investment, licensing and marketing partnership possibilities.Contact Jesse at: ting@iconnecte.com
Mobile: +65-9092-1163

SRI LANKA

FRIENDS

http://www.esrilankans.net/

TAIWAN

FRIENDS

http://www.wretch.cc/
In Taiwan, a site called Wretch stakes its fame on its list of celebrities — politicians, writers, athletes, top models, and artists — who keep member profiles on the site. It has almost two million members. http://yaleglobal. yale.edu/display.article?id=8303

SPECIAL INTEREST

Gaming & 3D

http://www.i-part.com.tw/
I-part first launched in Aug. 2003 in Taiwan. In March 2005, with one million USD or so seed funding from Taiwan-based IDT, they launched their Shanghai website. Now they have over 4 million registered users, including Taiwan sector. Although their business mainly designed for young females, but male users are also encouraged to register. In fact, hundreds of thousands of men and women are living as virtual couples on their website. Their service is monetized by virtual avatar. Their virtual money is called I-coin. It can be exchanged with Chinese Yuan in 1:1 ratio. To decorate your virtual house or to feed virtual pets, you should spend I-coin in I-part mall. Users can also publish diaries and photos. Besides leaving comments on other users' place, you can also send virtual gifts. http://www.cwrblog.net/393/female-social-network-i-part-raises-3m-usd-funding.html

THAILAND

BUSINESS

http://www.arenasia.com/
Mission: to offer the best business networking opportunities for professionals in Asia or those doing business in the region.

CEO and co-founder: Heidi Floeth
Contact: heidi_floeth@hotmail.com

President and Co-founder: Jan Geister
Contact: jan.geister@arenasia.com

Based in Bangkok, Thailand
Launched in July 2007.

FRIENDS

http://www.thailandfriends.com/ (LS)
Create your own profile and connect with thousands of Thai Girls and Guys around the world. It has never been easier to make new friends online.

Upload photos, create a journal, announce a party, meet Thai girls and guys, or chat live with someone new! A powerful, safe and simple way to be seen in Bangkok and everywhere else TF members are!

VIETNAM

FRIENDS

www.noiket.com
Vietnamese

www.vietspace.net.vn
A Vietnamese social network offering an Vietnamese interactive, user-submitted network of friends, personal profiles, blogs, groups, photos, music, and videos... With the 20,000th account being created on October 3, 2006, the site attracts new registrations at a rate of 150 per day.

http://www.vietdamcuoi.com/ (LS)
VietCircles.com is a Social Network website for our Vietnamese community. We believe that it's about time our community had one. Viet Circles has many purposes, from making friends, networking, keeping in touch with old friends, and community involvement. Our underlining mission for VietCircles.com is to unite our Vietnamese community.

Founded by Dillon & Chau.

DATING

http://www.vietroom.com/
VietRoom is a free Vietnamese dating and social network site to meet new friends and common interests.

GENERAL

http://www.saffronconnect.com/ (LS)
SaffronConnect.com is a South Asian social networking portal centered on audio and video content sharing and downloads. We are focused on serving the global resident and non-resident South Asian market.
SaffronConnect.com allows independent artists, music labels, and video content owners to upload, share and sell their content to a community of users rooted in South Asian culture.

The portal integrates features such as web profiles, blogs, instant messaging, music downloads, photo galleries, classified listings, events, groups, chatrooms, and user forums to create a connected community of South Asians. The website is also a destination for South Asian bands and upcoming artists to launch new albums, while enabling users to sample and share songs.

SaffronConnect is funded by Duggal, a NY based visual studio and computer imaging firm and is managed by Divine Arts, a California based, India focused digital audio and video distribution firm.

Founded in October 2006.

Press: sri@mypeepul.com

Alisha Patel
Public Relations

Manu Kaushish, manager, Saffron-Media

http://www.infeedia.com/
Infeedia is a South Asian Community based website. It allows the community rather than an editor to submit and review the content on the site. All of the content on Infeedia is submitted and voted on by users like you. Enjoy!

6 What about India?

India is an enormous country with over 1 billion inhabitants. Naturally, not all of them are connected to the Internet, but those who are, are usually technology-savvy. A good deal of India's internauts we meet on social networks work in IT outsourcing. They are used to working with Europeans and Americans and have no qualms in using social networks as a prospection tool. Usually, they come rapidly to the point by asking "Can we work together?". However, cultural differences remain visible in the approach: even on social networking sites, Indians remain courteous at all times and address their potential business partners with the same formalities they would in person.

Another thing which struck me when analyzing the Indian social networking market is that most sites are in English, not Hindi. This is remarkable because most countries this size usually prefer using their native language(s) exclusively or together with English.

Last but not least, it should be noted that in Indian culture, matrimony is mostly arranged by the parents and influenced by social conventions. This custom continues within the social networking phenomenon, where people can look for potential suitable partners through expert matrimony sites, update with social networking elements.

BUSINESS

http://www.siliconindia.com/
SiliconIndia is one of the largest content and community networks for Indian professionals, entrepreneurs and students worldwide. Since 1997, we have inspired successes for Indian professionals through our thought provoking SiliconIndia events and magazines. Now, through the addition of our online professional network, we combine the power of news, magazine, and events, with an online network that can exclusively help you develop deep professional relationships with the SiliconIndia member community.

The member benefits can be listed as:

Your own trusted network, discussion groups, Messages, and the Lounge to interact with the siliconIndia community and expand your professional network.

Write on what you are passionate about and publish to the entire internet using our professional Blogs.

Special web seminars and events on topics of interest exclusive to SiliconIndia network members.

Opportunities to get personalized one on one advice from experienced professionals for career growth, entrepreneurship, and higher education through our unique mentorship program. Mentors are invited from within the SiliconIndia network.

The opportunity to contribute to our leading magazine, online news and events, to help enhance your professional profile in the growing SiliconIndia community.

Contact:
India
SiliconMedia Technologies Pvt Ltd.
No. 124, 2nd floor, south Block, Surya Chambers
Airport Main Road, Murugeshpalya, Bangalore-560017.
Phone: + 91-80-41510601 Fax: + 91-80-41321359

For editorial queries: editor@siliconindia.com

For more information: india@siliconindia.com

U.S.
Harvi Sachar CEO
E-mail: harvi@siliconindia.com

Mona Sharma Business Development Manager
Phone: 510-344-0450 Cell: 510-798-5110

Email: mona@siliconindia.com

SiliconIndia
44790, S Grimmer Blvd, # 202 Fremont, CA - 94538
Phone: 510-440-8249 Fax: 510-440-8276

N.J. office: (732) 218-0831

http://www.techtribe.com/ (LS)
TechTribe is India's career networking platform. It's a place where current and future professionals connect to advance their careers.

Developing a career requires us to Network with people, share our Knowledge, and build our personal Brand — based on our identity, experience, and accomplishments. TechTribe is a platform which enables us to do that.

Networking
TechTribe provides a platform for members to network with likeminded people and build relationships that help with their careers. Networking on techTribe includes the ability to connect with people in "Tribes" — which focus on a common passion or an entrepreneurial idea. It includes the ability to seek Mentors, who can guide us through our career choices and decisions and share their experiences.

Knowledge
On techTribe, members share their knowledge and experience with others, helping each grow professionally. On topics ranging from technology and outsourcing to business management and corporate life, members express their thoughts in Blogs and share acquired knowledge through Articles.

Your Brand
TechTribe is a place where individuals get to build their personal brands. They showcase their achievements through Portfolios and gain credibility through their Expressions. The platform enables them to stand out from the crowd and be recognized for their strengths.

On techTribe, current and future professionals interact with people with similar and related interests, learn from each others' experiences, and, together, grow their careers.

TechTribe is headed by Rohit Agarwal, a seasoned Silicon Valley serial entrepreneur and former software marketing/sales professional. He is assisted by a seven member team which is based out of Silicon Valley.

TechTribe is funded by friendly "angels/VCs," who have been behind companies like Webify, Sybase, CommerceOne etc. Professional networking for ICT professionals in India.

145 Natoma Street, Suite 500
San Francisco CA 94105
USA
Phone: +1 (415) 974 0500

146-149 Tribhuvan Complex
Ishwar Nagar New Delhi 110 065
India

Media Inquiries - press@techtribe.com

http://educatorslog.in/ (LS)
Educatorslog.in was started by a handful of individuals unified by one overarching objective — to use the net to make a durable difference in India by creating ways to bring educators together — in this particular case, to give them a common platform for dialogue, and in the process, help build a community, or several communities, centered around organizations or passions in the field of education.

Our team comprises of alumni of Harvard Graduate School of Education, Indian Institutes of Technology, Indian Institutes of Management, BITS Pilani and Massachusetts Institute of Technology. The team has several years of relevant experience in various domains.

Hi An,

You will find a lot of information on the design and features of the community portal if you wander around it and read some of the section in About and Learn More, and FAQ. I am attaching a detailed bio at the bottom and also attaching a couple of photos — one western looking, one Indian looking — take your pic :). Here are our responses to your questions.

Please let me know if there is anything else.

Good luck with the book. Keep us posted! Thanks so much for connecting with us...

Best Regards
Shuchi
shuchi_grover@post.harvard.edu

Educatorslog.in aims to build learning communities among educators and is geared to bring together people associated with education in India to connect-share-grow: connect with other educators and those interested in education in India (pre-K through higher and adult education), share resources that are contextually relevant to educators and teaching in India, and grow through learning about exemplary practices and professional development programs that cater to the needs of Indian educators.

-Founders & management
Shuchi Grover, a graduate from Harvard Graduate School of Education, who has specialized in Technology, Innovation, and Education (full profile provided at bottom of e-mail) and a team of designers and developers from premier educational institutions in India and the US unified by one overarching objective — to use the net to make a durable difference in India by creating ways to bring educators together — in this particular case, to give them a common platform for dialogue, and in the process, help build a community, or several communities, centered around organizations or passions in the field of education.

Our team comprises of alumni of Harvard Graduate School of Education, Indian Institutes of Technology, Indian Institutes of Management, BITS Pilani, and Massachusetts Institute of Technology. The team has several years of relevant experience in various domains.

-Founding year & address/nationality
Nov. 2006; India

-Target audience & membership level (number of users)
Mainly teachers and educators, but anyone involved in education in India — Policy makers, Corporates, NGOs, and even parents.

The site has been up for two months now — in the first month it was open only to a small user base of about twenty (by invitation). It now has about sixty users.

We are still in the process of adding a few features and making the system robust and have not as such marketed the site in any way at all. The current membership has come about only through word-of-mouth. We hope to launch some marketing campaigns — viral and other — in about a month's time.

-Top three countries in which the community is used
India (although we get hits from all over the world)

-Main technical features and possible features in the near future

- *Developed on Drupal, the portal is built along the lines of a community blog. Any member can post. For each post, the following actions are possible:*
- *Add/view comments (and even comment on comments)*
- *Forward a post or comment as e-mail to any e-mail address*
- *See pdf version of post*
- *Print the post*
- *View all the posts/comments by a particular user*
- *Get an e-mail alert when a comment is added to any post*
- *Organization of posts by educational themes, resources by grades and subjects, and educational programs by type of program*
- *Tagging of every post by user-defined tags*
- *Viewing tag cloud and viewing posts by any tag*
- *Searching by phrases, words, tags*
- *Groups — public, moderated, and private. Anyone can create a group. Posts made to groups can be viewed only by people who are members of the group.*
- *Captcha authentication in all input forms (to protect from spam)*
- *A blog attached to the site to update the community on feature updates and other news*
- *The landing page shows latest posts, resources, questions, and comments, and the top twenty tags thus allowing the user several entry points into the site*

Upcoming features

- *RSS*
- *Posting to Blogger from educatorslog.in (this feature was there and worked with the old Blogger, but with the new Blogger API being somewhat unstable, it is still being worked on)*
- *Buttons (like del.icio.us or digg) to provide to other sites to post from there directly to educatorslog.in*
- *Classifieds section*

-Languages in which the service is available
Currently only in English (possibility of allowing other Indian languages).

Other comments

- *Read some of the testimonials (including from people not in India) on the blog http://newsblog.educatorslogin.com/ (under the post "Some comments that we've received)*
- *Given the type of comments we've received from outside India, we may in the future have a space for global conversations, while also allowing for spaces for country-specific conversations*
- *Shuchi Grover has been invited to present this project at an international conference on "Building Learning Communities" in Boston, US, in July*

Shuchi Grover Bio
A technologist and an educator by training, Shuchi locates her work at the intersection of technology and education. An alumna of Harvard University and a successful entrepreneur, she has over fifteen years work experience in the mainstream IT industry as well as educational institutions such as Harvard Graduate School of Education, Harvard Business School and several K-12 schools in India and the US. Her current professional pursuits include :

- Creating platforms for networking teachers, especially in India
- Designing curriculum for teacher education programs, and delivering courses for teachers on issues of technology in education
- Conducting workshops on educational technologies

- Assisting school management and teachers with technology planning and integration
- Identifying new trends in educational technologies
- Creating technology resources for teachers, particularly tools for networking teachers
- Coaching on Harvard's Wide World online courses
- Facilitating an after-school Robotics Club

She is invited to speak in conferences in India on issues of effective technology use in education. She has been invited to present her work on educatorslog.in at an international conference on "Building Learning Communities" in Boston, US, in July. She also maintains a blog — Education Musings (http://shuchi-edblog.blogspot.com)

She has undergraduate degrees in Physics & Computer Science from BITS (Pilani), India, an M.S. in Computer Science from Case Western Reserve University, Cleveland, and an Ed.M. (Technology in Education) from Harvard University.

Owned and operated by Hit Factory, Inc., d/b/a/ Educatorslog.in is a Delaware, U.S.A. corporation.

Press Inquiries
press@educatorslogin.com

FRIENDS

http://indyarocks.com/
Indyarocks.com is an online and mobile based social networking site for connecting Indians across the Globe. It allows members to build and leverage their network of contacts in incredibly powerful ways. It is a place where you can Invite, Connect, Share, Speakout and Have fun. The platform is designed to provide you with unlimited freedom of expression. Plus, you can invite your non-Indian friends to experience the rich Indian culture through Indyarocks.com.

info@indyarocks.com

Kalyan Manyam
kalyan@indyarocks.com

http://www.apundesi.com/ (LS)
ApunDesi is a social networking website that is exclusively dedicated towards Indians and Pakistanis commonly known as Desis. Create your own free profile, where you can publish blogs, create image galleries, communicate with friends and a guestbook where your friends can leave you comments. Apart from this, you will control every aspect of your profile, you can design it, upload mp3s, add music videos, and much more. You can also communicate using our forums, create interest groups, search for new and old friends, rate images uploaded to member galleries, play games, watch music videos, read movie and music reviews and submit or view current events.

ApunDesi was lauched on Dec 1st , 2006 with the idea of creating a desi community site.

www.orkut.com
Orkut is an Internet social network service run by Google and named after its creator, Google employee Orkut Büyükkökten. Until October 2006, Orkut was an invitation-only site, but it now permits users to create accounts without an invitation. Founded in January 2004.

http://www.hikut.com/
Hikut.com is a social networking service that allows Members to create unique personal profiles online in order to find and communicate with old and new friends.

Powered by Fm Infomatic Solutions.

Fm Infomatic Solutions is India's best IT Services Company. We are the web hosting and development company, based in India. We have the expertise of over five years in providing these services. Our clients range from India to USA, and back to the city of Noida. Our web designers have a keen sense of creativity in producing the maximum result-oriented contents. They first study about the client, his services, requirements and targeted customers. Then the outline is prepared by our theme designing dept. and then the website development took off. So here by all this we want to let you know that we are not just a company but a people-oriented system, a system for your business solutions.

To know more about our services, please visit www.xpcl.com, e-mail us at info@xpcl.com . Or call us at +91 98971-56789.

http://www.goyaar.com/ (LS)

Go Yaar! is an online directory that connects people in or from India through social networks at colleges, school, and work. Search and browse friends and classmates, find out who is in your class, look up friends' friends, create your own media through blogs, video, music, and much much more!

Phalgun Raju, founder and CEO.

http://www.snehah.com (LS)

The word SnehaH is a sanskrit word, which means Friendship.

Social Community Network from India, a social networking utility portal was launched recently. The portal, a stand out from others in its category, harps on the idea of knowledge sharing between people from creative and professional spheres apart from social networking.

SnehaH.com has been launched by Sravan, an software engineer cum web entrepreneur from Hyderabad, who has to his credit a list of successful ventures such as www.mavenarts.com – India's first digital online community—and www.Indiagram.com – A Social Bookmarking system, a utility portal. Managed efficiently by a talented team comprising Ram, a graphic visualizer, Xasu23 (Admin) and Kartik to customize the content of the portal. With an ever-growing team of contributors, the team seeks to improve and update the content of snehaH.com in every possible manner. Sravan's dream is to make snehaH.com a platform for resource and knowledge sharing for people from different parts of the world.

http://www.indiagrid.com/index.shtml

IndiaGrid.com web site is fully owned by TechnoSpring Software Development Private Limited. It is a Hub for people of Indian Origin in your area.

http://www.jhoom.in/ (LS)

Jhoom! is one of the first social software targeting Indian market completely, unlike Orkut. It has most of the features that the popular sites like MySpace has (minus the excessive customizations that MySpace offers). It has blogs, groups, forums, photo albums, blogrolls, polls, avatars, back-of-the-house administration tools and is adding many more features in the coming days.

A place where people come together to talk about movies, music and entertainment.

jhoom! – A Platform for Artists
Jhoom! provides the community platform for Indian artists to publish their music, publish their profiles and connect with their fans and audiences.

jhoom! - Buzz About Films
Check out what other users have to say about the latest hits and misses. Check out the latest videos, movie reviews, movie stills, and Gossip!

jhoom! is Local
Jhoom! is an extension to your offline life. With uptodate information on Entertainment events it helps you discover what is hip and happening around you.

Fantastic Parties
Jhoom! users benefit from exclusive jhoom! Parties and gigs featuring Top Indian DJs and Indian Artists. So look out for the next one.

press@jhoom.in

www.fropper.com
Fropper has recently launched a whole new site. On Fropper.com, you can create your personal Zone (Web page), upload and share your personal photographs, create & join groups, view & create your own ezBlog, and exchange messages to connect with people and make new friends.

Fropper.com
People Interactive (I) Pvt. Ltd.
Shiv-e-Numh, 2nd floor
205, Dr. Annie Besant Road

Worli, Mumbai 400 018
India

www.minglebox.com (LS)
Minglebox is a Bangalore based company in the consumer internet &
mobile space. Our intent is to create a leading franchise in the internet
and new media world. We are a team of highly motivated and energetic
individuals with complementary skills in business, technology, media, and
design.

Kavita Iyer, CEO
Sanjay Aggarwal, CTO
Sushma Abburi, Vice President
Sanjay Mittal, Vice President

feedback@minglebox.com

DATING

www.shaadi.com
In India there are lot of matrimonial sites. The complete list is available
at http://indiaupcoming.com/tag/matrimonial. Among them all, Shaadi.
com and BharatMatrimony.com are probably the most successful. Both of
these sites have plans to diversify into other regional languages too. http://
www.readwriteweb.com/archives/india_top_web_apps.php

http://www.naukri.com/

SPECIAL INTEREST

Sports

http://sixer.tv
An Indian social networking site for cricket fans.
Backed by LINUS Capital, a boutique investment and advisory firm based
in the San Francisco Bay Area. The Hyderabad-based website, currently in

beta, is expected to be launched before the ICC Champions Trophy 2006 games.

Sudheer Kumar, General Manager of 'Sixer', a Hyderabad based firm, says, "Our site will be an online hub for cricket fans with user-generated content, where a user can create content, share his or her profile and connect."

Students

http://www.batchmates.com (LS)
Cutting across geographical boundaries and bringing the far-flung corners of the world closer, Batchmates.com the premier portal of Allindia Technologies Limited has been the perfect platform for old school and college friends to stay in touch. Batchmates.com has successfully reunited nearly three million alumni through as many e-mails sent via batchmates.com since its inception in July 1997. We further receive 7,500+ members visiting batchmates (Batchmates.com) daily and over 1500 new registrations per day. Batchmates.com is wholly owned, developed, managed, and sponsored by Allindia Technologies Limited, a leading web solutions company in Eastern India and based in Kolkata, West Bengal.
support@batchmates.com

http://www.yo4ya.com/yo4ya/100_home.php

http://www.sulekha.com/
Sulekha is the biggest and most popular member-generated community and social/professional networking hub integrating social media and local commerce services. Millions of Indians express, interact and transact through Sulekha's portfolio of highly popular, complementary services in twenty-five cities in India and worldwide.

Sulekha.com is almost entirely member-driven and member-generated. Over ninety-five percent of Sulekha's more than ten million pages of content are generated by its participating members. What started as a simple idea and a tiny webzine – 'a place where Indians come to connect' – has now evolved into the most vibrant online community, winning unexampled emotional loyalty and global media acclaim both its ground-breaking innovation and business success.

Sulekha.com New Media Pvt. Ltd.
No. 484 & 485, Pantheon Plaza,
4th Floor, Pantheon Road,
(Opp. Commissioner's Office)
Egmore, Chennai - 600 008 (India)
Phone: 91-44-42103174/66789999
Fax: 91-44-42111956

http://www.rediff.com/
A key focus for Rediff.com is using world-class technology to drive community building. Through a single login facility, Rediff.com provides a combination of free and paid community features and products to consumers and businesses. These include e-mail, instant messaging, chat, e-cards, matchmaker, astrology services, blogs, message boards, mobile services, online shopping, and auctions.

Rediff Connexions is the Company's social networking platform and currently under beta testing.

Rediff.com India Limited
Mahalaxmi Engineering Estate
L.J. Road # 1, Mahim (West)
Mumbai 400 016. India
Tel: +91-22-24449144
Fax: +91-22-24455346

www.hi5.com
Hi5 is one of the top fifty most-trafficked sites on the Web, as ranked by Alexa.
More than 50 million people have registered accounts with hi5.
Our service has a unique, global footprint that touches North and South America, Europe, and Asia.

VIDEO/PHOTO

http://www.meravideo.com/
Popular video sharing online community hub for Indians around the world. MeraVideo is a part of BrainGain Entertainment Private Ltd., a privately held Mumbai based Media Company. BrainGain is a venture that aims at producing TV programs that help networks achieve top ratings through risk, originality and creativity. BrainGain is an expression of strongly networked, high caliber individuals from diverse backgrounds. MeraVideo is a personal video sharing service that allows people to connect, converse, and share their life experiences captured on video. In addition to serving as an entertainment platform, MeraVideo mission is to help the creators of videos to make money by sharing and distributing their work using the MeraVideo platform. MeraVideo mission is to build a community that is highly motivated to watch and share videos. With its strong, dedicated user base, MeraVideo is a fast growing video phenomenon. Feel free to e-mail us at contact@meravideo.com for your suggestions.

http://www.aapkavideo.com/
AapkaVideo is an online service that allows you to watch, upload, and share your videos with others.

MOBILE

http://www.yaari.com/index.php (LS)
Yaari (" Friendship ")- India's mobile social network!
Yaari is a social networking site created by Indian youth, for Indian youth. Our vision is to be India's largest social networking site. With your input, we are creating a site that is fun, hip and unique. Come join us and help make Yaari number one! We welcome your feedback, so do tell us what you think: feedback@yaari.com

Hi,

Here are my answers to your questions:

-Founders & management

Prerna Gupta, CEO

Prerna was working in venture capital when she had a vision of a social networking site that would change the face of Internet usage in India. So she decided to quit her job and go for it. And here she is today without a penny to spare but loving her new life as CEO of Yaari. Prerna graduated from Stanford University with a BA in economics and then worked restlessly in management consulting and venture capital until she finally discovered her true passion (bossing people around at Yaari). She also loves bananas, Cuban salsa dancing, yoga and other esoteric things, which you can read about on her Yaari profile.

Parag Chordia, CTO

Parag used to lie awake at night imagining a world where he could spend all his time listening to music, playing games and meeting beautiful women. Yaari is his attempt to create such a utopia. Parag now spends most of his time getting yelled at by Prerna and solving pesky technical problems. But in his spare time, he manages to teach at Georgia Tech, play sarod and party with one very beautiful woman. Parag received his PhD from Stanford University in artificial intelligence and music, and his BS in math from Yale. He hopes Yaari will provide Indian youth with a forum to freely express their views, propagate their passions and enjoy each other.
-Founding year & address/nationality
June 2005 in Palo Alto, CA

-Target audience & membership level (number of users)
Indian youth. Over 100,000.

-Top three countries in which the community is used
India
Pakistan
US

-Main technical features and possible features in the near future
Media upload, commenting, tagging, rating music

-Languages in which the service is available
Currently only English, but we will be offering it in many Indian languages soon

best
Prerna

Prerna Gupta
Chief Executive Officer
Yaari.com

Prerna Gupta, Chief Executive Office
Parag Chordia, Chief Technical Officer

press@yaari.com

7 What about the Middle-East?

People from the Middle East are as much interested in sharing knowledge, meeting new people online and communication as any other group. However, the 'policing' of social networks by Middle Eastern governments and the control within the networks themselves makes it harder for social networks to reach their audience. Strangely enough there are also a number of Muslim sites which are headquartered in the United States (e.g. Naseeb, Mecca, and Muslimica).

According to a Booz Allen Hamilton study (2007), Web 2.0 sites in the Middle East are not as prevalent as in Europe or the US; only fifteen percent of users in Arab countries report that they frequently visit Web 2.0 sites. Of the sites that Middle East users report visiting frequently, Amazon, Wikipedia, Hi5, and YouTube topped the list, followed sequentially by Mp3.com, MySpace, Blogger, and iTunes.

IRAN

FRIENDS

http://www.orkut.com
350,000 Iranians are a member of Orkut, despite the fact that the site is American.

ISRAEL

BUSINESS

http://www.themarker.com/
TheMarker Café is a community launched by a Jewish newspaper. It is aimed at professionals who are interested in the economy, finance, high tech, media, advertising etc and who read and write Hebrew. The main idea of the Café is to create social networks based on a common personal or professional interest. Once registered, people can ask any member of the

Cafe to join his or her circle of friends. If he or she agrees, he or she will join your list of friends and the system will send you notices about content he or she creates. TheMarker Café was launched in 2007.

http://hook.co.il/
Professional network that was launched in 2007.

FRIENDS

http://www.adamoreve.com/
The goal of AdamOrEve is to bring Jews together through social networks. Members contribute to the content of the site, building friendships, creating activity and discussion groups, and making business connections locally, regionally and globally.

AdamOrEve offers elite services such as Audio & Video Mail, Chat, and IM. Members receive a personal web-space, which supports music and videos and also contains areas for photos and graphics, blogging and comments.

I am Adam, and aside from the work I have done to create and build this site, I want to thank many of my friends both on and off line for their amazing contributions to this project. AdamOrEve is a collective effort brought to you from Israel. I created the space, but the membership fills it. Join, add content, connect, be Jewish, be happy!

The site is in English, Portuguese, and Hebrew.

Founded in September 2005. Based in Israel.

http://www.shox.co.il/
Blogging, hot or not ratings,...for teenagers in people in their twenties.

http://www.janglo.net/
Janglo was started in June 2001 as a free community service to help people in the Jerusalem area exchange information about "stuff", like jobs, apartments, events, and sales. About a year later, we launched a similar site,

Taanglo, for the Tel Aviv area. Both e-mail lists quickly took off and became some of the most popular sites for English-speakers in Israel, with many imitators. Janglo.net, combines the best of both lists and builds on them, strengthening their community aspects while expanding them to the entire country.

Janglo was founded by Zev Stub. Zev grew up in Chicago and made aliya in June 2000, right after he graduated from Yeshiva University. Zev now manages janglo.net on a full-time basis.

www.Shmooze.com (LS)
What do you get when you combine a JDate that's totally free, a Yahoo Groups for the 21st century, a facebook with a clean interface, and a MySpace just for Jews? Shmooze!
Shmooze is an online platform for social networking that people and organizations can customize to make connections with each other, to collaborate on projects, and to share content in a controlled and easy-to-manage way.

Although Shmooze software has thousands of possible uses for any purpose under the sun, we have decided to apply it first to further the interests of Jewish community and education, create connections among Jews in the Diaspora and the State of Israel.

Shmooze starts with individuals, enabling members to define themselves and their interests, sharing their photos, and creating blogs. Members can also create controlled access personal groups that enable them to create closed or open discussion forums and share files of all kinds with their friends and business associates.

Members also can enjoy access to a variety of high quality content about Israel and Jewish culture, including photo collections, online courses, ebooks, music, and movies.

If you manage an organization or business, Shmooze lets you set up groups for your enterprise, including blogs, discussion forums and file collections, including the ability to create sub-groups and to sell and advertise products and services. You can command a powerful tool to communicate with your members or your customers.

Shmooze is designed to be a commercial, ad-supported environment with all basic services at no cost to individuals. Sign up for free.

Organizations pay a licensing fee for a secure, full-service online community for their members or customers, but everyone can try before they buy. Soon Shmooze will be fully customizable to achieve consistency with the branding and interests of partners.

Shmooze is developed in Israel by Koret Communications, a privately-held Israel company, in partnership with the Jewish Agency for Israel and leading foundations and not-for-profit organizations.

biz@shmooze.com

http://www.klostu.com/
Klostu.com, developed by Pidgin Technologies, is a unique new platform which brings together existing disparate message board communities and their members into what is essentially a super social network — a network of social networks. Klostu provides members of boards (and even blogs) advanced profiles with a growing range of social tools and useful widgets. Klostu profiles appear within the boards and will move seamlessly from one board to another, wherever the user may travel on the boardscape. Klostu provides an advanced 'ajax desktop' style interface to manage user profiles and social activity, including finding friends, comments, instant messaging with jabber, rss reading and sharing, blogging, galleries, videos, and more.

Pidgin Technologies is based in Tel Aviv.

http://www.hevre.co.il/
Hevre is in Hebrew only and started as a Clasmates lookalike. Hevre means "gang" as in "band of friends".

http://dex.co.il/
Dex was launched in 2004 and caters mostly to teenagers. There is blogging, video, photos, music…

VIDEO/PHOTO

http://www.vringo.com/ (LS)

Dear Mrs. De Jonghe:

Thank you for contacting us. We would be very pleased for Vringo to find a place in your book.

Per your request, below please find the summary you requested of the Vringo community. If you have any comments or questions, please do not hesitate to contact me.

Kind regards,

Benjamin

Benjamin Levy
VP, Marketing
benjamin@vringo.com
mobile: +972 (54) 529-7500
US cell: +1 (646) 417-0127
www.vringo.com
Skype ID: benjamin_levy

Vringo is a cool new way to share video on your mobile phone. You share video by choosing what video ringtone plays on your buddies' handset when you call them.
Vringo is launching a video sharing community which allows you to share video ringtones (or Vringo's) with your buddies each time you call them.
You choose the clips you'd like your buddy to see, and they chose the clips they'd like you to see. These Vringo clips are licenced content from the best of movies, TV, music or are user generated and created from your own mobile phone.

Jonathan Medved
Chief Executive Officer
Jon is one of Israel's leading venture capitalists and a seasoned entrepreneur. Jon is a co-founder of Vringo and serves as the Chief Executive Officer.

David Goldfarb
Chief Technology Officer
As Chief Technology Officer and a co-founder of Vringo, David brings
over twenty years of industry expertise in the development of cutting edge
and innovative technology.

For more information please e-mail us at info@vringo.com

Vringo, Inc.
BIG Center
1 Yigal Allon Blvd.
Beit Shemesh 99062
Israel
Phone: +972 2 991-3381
Fax: +972 2 991-3382

http://aniboom.com/
AniBoom is a cross-media, cross-platform animation content project which
addresses wide audiences through a range of genres, techniques and means.
In order to get things started we chose the most democratic medium, the
Internet. In our next phase we intend to cross over to other mediums as well
as TV, Cellular, PC games, etc. AniBoom was launched on September 17,
2006.

www.bolt.com (LS)
With all the excitement about file sharing, blogging, camera phones, social
networks, video ipods, 'Really Simple Syndication,' and 'bigger pipes', we
started daydreaming about an online portfolio – a place where you could
store, organize and share all the media you create in the course of your digital
life. A place where home movies can attain cult status, where snapshots from
your last vacation might inspire a stranger to make the same trip, where
the most timid voice can find a listener, and the most obscure subject, an
audience. We built it and call it Bolt.

'We' are Bolt Media, a media company that for ten years has been creating
and managing some of the most popular youth-oriented sites online. Since
our inception we've focused on enabling people to interact and express

themselves in original ways. We think the new Bolt is a fitting new addition to that legacy.

bolthelp@boltinc.com

TESTIMONIAL *Idan Gafni*

Israel and Social Networks — Idan Gafni

As a small and technologically advanced country, Israel's participation in the social networks phenomena is unique. In a country of 7 million people, the 6 degrees theory is reduced to 3 or 4 degrees. Potential connections are never too far. In such an ecosystem, social networks become structured tools of relationship management and people search, and less of finding a path to contact a distant member.

Israel's personal social networks include dedicated networks for children (Merushatim), youth (Mekusharim, Tapuz), soldiers (Bona), and adults (Beshutaf). An interesting story from this market is of a TV production company that paid social network "Mekusharim" to create profiles in the network of characters from a planned TV show. The profiles were ordinary profiles, and only after the launch of the show people were informed this was a teaser to the show. Another special form of network is a hybrid network. Hybrid networks use personal networks and financial reward programs. These networks are pyramid shaped social networks that reward members on advertisement watched by their network (SMSer, S4M).

Israel's professional networks include: TheMarker Café, Pinpoint, Thecoils, and a dedicated closed network of Israel's technology market in Ning. The most significant network full with articles and blogs is TheMarker Café, which belongs to Israeli leading business newspaper TheMarker.

The technological characteristics of the Israeli market have incubated several services and products such as: movie-centric network "TrustedOpinion", professional rewarding network "VShake", mobile media-rich network PeerBox, Xing's partner ZoomInfo, and int2001 with their contextual network search solutions (ICQ directory search).

The Israeli participation in global professional networks was proven to be an effective tool in reducing the effect of the geographical distances to America, Europe, and Asia and a valid method to create business leads. Social networks came to be an essential tool for start-up companies with limited resources when exploring new markets or in business development initiatives. Israeli presence is significant, especially in LinkedIn and Xing (formerly OpenBC).

Israel is a good example to a society that embraced social networks, adapted them to the specific needs (like soldiers' network), and used them to break geographical barriers. Israel demonstrates that social networks function as enablers and not as services; networks get different forms, address different needs, and comply with different cultural customs. Social networks should not be duplicated from one market to another but should vary just like culture does.

There is a lesson to be taught from the dynamic nature of social networks. There are no "rigid" best practices in networking. Successful networkers are the members that constantly take the time to monitor and observe the network and dynamically adapt to the new forms of the network. For successful networking it is crucial to remember that every social network is built on individual members. You should always try and combine active and passive networking to get the optimal results for your network's growth. Active networking is done by taking a personal approach when contacting unconnected members of the network. Passive networking is done by finding a way to be discovered by other members and to attract the relevant members to connect. Networking is just like any other social activity whether it is online or offline you should be dedicated to the process in order to succeed.

Idan Gafni — Serial Entrepreneur, Connecting the dots between Users, Content, and Technology.
www.CellXpert.com

JORDAN

http://jeeran.com/
Established in 2000 as the first Arab web hosting community, Jeeran's continuous mission is to allow members the effective harnessing of the internet. Web hosting and design, online storage, image management, and e-mail are some of the tools that make our website unique in addressing members' needs. Jeeran counts 1 million users.

Laith Zraikat: Director of Innovation & co-founder of Jeeran
Omar Koudsi President & co-founder of Jeeran

LEBANON

FRIENDS

http://www.lebvillage.com/ (LS)
Hi! We're Ron & Marc, welcome to Lebanesevillage.com. We're hosting this community website because we feel it's important that we have a place of our own to do all those things we do online: Blog, chat, forums, music, videos. This is an invite only website; you are here because either we invited you or someone else in our great Lebanese community decided you should be a part of our community. Enjoy your time here, and remember, you are here with friends.

http://beirut4ever.com/
Beirut4ever.com is an online social networking community that allows you to set up a unique personal profile, communicate with old friends and meet new friends on the service, view Beirut4ever members' profiles, share photos, post journals, profile comments, photo comments and many other features.

info@beirut4ever.com
beirut-4-ever@hotmail.com

DATING

http://profile.com/ (LS)
Profile.com is an interactive online community! Meet lots of new interesting people for dating or just get to know them. There's lots of things here to keep you occupied, including forums, photo rating, games, blogs, and more. Whether you are looking for a friend, a date, or love, our site is always free to browse, free to post, and free to respond! Use your profile as a personal ad or as your home on the web. Either way, the social networking features of our site allow you to build your own circle of friends (or lovers) and create more friendships and relationships all the time.

http://www.mylebnet.com/

MyLebNet.com is the place to keep in touch with friends, family and to create a business network between other Lebanese around the globe. It is the first social networking site dedicated to the Lebanese community and is intended to promote and bound the Lebanese and their friends in order to keep in touch and promote the Lebanese spirit and way of life. MyLebNet.com is a trusted network, where you decide who is in your circle of friends or business. You can read and send messages, post photos, collaborate in group discussions, schedule calendar events, keep a personal journal (blog), post classified ads, chat in real-time, create a private family area, share music and videos plus many other features!

TUNESIA

FRIENDS

http://amiz.fr/ (LS)
Founders are Sebastien and Olivier.
sebastien@amiz.fr

Dear An,
You'll find the information in the attached document.
If you have any further questions, never hesitate to ask.

Good luck with the book,
Sebastien

Founding Process

Amiz was founded by me, Sebastien Moeys, in July 2006, right after graduating from high school in Amsterdam. Perhaps it's surprising to read that the founder of one of France's most popular social networks is in fact Dutch, so here's some explanation. I've always been a frequent visitor of France during holidays, visits, etc. Me and my family have friends and family in France, so ever since I was born I spent several weeks of the year in a French environment. This is how I learnt the French that would later come in very handy running Amiz.fr.

With the uprising of social networks in the US and the Netherlands (where I live), I started becoming an active user of those networks. I was actually visiting my American friends' MySpace profile to check out what they were up to, I used a Dutch social network to keep in touch with my Dutch friends, but for the many friends and relations I have in France I didn't see a good way to keep in touch. The existing French social networks were simple and didn't have any nice features at all.

This lack of possibility to keep in touch using a social network was my reason for deciding to start Amiz in the spring of 2006. I approached a friend who was going to help me out doing the programming. After some months of development and work, the first version was launched in July 2006. Traffic and popularity rocketed since the launch, and we were constantly developing new features to meet with our members' demand. This made Amiz what it is today: a constantly growing network under constant development.

Perhaps an interesting fact: the founder behind one of France's largest social networks is seventeen years old.

Founders and management

Founded by Sebastien Moeys with the help of my friend Olivier. The project is currently managed by me, while Olivier does the programming. Our team consists of:

- Sebastien, managing the project
- My friend Olivier, responsible for programming
- Several freelance programmers helping out when needed
- A French online media expert consulting us on marketing strategy
- A number of loyal volunteers working hard to keep Amiz a safe, erotism-free network
- A large group of loyal members beta testing and debugging new features under development

Founding year & address/nationality

Launch date: 11-07-2006
Company location: Amsterdam, Netherlands

Target audience

Most of our users are in the 15-25 age range. This is our main audience. However, a group of younger as well as a group of older people (in their forties and fifties) have started to actively use Amiz. Our audience is getting more diverse by the day, which is a good thing.

This month (March 2007) the number of two million members will be reached.

Top countries in which the community is used

- *France*
- *Northern Africa (Tunisia, Morocco, Algeria)*
- *French-speaking Canada*
- *French-speaking Belgium*
- *Switzerland*

Main technical features and possible features in the future

Our features at the moment.

Personal features:

- *Creating your personal page with your personal information.*
- *Adding a blog to your page.*
- *Adding albums with an unlimited amount of photos to your page.*
- *Adding youtube videos to your page.*
- *Completely customize the look of your page using our easy to use page personalisation feature.*

Social features:

- *Adding other users to the friends list on your page.*
- *Add and receive public friend comments.*
- *Communicate privately using our private messaging system.*
- *Create or become a member of public or private member groups to discuss topics in their forums.*
- *Search for people in the same city. Search for people sharing the same interests.*

Possible future features:

- *Possibility to add music to your page.*
- *Support for video sites like dailymotion, google video, etc.*
- *Possibility to tell us which schools you attended, allowing you to connect to former classmates.*
- *More advanced page customization options.*
- *Instant messaging (chat).*

Languages in which the service is available
Because Amiz is a Francophone network, it's only available in French.

DATING

http://abcoeur.com/
Dating site.

UNITED ARAB EMIRATES

FRIENDS

http://uaewomen.net (LS)
Online community website dedicated to the UAE women and families
uaewomen@uaewomen.net

General

FRIENDS

http://www.dIg.com
DIg wants to be the Facebook of the Arab world. Their prime demographic is Arabic youths between 14–24 years. Founded in February 2007, the site has 150,000 registered users. The default languge is Arabic, but the site can be consulted in English as well. DIg is Internet speak for "deewanji, from the Arabic word "dewan" , a term used to describe a place where Arabic

communities come together to converse, share information, and chat to each other.

CEO: Majied Qasem
Chairman: Rudain Kawar

http://faye3.com/
'Faye3' is an Arabic colloquial term for "cool" or "hip". The site was founded by Sohaib Thiab and Hussam Hammo and won first place in the Queen Rania National Entrepreneurship Competition (QRNEC). This is an annual competition that invites student teams from different universities to present a business plan for a technology-based entrepreneurial project of their choice. Faye3 will be backed up by Maktoob, a webportal for the Arab user.

Naseeb, Mecca, and Muslimica are also important social networks for Muslims in the Middle East, but due to the location of their headquarters they are listed under "USA- miscellaneous".

VIDEO/PHOTO

www.IslamicVideos.net
Islamic video service, owned by Muxlim (The company's headquarters are located in Espoo, Finland, and we are planning to open regional offices in the US, UK, and U.A.E. during 2007, says Muxlim's CEO and Co-Founder Mr. Mohamed El-Fatatry. Muxlim Inc. is privately owned by its co-founders and the company is currently looking to close its first financial round after receiving initial funding from an independent angel investor.)

http://www.muslimr.com
Share Photos, Videos, Links & Blogs With Muslims

http://ikbis.com/
Ikbis is the first photo and video sharing service in the Arab World. Ikbis is part of TootCorp, a media company based in Arabia and founded in September 2005. TootCorp has special interest in citizen media and

self-publishing. Other services by TootCorp include Toot and Toot Advertising Network (TAN).

What is Ikbis?

Ikbis is a photo and video sharing service geared for the Arab audiences around the world. With Ikbis, you can upload and organize your photos and videos that you've taken with your digital camera or mobile phone. Moreover, you can share your photos and videos with friends and family, interact with other Ikbis users and rate photos and videos.

Ikbis headquarters are located in Amman, Jordan. We spend most of our time in a shared office space with Syntax, a branding and design firm.

Ikbis representatives are also located in Dubai, London and Berlin too.

8 What about Russia and Ukraine?

When talking about Internet penetration in Russia, there is a big difference between Moscow/St Peterburg and the rest of Russia. Overall Internet penetration is about 25% according to the Public Opinion Foundation of Russia but is probably much higher in the big cities. Interestingly enough, mobile phones are highly popular in Russia and many people use their mobile phone to access the internet.

Russia does not have a clear number one when it comes to social networking. Sites like odnoklassniki.ru (classmates), moikrug.ru ("Russian LinkedIn"), have been growing fast but have only 1 million users (less than 5% of Russia's 30 million users internet community). Dating sites like loveplanet. ru, mamba.ru, and damochka.ru have been more successful by getting 3–5 million profiles, but they cannot be called true social networking sites.

Blogging is reasonably popular in Russia with LiveJournal taking first place. According to a survey conducted by Yandex and released in Sept 2006, 60% of Russian bloggers are female, 40% are male. Their average age is 21, several years less than the average age of a Russian Internet user. Nearly 80% of all Russian bloggers are from Moscow and Saint Petersburg.

BUSINESS

http://moikrug.ru/
Bought by Russian portal Yandex in March 2007. Local "Linkedin". It was founded on 18 Nov 2005 and has ten thousand users.

FRIENDS

http://toodoo.ru/
Each user indicates his/her favorite sites and can then find other users who enjoy the same sites.

http://www.limpa.ru/

Limpa.ru is Rate.ee's Russian equivalent (Rete.ee is Estonian). Limpa. ru has gained users, but many are not so active as Rate.ee.0 days). Limpa's users are mostly Baltic Russians, who are different from "true" Russians.

http://vkontakte.ru/

Facebook clone. Launched in September 2006 by Pavel Durov, it has 1 million members. Vkontakte is one of the top five communities in Russia.

http://www.fakultet.ru/

Social network geared to students. One percent of the company's ownership capital will be distributed among the users.

http://comby.ru/

Social network for friends, My Space clone.

http://www.damochka.ru/

Rambler, the No.2 search engine in Russia with a 20% share in the market, owns 51%.

http://www.doodka.com/

Doodka.com is property of ClosoSolutions and offers free blogs, photo albums, etc in Ukraine, Russia, and the countries of the former USSR.

http://www.odnoklassniki.ru/ (LS)

Odnoklassniki.ru is the community site for Russian speaking people all across the world. Launched on the 5th of March 2006, it is now one of the fastest growing sites in Russia, and probably the biggest social network already. Developers of the site have previously done 192.com – the largest directory enquiries site in the UK, and passado.com – popular social network site in Germany in Spain.
pr@odnoklassniki.ru

http://mamba.ru/

DATING

http://dating.ru/

http://jdu.ru/

SPECIAL INTEREST

Film

http://www.kinobaza.com/
Russian social network for movie fans

TESTIMONIAL

Igor Kovalev
Chief of IT department, Ford of Russia
IT blog: http://itblogs.ru/blogs/kovalev/default.aspx

The first social network in Russia was the technical one – FidoNet. There was not Internet in Russia at the time (1990), and even when I joined it in 1994 the only available Internet technology was UUCP (simple technology to send e-mails off-line). It started with the point in Novosibirsk, but soon Moscow and St.Petersburg grew to become the biggest nets in Fido. Configuration and support of a FidoNet station required at least some level of technical skills, so it was comprised of mostly IT specialists of various levels and their friends.

The network was the only source of the IT news at the time, and I dare say that most of the people who launched Internet in Russia come from the Fido roots. Internet was launched when the Fido was in its bloom and was the main reason for its decline. Another reason was described by Clay Shirky, who himself was the part of the bloom and decline of usenet – you need barriers for participation. Barrier to participate in Fido appeared to be too low. Besides that, we (I was one of the hubs of Fido in St.Petersburg) "grow up". Anyway, the child, which Fido helped to be born so much, was the main killer.

Fido was a different technology compared to the Internet. Since the web came to Russia, all other social networking projects were based on Internet technologies and same as with Fido were replica of the projects started in US.

Certain parts of ex-Fido members started the Internet and continue to bring in anything new and interesting they find in the global web. Most of the first irc, icq, livejournal and linkedin members were ex-Fido. It so happens that I personally know some of them, and I still have the fire to keep up — so I'm involved or at least informed about the new projects. Participation barrier was one of the reasons for Fido's decline, but new projects are open to the public, and it looks like it is not a bad thing. Some of the people I know even complain that new projects fail to enlarge their networks significantly, especially in the begining – it's all the same people who are eager to try the new staff.

What is the status now? Most of the succesfull global projects have significant participation from Russia, usually limited by the need to at least read in English, e.g. livejournal users with the highest quantity of friends are certain Russian writers and journalists. Amusing that their first exposure to the net was in Fido times. The language and alphabet barrier also lead to the fact that most of the social networking projects have their replicas with Russian interface: liveinternet.ru for livejournal.com, moikrug.ru (my circle in Russian) for linkedin. com. There are numerous blogs and wiki projects in Cyrillic as well. At the same time, in spite of the language barrier, international projects still enjoy higher participation by Russians, comparing to the local replicas.

If Fido took six years to become successful, the latest ideas take only months. The current questions of how social networks, blogs and other internet tools will affect real life society, Russians will solve together with and at the same time as the whole world.

UKRAINE

FRIENDS

http://atlaskit.com/ (LS)
Atlaskit
KueB 2222,
Yr. Merbhnkoba 12-A
0 one 8

info@atlaskit.com

http://www.i.ua/

http://www.droozhi.com/

Droozhi.com is a global online Ukrainian community that connects young minded, educated Ukrainian professionals through networks of friends and business contacts. Droozhi.com provides a safe, fun, discreet, and trusted environment for meeting Ukrainians for personal, social and business networking. Droozhi.com aims to unite the Ukrainian global community by bringing the power of social and business networking to every aspect of Ukrainian life and culture, one "droozhi" at a time.

Droozhi.com is for Ukrainian singles, Ukrainian's who are married, and anyone who wants to connect with Ukrainian professionals or help their friends expand their business and social networks through a trusted online network.

What does "Droozhi" mean?

"Droozhi" is a fun and creative interpretation of the Ukrainian word "Druzi" for "friend(s)." We believe that whether you're here looking to connect with Ukrainian professionals, meet your Ukrainian soulmate, find a job or service, etc.– it's all a matter of networking with "Droozhi"!

Who's behind Droozhi.com?

Droozhi.com is founded by Markian Kaczaj with Headquarters in the San Francisco Bay Area. Markian's experience in software and high tech sales management spans over fifteen years. Markian has spent the past ten years in Silicon Valley/San Francisco in senior sales management positions at companies such as Akamai Technologies, Savvis, Itochu Technologies-Netvein Division and Qwest Communications. Markian holds a BS Degree from La Salle University, Philadelphia with a Dual Major in Marketing and Russian Language and a Minor in International Business. Markian also graduated from Ukrainian School "Ridna Shkola" in Philadelphia and was a member of Ukrainian "Tryzub" Soccer Team and Youth Organization "Plast". His Droozhi.com profile lists his interests as "promoting and uniting Ukrainian awareness, identity and cultural pride", international business, online gaming, surfing/snowboarding, martial arts and fitness, volunteering at the local humane society, and enjoying freshly homemade potato Varenyky with extra sour cream:)

VIDEO/PHOTO

http://www.areaface.com/ (LS)
AreaFace is for people from all over the world. Gallery of portraits of every country made by people. Portrait of country is the big page consisting of hundreds of small portraits. It has an extremely simple and usable interface for fast photo adding. Registration will take only one minute and the same for your portrait uploading. As a result, you'll be the part of portrait of your country, which is in our world gallery.

Hello An De Jonghe,

Areaface is founded by me, Oleksandr Bondar. All management of the service is made by me also.

The main idea of the service is to show portraits of countries. Portrait of country is a page where there are a lot of small portraits of registered users from this country and their friends.

Service became available from March 2006. It is registered in Ukraine, Lviv.

Areaface provides service to people with different age and interests. Now on site there are 140 active registered users from thirty-one countries. Most active countries — Ukraine, Belarus, and Russia.

Registered users can upload theirs portraits and portraits of friends. Members of the service can send messages to other users. There is the possibility to create a friends list and to browse portraits of your company. Each portrait can be rated. In the near future, wait for big changes; they will be nice changes;) Areaface is available in English and Russian languages.

Best regards
Oleksandr Bondar
areaface@gmail.com

9 What about Europe?

Europe is a patchwork of old (Western) and new (Eastern) countries, which results in a fragmented market where social networking is concerned.

Social network sites are used by 17% of the European online population: In the UK, 34% of online consumers are members, making them Europe's biggest users of social network sites. (*Source: ForresterResearch, October 4, 2006*). France has also embraced social networking, probably because the French are keen bloggers and therefore interested in all things Web 2.0. (An interesting detail in that respect is that the popular UK site *Mashable* has been localized for a French audience in 2007.)

The new European countries in the East have sprouted quite a number of well-made social networking sites in just the last few years, leaving the door open for more to come. Certainly there is still room for more business related communities and more internationally-oriented sites, e.g. by adding English as a second language option.

Contrary to popular belief, a mature Internet market (countries where Internet has been adopted for many years) or widespread access to the Internet (number of connection points) does not equal a proliferation of social networking sites. Probably culture and the presence of venture capital are at the origin. If we take a look at Estonia, for example, we see a small, rich country (1.3 million inhabitants) where Internet is omnipresent. Every school has PCs with an Internet connection, all citizens enjoy free Internet at over seven hundred access points and even the government has created a website where draft bills are accessible to the public and citizens can make suggested amendments. Nevertheless, when we look at the social networking market in Estonia, we find precious few Estonian networks.

As a whole, it is surprising to see that no real pan-European social network has seen the light until now, especially with the growing number of countries which are a member of the European Union (EU). With twenty-five members in 2007, there is a market to take.

AUSTRIA

BUSINESS

http://www.unternehmerbund.com
Entrepreneurs of the most diverse industries united into a large, politically
independent co-operation network.
gh@unternehmerbund.com
contact: Gerald Hangweyrer

FRIENDS

http://www.szene1.at/
Management
Franz Tretter
Management, Technical operations & Development
Phone: +43 (0)699/113 210 21
E-mail: f.tretter@szene1.at

Josef Voglsam
Management, Marketing & Sales
Phone: +43 (0)699/148 884 44
E-mail: j.voglsam@szene1.at

Rudolf Rabenhaupt
Management, Eventcoordination & Purchase
Phone: +43 (0)699/155 400 42
E-mail: r.rabenhaupt@szene1.at

Szene1 Entertainment GmbH

Szene1 Office Linz
Franzosenhausweg 49a
4030 Linz
Austria

Szene1 Office Waldneukirchen
Hohe Linde Strasse 13
4594 Waldneukirchen
Austria

http://www.eventshooters.com/
Founded by Thomas, Johannes, Christoph, and Erwin.

http://www.7just7.de/
Networking portal which focusses on Video/Photo-Sharing, Blogs &
Forums, News, Classmates & Jobs, Music, Art & Style and Parties &
Events.

Contact:
"Just-Network" Handels GmbH
Favoritenstrasse 80/Top1
A - 1100 Vienna

Tel: +43 (0)1 890 88 00
Fax: +43 (0)1 890 88 00 - 77

E-mail: office@justnetwork.at

SPECIAL INTEREST

Arts & Crafts

http://derwienersalon.com/ (LS)
salonieren@derwienersalon.com
contact: Christine Reiterer

http://sanga.sossoon.net/ (LS)
contact: Hannes Offenbacher
news@sanga.cc
Cultural Creative Platform

BELGIUM

BUSINESS

http://www.join2grow.biz/
Join2Grow.biz is an on-line networking community for European entrepreneurs.

The site provides a platform where entrepreneurs can interact and exchange ideas with others who share similar life-goals, ambitions, and dreams. It is also a place of opportunity, where entrepreneurs can discover and make contact with potential partners and collaborators throughout Europe.

The starting point of Join2Grow.biz is the Enterprise and Entrepreneur Survey, initiated by Fortis Commercial & Private banking and conducted in partnership with TNS Sofres and McKinsey. This comprehensive study of the needs, habits, and motivations of today's European entrepreneurs is the first of its kind — no previous survey has focused specifically on entrepreneurs in order to develop a complete and accurate picture of who they are and what drives them.

Visitors are invited to participate in an ongoing discussion about the results of the survey by posting comments and questions for further discussion. The site provides a forum where entrepreneurs can reach out to the entire on-line community of European entrepreneurs, or connect on a one-to-one basis with their peers.

Join2Grow.biz is a place where the professional and personal lives of entrepreneurs intersect.

http://www.elan2.be/
Network for students and young entrepreneurs and retired seniors who want to exchange knowledge.

http://www.hrminfo.net/iRamblas/index.asp
The platform for networking, interaction, and knowledge-sharing of
HRMinfo.net. IRamblas is only open to PASSport holders (paying
members). Available in Dutch and French.

http://www.biztribe.be (LS)
Biztribe mission is to promote, improve, and enable business relationships
between entrepreneurs and decision makers in the European Union. Biztribe
is a European project with a strong local and regional focus.
Biztribe is an independent business network. We highly value our
independency, so we can remain objective in our communication. Biztribe is
not directly or indirectly affiliated to any company and/or organisation.
Access to the Biztribe community is limited to decision makers; entrepreneurs,
managers, directors, and board members. Salespeople, headhunters and such
will only be tolerated if they have a networking attitude.
Press: press@biztribe.com

It seems this network has not been maintained and has lost the battle to
Linkedin, Xing and Ecademy on the professional networking market in
Belgium.

http://www.cionet.com/
Network for CIOs in Belgium, based on the Xing platform. Annual
membership fee.

http://www.euromarketers.net/
Euromarketers.net is a free virtual Community created to promote
networking among professionals and academics of the marketing and
sales arena. Euromarketers.net is an initiative of the European Marketing
Confederation (EMC), the umbrella organisation for marketing and
sales associations in Europe, in partnership with Neurona.com (Grupo
Intercom). Operating since the 1960s, the EMC Brussels' headquarter was
established in 1993. The mission of the EMC is the promotion and the
development of marketing as the fundamental business process leading to
economic growth and prosperity and the improvement of the competitive

position of Europe's trade, industry and commerce. Euromarketers.net is open to anyone working, or simply interested, in the marketing or sales communities. To participate in Euromarketers.net is easy: simply register (for free!), tell us about yourself and your contacts and start looking for other profiles of interest to you... then invite them to be part of your personal network.

FRIENDS

http://www.lnm.eu
LNM.eu is the social network based on the new generation social networking technology. LNM.eu combines the classic social networking tools with instant messaging. LNM.eu is part of LNM Media, a privately-held company based in Brussels. LNM.eu is operated and managed by After The Hype bvba, Korenlei 22, 9000 Gent, Belgium (BE 479.432.101).

LNM.eu staff can be reached by feedback@lnm.eu. Please note that this e-mail address may only be used for non-technical or non-support questions.

http://www.looknmeet.nl/ (LS)
Operated by After the hype bvba which is located Korenlei 22, 9000 Gent support@afterthehype.be

http://www.schoolbord.be/ (LS)

www.digs.be
Operated by Telenet.

http://www.netlog.com

ex http://nl.facebox.com/
Facebox is the social medium for over six hundred thousand Dutchspeaking youngsters. Over 2 million people check out 60 million pages on Facebox.

Facebox has developed a unique localisation technology, permiting all content to be adapted to the location and profile of each member. This guarantees that members immediately feel at home and see only the profiles of other members within the same age category and region. Members can create their own webpage, increase their network of friends, publish playlists, share videos, post blogs etc. Facebox.com is the ultimate tool for young Europeans to communicate with their social network...their own language. Facebox.com was launched in September 2006 but was invented five years before. Toon Coppens started ASL.TO in '99, one of the first social internet comunities with European roots. Lorenz Bogaert (CEO) joins, and a little while later ASL.TO is rebranded to Redbox, which was primarily focused on Belgian youngsters. By the end of 2005 other European countries got their own communities (e.g. coolbox.be, xobox.de, fr.facebox.com, gentebox.es). Since September 2006, these sites are hosted under Facebox.com.

Incrowd bvba
Albert Liénartstraat 16
B-9300 Aalst
Tel: +32 70 66 07 28
Fax: +32 70 66 07 29
VAT: BE 859 635 972

SPECIAL INTEREST

Gaming & 3D

http://www.taatu.com/
Founded on January 28, 2005 and currently active in Belgium, the Netherlands and France.

Chée de Louvain 490
1380 Lasne
Belgium

info@taatu.com

VIDEO/PHOTO

www.garagetv.com
Operated by Telenet.

http://moblr.com (LS)
Moblr launched just before Christmas and aims to be the mobile YouTube. The problem for the UK-based company is that YouTube Mobile has already gone live. If some of YouTube's established competitors can't break its stranglehold on the video sharing market, it doesn't bode well for this new mobile service.
info@moblr.com

Moblr is published by
Kiboo sprl
Chaussee d'Alsemberg 995
1180 Bruxelles
Belgium
Tel: +32 (0)2 332 32 22
info@kiboo.net

TESTIMONIAL

Networking in Belgium — Geert CONARD

Although the UK and France are seen as the cradles of networking, Belgium also has a rich past in what I'd like to call 'Old-school' networking. The typical 'chamber of commerce' style societies like VOKA and Unizo have been organizing business meetings and receptions for centuries. Next to this, all important service clubs also have Belgian chapters (Lions, Rotary...).

Since 2004, a new wave rushed through Belgium and new-style, more "open" networking clubs started to blossom. Some of these new clubs also have an online part, a platform on which their members can communicate and share their thoughts. In twelve months, every business club in Belgium started to feel the need to have such an online part to complete the networking experience for their members. Some networking clubs built their own online networking platform, others knocked on the door of an already established online platform and open a sub-club or forum on such an existing network. Examples: In Belgium M4M opened a Premium Club on Xing. In the UK both BNI and BRE use Ecademy as their online platform.

Today, in my opinion, the three most important online social business networks in Belgium are Ecademy, LinkedIn, and Xing. The most important offline clubs, next to the earlier mentioned VOKA and Unizo, are clubs like M4M and Business Network Cafe, or the more regional initiatives like Via Via (Herentals), A12 Business Club (Antwerpen), Unlimited Business Club (Mechelen) or Leuven Inc (Leuven).

The way forward for networking in Belgium and even networking in general is to lose a few prejudices. Networking is not just meant for top managers; networking is useful and valuable for everyone. You cannot only gain business opportunities through networking, you also gain contacts, acquaintances and friends. You'll have 'a friend in every city' around the globe, if that's what you wish . . . You'll always have someone to pick you up from the airport and show you the best restaurants in town, wherever you are. You'll find likeminded souls for deep and meaningful discussions about business topics, your hobbies and passions or even life itself. The new 'open' style networks have really opened up a new world for those who are a bit shy and were left out in the dark at a conventional networking event. The new networking concepts will invite them to actively participate and have a positive experience.

In my opinion, the world of economics is changing. Not even forty years ago, most people were employed in a factory. Professional life was ruled by unions. Today more and more people become self-employed and lose the social security and the social contact with their colleagues. Online social networks can be a valuable alternative for this. Marketing economics are also changing. Large companies were able to spend big marketing budgets to promote their products and services. Even a national campaign is impossible for most self-employed people and small companies. Gaining business through proactive networking is budget-friendly and effective. People will also experience the need to train themselves into using their network. Always listen for keywords and connect people to the contacts they need, day by day. To make sure you're not left out you'll have to introduce yourself in a way which isn't "hardselling", but instead keeps top of mind because of the 'twist' or angle you bring to your story. If a third party needs your products or services and one of your direct connections hears this, you must be the first contact they want to connect this person to.

The only negative side to this whole story is time. Lots of people aren't patient enough to build and nurture their network until it's grown into a valuable asset. For a businessman who starts building a network from scratch it takes an average of three years to build a network. Lots of people abort sooner because of impatience. In school we are taught to go for the sell. We are used to forcing our products and services down people's throats. This just does NOT work anymore in today's society. Networking is a gentle and civilised way to gather contacts and learn to know people. Never think of your network as potential customers. Your network is a group of people who will, once they trust you enough and your reputation proceeds you, refer you to other people. I want to conclude with the best networking tip I can ever give: "Never sell."

Geert Conard
www.geertconard.com
Author of the book on social business networking "A Girlfriend in Every City"
www.agirlfriendineverycity.com

BULGARIA

FRIENDS

http://one.bg/

17A Tintyava Str.
1113 Sofia, Bulgaria

Phone: +359 2 862 41 84
          +359 2 868 90 79
Fax: +359 2 868 32 87
E-mail: info@one.bg

http://www.neogen.bg/
Part of the Romanian Neogen network.
Contact person: Gergana Tsonkova

E-mail: pr@neogen.bg
Phone: 082/833 584 0885/046 268

CROATIA

FRIENDS

http://povez.com/

http://ekipa.hr/ (LS)
Ekipa Internet d.o.o.
HR-10000 Zagreb
Trg bana Jelacica 5
info@ekipa.hr

http://www.stariprijatelji.hr/ (LS)
Reconnect with old friends.
pomoc@StariPrijatelji.hr

http://www.tulumarka.com/

DATING

http://www.iskrica.com/ (LS)
Founded in 2002 as a dating site.
iskrica@iskrica.com

VIDEO/ PHOTO

http://www.pticica.com/ (LS)
Photosharing site.

CYPRUS

MOBILE

http://wadja.com (LS)

Well, my name is Alex Christoforou, and I am one of the founding members and Managing Director of Wadja Media Limited, which owns www.wadja.com .

I am happy to contribute whatever help I can for the book on social networks. I believe the project will be very comprehensive and informative, given the growth and significance of social networks in today's web space.

So I guess I will jump right in and try best as I can to answer the information below. I hope you will find it helpful and please let me know if there is anything more I can help with.

-Founders & management
The founding members are myself (Alex Christoforou), Theodore Mouratides, and James Christoforou.

-Founding year & address/nationality
Wadja Media Limited is a Cypriot Company headquartered in Nicosia, Cyprus with a development and operations arm in Athens, Greece. We incorporated in March of 2006.

-Target audience & membership level (number of users)
Wadja.com is a mobile social network that is open to users worldwide. Our target audience is 14-34 year olds actively involved in social networks and who love using their mobile phones and devices to communicate with friends. We launched the service in September of 2006 as a bare bones BETA. To date we have 110,000 users and are adding over two thousand users daily. We are actively involved in moving towards a version 1.0 release and a full scale launch.

-Top 3 countries in which the community is used
1, 2, and 3. All of Eastern Europe (we are growing at record speeds :-)
Also a strong presence in the UK and Middle East.

-Main technical features and possible features in the near future
Our main technical feature is absolute device independence. Geography, service provider, handset, screen size...it doesn't matter, Wadja is accessible on any web enabled mobile device and out profile interface is consistent in design whether someone is viewing it from the web

or from a mobile phone. We offer many avenues of communication for users which bridge the gap between web and mobile, including global SMS (Texting), Mobile Messaging, Mobile Instant Messaging and of course Media File Sharing. We will be offering a wide array of media solutions in the future compatible with any mobile device as well as Premium SMS services, and Ads on SMS services for interested mobile advertisers. Likewise we are in heavy development to gear up for an official version 1.0 launch which will offer a sleeker design and improved web and mobile interfaces.

-Languages in which the service is available
Currently our interface is available in the English language; however, all user generated content and messages within the community can be any language a user wants.

Thank you again, and I look forward to learning more about the book as it moves forward. Best of luck!

Cheers,

Alex Christoforou

Wadja Media LTD.
Home of the Blue Kangaroo
www.wadja.com
http://www.wadja.com/alex

20-22 Ypsilantou Street
106-76, Athens, Greece
Tel: +30 210-72-17-292
Fax: +30 210-72-17-294

Wadja is all about the internet on your mobile phone. Our number one goal is to make it as easy as can be for you to have as much fun with your mobile device as humanly possible! With Wadja your mobile phone becomes so much more than a gadget. You name the device, and chances are your Wadja Services will play on it. Make friends, send free text (sms) messages, share photos, music, and video clips from one mobile phone to another. Geography, service provider, handset, screen size...it doesn't matter, Wadja goes where you go.

Wadja Media LTD.
Home of the Blue Kangaroo
20-22 Ypsilantou Street
106-76, Athens, Greece
Tel: +30 210-72-17-292
contact@wadja.com

CZECH REPUBLIC

FRIENDS

http://libimseti.cz/
Libimseti
Contact: info@libimseti.cz

http://px2.xchat.centrum.cz/~guest~/index.php
Xchat

http://www.lide.cz/
Lidé ("people") was launched in 1996. It has 1 million users.

DENMARK

BUSINESS

https://www.zaple.dk/
Zaple was born out of a frustration with current SAP recruitment methods.
Trying to recruit the right SAP consultant at the right time is a major cause
of concern for the industry and can often result in project slip. Similarly,
trying to identify SAP consultants with specific industry and/or product
specialisation for ad-hoc assignments is just as difficult.
After extensive research, Zaple decided that there was a better way of doing
things and that the creation of a network would better facilitate recruitment

of SAP consultants and also provide additional benefits to the SAP industry which are not currently available.

This resulting network is Zaple, which has grown to become a unifying hub where SAP professionals can communicate with each other, exchange knowledge, gain a useful insight into the SAP community and identify job opportunities. Companies using SAP can join the network and feel confident that they will be able to access the right people for their projects and also communicate with them through a credible and respected forum.

Zaple refers to Zaple A/S, CBR no. 28130023, with an address at Brolæggerstræde 6, 1211 Copenhagen, Denmark. Zaple A/S operates through Local Country Partners. The Local Country Partner in Denmark is MatchMaker, CVR no. 83141212, with a registered office address Leopold Damms Allé 1, 2900 Hellerup, Denmark.

Zaple in the Netherlands
Rowald Pouderoyen
Oude Bosscheweg 11z
5301 LA Zaltbommel
Tel: +31 (0) 418 511 335
www.zaple.nl

Zaple in the United Kingdom
Chapter House
33 London Road
Reigate
Surrey RH2 9HZ
Tel: 01737 230 003
https://www.zaple.co.uk/

FRIENDS

http://www.arto.dk/

Arto was founded in 1998; the social networking element was added a couple of years later. They have six hundred thousand accounts and focus primarily on teenagers.

Address:
Sct Leonis Gade 5, 8800 Viborg
kundeservice@arto.dk

http://www.meetyourmessenger.dk/
Managed by Mym a/s
JF Kennedys Plads 1E3 sal
9000 Aalborg
Denmark

SPECIAL INTEREST

Miscellaneous

http://dwank.com/
Dwank is all about people showing their homes to the world. You can't buy or sell homes though. But you can get some great home design and decorating ideas from browsing this web site. You can also give and get do-it-yourself advice.

Enjoy all the very different homes and please upload images of your own home. All homes are welcome – from modest houseboats in the canals of Amsterdam to million dollar Beverly Hills mansions.

Dwank.com
Attn: Jakob Jelling
Eckersbergsgade 38, 2. sal
8000 Aarhus C
Denmark

E-mail: info@dwank.com

http://www.expatnet.dk/
Former ForeignHelp.dk – Denmark's leading expat community for expatriates living in, working in or moving to Denmark. We are helping people to get information about Denmark, meeting likeminded individuals, networking, news, events, online dating, job searching, house hunting... and make the most of expatriate life in Denmark!

VIDEO/ PHOTO

http://www.vix.dk/
Video and photo network
In Danish only.

MOBILE

http://www.imity.com/ (LS)
Imity is a free application for your mobile phone that uses Bluetooth to sense other phones around you. That information forms a social network – online, offline, and all the other lines.

Hi An - here's our response

-Founders & management
Morten Just
Claus Dahl
Nikolaj Nyholm

-Founding year & address/nationality
Danish
2006
Copenhagen, Denmark. Office at the IT University (Rued Langaardsvej 7, 2300 Copenhagen S)

-Target audience & membership level (number of users)
Five hundred users

Target audience: a) Young people who socialize a lot during a week. b) Business people who go to conferences

-Top three countries in which the community is used
Denmark
Germany
US

-Main technical features and possible features in the near future
We combine real-life and online by registering who people meet in real life, then form an online social network based on that information. The technology is currently an application for mobile phones that uses Bluetooth to sense other people's phones within ten meters.

-Languages in which the service is available
English only.

Imity
ITU, 5te
Rued Langgaards Vej 7. 5D25
2300 Copenhagen S
Denmark

We love e-mails, too. Send them to Morten, Claus, Ricki or nikolaj@imity.com.

ESTONIA

FRIENDS

www.connect.ee (LS)
Popular local social networking and online video and contacts sharing site in Estonia. Launched at the end of 2005. Registration via invitation.
info@connect.ee

www.rate.ee

An online social networking deal in Estonian. Eesti Telekom, 51 pct owned by Finnish-Swedish TeliaSonera, has bought a 51 pct stake in Serenda Investment, parent company of Estonia's leading teen social networking website Rate.ee. The site has around 360,000 members and Andrei Korobeinik, the founder, will hold onto the remaining 49 pct of his company. The deal is valued at around 2.5mn euros. Korobeinik also runs leading teen websites in Latvia (www.Face.lv) and in Lithuania (www.Point.lt).

http://minugalerii.ee/
MyGallery is an Estonian on-line community through which it is possible interact with your old friends and to find new ones, as well. In addition, it is possible to comment on the photos of other users, to have your own blog, to join different communities and to create your own photo gallery. MinuGalerii also works in Lithuania, Latvia, Russia, and Ukraine.

SPECIAL INTEREST

Pets

http://uniteddogs.com/
Here you can make a website for your dog, take a look at other people's dogs, rate their pictures, post comments and communicate with other dog lovers. Uniteddogs.com is free for everyone.

Ragnar Sass, CEO
Martin Tajur, head designer

info@uniteddogs.com

http://www.unitedcats.com/
Unitedcats.com is the cats' social revolution on the web. You can create a very own website for your loved one, share photos with friends, comment, communicate and rate everything and everybody.

VIDEO/ PHOTO

http://kroxa.net/ (LS)

FINLAND

FRIENDS

http://www.ii2.org/
Ii2 is a community designed for young people. By using ii2 you can create your own profile with images, browse other users' profiles, comment on other users' profiles and of course chat with other users.

SPECIAL INTEREST

Gaming & 3D

http://www.habbo.com/
Habbo Hotel is a virtual community owned and operated by Sulake Corporation, the 12th fastest growing technology company in Europe. It combines the two concepts of a chat room and an online game. The original conception of Habbo Hotel, Mobiles Disco, was created as a small project by two Finnish men: Sampo Karjalainen and Aapo Kyrölä. It was intended to promote a rock band called Mobiles. The pair later sold their project to the Finnish telecoms giant Elisa Oyj. The game is centered around Habbos, virtual representations of its members. Habbos can be dressed by each user individually using pre-supplied virtual clothing. Each character has a different name and is identified solely by this name. The service's other focus point is virtual furni, which can be bought by Habbos using credits via a variety of payment methods, including, but not limited to, SMS, home phone, pre-paid cards, credit card, and money order. This furniture can also be traded between users.

http://www.aapeli.com

Gaming community site by the company Apaja. Started in 2001, they have about 1.2 million accounts.

Religion

http://www.muslimspace.com/ (LS)
Welcome to MuslimSpace.com, a new and rapidly growing social networking site catering to the 1.2 billion Muslims worldwide. MuslimSpace is the brainchild of Mohamed El-Fatatry, an Egyptian professional Web developer, designer, and programmer living in Finland. A former MySpace user, El-Fatatry created MuslimSpace in March 2006 because he said he was tired of the un-Islamic content of popular social networking sites, such as adult advertisements, and the aggressive behavior of some of their users, not to mention the racist and offensive comments he sometimes encountered on such sites about Islam and Muslims. After the U.S., the bulk of its members are logging in from Malaysia, the U.K., Canada, Turkey, Egypt, Singapore, Australia, and Germany.

Site: MuslimSpace.com

- Brief Description: Muslim Social Networking Community
- Founders & management:
    - o The site was founded by Mohamed El-Fatatry, a young Muslim media technology professional who was called the "Linus Torvalds" of the Muslim world due to his innovations in computer science that positively affect Muslim users worldwide.
    - o The site was managed by a group of volunteers, till it was acquired in December 2006 by a new technology company called Muxlim Inc. It is now managed by the company's directors and co-founders Mohamed El-Fatatry and Pietari Päivänen.
- Founding year
    - o The site was founded in March 2006.
- Target audience & membership level (number of users)
    - o Target audience is technology-literate Muslims from all age groups, especially the younger generations.

- o The site currently has over 21,000 members purely by word-of-mouth (no money has been spent on advertising the site since its launch).
- Top three countries in which the community is used
  - o United States
  - o United Kingdom
  - o Malaysia
- Main technical features and possible features in the near future
  - o The site offers basic networking features like messaging, commenting on guestbook, pictures and blogs, blogging, polls, games, videos, music, quizzes, forums, picture rating, classifieds, groups, events, gallery and member search along with custom profile creation to enable members to design and decorate their profiles to their liking.
- Languages in which the service is available
  - o The site is currently available only in English. However, plans are in place to offer an Arabic and French interface in the near future.
- Positive stories from MuslimSpace:
  - o A member who posted a blog about his financial trouble got advice from an elderly member of MuslimSpace to use his drawing skills to make paintings and sell them on eBay. Following the advice, the member is now successfully running an eBay store selling his art and is in good financial standing.
  - o Jennifer, a Christian, who is a former MySpace.com user and is now a member of MuslimSpace says: "I love that I joined because it's such a safe network and, unlike MySpace, I am actually benefiting from this site," she said. "I don't have to worry about receiving junk, or about stalkers."
  - o Rachel, a Muslim user of MuslimSpace, said that she had nobody else to turn to with her marital problems and her mother's failing health, but that she had found support from MuslimSpace.com members.
  - o The site is also a place for policy makers and organizations to reach Muslims. As an example, Florida Governor Candidate for the year 2010, Mr. Atlee Yarrow is an active member of the community to connect with Muslim youth who will be

of voting age when he is officially running for the position. NGO's can also find talented individuals to volunteer to their activities.

o Muslim internet users along with Non-Muslims who wish to interact with Muslims, know more about Islam, or find out more about different cultures usually enjoy their stay at MuslimSpace.

- Media Coverage:
  o Helsingin Sanomat, Finland's largest newspaper interviews Mohamed El-Fatatry: http://www.hs.fi/english/article/A+Muslim+MySpace+based+in+Espoo/1135222538803
  o ABC News interview: http://abcnews.go.com/International/International/story?id=2133403&page=1
  o World Politics Watch interview: http://www.worldpoliticswatch.com/article.aspx?id=90
  o MuslimSpace ranked 4th social networking website in the world: http://www.vee.fi/lehti/ilmio/top_v_15

http://kuvake.net/

Mission Angels Network Executive Summary

Mission Angels Network is a network of people and groups (i.e. missions) that are fulfilling the Great Commission presented in the Bible. Great Commission is the greatest command mankind has been ever given in scope and effects. The name Mission Angels means people who support the missions like the business angels support businesses. In the biblical world there have always been supporters to the various missions and in the end nearly all missions are done at least by partial support of individuals, including workforce, supplies, and funding.

In spite of heavy dependance of supporters, biblical missions have so far used modern technological possibilities to communicate, unite and work together with their supporters modestly. What comes to individuals, a key element living a Christ-centered life is a connection to others (unity, fellowship) and working as a group (congregations and missions), which are in continuous danger due to individualistic western lifestyle megatrend. Mission Angels Network will offer the supporters and missions with a high-end social network taking its stand to answer these needs.

Mission Angels Network has been founded in 2007 by Olli-Pekka Jalovaara, and it works at the moment through website www.missionangels. com and does have a company "Jalovaara IT" behind it. Later, a non-profit organization can be formed to handle at least a part of the Mission Angels Networks tasks.

Address: Heinäahontie 4, FI-41330 Vihtavuori, Finland, EU
Target audience: People and mission that are fullfilling the Great Commission in the Bible
Target countries: Worldwide
Registered people: At the moment only beta testers.
Registered missions (groups): At the moment only beta testing missions.
Languages: English, Finnish and can easily be translated into other languages.

VIDEO/ PHOTO

www.irc-galleria.net
Photogallery. Founded in December 2000 by Tomi Lintelä and bought by Sulake (the company behind Habbo Hotel) in May 2007. One of the largest (the largest?) online communities in Finland. In Finnish only.
They have about four hundred thousand accounts.

MOBILE

http://europe.nokia.com/A4144923
Nokia Senor aims to help users form spontaneous social circles through their Nokia brand phones. (mososo)

Nokia Sensor

- Spontaneous social circles
- Your portable personality
- Instant communities and networks
- Free to download, free to use
- Free file sharing

http://www.jaiku.com/ (LS)
Jaiku's main goal is to bring people closer together by enabling them to share their presence. For us, presence is about everyday things as they happen – what you're up to, how you're feeling, where you're going. We offer a way to connect with the people you care about by sharing presence updates with them on the Web and mobile.

We're a young company and developing constantly, so check out the Jaikido blog for the latest updates. We appreciate your feedback, so feel free to comment away on the blog.

We're based in Helsinki, the capital of Finland up in the very north of Europe. The address of our office is Lönnrotinkatu 32 D 51, 00180 Helsinki, Finland.

If you'd like to get in touch with us, please contact the founders Jyri (+358-40-52 28 496) or Petteri (+358-40-77 27 007). We are all reachable by E-mail at firstname at jaiku.com.

FRANCE

BUSINESS

www.viadeo.com (formerly www.viaduc.com) (LS)
Viadeo is one of the world's largest business social networks with over one million two hundred thousand members across Europe and three thousand new members joining every day. Members use Viadeo to find clients, suppliers, business partners, jobs and employees from all over the world online.

Originally founded in 2003 by two hundred high-flying entrepreneurs in France, Viadeo started as a private network of business people who realised that they could share key business information and solutions to day-to-day business problems if they networked together on the Internet. The network was opened to the public in 2004 and grew to over one million members in less than two years and has now become a truly international network where users can create profiles and network in English, French, Spanish, German, Portuguese, and Italian. It will soon be available in other languages including Chinese.

Ariel Messas, Directeur des Etudes, Fondateur Viadeo
Arnaud Lemaître, Fondateur Viadeo
Thierry Lunati, Directeur Général, Viaduc – Viadeo
Dan Serfaty, CEO Viadeo
Eric Didier, COO Viadeo - International
Peter Cunningham, Country Manager Viadeo UK
Gerhard Brink, Viadeo Deutschland, Direktor Business Development
Pedro Sánchez Pernia, Country Manager Viadeo Españay Portugal

http://www.europeanpwn.net/
Dear An,

I'm happy to send you a contribution for your book about social networking.
Please find below the testimonial I gave on European Professional Women Network. It was intended for the members of this network, but I'm sure it would also be of interest for your readers.
I copy Margaret Milan, founder of the European Professional Women Network as well as Mirella Visser, Vice President of European Professional Women Network and author of the article, as I don't know if you already had the opportunity to interview her for your book.

Best of luck and talk to you later,

Diana Derval

We are a pan-European network of women's organisations whose objective is to promote the professional progress of women and their presence in corporate leadership.

For women: we provide a cross-sectoral networking and training platform for professional women with an international outlook.

For companies: we provide a network for their high-potential managers and a unique source of best practice across Europe.

Our mission

Promote the professional progress of women through all their career phases.

Promote sustainable and innovative professional career paths.

Encourage companies to recognise the necessity of diverse management approaches.

Raise the visibility of European women in business.

EuropeanPWN
4, rue Galvani
75838 Paris Cedex 17
France
Phone: +33 (0) 1 39 75 49 66
E-mail: contact@epwn.net

http://www.6nergies.net/ (LS)
Alain Lefebvre / alain@6nergies.net

http://www.piwie.biz/
French business network

FRIENDS

http://neurofriends.net/ (LS)
Founded by Benoît Chesneau. Social network for friends. It is only possible to connect with people you know or have been introduced to: your profile and picture are only accessible to your friends.
contact@neurofriends.net

http://www.netoo.net/
French social network.

http://dotnode.com/pub (LS)
Node is an online community connecting people through a trusted friends network.
We wish to create a worldwide friendship network without any language barrier.
By joining .node, you can use lots of little services based on trusted friends.
alexandre@dotnode.com

http://www.ubiplanet.com/
Social network and media sharing site. The target audience is 25 to 50 year olds who value privacy and control.

http://www.convillial.com/ville/index.php
The team
Convillial has been founded by three friends: two from Paris, Thomas and Hugo, and one from Provence, Catherine, to help people from the same region or city to meet and discuss their projects.

The idea
Too many people live next to one another without ever knowing one another: to organize a trip, exchange cooking or language tips, to study together or to organize a party. That's why we've created Convillial!

Contact: inscription@convillial.com

http://www.my-communities.com/
The project My-communities was born in Angoulême in 2006.

We didn't find any community sites where the services were built around a community and not around individuals, so we decided to start My Communities.

We are three friends who are working on the concept since one year. One of us is responsible for development, another for graphic interfaces and another for the marketing. My Communities is today a project that is being developed at night, during the night and during the weekend.

contact.mycommunities@gmail.com
contact@my-communities.com

http://www.yootribe.com/
Web and mobile service by SwitchMod.

Contact:
Philippe Framezelle: pframezelle@m6.fr
M6 Web
60 avenue Charles de Gaulle - 92200 Neuilly sur Seine

contact@yootribe.com

www.skyblog.com
Skyblog is a free blogging platform which started in 2002 by the French rap radio station Skyrock to let listeners interact with each other and the station. Today Skyblog is in the top five of most viewed websites in France and is the number one website for French teenagers (15–24 year-olds).

http://www.citycita.org/
Citycita is a group communications and networking tool designed for organizations of all sizes. Whether you have twenty attendees or 1200, Citycita can help you coordinate and communicate more effectively. At its heart, Citycita is a social platform that encourages your group members to network and build deeper working (and personal) relationships with each other.
Philippe Guillard, Jamin Rubio, the two founders, and Fola Williams run the site.

http://peuplade.fr (LS)
Hi,

As promised, please find the answers to your questions. Don't hesitate to contact me if you need anything else. I look forward to discovering your book!

Best regards,

Jérémie

-Founders & management

Peuplade was founded by Nathan Stern, Stephane Legouffe and myself, Jeremie Chouraqui. Nathan is a sociologist (he was a professor at La Sorbonne, where he studied) who also managed a Marketing company; Stephane is the IT developer who designed our website, and he is an expert in IT social website technologies; before Peuplade, I practiced law and founded a movie company, Digiprod, and I studied at HEC School Management and La Sorbonne law school.

We are an eight person company, and being an Internet company, innovation comes from everyone in the company.

-Founding year & address/nationality

Peuplade was founded in 2003 in a small Parisian district, Les Epinettes, as an experiment and was extended to Paris in late Sept. 2006. We are planning extension to every major French city during the first two semester of 2007 and to international cities by the end of 2007.

-Target audience & membership level (number of users)

Before opening in Paris, Peuplade had 20% of the Epinettes' people connected. In February 2007, more than fifty thousand parisians are members of Peuplade. By the end of 2007 our target is three hundred thousand French members.

-Top three countries in which the community is used

The comminuty is today used in France only. Yet we are being solicitated by various international media (BBC, Time Magazine, Der Spiegel, RTL, Il Foglio, Nikkeï Trendy. . .), and we receive hundreds of e-mails by people asking us to open Peuplade in their country.

-Main technical features and possible features in the near future

Peuplade offers five major features fed by people, and anyone can become a free member.

- *Neighbours : discover the neighbours of your districtTheir favourite addresses, their talents, their services, . . .*
- *Classifieds : goods exchanges, services close to your house, giving a hand. . .Childcare, cat to feed, plants to water, computer help, ...*
- *Appointment: meeting up between neighboursWelcome drinks, romantic strolls, topics meetings and many more...*
- *Peuplades : taking part in district projectsLocal newsletter, district open house, solidarity groups, neighbours' concerts...*

- *Parents : help each other among parentsSharing toys, going out with kids, sharing child care ...*

In the near future we will offer a "library" to propose new projects and share best practices, a neighbourhood Instant Messenger, and much more...

-Languages in which the service is available
The service is currently available in French. It will be available in English by May 2007.

http://www.my-communities.com/ (LS)
Social network for friends and family.

Dear Mrs An De Jonghe
This is our short text in English for www.my-communities.com social network.

Yours truly

Cyril Béchemin
bechemin@gmail.com

My-Communities

Above all, conceived for family and friends, My communities is a social web community. We offer to our members to create virtual private communities where everyone contributes collectively to the development of the content (pics, texts, links, vids, music). It's the community and not the individual which is in the center of my-communities website.

Founders & management
Christophe Perier Engineer
Loïc Lafarge Art Director
Cyril Béchemin Marketing

Founding year & address/nationality
Nov 06
contact.mycommunities@gmail.com
Angoulême-France

Target audience & membership level (number of users)
Small and average communities' : family and friends
February 07:2000 users

Top three countries in which the community is used
- France
- United States

Main technical features and possible features in the near future.

PHP Ajax MySQL postgreSQL, java, Smarty, HTML

In the future:
Syndicate the all best services : RSS, Webradio. . .
Travel module.

Languages in which the service is available
-English
-French
(Spanish, Italian in 2007)

contact.mycommunities@gmail.com

DATING

http://www.meetic.fr/
Founded in 2002.

Millions are already subscribed to meetic, making it the leading site in Europe and one of the biggest sites worldwide.

Whether you are looking for your soulmate in your city or state, or whether distance is no object, you will always find meetic members who share your desires and who long for successful relationships.

http://www.ulteem.fr

Who are we?

Ulteem is a service that matches people psychologically, provided by meetic, the European leader in online dating.

Ulteem was created to offer a new way of meeting people for those who are looking for a solid start to a long-term relationship. We match our members using psychological profiling in order to give new couples the best possible start.

The Ulteem philosophy

We think that clarifying our ideas about ourselves — such as what we expect of other people and what common interests could link us — is a great start when hoping to meet a future partner. Our role is to give you the means to meet the right people and to provide good service. In this environment, we are confident that you can find that special person and start to build a relationship together: you will know that it is based on the best possible foundations.

Ulteem is there to ask you these questions without ever being judgemental. We use your answers to the Ulteem Test to produce a twenty page report assessing your character. We also provide a detailed compatibility report for each of the members who are a strong enough match to be presented to you on your MatchList. Of course, while we believe that for most couples, success is based on having similar values and expectations, complimentary character traits are also important.

Meeting new people is not always easy, but we don't believe you should miss out on opportunities that could change your future just because of the constraints of day to day life. This is why we have created Ulteem, and this is our philosophy.

Ulteem is a service provided by meetic, a company with share capital of €1,648,542.80, registered in the Trade and Companies Register of Nanterre (France) under number 439 780 339, located at BP 109, 92106 Boulogne Cedex, France, represented by Mr Marc Simoncini, Chairman and Director of publication of the Ulteem site (Tel: 0871 4250 455).

SPECIAL INTEREST

Gaming & 3D

www.minifizz.fr
Hi An,

Here are the answers to your questions; I also sent a presentation for your convenience. Have a nice weekend, Sabine.

MiniFizz, a concept by Sabine Allaeys (Belgian) and François Grimonprez (French), the founders of Flow. Flow CmM started its mobile phone game editing activities in 2001. The games are primarily targeted at young women/girls. Flow CmM is very much aware of the fact that repartition of hardware, i.e. mobile phones, between boys and girls is 50/50, whereas for software, i.e. games, this is not the case.

Minifizz itself is a game/activity portfolio developed to meet the interest of young women/girls. It can be played on a mobile phone and is supported by an online community (website) and a girl magazine in print.
MiniFizz is certainly not a remake of traditional boys games painted pink. It is a series of ideas where feminine values are highlighted. Important factors in the game are communication (MF MISSION), psychology and affection. Looks, society, fashion (MF Avenue) are present in a just and contemporary way, topped by a good zest of humor. The girl is not seen by male eyes (most of the game creators) neither through the usual cliché that girls only exist for boys. Users can register a MiniFizz account and create a MF Popp's for free. When connecting to Canal MiniFizz, the user will become a MiniFizz herself with the creation of her own avatar with her own looks (including piercing, tattoos…) using "MiniFizz Popp's" ; then she can share her life and her emotions with other members of the community in her " FizzBlog " , a web and mobile based blog. She can also post an image by MMS or a live comment.
MiniFizz stands for multinational and multicultural values and proclaims variety. Each MiniFizz has her own character, her history and her preoccupations. Culture, art, science are part of the passions and interests of these heroines as well as relationships and this famous sensibility that is the kernel of the MiniFizz secret.

Www.minifizz.fr was born in June 2006 on the Web and available on mobile phones in July 2006.

After 6 months:

- 20.100 members
- 9.000 blogs
- 1.200.000 page views/month on the Web
- 23.600 unique visitors per month

On February 10, 2006, Flow – content creator – partners with Cityneo– services for mobile phones – to launch "Canal MiniFizz" targeting young, mobile phone, feminine users (14–25 years old).

On March 21, 2007, Minifizz also launches a Belgian (French speaking) version together with the fashion magazine Gimik.

Contacts concept & creation:
Sabine Allaeys allaeys@minifizz.com
Tel: +32 475 69 20 58

Canal Minifizz is edited by Cityneo:
43, rue d'Amsterdam
75008 Paris
Tel: + 331 49 49 03 88
Fax: 01 49 49 04 08
Press inquiries:
Romy Kikano
Romy.kikano@cityneo.com
www.cityneo.com

Sports

http://www.widiwici.com/ (LS)
Sports network created by Arnaud Latourrette and Benoît Mouren.

arnaud@widiwici.com

benoit@widiwici.com
widiwici
21, rue d'Austerlitz
69004 Lyon
France

Students

http://reseaucampus.com/ (LS)
Founded in May 2006 by Nicolas Vauvillier and Julien Pascual. Facebook lookalike for students.
communication@reseaucampus.com

http://www.bahut.com/
Bahut.com is a community site that wants to represent all French-speaking students. Founded by students, for students, Bahut aims to create relationships between students of all high schools and universities in France and at a later stage in Europe.

Every" bahut " will have his own space with News, Forums, Chat, Surveys, Visitor's book… The idea is to share our experience, exchange our point of view, relive our best memories, help one another, …

Every student can meet students from a neighboring " bahut ", reconnect with old friends, share pictures, talk to ex students,…

Becoming a member of Bahut is free of charge.

Website: www.bahut.com betaversion launched in September 2006
Founder: Stéphane Soler, student at EPITA Paris
Team: Mélanie Tassi & Fabien Guirau
Number of member schools :4012
Contact: Stéphane Soler
Tel: +33 (0) 6 18 46 35 62
E-mail: presse@bahut.com

http://copainsdavant.linternaute.com/
Get in touch with your old school mates on Copains d'avant and share your old yearbook pictures. Find out what became of your friends and get in touch: your e-mail address will never be revealed on the site.

Copains d'avant is:
- 4 Million members
- I Million pictures

http://www.copaing.net/
This site was designed to let you reconnect with old classmates through the schools they've attended. Membership and all functionalities are free.

http://www.trombi.com
I created trombi.com in May 2000 to get in touch with my old schoolfriends. I was still a student at that time, when I invited all my friends to become a member. They invited others and so on...Today we have over six hundred thousand members and thousands of us have reconnected with old friends. Each month, I million people visit the site.

André Pitié
Founder of trombi.com

Trombi
61, rue La Boétie
75008 Paris

http://www.studiqg.fr/ (LS)
StudiQuartierGénéral
Social network aimed at students.
Saarbrücker Strasse 38
75009 Paris
France

Phone: 0 144 300 521
Fax: 0 144 300 522
E-mail: aide@studiqg.fr
presse@studiqg.fr

Miscellaneous

http://www.intrainduction.com(formerlyhttp://www.traindunion.com/)
(LS)

Social and professional network for people who take the same train.
Founded by Virgile Rault on 15 December 2006
Tel: + 33 (0) 6 71 46 63 49
E-mail: contact@train-union.com
83 rue du président Wilson 92300 Levallois Perret

Dear An,

Enclosed please find a short text about Intrainduction/Train d'union.

*The English version is not yet released (it will be coming out within two
months), so you can replace Intrainduction by Train d'union in the text if
you want to. It is up to you.*

*I've talked also about functionalities that are not already in place on
our website. I thought it could be interesting to share the evolution of
Train d'union.*

If you want me to change anything, just let me know.

Sincerly,

Virgile Rault

*+33 6 23 96 36 21
skype:virgilebem*

Intrainduction is a social network for European train passengers. Its
purpose is to match people who have booked a ticket on the same train. The
main idea is to take advantage of the journey time to meet your seatmates,
exchange tips, share a cab and to a greater extent have a different behavior
towards public transport. Professionnal as much as personal driving forces
could be involved.

The train is a very rich social environnement, but its networking potential
is still untapped. Most people don't dare to talk to their seatmates. Why?
Because the train is a limited-freedom environment. Therefore, it splits train
passengers into two categories:

-On the one hand, there are people willing to enjoy a train as a place where the hustle and bustle of city life cannot step in. Therefore, they really appreciate to switch off the cell phone, look at landscapes, or give a second thought to their concerns.

-On the other hand, we find people trying to balance this limited-freedom environnement with a more open-minded attitude and who are more prone to share the journey time with somebody else.

As a matter of fact, Intrainduction easily escapes from train environment to connect people after the arrival also.

In the very near future its members will be able to set-up their own community on two criteria:

1) A connecting link: Paris – London
2) Any kind of topic that a member wants to put forward. We would say a tag or a key-word such as "surf, travel, look for a job, lawyer," etc.

As a result everyone will be able to set-up a same community on two different places. Being part of a community in your home city doesn't prevent you from belonging to this same community to another place, especially when the latter is a place where you often go on holidays or for business trips. The main advantage is that we will have additionnal clues to find people on site sharing the same interest, passion or business. As a train is often regarded as an economic vector, such communities revolving around business matters could be also of much interest.

Public transports are just like education backgrounds, cultural contents or personal tastes; it's part of our identity; it shapes the daily life of millions of commuters. Trains convey scores of passenger profiles, expectations and a fundamental need of local information. Intrainduction aims also at gathering people outside the train and giving them the most relevant information for their trip.

For more info: www.traindunion.com (French)
www.intrainduction.com (English version coming up soon)

VIDEO/ PHOTO

http://www.dailymotion.com/
Team:
Benjamin Bejbaum, Co-founder and Chairman & CEO.
Olivier Poitrey, Co-founder and CTO.
webmaster@dailymotion.com

http://corp.vpod.tv
Vpod.tv is an innovative Video Publishing On Demand service, enabling customers and corporations to very easily create their own private Internet and mobile TV channels.

Video Publishing On Demand SA
22 rue de la Pépinière
75008 Paris, France
Tel: +33 1 43 87 54 22

Video Publishing On Demand Spain SL
Avenida de Bruselas, 7
28108 Alcobendas (Madrid), Spain
Tel: +34 914 84 14 27

http://www.eyeka.com/
Founded in 2006 by mobile and media experts, Eyeka's vision is to take a leading role in this new of Web Tv and Mobile Tv. Eyeka's goal is to provide a web and mobile platform and it content to broadcaster or brands. Eyeka wants to innovate the traditional media industry by promoting and redistributing that user-generated content.

Contact:
Magali Gatel
PR Manager
Magali.Gatel@eyeka.com
Tel: 00 33 1 44 76 80 80

Address: 34, boulevard des Italiens 75009 Paris, France.

http://www.trivop.com/

Videoagency, a new European venture, has launched the first online hotel video portal called Trivop.com in April 2007. The site was founded by Thomas Owadenko.

Today, Trivop.com offers hoteliers the free distribution of their own hotel videos. Videoagency is already working on the 2nd version of Trivop.com whereby user generated content (UGC) and customized functionalities will be available to the end users. The value-added element of Trivop's proposition to the consumer is simple: The portal will allow consumers to view the official hotel video whilst giving them the opportunity to upload their own private hotel videos. Thus, you will be able to compare what the hotel would like to show you and what travellers have actually experienced during their recent stay.

Contact Trivop:

press@trivop.com

+33 (0)143250390

22, rue de Seine

75006 Paris, France

http://www.kewego.com/

French, ex Pulsevision.fr

http://www.skema.fr

Thanks to our assistants and audiovisual forms, the enduser can create high-quality videos in just a few minutes, starting from a webcam or a mobile phone. The videos will automatically be edited, produced, indexed, and post produced.

66 Avenue de Landshut

BP 50149

60201 Compiègne Cedex

Tel: + 33 (0)3 44237931

Other agencies in UK and Brazil. Olivier Dufour is its president.

http://www.wideo.fr
Contact
- by e-mail: Philippe Framezelle (pframezelle@m6.fr)
- by mail: M6 Web – Philippe Framezelle – 60 avenue Charles de Gaulle
92200 Neuilly sur Seine

GERMANY

BUSINESS

www.xing.com (LS)
Xing makes your professional network an active part of your life. Far more than a directory of business contacts, Xing enables its members to discover professional people, opportunities, and privileges through its unique discovery capability and advanced contact management tools.

Its novel approach to professional services has resulted in Open Business Club AG being named one of the world's hottest Web 2.0 startups by Business 2.0/CNN Money and one of Europe's "Top 100" by Red Herring.

Founded in August 2003, Open Business Club AG's global network manages tens of millions of member-to-member connections across 16 languages and all industries, with "real world" events held around the world.

Open Business Club AG currently employs an international team of 62 people from 13 nations, with its headquarters based in Hamburg (Germany), and offices in Beijing (China) and in Zurich (Switzerland).

Lars Hinrichs founded the company in 2003 and has headed operations since in his role as CEO.
Eoghan Jennings is responsible for the planning, controlling, and evaluation of corporate performance at OPEN Business Club AG.

presse@xing.com

http://socialbc.com/ (LS)
Our Social Business Club network aims to support you in developing a sustainable and socially responsible, profit or a not-for-profit business in both the private and public sector. We provide a home for the "meeting of minds" to share experiences in areas like entrepreneurship, corporate social responsibility, long term sustainability, innovation, and leadership.

Our online networking portal provides you with a unique combination of online discussion and marketing tools to enable you to:

Create, moderate, and participate in specialist discussion forums,
Access various newsfeeds,
Post press releases and news stories to international news agencies and to automatic news-feeders,
Create your own weblog (a journal that is frequently updated and intended for general public consumption),
Post and read job advertisements,
Post and read details of events.

Alexander Dort – Founder and COO of socialBC
He can be reached by mail:
alexander.dort@socialBC.com

http://www.brainguide.com/ (LS)
Portal for knowledge management where experts meet.

brainGuide AG
Hauptstraße 19
82319 Starnberg
Fon: 08151-6558-0
Fax: 08151-6558-29
Brunnstraße 1
80331 München
Fon: 089-26 26 29 00
E-mail: info@brainguide.com

Dr. Florian Schmid (CEO)
Tim Wagner (CTO)

http://www.theweps.com
Platform for business people worldwide from different industries.

2005-04-10 Inoffizieller Start der Webseite im Netz – Test-User
theWEPS.com is international – English and German, other languages will
follow later
theWEPS.com is a project of the company Bayartz AG, represented by the
CEO Mr. Hans Bayartz, Bennostraße 6, 52134 Herzogenrath

http://www.ciwi.biz
CIWI is a network for artists, creatives, innovators, entrepreneurs, innovation
professionals and those interested and engaged in creativity and innovation
worldwide.
If you are a creative professional, either a creativity consultant, an artist or
art worker, CIWI offers you a powerful platform to develop the network
beyond the limits you have experienced so far. Here you find the tools to
strengthen the ties to organizations in other countries as well. CIWI is
a brainchild of IM-BOOT founder Steffen Konrath. People can become
members of CIWI by invitation of its founder or its members only. It is a
closed user group. Registration on CIWI is free, but premium membership
costs 6 EUR/month. CIWI's primary purpose is to promote networking
among its members and to offer a global marketing platform with media
support. CIWI is the abbreviation for Creativity and Innovation Worldwide
Initiative. It is a brand of IM-BOOT. IM-BOOT, Franz-Huber Str. 33,
D-83088 Kiefersfelden.

http://www.global-electronics-club.com/ (LS)
The Global Electronics Club (GE Club) gives professionals in the electronics
and photonics industry an opportunity to maintain personal contacts and
exchange information with people from around the world. Global electronics
is the electronics and photonics network established by Munich Trade Fairs
International. It includes electronics trade fairs around the world and an
Internet platform. The international exhibitions electronica, Productronica

and LASER. World of Photonics presents major international trends at the trade-fair center in Munich.

Legal Information on Messe München GmbH

Supplier
Messe München GmbH
Messegelände
81823 München
Germany
Phone: (+49 89) 9 49-2 07 20
Fax: (+49 89) 9 49-2 07 29
E-mail: newsline@messe-muenchen.de

Names of persons authorised to represent the company:
Manfred Wutzlhofer (Chairman & CEO)
Norbert H. Bargmann
Klaus Dittrich
Hans-Joachim Heusler
Eugen Egetenmeir (Deputy Managing Director)

http://www.decayenne.com/
Decayenne is a private network founded in 2001. Originally established as a way for a group of close friends to stay in touch and coordinate activities, it has developed into an innovative worldwide project. Today, Decayenne connects various individuals with the aim of promoting international social and business contacts. It enables the free exchange of ideas between members, ideas which support strategies for achieving personal and professional success. Decayenne is a valuable intermediary between like-minded individuals who are often continents apart but share the same interests, backgrounds, and relations.

Decayenne, with its resourceful website and special events, creates opportunities to access and exchange inside its unique network. The system offers outstanding features that apply to all facets of modern networking, from travel to trade, and from friendships to business partnerships. Decayenne's primary objective is to build long-lasting bonds between its members and to support their professional development and social activities. Decayenne members are part of a global family, meeting regularly to share culture, business and entertainment in suitable convivial environments.

FRIENDS

http://www.amitize.com/
Amitize.com is an online community that lets you meet friends around the world.
You can create your own community, private or open, and you can share photos, blogs, journals, music and many more.

www.fruehstueckstreff.net
Frühstückstreff was founded in the summer of 2001 in Darmstadt, Germany, and the idea has spread to over forty cities in Europe since. Fruehstueckstreff. de publishes events for gentle people interested in expanding their circle of friends in the course of stimulating leisure activities. Our Frühstückstreff volunteer staff members are vibrant women and men who in their spare time enjoy organizing events for other people and inviting them at no cost. Our award-winning website, Fruehstueckstreff.de, is one of the six thousand most valuable German internet addresses 2004, 2005 and 2006.

fruehstueckstreff
Publisher
IDL Software Publikations-
und Verlagsgesellschaft mbH
Postfach 130104
Isselstraße 43c
D-64297 Darmstadt

+49 (0)170-3554604 mobil
+49 (0)6151-954910 fon
+49 (0)6151-954911 fax
Editorial staff:

Klaus Schultheis (ks), Chief editor
redaktion@fruehstueckstreff.de

http://www.friendsbay.de (LS)
Founded in 2004 by Danny Troll and managed with Dominik Mühl and Marc Stirnweiss.

Nordweststr. 47
63128 Dietzenbach
Germany
press@friendsbay.de

http://www.meinefreunde.de/ (LS)
Social network based in Berlin. German only.
Bild.T-Online.de AG & Co. KG
Axel-Springer-Straße 65
D-10888 Berlin
info@bild.t-online.de

http://www.t-community.com (LS)
Deutsche Telekom AG,
T-Com
Friedrich-Ebert-Allee 140
53113 Bonn
E-mail: info@t-community.com

http://schwarzekarte.de/ (LS)
Schwarzekarte is a private lifestyle community. Membership is by introduction only. Members are kept updated on important Media, Sports and Artevents and will receive invitations to afterparties.

SK Media GmbH
Hansaring 63-67
D - 50670 Köln
Fax: +49 (0)221-35586619
info@schwarzekarte.de
presse@schwarzekarte.de

Geschäftsführer: Julia Schneider, Jan Becker, Felix Baltes

http://flork.com/ (LS)
Via this system you can create a personal profile and publish information. Additionally, you can use this profile to log into other services like www. gnoosic.com, www.gnooks.com and www.gnovies.com and use your choosen Username for example when posting messages on the discussion boards of these sites. Other users of these sites then will be able to look up your profile.

Marek Gibney
Scheideweg 39b
20253 Hamburg
Germany
Tel: +49 40 200 45 36
E-mail: marek@gibney.de

http://www.alooha.net (LS)
We just want to offer an easy and simple way to do what people did the last couple of thousand years – keep in touch with each other and extend their network by meeting others related to their friends. Another difference is that we want to offer an international service, so we offer a German version beside the English one and try to expand the supported language.

AndTeK GmbH
Moosstrasse 16
D-82319 Starnberg
Germany
Phone: +49(0) 700 26383500
Press: press@andtek.com

http://lokalisten.de
Network of friends; especially active around Munich.

Founded on May 2005
Members: 700.000 (April 2007)

Founded by five friends : Andreas Degenhart, Peter Wehner, Jürgen Gerleit, Norbert Schauermann, Andreas Hauenstein

Müllerstrasse 3
80469 München

Tel: +49 89 2388 755-10
fax: +49 89 2388 755-15
E-mail: kontakt@lokalisten.de

http://www.beonit.com/
beonit - the world of portals

A world of portals for people with a mission.
Wherever people live, and whatever people do – they look for partners to find their way and solve their mission. Nobody has all the answers.

Beonit is a world of personalised Web Portals, which will improve the social network movement.

Beonit is a community of entrepreneurs who establish various theme portals.

Beonit will therefore carry a vast amount of individual themes.

Besides a Business & Personal Network we think of portals for:

Partners & Friends,
Family Affairs (au pairs, babysitters, housekeepers, insurance, places to go with kids),
Food (vegetarian, lifestyle, food for kids)
Golf , Sports in general, Services, Clubs, Pilots & Aircrafts, Wellness, Travelling, Local area portals, Cars & Bikes, Model Building and many more.

We want to give everyone with a mission and content knowhow the opportunity to start and grow his or her own portal.
Beonit is a franchise business.

BeonIT GmbH & Co. KG was founded in October 2004 by:

Dr. Andreas von der Eltz, Managing Director
Roger Ziems, MP, Technical Director
Klaus Schultheis, MP, Marketing Director

BeonIT GmbH & Co KG
Willibrachtstraße 14
60431 Frankfurt am Main
Germany

+49 (0)69 52 45 34 fon
+49 (0)69 7 91 22 10 57 fax
info@beonit.com

http://www.myfriends.de/
mobilcom Communicationstechnik GmbH

Hollerstraße 126
Postfach 520
24753 Rendsburg-Büdelsdorf

http://www.openpeople.de/ (LS)
OpenPeople is an internet community which can only be joined if an existing user invites you. After registering, you will be able to invite your friends, get in touch with other members and find people from your past, your present and maybe even your future...

Dear An,

I'm really sorry about the delayed answer to your e-mail. One of our support employees forwarded it to a wrong e-mail address, so I received it yesterday:-

If you have any questions feel free to contact me.

Best regards,

René-Christian Glembotzky

Managing Director

typographia media GmbH
Tiestestr. 36
30171 Hannover
Tel: 0511/475398-10
Fax: 0511/475398-29
Mobile: 0170/8777777

Networking:
https://www.openbc.com/hp/ReneChristian_Glembotzky/

openPeople – Corporate Profile

Summary

OpenPeople is a social network for all those who want to stay in contact with their friends and make new contacts about their existing circle of friends. Different to most other networks with the focus on private networking, openPeople is a real-name based network. So it's easy to re-find old friends by entering their prename and family name.

Beta-Launch
July 2006

Founders
René Glembotzky, Chairman
Andreas Nikolai, CFO
Inka Höfert, Co-Founder

Corporate Overview
Chairman René Glembotzky is the official face and voice of openPeople. Following a successful sale of the market leading community free-sms.de to the quoted wallstreet:online AG in late 2005, René Glembotzky spent several months in consulting and analyzing social networks around the world. He has authored several articles about viral marketing and futurism of social networking and marketing. His co-founders Andreas Nikolai and Inka Höfert round the management team.

OpenPeople has been privately funded with a total of 800.000 euro ($ 1.05 million) invested since early 2006. The management is considering no initial public offering.

The management team is nothing if not ambitious, but they are not crazy. Instead of a long-term plan to become "the leading social network on earth", openPeople wants to be a friendly place where members value the home-like atmosphere in a trusted circle of friends and acquaintances.

Features

User Profiles—openPeople profiles are flexible and easy to personalize. Basic demographic and individual information is captured in a structured way. It's not possible to create your own layouts to keep the look feel in a clear way.

Personal Networks—The essential feature of openPeople are personal networks where users can group and classify friends and acquaintances they know from real life. It's easily possible to find people by browsing their friend's friends, by entering a name or using one of the search agents. Getting in touch with an interesting person from last week's party has never been so easy.

Weblogs Articles—Each user has its own blog, but articles are also published in a global blog so other users can easily find, read, and comment new articles.

Clubs—openPeople users have the possibility to create up to ten individual clubs. Clubs are a mixture between a discussion forum and gallery where users can communicate with other people who have the same interests.

Events Meetings—openPeople offers a robust event and meeting system where users can post public & private events, as well as arrange meetings with other openPeople members.

Privacy Notes

As a difference to other social networking communities for private networking, openPeople uses real names instead of usernames to make it easier to find and be found. Due to the fact that it's essential to secure the privacy and guarantee the safety of under aged members openPeople uses a highly developed privacy control system and uses special non-public algorithms to protect members against any disturbing or annoying impact. OpenPeople also has a qualified security team to detect fake accounts or anomalies of the normal usage.

General Notes

What is perhaps most remarkable about openPeople is the extraordinary loyalty of its members and commitment to the platform. A major part realizes the advantages of inviting their own friends to get in touch with more people they know from their past or interesting people they've met in "real life networking".

The platform is currently available in German and English and running as a private beta. It has twenty-seven thousand registered members generated through the viral marketing effect of one hundred direct contacts the founders invited in July 2006. Over 90% of the members are from Germany, Austria, and Switzerland.

typographia media GmbH
Tiestestr. 36
30171 Hannover
crew@openpeople.de

http://www.lovento.com
Birkenweg 41
53343 Wachtberg, Germany
CEO: Marcel Aulenbacher

Founded in July 2005.

http://www.netzclan.de/ (LS)
Project of
Fruetel Media Services
Thomas Frütel
Von-Ossietzky-Ring 51
45279 Essen
Tel: +49 (201) 80 68 784
Fax: +49 (1212) 5 114 12 007
E-mail: info@fruetel.de

DATING

http://amiamo1.com/ (LS)
How it works: You enter things you like – can be everything: bands, films, hobbies, stars, cities, and more. Amiamo then shows you members who like the same things. After that, you can contact them.

responsible:
Nico Wilfer
Wiener Straße 19
64521 Groß-Gerau
Germany
nico@amiamo.de

SPECIAL INTEREST

Books

http://reliwa.de/
For book and movie lovers.

Fashion

http://www.burdastyle.com/
Nora Abousteit and Benedikta Karaisl von Karais, Makers of BurdaStyle
BurdaStyle, your destination for do-it-yourself style. We like to think of
this website as a virtual sewing circle, an open-source hub of ideas, expertise,
and amazing patterns you can download and sew at home. Launched as Beta
at DLD 07 on January 21st, 2007, BurdaStyle is a project of Hubert Burda
Media Marketing & Communications Research & Development department.
BurdaStyle is inspired by Burda Mode, which was founded by Aenne Burda
in 1949. It's not entirely coincidental that BurdaStyle headquarters shares
office space with Etsy.com. Not only is BurdaStyle's selling enabled through
Etsy — when users put one of their designs up for sale, it's sold through
the Etsy.com website — but we like to think that both BurdaStyle and
Etsy are in the business of using new technology to drive old-fashioned
craft.

Burda Media Marketing & Communications
Arabellastr. 23
80333 München
Germany

Students

www.studivz.net
Studivz is short for "Studentenverzeichnis" or Student directory. It was launched in October 2005 by two students. In January 2007 Studivz has been sold to one of its investors, Georg von Holtzbrinck GmbH, a German publishing group. They have about 1 million users.

Saarbrücker Straße 38
10405 Berlin
Germany

Phone: +49 (0)30-280 974 31
Fax: +49 (0)30-40 50 427 34

http://www.schuelervz.net/
Schülerverzeichnis is a German-only site for teenagers, started in 2007. It is from the same company as Studivz and counts approximately five hundred thousand members.

kontakt@schuelervz.net

http://zeeya.net (LS)
International community for students.
Founded by Vera and Sam Brannen, a German-American couple from Frankfurt am Main, Germany.

Further information regarding Zeeya.net:
Vera Brannen, Konrad-Adenauer-Straße 44,
D-63073 Offenbach am Main, Germany
Telephone: +49 (0)69 - 95 93 26 60, E-mail: vera.brannen@zeeya.net

Press contact for Zeeya.net:
textstark Unternehmenskommunikation, Homburger Straße 29, D-65197 Wiesbaden, Germany
Tel: +49 (0)611 - 890 50 34;
Fax: +49 (0)611 - 890 50 39;
E-mail: zeeya@textstark.de

http://www.studylounge.es/ (LS)
Hi,

My name is Christoph Berger. I am 27, a student of the university of Cologne, an entrepreneur with intergenia AG (founded in 1999) for more than seven years and also the founder of Studylounge. I want to give you some information about our social network.

Studylounge is a social network for students founded in April 2006 by the Studylounge GmbH, a joint venture by the intergenia AG and the i12 AG, as a German social network for students; in August 2006, we started a French, Italian, and Spanish version of studylounge.

The features found in Studylounge are similar to the successful formula of prior social networks — friendships, discussion groups, picture albums, profile pages, messaging (though Studylounge also offers personal chat capabilities), guestbooks and the option to "wink" to other members. When viewing the profiles of other members, you see every single shortest link/connection to this member (extended network).

Since in Studylounge you have no nickname — our members use their real names — we put increased effort in privacy protection. Studylounge offers extensive and diversified options to control the information you give about yourself. Everybody can decide which information he or she wants to share with whom. For every single item you may decide which user group may get access to it — just your friends or every Studylounge-member.

However, Studylounge differs from many other student-focused social networks in the increased ease and simplicity we try to implement in getting to know other members. From the homepage you have direct access to a list of online members and latest activity (new members, groups, postings); basically, even if you have no clue as how to really use the site, a few clicks can give you a good idea of how the network and the site work. At the same time we strive to create — beyond the simple social networking — a true online community where students from different universities can get in touch and share.

The top three countries are at the moment the Studylounge-Networks in France, Italy, and Spain. We not only have different language versions to access the same network, we have different communities for each country. All Studylounge-Networks together have already more than one hundred thousand members.
In the future we will bring even more features to our already very successful page.

I hope to have answered all your questions.
If you do have any more questions, do not hesitate to contact me.

Best regards Christoph

Christoph Berger
Vorstand

Intergenia AG
Daimlerstraße 9-11
50354 Hürth

Fon: +49 (22 33) 612-215
Fax: +49 (22 33) 612-225
E-mail: c.berger@intergenia.de

Studylounge GmbH
Turmstr. 5
35578 Wetzlar (Germany)
Tel: (+49) 6441-2089392
Fax: (+49) 6441-2102257
E-mail: support@studylounge.es

Management: Christoph Berger, Oliver Kruse

Travel

http://www.cosmotourist.com/
Cosmotourist gives consumers access to a broad variety of travel information.
We guide our users to exactly the locations they are interested in by offering
a multilevel search feature. Travellers find all kinds of specific information
on more than 1 Million locations provided by the most reliable partners on
the web and our traveller community.

We make planning and booking your next vacation as easy as possible
by offering the best deals currently available and an easy to use booking
engine.

Cosmotourist has its headquarters in Munich, Germany. We operate websites in nine different countries, including the US and major European countries like Germany, France, and the UK.

For questions and general inqueries you can contact us at: info-en@cosmotourist.net

http://yumondo.com/
Yumondo is a social network where you can share everything about your city: photos, events…

Yumondo is a service of Metaversum GmbH

Metaversum GmbH
Rungestrasse 20
D-10179 Berlin (Germany)

Contact:
Phone: +49 (0) 30 847 12 25 0
Fax: +49 (0) 30 847 12 25 29
E-mail: info@metaversum.com

Managing Directors: Dr. Mirko Caspar, Dietrich Charisius, Jochen Hummel

VIDEO/ PHOTO

http://www.myvideo.de

GREECE

FRIENDS

http://zoo.gr/
Started in 2004 by five friends. In Greek only.

http://joy.gr/
Sixty-five thousand registered members. In Greek only.

http://www.fatsa.gr/
Founded on February 6, 2006. In Greek only.

http://social.dailyfrappe.com/ (LS)
Welcome to DailyFrappe Social, our newest addition to the DailyFrappe community.
With DF Social you can:
Meet like-minded Greeks from all over the world.
Use our community for friendship, business, or romance. You're in control!
Share pictures and on-line photo albums.
Write and read on-line Travel Journals about Greece & Cyprus.

For the time being, DailyFrappe Social will be in private beta and accessible by invitation only. If you'd like to be added to our e-mail list for further updates please contact us at beta@dailyfrappe.com

www.worldwidegreeks.com
In English.

HUNGARY

FRIENDS

www.iwiw.net
The biggest web 2.0 service in Hungary is iWiW.hu, a social network. IWiW means International who is who, and according to Wikipedia it currently has over five hundred thousand registered users with real names and over fifteen million connections between them. The site is invite-only.

http://myvip.com/index.php (LS)
info@myvip.hu

VIDEO/ PHOTO

http://videa.hu/main.php

www.videobomb.hu
Video sharing site, run by Blogter.hu

www.videoplayer.hu
Video sharing site, run by Sanoma Media Company

ITALY

BUSINESS

www.neurona.it
Neurona.it is the most important Network in Italy for Business Users. It's the major "competitor" to LinkedIN and Xing, but both Xing and LinkedIN are in English that restricts too much the use of those Networks by "normal" people. The country manager of Neurona is Silvia Aznar.

http://www.milanin.com (LS)

Hi An,

We want to be innovators in Social Business Networking.
Our Web Platform is an Open-Source solution. It's free also for the other Small Groups/ Communities (!), and of course the participation in MilanIN eGroupWare project is open to everyone. I believe that sooner or later this Project will become popular and many strong IT professionals will contribute to it! (I will then have to buy lots of beer for my friend Michael Tabolsky since it all happens also thanks to his great belief in this crazy idea!)
The idea is to propose for free our on-line platform for Social Business Networking to others, to let them not be dependent on the commercial platforms for Networking: Social Networking should be free! It belongs to communities. Of course if one then wants to earn some money on the premium services, it's just a great idea! But the base networking must be free and available to any group that wants to launch their own social networking (for closed-groups or open groups) and would need an on-line platform to support it.

Of course, we know we're not (yet) perfect. We know we should improve MilanIN from all sides. And we know how to do it :) It's for all Project areas—from real-life events organization to knowledge sharing on our Web platform. And we're improving day-by-day!

Can you tell me anything more about Milanin?

Pier Carlo is the President of Milan-IN. Here is his profile on our Platform:
http://www.milanin.com/members/piercarlo.pozzati/. But he was not the only one to create MilanIN, there was a group of people interested in Social Networking in Italy, so Pier called them to join forces to create this Club. Now this group is known as the Board: http://www.milanin.com/egroupware/sitemgr/sitemgr-site/The-Board.

These days we're registering a National Association of Business Networking in Italy, and Pier Carlo will probably be moved to that direction (together with me), leaving some space in Milan for somebody else. But it's for "tomorrow", not today. The Association Club-IN will cover the network of local Open Business Networking Clubs in the most important cities of Italy (Rome, Torino to come ASAP and few next in the following months). We call this movement "Milan IN-2.0":=)

MilanIN, as you probably already understood, is very different from the others. We're not a Social Network; we're a Business Networking Club, with real-life events, with sponsors/partners that make presentations, with lots of properly organized entertainment for Club Members (sport, social, cultural, business). We declare ourselves as Business Networking events experts and so on. We have some particular programs as "Advantages for Members-Trusted Service Providers".

We have business partners for office/ networking/ hosting/ etc from the Italian leading businesses, among them the leading Business School MIP as our Sponsor.

Also we have MilanIN-TV Project, and we're preparing now live broadcast from our Events that will be also re-broadcasted by the leading Web-TV sites in IT-Web. Here is the MilanIN-TV home:
http://www.milanin.com/egroupware/sitemgr/sitemgr-site/Broadcast-channels

We have on-line partners program to declare the Networks we officially collaborate with (like LinkedIN, Viadeo, Comunitazione, etc). Here is the right page: http://www.milanin. com/egroupware/sitemgr/sitemgr-site/Online-Partners

About the MilanIN hubs/groups: we've started with LinkedIN Group, then we created a Hub on Viadeo, now there is also a group of MilanIN (Social Business Networking in Italy) on Neurona and in a few days also on konnects.com. We want to keep strict relations with the most important Social Networks since our business model is offline Events, and we do not compete with them, we propose a collaboration to turn their Virtual Communities to the real emotional Clubs.

Btw, you may be interested to check our "Advised Social Networks", which is a result of the "Not-only-MilanIN" project, that's on our Web Site. We have a project that allows Club Members to share with others the Social Networks one knows/is a member of. We have categorised those Networks by location- Italy, World, on-line only and Milan. And all those Networks have been checked (at least by myself and president) in the sense we have contacted them and discussed something about partnership. Here are the results:

http://www.milanin.com/egroupware/sitemgr/sitemgr-site/Milan
http://www.milanin.com/egroupware/sitemgr/sitemgr-site/Italy
http://www.milanin.com/egroupware/sitemgr/sitemgr-site/World
http://www.milanin.com/egroupware/sitemgr/sitemgr-site/Online-Clubs

An, I am always happy to collaborate, and let's keep in touch for sure! As you may have understood from my profile, I am one of the major Milan-IN Evangelists and Spirit

Owners, since I am co-founder, IT Manager and Member of Marketing Team as resp. for Web Markering/SEO/Promotion... So it's my duty to know all about Social (Business) Networking and keep the relations with the most valuable of them.

Btw, lots of thoughts about Social (Business) Networking in Italy in my Blog, here: http://www.milanin.com/members/andrey.golub/weblog/ Some posts are in Italian, but most are in English.

Let's keep in touch. I am always on skype, "avg_milano". And I'll try to find you on LinkedIN.

Andrey Golub

Team:

Pier Carlo Pozzati
Founder

Andrey Golub
Co-founder and IT/ Web-Promotion manager
andrey@milanin.com

Luca Zambrelli
Marketing Manager
(The ex marketing manager, Andrea Falzin, is now Country Manager Italia at Viadeo while remaining on the board of Milanin.)

The other Board members and non-Board members can be found on Milanin's site.

Contact:
ufficiostampa@milanin.com
Business Club Milan IN
Via Tanaro, 22-20128 Milano
CF 97413780152

http://www.bizbureau.org/CMS/
BizBureau (www.bizbureau.it) was launched in 2003 by Carmelo Cutuli (www.cutuli.it), a notorious ICT Consultant in Italy. The venture has quickly attracted a strong attention from the Italian ICT community. The core concept behind BizBureau is the following: organizing informal meetings where entrepreneurs, managers and professionals can freely meet and debate on ICT themes.

Bizbureau was the first networking attempt in Italy but does seem to have lost traction since.

FRIENDS

http://www.italiansonline.net/

http://it.dada.net/home/
Dada S.p.A. is a leading international provider of Web and mobile community and entertainment services and is the controlling company of a Group which is entirely dedicated to the development of Internet services. Dada services to over 7 million people in twenty-three countries of the World. Approximately twenty thousand new users join the Dada.net community every day mostly in Italy, USA, Spain, and Brazil.

Dada operates three communities:
Personal Space & Social Network (life.Dada.net)
Mobile Entertainment (mobi.Dada.net)
Dating (love.Dada.net)

The Dada group currently employees 450 people and has offices in Florence, Milan, New York, Beijing, Barcelona, Rio de Janeiro, Bergamo, and Treviso.

Marketing Manager for Italy is Laura De Benedetto

http://www.socialdust.com/
Friends network in Italian only. Founded by two friends: Tiziano L. U. Caviglia and Chiara Bruzzone.

VIDEO/ PHOTO

http://zooppa.com/
Zooppa.com originated from the idea of creating a space for social advertising through user-generated content.

It is committed to the vision of real people and real companies conducting business in a creative and rewarding viral context. This means stimulating the creative talent of those who have no voice in the traditional advertising setting.

Zooppa is housed by the technological incubator H-Farm, a center for research and innovation in technological and new media fields, placed near Venice. H-Farm develops Zooppa, by providing venture capital and graphical design, technical and strategic services to the project.

Zooppa.com partners with international companies to sponsor their brand through Zooppa's video competitions. Based on the briefs companies provide, users are invited to create their own commercials for that brand. This can mean designing an animated sequence, writing a script or concept for a potential ad, or actually shooting their own video.

For each company that Zooppa partners with, a new contest is launched for users to compete in. Users are also encouraged to create their ads using concepts or scripts posted by others. As an incentive to share one another's creativity, Zooppa rewards this type of collaboration with Bonus Team.

Once users have uploaded their commercials, it is up to them to decide the winners. Users rate the videos, and it is based on these ratings that Zooppa awards the cash prizes.

What makes Zooppa unique is how the winners are rewarded. Each Zoop$ that users earn are equivalent to real US dollars. Once users have accumulated a minimum of 1000 Zoop$, they can convert their Zoop$ into a real cash pay out.

After running a beta version of the site for a month and sponsoring a promotional contest, Zooppa.com was officially launched on March 1, 2007.

mailto:press@zooppa.com

H-Farm S.p.A.
Tenuta Ca' Tron Via Sile
51 – 31056 Roncade (TV) – Italy
Ph: +39 0422 789.611
Fax: +39 0422 789.666

LATVIA

FRIENDS

www.draugiem.lv (also www.jouwvrienden.nl and www.frype.com)

http://c2.one.lv/ (LS)
The fifth most popular site in Latvia – it's mostly popular in the Russian community.
one@one.lv

http://orb.lv/ (LS)
In Latvian and Russian.
kontakti@or.lv

http://amigos.inbox.lv/ (LS)
In Latvian, English and Russian.
Operated by Sia "Inbokks".

Contact:
39- 7 floor F. Sadovnikova street,
Riga, LV-1003
Latvia

E-mail:
Business information: sales@co.inbox.lv

www.Face.lv (LS)
Face.lv is one of the biggest sites in Latvian internet. There are 111.973
active users at Face.lv, plus some owners of the hidden accounts and
unregistered visitors. The number of our users is increasing. We also have
successful projects in Estonia (most popular website there) and in Lithuania
(within top 10).
There are more than 4 million page views daily.
sales@face.lv

SPECIAL INTEREST

Students

http://klase.lv/ (LS)
Social site for schoolmates. In Latvian and Russian.
help@klase.lv

Miscellaneous

www.expatsnet.net (LS)
The site Expats Network International has been established with the main
goal to serve the English speaking expatriate community residing in the
Baltic States by providing trustworthy and easy to utilize, informative
and interactive means. This site offers an explicit range of Internet tools
and is both qualitatively informative and amusingly entertaining. The
international community in the Baltics can be assured that facts, figures, and
news published in the site concerning immigration, employment, real estate,
health care, travel and business prospects are of leading status, knowledge
and quality, hence, guaranteeing daily success and long term benefits of
living in the Baltics. In addition, the site is also designed to be interactive,
thriving to be the basis for a flourishing network of the English speaking
expat community in the Baltics. On behalf of the site, we welcome all
new members to the expat community, be they a whole family or a single

individual, a business leader or a lecturer, an employee or a student residing in the Baltics.

Latvian Office coordinates: Expats Latvia Ltd.
Address: Brivibas str.95, Riga, LV-1010
Phone: +371 7273127
Fax: +371 7273227
Mail: expats@expatsnet.net

VIDEO/ PHOTO

http://latvija.tv/
Latvian You Tube. In Latvian and Russian.

http://mansvideo.lv

http://fotki.lv/
Photosharing. In Latvian and Russian.

http://www.poga.lv/ (LS)
Photosharing.

http://foto.inbox.lv

http://myfoto.lv

LITHUANIA

FRIENDS

http://www.point.lt/

http://pazintys.lt/main/index.php
"Pazintys.com" is owned and operated by Enit Invest S.L.

http://www.draugas.lt/
Paneriug. 51-321, LT-03202 Vilnius
Tel: (8-5) 2104330
Contact: info@draugas.lt

http://www.ieskok.lt/lt/
info@ieskok.lt

Tel: +370 8 37 300838

LUXEMBOURG

BUSINESS

http://www.codex-online.com
Legal information site functioning as a community tool for publishing, consulting, and commenting legal documents.

The website offers:

- The possibility for any user of the site to publish legal documents online
- A fully searchable database
- A legal news alert service
- A professional directory

The site is designed to constitute a global forum of interaction for professionals, who can publish their materials online and, through the registration and referencing process, be identified as the author of any document to other users of the site. Registering as an author at www.codex-online.com makes the writing user a member of the site community.

We would like to invite you to become a member of our community by publishing your documents on the site. These are not only searchable in the database but are also included in our legal news alert service, which provides customers with weekly e-mails containing all new documents entering the site, on the topic(s) and in the language(s) of their choice.

The site has European origins (it was designed and is managed in Luxembourg), and the materials currently available cover mostly European countries and topics. The site community is expanding, however, and beyond Europe, we are naturally looking for materials to widen and enrich the scope of professional information available on www.codex-online .com.

Please visit the website for further information on its purpose and coverage. You can also contact us at marc.rauchs@codexnews.com for any question you might have regarding the website and the services offered.

Marc Rauchs
Codew Online s.a.
36, rue de Luxembourg
L-8077 Bertrange
Tel: 00352 31 21 18 20
Fax: 00352 31 21 18 50
E-mail: marc.rauchs@codexnews.com

NORWAY

BUSINESS

http://www.nettverket.org/forum/
Hi An,

The only virtual open for all networks is a userforum for Norwegian LinkedIn users calles nettverket.org (where I am chairman). There is no specified Norwegian social or business virtual network, and we usually use LinkedIn, Xing, and Ecademy.
John-Patrick Skaar

FRIENDS

http://www.bloc.no/
Bloc is a Norwegian networking site calling themself "Norways largest gang of friends".

http://www.meside.no/
Norwegian social networking site run by TV2

http://blink.dagbladet.no/
Norwegian networking site made by Dagbladet.
Postal adress: Boks 1184 Sentrum, 0107 Oslo
Visiting adress: Akersg. 49, 0180 Oslo
Ph: 22 31 06 00

POLAND

BUSINESS

http://www.goldenline.pl/ (LS)
Marek Zagajewski is Head of Customer Service.
info@goldenline.pl
media@goldenline.pl

http://biznes.net/

http://ogniwo.net/

info@ogniwo.net

FRIENDS

www.grono.net

http://www.spinacz.pl/

http://www.epuls.pl/

VIDEO/ PHOTO

http://www.photoblog.pl/

PORTUGAL

SPECIAL INTEREST

http://vivapets.com/
Vivapets.com is all about pets and the people who love them, a place for everybody to communicate and share the love for our animal friends!

The project (born "Arca de Noe") was originally launched in 2000 and is the original online Pet Community. You can create your own personal pages for your pets, called "Petsites", "Petblogs", photo albums, build your network of pet and human friends, and engage with them via forums, chat, or personal messaging among many other features, and fun stuff.

We also take great pride in using the latest cutting edge web technology to bring you the best browsing experience possible, so you can browse and express yourself using the smartest web tools and technology around!

In English, Spanish & Portuguese.

CEO: Marcos Cerqueira
Location: Oporto, Portugal
Launch date: 2003
The site has 100,000 members.

ROMANIA

FRIENDS

http://www.neogen.ro/
Contact person: Maria Suciu
E-mail: pr@neogen.biz
Phone: 021-3184084

www.porkolt.com

http://www.bascalie.ro

http://www.simpatie.ro/

DATING

http://www.nevedem.ro (LS)
Dating site in Romanian, English, and French
Bucuresti, Romania
Tel: (+40) 722 408 215
E-mail: contact@nevedem.com

http://www.romance-cafe.com/

SPECIAL INTEREST

Books

http://www.tagabook.com/
Site for bibliophiles.

Founded by a student, 4th year at Politechnica University in Bucharest in September 2006.

str. Gradina Postei, nr. 28/A, Arad
jud. Arad, Romania, Cod Postal 2900
E-mail: contact@tagabook.com

George
Architecture and Development
E-mail: george@tagabook.com

Students

http://www.colegi.ro
Provides e-mail directories of alumni from hundreds of schools and universities throughout Romania. It only contains contact information for alumni who have registered with the system. Many Romanians use this resource to re-establish contacts. In Romanian.

SERBIA

FRIENDSHIP

http://www.urbae.com/
Part of the Romenian neogen network.

DATING

http://poljubac.urbae.com/
also in English

VIDEO/ PHOTO

www.kobajagrande.com

SLOVAKIA

VIDEO/ PHOTO

http://www.myubo.com/
Myubo lets Slovak and Czech users upload and watch videos. The site has two thousand users and was launched in 2007.
CEO: Igor Rintel
Location: Bratislava, Slovakia

SLOVENIA

FRIENDS

http://www.simpatije.com

http://www.glasujzame.com/
Youth portal/community

DATING

http://ona-on.com/SVN/europage.jsp
Ona-on.com is a leading dating service in Slovenia offering online & mobile dating, offline parties & social events. The ultimate place to find your soulmate and meet lots of new friends.

PP 3920
1001 Ljubljana
Tel: 01 565 79 55
Fax: 01 565 79 50
info@veneti.com

VIDEO/ PHOTO

http://www.mojvideo.com/

SPAIN

BUSINESS

www.neurona.com (LS)
Neurona is a free virtual community launched in August 2003. Its aim is to promote meeting old classmates and colleagues.

We offer you the possibility to build your own contacts network, both personal and professional. Our goal is to help you find or gain new working opportunities.

Neurona.com may be useful to:

- Progress in your professional career
- Find partners and co-workers
- Broaden your clients and suppliers portfolio
- Contact professionals and request advice.

If you are considering getting a new degree or changing your job and you need a piece of advice, not only can you obtain feedback from our users, but you can also contact people who may be able to help you make up your mind, recommend something or provide you with all the relevant information on the issue.

The active participation from our users is essential to Neurona.com. We offer you a Communication Centre so that you can contact your friends and other members from our Community in a private way or through public forums where you can participate and open new debate topics.

https://www.linkedin.com/e/gis/1296/287636468944/

This is a group that is for all SAP Certified Consultants, regardless of Module (or those pursuing certification). We all studied very hard for this certification, and I thought it would be handy to make sure we all knew each other and could use this forum as well as LinkedIN to discuss relevant issues, i.e., job openings, rates, etc.. Remember, he who has better information, wins...

-Founders & management

Founder and Manager Lonnie D. Ayers

-Founding year & address/nationality
Founded July 15, 2005
C. Hartzembusch 33
Barcelona, Spain, 08014
American

-Target audience & membership level (number of users)
I formed this group for SAP Certified Professionals and have expanded it to include consultants who are working on certification. The purpose of the group is for SAP Consultants to share information, either Technical, or on current rates, and hopefully, to get higher rates as a result.

I currently have 255 members in the group.

-Top three countries in which the community is used
I do not have a way to actually count this characteristic; however, I am guessing that it would be America, the UK, and Germany; however, I have members from all over the world in it.

-Main technical features and possible features in the near future
Membership in the group is by invitation only. Members have a small icon that shows up on their LinkedIN profile when they are members. You can search for specific members by keyword, for example, and limit it to members of this group. As long as you are connected, you can contact that member directly.

-Languages in which the service is available

English

https://www.econozco.com/
EConozco is a professional network. Founded by Arnold Armengol Bertroli and Horaci Cuevas Jiménez. Bought by Xing on March 27, 2007.

Founded in 2003, the eConozco network recently reached approximately 150,000 members in the Spanish and Latin American markets and has posted an average monthly growth of eleven percent in the last half year. Like XING users, members of eConozco mainly use the network for business purposes. Both parties agreed to keep the purchase price confidential. The takeover will allow XING to rapidly expand in the Spanish-speaking market and to gain access to key Spanish economic centers, like Barcelona and Madrid.

FRIENDS

http://www.bepin.com/

Made by Adoos with Julian Martinez as CEO.

- Connect to and keep in touch with your friends.
- Make new friends and find old ones.
- Meet people from your town / city and from around the world.
- Meet people who share your interests.

http://nosuni.com
NosUni is an interactive facebook that allows you to better know people around you. Through nosUni you can share fotos, interact with friends, find people with interests similar to yours and exchange all types of information and pictures in a secure environment. NosUni is free. Among other things, in nosUni you can upload and share fotos, find people according to different criteria, messages, wall, and detailed privacy settings. We are working on additional features such as blogging and groups, which will be available soon.

http://tuenti.com/
Tuenti was originally called Who is Who. It was created by a group of university students who wanted to create a link between people with hobbies and interests in common. On September 28, 2006, it was renamed as Tuenti.com.

Tuenti is a virtual community, not open to the general public, to help people understand a bit better the world surrounding them. Tuenti allows you to pass on information between users in a funny and quick way. This enables you to extend your real life and build a stronger contact network that makes your everyday life easier.

This community offers you the possibility to contact old classmates and meet new people. You will be able to have chat conversations, send and receive e-mails, share pictures, and more features that you will discover little by little.

http://www.linkara.com/
The leading community on culture and hobbies.
Linkara is a free online community which was born with the purpose of creating a personal network where the members can get to know other members of their interest and share all kind of information.

In order to do so, Linkara.com provides its members with the ideal space to participate actively, and it intends to be a meeting point where the members can rate films, books and songs and read the comments made by other members.

Moreover, Linkara.com offers the option of searching other members according to their hobbies, interests and features, and they can be reached by an internal e-mail system or by instant messaging.

Contact details:
Linkara S.L.
Avenida Diagonal, 612
Barcelona
(Spain)

http://www.cielo.com/mundo/

Cielo.com is the best online community that connects people worldwide through networks of friends and family for everything from following local soccer matches to finding an exercise partner to learning about travel destinations in South America. While Cielo.com networking online has grown in popularity over the past year, now Cielo.com is reaching out to distinct international communities, namely the Italian, Portuguese, French, Romanian and Spanish-speaking global community from Argentina to Sweden, from Mexico to Spain or Japan. Cielo.com will help you to find friends all over the world.

With Cielo.com you can:

-build your own network of contacts who share your interests
-use built-in communication services
-create classified ads and get responses
-create your own event or attend to other members' events
-create clubs and invite people, who share your interests

http://conectados.com/

Conectados.com is the Spanish speaking community that brings you closer to your friends and makes your social network grow.

You can create your own space, share pictures, interests, feelings and meet the friends of your friends.

Conectados.com is your meeting point with people worldwide.

Everyone takes part in Conectados.com:

People who want to connect with friends

People who are searching for new friends

Study groups who need to communicate online between them

Working groups who want to interact in a virtual way

Families who want to keep in touch

Anyone willing to share something!

Run by a working group in different continents, Conectados.com does not have general headquarters.

http://www.egrupos.net/

EGrupos is one of the most vibrant and complete Spanish-speaking users community.

Create your own page, mail lists, *blogs*, polls, organize meetings, post your photos, favourite videos, songs, and artists, keep your friends list up-to-date and meet other people, post ads or auctions, take a look at what other people post or sell, chat, etc.

EGroups gets over a thousand new users a day. Currently they have 2,4 million users.

EGroups is an AR Networks and eListas Networks service.

AR Networks is a company founded in April 1999 in Sunnyvale, California, in the heart of Silicon Valley, by two Spanish internet experts who had previously worked in Harvard University, Nestcape Communications and eBay Inc. EListas Networks is the subsidiary company of AR Networks, founded in Spain in April 2000. AR Networks is one of the providers' leaders in cooperative services to management and distribution lists, offering to both big and small companies through www.eListas.net the most complete package available in the market to manage all communication needs and distribution tools for message and survey generation. In December 2003, eListas hosted more than twenty-five thousand distribution lists from hundreds of customers, distributing information to more than 42 million subscribers worldwide. EGrupos is an appendix to the eListas service. The mail lists (called "groups" in eGrupos) include tools for social and business networks.

http://www.wamba.com/
Wamba is a new wave and a new internet community founded in Palma de Mallorca, Spain. It was founded by two young businessmen in the internet sector — Matías de Tezanos (well known internet businessman) and Enrique Dubois (music amateur, founder of the technology enterprises Premium and SXNetworks and visionary and manager of Wamba).

It was created to compete with American corporations in the social network services market, as well as in video, photo and blog viewing and storage, from a local focus that encourages user generated content.

In Spanish, German, French, and Italian.
Social adress: Palma de Mallorca, Balearic Islands, Spain. C/ Jaime III, 5, 4°B. 07012.
E-mail: wamba@wamba.com

DATING

www.gentenotable.com
This online personals service is a way for adults to meet each other. The service is provided by the owner of this web domain, and it includes forums, chats and internal mail messaging system, amongst others features.

Contact details:
E-mail: info@gentenotable.com
Tel: (+34) 952 814 317

http://moviligo.com/
Moviligo is a mobile dating service, which allows you to meet people, anytime and anywhere. The only thing that you need is a mobile to search for girls and guys worldwide and send them messages, flirt, chat and many more things.
This web site is powered by Mobile Dreams Factory, S.L., a leading company in content development, marketing services and technology operating in the mobile business. Founded in 2004 by a group of marketing, media, internet, and technology professionals, Mobile Dreams has offices in Spain and Mexico, along with a distribution network in the main regions of Europe, America and Asia, and USA.

Contact Details:
C/ Zurbano Nro. 92. 4°
28003 Madrid
Spain

Tel: +34 91.395.22.99
E-mail: europe@mdfactory.com

SPECIAL INTEREST

Sports

http://www.mybestplay.com/ (LS)
Sports network for players, coaches, trainers, managers or clubs worldwide, which offers the following services:

Spain
Gavanza, S.L.
Plaça Tirant lo Blanc, 7
08005 Barcelona
Tel: +34.93-224.04.84

Chile
Augusto Leguía, 100 oficina 801
Las Condes (Santiago)
Tel: +56.02.657.2517

Argentina
Av. Cordoba 3239 PB Of. C
C1187AAK Buenos Aires
Tel: +54.11 4963.0992

E-mail: info@mybestplay.com
Sports network for players, coaches, trainers, managers or clubs. info@mybestplay.com

Students

http://www.unilocus.com/
Unilocus is a social network specifically designed for college students. Imagine a giant and interactive graduation photograph with every student

in Spain. Aren't you curious? Unilocus is you, your friends, your classmates and every activity you might do together.

Contact: info@unilocus.com

http://www.estudiln.net/
EstudiLN.net, estudienlenco.net, domain in other countries and every sub domain belongs to the Ehssan Dariani, Dennnis Bemmann and Michael Brehm project. The goal of this project is to promote the creation of European universities networks, decrease the anonymity in universities (big ones) and offer an easy to use platform where students and their initiatives on local issues can be shared and organized for free.

Gran de Gracia, 15, 1° Ia
08012 Barcelona
Spain
ayuda@estudiln.net

Our address:
StudiVZ Ltd.
Saarbrücker Str. 38
10405 Berlin

Travel

http://viamedius.com/
Viamedius is a travellers' community based on the contributions made by all its members, whose main objective is sharing their travel experiences with each other. In Viamedius we think that travelling is a unique experience and only those who have the honour of having lived this wonderful experience are able to tell it. Travelling means a particular state of mind, a source of feelings that may be aroused both by a long trip around Africa and by a simple troll around the secret corners of your neighbourhood. In Viamedius you can easily get all the information related to these trips and get in touch with other travellers in order to share information of your interest.

How does it work? What kinds of trips are you looking for? You can find out about other travellers' experiences by searching by destination, type of trip or type of traveller. In the case of a more specific research, please use our search engine in order to get a more specific result.

Add a trip: your trips are our raison d'être, and you build www.viamedius. com Thanks to this option you can make your contributions to the webpage. First of all, you summarize your trip in a couple of lines, give it a title and add the pictures (in the case that you have them). Afterwards, you just select your destination, type of trip and type of traveller. These categories make it easier for other users to find similar trips. Eventually, you fill the form with your personal details. In the case that you have already done it, you just type your user name and your password.

My travel journal: This is a space where you can save your trips. And what's more, you have a private menu where you receive messages from other members and where you can share your pictures with the members of your choice.

Community: You can contact every member of the community.

Blackboard: An open space to leave your messages.

Advantages of using Viamedius: You have your own travel journal, a private space to save all the information and pictures about your trips. You can share the pictures of that special trip with your traveller companions; contact all those travellers who are registered in the page to get information about your next trip destination. Other travellers' experience is first-hand information about the destinations you are interested in, and this information could be very useful to start planning your trip. The different categories in which information is divided into will allow you to find a trip the suitable trip for you. So don't hesitate and share your travelling experiences!

Contact :
contacta@viamedius.com
viamedius@hotmail.com

Powered by Signia Technologies
Signia Technologies
C/Balmes 184, àtic 3ª
08006 Barcelona
Tel: 93 342 72 72
Fax: 93 394 04 32

Miscellaneous

http://www.mapalia.com (LS)

Hi An,

Here are our answers,

Yours,

Jose A. del Moral

-Founders & management
Alianzo Networks, which is a company based in Bilbao, Spain.

-Founding year & address/nationality
We are in the betatesting period, with one hundred people trying it out. We should start the network around the end of January. It is addressed to people living in the main cities of Spain.

-Target audience & membership level (number of users)
No data yet about users.
Target audience: people living in the ten largest cities of Spain.

-Top three countries in which the community is used
Spain

-Main technical features and possible features in the near future
Google Maps and Flickr mashup, personal contacts, personal ads, RSS, tags...

-Languages in which the service is available
Spanish, Catalan, Galician, and Basque, all of the languages officially spoken in Spain, together with English.

Alianzo Networks, S.L.
Madrid
Cava Baja, 27/4 - 28005 Madrid
E-mail: info@alianzo.com

Bilbao
Edificio Ilgner, C8 - 48902 Barakaldo – Bilbao

http://www./spaniards.es
Our mission is to help and connect all Spanish people who are living abroad, whether to study, for business or for pleasure, and those Spanish people who want to leave Spain temporarily or permanently.

VIDEO/ PHOTO

http://www.esflog.com/
EsFlog.com is a community of photologs. Members can create their own photolog, which is then connected to the favourite photologs of other members. You can then add comments to each photolog and watch other members comment on your photolog.

AZ Interactive S.L.
CIF n° B-61119442.
Apartado Correos 21027,
08010 Barcelona (España)

http://tu.tv

http://dalealplay.com/
Dalealplay is an online video streaming service that allows anyone to view, rate and share videos that have been uploaded by the members.

Powered by AdverNet S.L. Copyright (c) 1996–2006. This site is only available in Spanish.

Contact details:
C/ Juan Ignacio Luca de Tena, 7, 2nd floor.
28027 Madrid
Spain
AdverNet S.L. C/ Juan Ignacio Luca de Tena n7 segunda planta 28027 Madrid
Spanish YouTube clone (only in Spanish).

MOBILE

http://www.festuc.com/
Founded by the same management team behind eConozco, Funtropy Sl is a consulting company specialized in games for your mobile phone (mososo).

Festuc is a community of friends which allows you to communicate where you are, whenever you want, to your circle of friends. You can chat, meet, make a profile, look for new users...

Festuc is a mobile community made up of groups of friends. By using your mobile phone and the potential of social networks you can contact new people and get to know friends of friends.

Festuc offers you one of the newest services in mobile social networking: you tell Festuc which bar or club you are in at that moment and this allows you to know which bar, area and city your friends are partying at. This also enables you to view profiles of other members who are nearby. Festuc will only locate you under your request.

Festuc is a service offered by Funtropy sl, a Spanish consultancy firm for the development and distribution of Mobile Phone games and applications. This company was founded in Barcelona in 2004.

Festuc was founded in May 2006.

SWEDEN

FRIENDS

www.playahead.se
Playahead is a community that was founded by three teenagers in Helsingborg, Sweden, in 1998. At that time there was no meeting place for teenagers on the web. The site grew rapidly and became very popular and was sold to a company in Stockholm. Playahead was re-acquired in 2002 and rebuilt, using completely new technology, and the old idea of an online meeting place was revived.

http://trig.com/
Communities thrive on networking. The first step of networking is finding others to network with. Trig has a good browse page, where you can add more browse categories if you think any of them are important. It's an easy way to find exactly what, or who, you are looking for.

Since you can put tags on almost anything on Trig, we also made it possible to find friends, post blogs, and images, by tags. It makes browsing Trig a little more creative, since you can look for people (and other things) who have been tagged, for example, "stylish" or "hilarious".

"The next step is to actually do the networking. Besides sending messages, comments and friend requests, you can chat with people directly with the inbuilt instant messenger."
Trig also makes it possible to let your personality show. Here are a couple of things you could start with:

- Skins: You should decide what your profile looks like. By changing profile skin, your profile will look original and new.
- Blog: Creating your own blog is easy. Your thoughts are as important as anyone else's, so start posting.
- Gallery: Fill your gallery with images. Private ones for your close friends, public images for the rest of us.

press@trig.com

Trig.com is owned and run by Adocca Entertainment AB and is based in Stockholm, Sweden

www.lunarstorm.se
1.2 Members. In Swedish only.

http://www.buzzpal.com/
If you love music and partying, then BuzzPal is for you.
BuzzPal offers a revenue sharing program, which means you can get paid when other people view your pages. The better your content, the more your page views, the more you make. City guides and local music and entertainment features will launch by the end of the year, starting with the USA and Europe.

What Other Sites Will Be In The BuzzPal Network?
BuzzPal.mobi (mobile), BuzzPal.tv (TV & video), BuzzLove.com (dating) and LatinBuzz.com (Hispanic).

Founded by Chris Comella aka Chrisco, an American living in Sweden. Our office will likely be in San Francisco / Silicon Valley or Europe (Sweden or London). We're currently circling our investors, partners and team members and expect to launch by July 4th, 2007.

DATING

http://e-kontakt.se/
Dating site operated by Intodate International AB
Postadress:
Box 2235
600 02 Norrköping
Contact: info@e-kontakt.se.

SPECIAL INTEREST

Gaming & 3D

http://www.entropiauniverse.com
The Entropia Universe is a massive online virtual universe. Set in a distant Sci-Fi future where man has developed amazing mind powers, participants assume the roles of colonists who must develop the untamed planet of Calypso. Adventure across continents from snow covered mountain tops to ancient underground caverns. Discover an outback populated with fierce and dangerous creatures; the wilderness on Calypso is also rich in minerals and ore, all of which can be lucrative sources of income for would-be colonists. The Real Cash Economy means that the Entropia Universe currency, the PED, has a fixed exchange rate with the US dollar, where 10 PED = 1US$. Real funds can easily be deposited and exchanged for PEDs; the currency that allows participants to acquire virtual land and equipment to develop their virtual character (avatar) inside the Entropia Universe. The outposts, cities, and auction on the planet Calypso are busy trading hubs where tools, weapons, minerals and a multitude of other items are bought and sold by adventuring pioneers. The wide range of professions available to colonists allows hairdressers, crafters, and store owners to find a spot on the bustling frontier. Skills and resources make lively trade on Calypso. All your economic data is securely contained in your own personal account and withdrawals of accumulated PED can easily be made into your own currency.

SWITZERLAND

BUSINESS

www.rezonance.ch
French speaking professional network in Switzerland.

FRIENDS

http://genevaonline.ch/ (LS)

Will soon be transferred to www.glocalpeople.com

The community was founded by members SiteAdmin & Nir (who also set up Sindy). Both of us have (semi) respectable and (very) stressful full time day jobs. GenevaOnline ('GoL') is a community of friendly people who want to meet & help other friendly people. The minimum age is 23. This is not a dating site. The site is in English.

Hello An,

Some info about GenevaOnline.ch below.
Please let me know if you need additional info.

Thanks

Oded

GenevaOnline.ch (soon to be re-named 'Glocals.com') is a niche community for 'Glocal' people: people who are well travelled and 'Global' and who want to feel 'Local' wherever they are. We specifically cater to 25–35 y/o English speakers who work for multinational companies and their families.

The idea was born of its founders own needs. Nir and Oded Ofek (brothers) are both 'Glocals', who moved to NYC and Geneva, and there felt the need to connect with more people like them and to quickly feel 'Local' in their new cities. GenevaOnline.ch was launched in March 2006, in Geneva Switzerland, and quickly gained a loyal following among the Glocals in Geneva.

Currently (March 07) we are present in Geneva only, with 10K members (5% of the local population!). Of these 10K members:

95% live in Geneva.
9% are Swiss, 91% originally come from other countries.
50% logged in last week, 70% logged in the past month.

The community currently generates 1.1 Million page views per month and is ranked 35,000 by Alexa.com.

Membership on GenevaOnline.ch is free, and Revenues are generated via advertising.

The technology behind the site is proprietary, but pretty standard, and the key thing that makes the community stand out are the members, who are all indeed Glocals and who generate all content and activity. We do not accept members under 23 years old, the site is in English only, and members who are not active are deleted in order to maintain a real and active community.

In 2007, we will roll out the platform into five more cities, to spread the joy...we hope by the time the book is out and you read this, there will be a local Glocals.com chapter next to you already...(-:

mailto:admin@genevaonline.ch

http://www.meinbild.ch/ (LS)
Scooba GmbH
meinbild.ch head office
Artherstr. 60
6405 Immensee/SZ
E-mail: info@meinbild.ch
Fax: ++41 (43) 433 02 84

SPECIAL INTEREST

Travel

http://www.youtourist.net/
Social Network Platform for the Tourism Industry

UNWTO and WISeKey announced an agreement today to expand the use of traveller identification and authentication technologies in the multibillion dollar tourism sector.

This collaboration builds on the Public Private Partnership agreement signed by UNWTO and Microsoft in 2006. The partners will seek to deliver YouTourist as a unique e-Tourism Social Network (youTourist. net). Based on WISeKey Digital Identification and Microsoft Cardspace technologies, this platform allows tourist to connect with one another to exchange information based on the UNWTO's Global Code of Ethics for Tourism.

The Code is a blueprint for safeguarding the resources upon which tourism depends, ensuring that its benefits are equitably shared in the spirit of the Millennium Development Goals. It sets out guiding principles for governments, destinations, tour operators, travel agents, tourism workers, developers, and travelers themselves.

YouTourist will encourage tourist exchanges of pictures, videos, and comments and give special communication opportunities for local communities and travel companies involved in the whole chain of tourism development. Crosscutting areas in poverty alleviation can be greatly aided by introducing the type of technology available for travel industry Trusted Social Networks. Digital Identification for secure participation will be a key element.

Marcelo Risi, UNWTO Press and Communications Department,
Tel: +34-91-567-8193 / +34-91-567-8194 / Fax:+34-91-567-8218,
comm@unwto.org
www.unwto.org

Miscellaneous

http://lautundspitz.ch
Social network for partying

http://beta.plazes.com/
The Plazes website automatically detects your location via your computer network and connects you to people and places nearby. See people in your area, discover other locations and follow the whereabouts of your friends.

Based in Zurich, Switzerland.

THE NETHERLANDS

BUSINESS

http://www.picnicnetwork.org/
In a true high level conference tradition, Picnic has created a network for Picnic delegates. The exception is that the Picnic Network functions also as an online social network, bringing together entrepreneurs, researchers and creatives from the cross media world.

As an online social network, its sole purpose is to amplify individual member's visibility internationally. It serves them as a database of affiliated persons and organisations, used to build lasting social and/or professional relationships with other participants.

This website consists of a public face-book, containing profiles of Picnic speakers, partners, delegates and Picnic team members. The Network's focus is on individual persons, simultaneously supporting the presentation of their organisations and projects.

For questions about this website, please mail to PICNIChelp@mediamatic.nl

Cross Media Week Foundation
Herengracht 386
1016 CJ Amsterdam
the Netherlands
E-mail: info@crossmediaweek.org

Tel: +31 20 320 5813
Fax: +31 20 797 7901

http://www.bizzies.nl/
Founded on June 4th 2007 by Diederik Heinink. Professional online network by and for Dutch people.

http://www.dgacontact.nl/

Two Dutch entrepreneurs met in May 2004. André Maljaars from Leaderboard and Coen Meischke from JCMPensions were both convinced that networking for SME-entrepreneurs could be organised more effectively, without extensive traveling. Their vision was to provide an onlinebusiness club for entrepreneurs only where 'no salesman will call'. Like all entrepreneurs they visited numerous network events and became frustrated by how little effective these meetings are. As a result, they founded dgacontact bv.

DGAcontact is a Dutch online business club where entrepreneurs write their own profile. Members can search throughout the protected database and connect and communicate with entrepreneurs with two clicks of a mouse. The membership offers you a mix of online and 'traditional networking' where interesting events are organised and where you can meet fellow-entrepreneurs. On the website you can check who is who and who is coming to these events, which increases the effectiveness of networking.

In summer 2005, they decided to partner with Stephen Howard and Bas Welles from BDIS Ltd. and founded Foundercontact International Ltd. That is the international networking initiative for European entrepreneurs. Foundercontact now has offices at Amsterdam, Budapest, London, New Delhi, and Maarn in The Netherlands.

president: Coen Meischke
Amersfoortseweg I
3951 LA Maarn
Tel: 0113 21 85 66
E-mail meischke@dgacontact.nl

http://www.foundercontact.com/

Foundercontact is a personal tool for better contacts, more competence and the provisioning of capital. Our database with entrepreneurs is growing every day. Currently we communicate regular with approx. five thousand entrepreneurs coming from fifty-six countries all over the world. You can choose the service level that fits you most with FC Guest, FC Xpress, FC Business and FC Executive. Our customers have companies in business segments like industry, bio-chemical, medical, production, business services, financial services, export, construction, wholesale, and raw materials.

Unique Proposition of foundercontact

1. Membership only possible for entrepreneurs and business owners
2. foundercontact stands for
    -better quality of contact moment
    -customer intimacy (1 on 1 marketing)
    -sharing of competence, innovation (co-production)
    -international network linked with national networks
    -personal tool for contacts, competence and capital
3. It multiplies individual networks of entrepreneurs.
4. With our capital gate service we can bring you into contact with
    otential investors (network of 3,500+(!) and still growing).
5. Foundercontact is an online business club for entrepreneurs.
6. The entrepreneur is in the driving seat (no salesman will call).
7. Foundercontact is an easy-to-use search and communication
    platform for business development abroad.

Foundercontact International Ltd.

Andre J. Maljaars, ceo & co-founder
Mobile: +31 6 22 780 399

Klaus Oestreicher, marketing & communication
Tel: +49 92 41 808 28 50

Registered Office:
72 New Bond Street
Mayfair
London W1S 1RR
United Kingdom

Visiting address:
WTC Tower C, floor 3
Schiphol Boulevard 107
NL 1118 BG Amsterdam Airport
The Netherlands
Mail: info@foundercontact.com

http://www.aglocoworld.eu

Dear An,

I put in my best effort to describe Agloco, because I wanted to uphold the quality of your book. I am very pleased with the result and hope the text will find a good spot in your book. Thank you again for your offer to contribute and please keep me in the loop as to when your book is ready so I can order a few copies!

Warmest regards,
Ray Germers

Agloco is an Internet based infomediary that enables businesses to deliver highly targeted messages to consumers. It is also an international community of Internet users whose active members are rewarded for surfing the Web with the Agloco Viewbar software and for referring their friends to join Agloco. These rewards take a number of forms. By becoming an Agloco member and downloading the proprietary Viewbar software, you benefit from Viewbar content tailored to your interests, as well as discounts and deals offered by its sponsors, and useful Internet navigation tools built into the Viewbar software.

Many of us are familiar with online social networks, such as MySpace and Facebook, as well as online professional networks, like LinkedIn and Ecademy. These networks are based around communities communicating with one another in the personal (social) or professional environment.

Agloco is an Economic Network. An Economic Network is based on similar roots, but also *adds* the driving principle that individuals who have joined together as a group can be economically stronger than the individuals alone. This is the driving principal behind any group trying to become stronger by joining forces: business groups (like trade associations and the Chamber of Commerce), countries (like the formation of NAFTA and the EU), or people (like labor unions and buying co-ops).

For individuals it is simple. They can demand more from the entities that have been controlling them and finally achieve the power they deserve. Much like segments of the labor force saw they were being exploited one hundred years ago, today we see the Internet consumer being economically exploited by many Internet companies. Agloco wants to change that.

Individual Internet users are already creating value all over the Internet, and only now are they coming together as members of Agloco to claim that value. The purpose of an economic network is for the members to acquire as much of the value they create as possible, and they shouldn't have to change their Internet usage behavior to get it.

This is the whole basis for creating this company. The Internet holds many unique and valuable ways for individuals to "interact with each other and with groups." Wikipedia is showing this with free access to information on the Internet. Agloco can accomplish the same thing with free access to value created on the Internet.

Earning money for surfing the web is just the beginning. The Viewbar software allows you to have your own personal Internet infomediary. A revolutionary tool that delivers content, deals, faster searches, special discounts, and shopping off- and on-line that's relevant to you. And even though the Viewbar software works for the user, the user is the one who gets paid.

Plus, you are completely in control. The Viewbar does not require you to change your Web viewing habits in any way and simply sits at the bottom of your screen while you surf the net. You can minimize or close the Viewbar at any time, simply by clicking on the minimize button. Most importantly, surf with the confidence that Agloco will never divulge your personal information.

Agloco makes money for its Members in many ways:

Search: Every time you use the Viewbar to do an Internet search, Agloco earns money from the search engine providers (for example, Google pays as much as $0.10 on average for each search that is directed to its search engine).

Advertising: The Viewbar itself displays ads that are targeted based upon the websites you're visiting. When you click on an ad and make a purchase, Agloco receives a referral fee, which is passed on to their members (individual members do not receive any compensation for clicking on ads in the Viewbar, and the Viewbar can detect if someone is clicking ads in a fraudulent manner).

Transaction commissions: Many major retailers pay commissions when you refer customers who make a purchase. Agloco collects that commission and passes it on to its members (for example, Amazon pays an 8.5% commission to most websites who refer customers and has cut deals for even larger percentages. The bigger the Agloco community, the better commission can be negotiated for its members).

Software distribution: Numerous software companies pay websites to encourage the download of new software releases (for example, Adobe's Flash and Acrobat Reader software), and trial versions of new programs. Agloco members not only get access to the latest and coolest software, they get paid for it.

Service distribution: Many online service providers will look to the Agloco community as a source of new and active users for their services (for example, eBay, Skype, and PayPal, among others, all pay fees to people who help them recruit new active users to their services).

Product distribution: When members agree to use a product, such as cell phones, high-tech gadgets, office supplies, new credit cards or financial services, Agloco can collect referral fees. Some companies even offer special rebate and cash-back programs.

Agloco recognizes the value of the community

Today's hottest Internet businesses are all about the power of social networks. Companies like MySpace, Facebook, and YouTube have become worth billions because businesses have realized that these social networks are generating huge advertising and marketing opportunities. As these social networks grow, the economic potential for its owners — and the advertisers who target the site's users — is remarkable.

The users created the community, but where's their share of the profit?

It was from this question that Agloco set out to create the Internet's first Economic Network, harnessing the power of Internet-based social networks to directly benefit the members who help to create the community.

Sincerely,

R.L.J. Germers B.Sc.
The Netherlands
www.aglocoworld.eu

FRIENDS

www.jouwvrienden.nl

http://funkybabes.nl/ (LS)
Joop Geesinkweg 125
1096 AT Amsterdam
mailto:emanuel@funkybabes.nl

http://www.xseno.nl
Targetgroup is 13 to 21 year-olds. People older than 30 years are not admitted to the site. Founded on January 1st 2006.

http://www.whoozz.com/
Portal with community for youngsters.
Address:
Jan van Galenstraat 25
3115JG te Schiedam

http://www.workmates.nl/

http://www.nieuwemensenlerenkennen.nl/

www.cu2.nl

http://www.sugababes.nl/

www.hyves.nl (LS)

Ex Startphone founded by Koen Kam (ex- Hubhop), Floris Rost van Tonningen and Raymond Spanjar (both ex-IEX) in 2004. They have around 3 million accounts.

hyvers@hyves.nl
raymond@hyves.nl

www.facepic.nl
From Koara Media. Owned by Nick Long.

http://www.connected2friends.nl (LS)
Founded by Roy Christiani. Targeted to 13 to 23-year-olds.
info@connected2friends.nl

http://www.ilikeu2.nl/ (LS)
ILikeu2 started a couple of years ago as an English-speaking datingsite on www.ilikeu2.com, which became an instant success.
Through listening to our visitors we decided to start a Dutch-speaking version, which became a social network rather than a dating site. ILikeU2.com is still owned by us but is being managed by a third party.
info@ilikeu2.nl

ILikeu2.nl is one of several projects of Erik Hoekstra en Chris van de Steeg.

http://www.apura.org/ (LS)
Welcome to Apura Networks, the network to Suriname and the rest of the world.

Apura is the name of a native Indian village in the heart of West-Suriname, a beautiful part of the country inhabited by the indigenous people of Suriname, the Indians. Apura is also the name of the first Indian Arowak captain of the village. Networks is derived from 'networking', something we see as an effective way to bring people together.

Apura currently has: 1256 active members

Management:
Michael Loswijk B.Sc., Secretary, Treasurer and Director Content

Miguel Rodrigues B.Sc., Founder, President and Director Networks
Ir. Steven Coutinho, Board Member and Director Research
Michael Dooijes, B.A., Economics, Director Business Development

Post address
Berlaarstraat 175
1066 PL, Amsterdam
The Netherlands

Tel: +31 (0)6-24736961
Fax: +31 (0)20-6154083
E-mail: info@apura.org / miguel@apura.org

DATING

http://paiq.nl

http://www.desnackbar.nl/
Datingsite
De Snackbar was created by TED.
TED is a free newspaper for teenagers which is distributed at three hundred locations in the Netherlands. More info on TED can be found at www.ted.nl .
In De Snackbar "snackies" (members of De Snackbar) are weekly introduced to one another based on their profile and click and surfbehavior.

SPECIAL INTEREST

Good Causes

http://www.aidpeople.org/
Why Aidpeople.org?

Did you also lose track of most people you worked with in the past, in your home country or when you worked overseas in a developing country or disaster zone? Well … we often did, so.. let's search, find and re-connect at www.aidpeople.org !

What is Aidpeople.org?

Aidpeople.org is an exciting new online community for people involved in humanitarian aid and development work, where we all can keep in touch, network, find info and share knowledge.

Main Features of Aidpeople.org:

Find people like former colleagues or people that share the same interests as yourself.

Share Aid Info in the aidpeople.org forums and theme groups.

Publish your personal Blog with your writings about humanitarian aid.

Members can also search and add training and study info and links to other interesting humanitarian information available on the web.

Who is aidpeople.org for?

Anyone who has any links with the humanitarian sector, from people working in relief and development, to universities, to suppliers. Whether you're looking for an old colleague, want a new job, have a position to advertise, a product to sell or need some advice about the program you're working on, this site is the place for you.

How is aidpeople.org different to anything else on the web?

Almost all other sites for the international aid community are information-based. The kind of work done by the humanitarian sector is all about people: beneficiaries, colleagues, governments, suppliers, and donors. Aidpeople.org is the first ever website for the humanitarian sector to recognize this aspect and to bring people together so they can network. The more people you know, the bigger access you have to information and resources.

Aidpeople.org is just starting out on its journey to connect people from all over the world of relief and development work. The more people who join this online community, the more contacts can be made and the more information and experience can be shared. Currently there are already 1,500+ members from all over the world who signed up as members. But within the first year, we expect to have more than twenty-five thousand members sign up. If each of those introduces just four friends and those four introduce again four more friends, well, you can see how quickly the network will grow.

Who is behind Aidpeople.org?

The idea of an online community for people in the humanitarian sector was that of Dutchman Martijn Hekman. Martijn, who is currently working in Sri Lanka for an international relief and development agency, has enlisted the help of other aid workers who are as excited about the future of aidpeople. org as he is. Aidpeople.org is an initiative of the 2inspire Foundation based in the Netherlands.

Music

http://www.twones.com/ (LS)
Twones is an online matching platform where people meet people though their music taste. Music is sticky, personal and your music taste is changing all the time. Everybody can join and find out who they match with. Who doesn't love music?

How it works:
The Twones application software uploads a users playlist to the Twones database. At Twones.com you can view other users' tunes and see with whom you match by music taste. You can connect with their connections, read their profiles and make new friends.
diederik@twones.com

Parents

http://www.zooof.com (LS)
With Zooof you can discover, expand and maintain your family ties!

Hi An,

We are still beta, so we are really in the beginning. Some information:

Zooof.com b.v. was founded on 22-09-2005 in Amsterdam by:

Rob Asmus
Stefan Leenen
Jean-Paul Busker

Management:
Jean-Paul Busker

All Dutch nationality

Address:
Zooof.com b.v.
1 Helmersstraat 177
1054 DS Amsterdam
0031-206208888

Target audience: worldwide 14–90

Languages: 35

Technical features: try it :-)!

Users: at the moment it is invitation only, we have four hundred beta users in forty-nine countries. After the beta stage, the site will be open for everybody.

Zooof.com
Max Euweplein 44
1017MB
Amsterdam
The Netherlands
+31206208888

info@zooof.com

Students

http://www.schoolpagina.nl/

www.schoolbank.nl
Founded in 2002.

Miscellaneous

http://www.dienstmakkers.nl
"Classmates" for the Dutch army

http://www.edacteur.com (LS)
As a user of this website you can freely publish multimediafiles, such as: texts, documents, pictures, videos, sound, music, software, and games. You determine the subject of your publications. You are rewarded by your viewers with coins. These coins can be changed into euros afterwards. You can download, read & play the files of others as well.

Feiko Clockstraat 166
9665 BJ Oude Pekela
info@edacteur.com

http://www.yelloyello.com/ (LS)
YelloYello is an alternative to the Yellow Pages; it is a social network and a business guide all in one. YelloYello was founded by Joost Hietbrink and Mik Nijhuis.

Hoogstraat 31d
3011PE Rotterdam
Tel: +31 06-41216660
feedback@yelloyello.com

http://www.djguide.nl/

http://www.seeyoudance.nl/

Launched in February 2007. Social network for the dance scene; you can make your profile, win free tickets...

http://globaldutch.com
Online invitation only community that connects Dutch people abroad

http://nlborrels.com
NLBorrels is an independent global network of Dutch expatriate professionals and entrepreneurs dedicated to increasing social interaction, career advancement, and exchange of information of interest to the Dutch community living abroad. The NLBorrels organization was founded by Sander Raaymakers in 2001.

What we do
NLBorrels organizes frequent formal and informal "borrels" (networking events), parties and sporting events through its network of local chapters, and we are represented in eighteen cities: Amsterdam* (NL), Barcelona* (ES), Boston, Cannes (FR), Chicago, Cincinnati, Houston, Los Angeles, London (UK), Milano (IT), New York City, Palo Alto, Philadelphia, Rio de Janeiro (BR), San Francisco, San Diego, Seattle, St. Petersburg (RU) & Washington DC.

Membership
We presently count roughly 3800 members in the USA and another 2200 in fifty countries world-wide* (Nov '05). Only registered members receive an invitation for the events we organize, but guests are always welcome. Registration and membership are presently free.

VIDEO/ PHOTO

www.videostart.nl

www.filmpjes.nl

TESTIMONIAL

Virtual Holland by Michiel Gerbranda

The Dutch increasingly seem to find their way to virtual social networks. Especially private networks such as Hyves attract a large following. The reason: the Dutchman seeks attention.

Virtual social networks are largely used to maintain existing contacts and to find new ones. By collecting a large number of 'friends' and the intense communication through text, image and sound, users build their personal image. Because this image is visible to the outside world, social networks are capable of supporting the personal identity of its users. Hence why these networks will increasingly play an important role in our daily life. Apart from Hyves, MySpace, LinkedIn, Xing, and SecondLife are the most widespread social networks in the Netherlands.

The popularity of virtual social networks has caught the attention of Dutch companies as well. By way of experiment ING and Randstad have already opened up on SecondLife. In an attempt to be innovative, more and more Dutch companies try to do 'something' with virtual networks, unfortunately without having an idea of the goal they want to reach. Because of this, the potential of virtual social networks is still largely untapped. Companies choose to use virtual social networks but relapse into traditional ways when using them. The power of social networks lies in communication and knowledge sharing between the users — companies should not expect to influence this process as they can in the traditional media. It doesn't make sense to push a commercial message into a network (traditional communication) when companies should be earning the attention of these online users. Companies should build their image (create a message) and then give the users a reason and a platform to communicate.

Michiel Gerbranda; Afgestudeerd aan de opleiding Marketing Management te Tilburg (Holland). Specialisme: virtuele sociale netwerken en arbeidsmarktcommunicatie.

TURKEY

BUSINESS

http://www.cember.net/login.php

FRIENDS

www.zurna.com

http://www.yonja.com/
Yonja is founded and operated by a handful of entrepreneurs and technologists in Silicon Valley. Our investors and founders have backgrounds with leading technology companies such as IBM, Microsoft, Oracle, Siebel Systems, AMS, Sybase, and Digitas. Yonja's members range in age from 18 - 55+, more than 80% of whom are between 18 and 30. Yonja has 4 million members.

http://www.daveti.com/

DATING

http://siberalem.com/bulustur/anasayfa.asp

VIDEO/ PHOTO

http://www.vidivodo.com/
In Turkish and English. Launched on 25 December 2006. Vidivodo is the leading video sharing and broadcasting website that has stunning features like video mix, direct webcam recording, partner powered channels. Vidivodo aims to reach a broader scale of users and provide TV like experience to its subscribers. The company is privately held with funding from Itamae Interactive Technologies and strategically partnered with Retroturk Interactive Technologies in EMEA countries.

UNITED KINGDOM

BUSINESS

http://www.jaketm.org/site/dsp_default.cfm gay men
"The world's largest gay professional community"

Unlike any other gay site, we actively encourage members to get as much commercial benefit out of our technology as possible. Feel free to advertise your company, for jobs, sell stuff on the forums, or just use it to meet new people. Jake can be a really useful tool – and we're happy for anyone to benefit from it for free. When you login, you'll notice that people's profiles are divided into 'trusted' and 'constructed'. Trusted profiles are those where members use real names, a decent photo and where the intro doesn't read like a dating ad (we love Gaydar type sites – but Jake is different). You will find everyone from city boys and media people through to politicians on this site because it doesn't have any of the stigma usually attached to gay sites. Founded by Ivan Massow.

http://www.academici.net/
Address: 33 Grove Avenue., Birmingham B13 9RX, UK

http://www.projectstars.com
Projectstars is an online business community for enterprise professionals to share expertise, build relationships, and find projects. The projectstars network consists of over three hundred communities covering enterprise departments, topics and issues. We are dedicated to improving the careers of corporate professionals. Those who participate in the community own it. Every quarter we reward the top contributors with shares in the company. Membership is free and by invitation from an existing member.

Founded by Steve Purkiss in 2007.

http://www.firsttuesday.com/

First Tuesday was originally started as a UK networking forum for technology entrepreneurs and venture capitalists, which flourished during the dot-com era.

First Tuesday was started in London in October 1998 by Nick Denton, Adam Gold, Mark Davies and Julie Meyer and in Dublin by Marc Butterly and David Neville to hold networking events on the First Tuesday of each month.

In Ireland the First Tuesday Network is still successfully managed by Investnet ltd and has proved its value to the ICT community by thriving for over seven years and still not charging for membership!

The startup networking concept was without borders and rapidly, and organically, globalised based on very simple rules, however, with minimal formal structure. It rapidly became well-known globally as an important meeting place for dotcom entrepreneurs and investors.

First Tuesday organisations run by independent individuals and their companies developed in numerous other cities around the world, to develop a unique global network of affiliates.

At its height during the dot-com era, First Tuesday had five hundred thousand registered members on its websites through a branch network run and owned by local organisers in over one hundred cities. In Ireland the First Tuesday Network has approximately seven thousand members. You can contact us by e-mailing: david@firsttuesday.ie

First Tuesday and its affiliated networks continue to be run in a number of countries today, including the Czech Republic Prague Brno, Hungary Budapest, Ireland Dublin, Luxembourg Luxembourg, Norway Oslo, South Africa Johannesburg, Spain Barcelona, Switzerland Zurich Geneva, and others.

http://elgg.net (LS)
Elgg.net is the online social network for those interested in education, learning technology and new approaches to teaching and learning.
system@elgg.net

www.soflow.com (LS)
Soflow was founded in 2004 by Robert Loch and Paul Birch. Initially set-up as an online business network, Soflow has expanded its horizons

and today provides a space and tool-set to help people solve everyday business challenges. At the core of Soflow is Soflow Solutions including Soflow Missions, Soflow Connector and Soflow Ads. Soflow complements its Solutions package by hosting a number of Groups across a range of industry classifications. Soflow Solutions and Soflow Groups combine to form the backbone of a new and powerful force in digital media.

Our Address: Soflow Ltd, Wilmot House, St James Court, Friar Gate, Derby, DE1 1BT, United Kingdom

http://www.streakr.com/
London based
Neil Gould

http://www.business4brunch.com

http://www.network2connect.com/ (LS)
Online Business-2-Business networking website. Free and paying module.

Geoff Cox
Managing Director

Network2Connect is operated by N2C Limited, of 64 Castle Road East, Oldbury, Warley, West Midlands, B68 9BG

http://www.marzar.com/
Marzar is a social media platform for businesses and professionals. It was launched in August 2007 and has about one thousand members.

Marzar allows you to communicate with other professionals, create work groups and share files, source suppliers, access skills, syndicate press releases, and business articles, advertise your services, and much more.

Founded by John Horsley

Marzar Ltd
9 - 13 Cotton's Gardens
Shoreditch
London
E2 8DN
info@marzar.com
Ph: +44 (0)20 7729 9269

http://www.ecademy.com
Dear An,

I would be delighted to work with you on this. Thank you for your interest.
I have attached two Press Releases and also our Media Pack, which has not been finally edited yet, but for matters of speed, I have attached it.
Regarding your specific questions:

-Founders & management – also see attached Press Information for brief Biography

- *Penny Power – Founder*
- *Thomas Power – Chairman*
- *Glenn Watkins – CEO*

-Founding year & address/nationality

- *1998*
- *British origin, now in over eighty countries*

-Target audience & membership level (number of users)
See attached demographics report, av. Age 46, married, family, self employed, is the most frequent member.

-Top three countries in which the community is used

- *UK*
- *USA*
- *Belgium*

-Main technical features and possible features in the near future

- *Blogging*
- *MarketPlace*
- *Clubs for more intimacy*
- *Private messaging*
- *Skype and YouTube integration for increased communication*
- *Meeting Management for personal or group meetings, allows you to set up meetings for others to register to (in the future, we will add a feature to allow them to be chargeable so members can charge their time or for events).*

-Languages in which the service is available

- *English, as this is the Internet language and encourages countries to cross-fertilise and find common interests and business opportunities*

One thought for you and your revision, when reviewing the sites, I would suggest you look at whether they are community led or tools led; this has a bearing on whether members say they 'use' or 'belong' to a social network. Happy to have further talks about this, An.

Thank you again, An. I hope this is helpful. Have a great weekend.

With warm regards,
Penny Power
Founder and Director -Ecademy Limited

Read my Ecademy profile here:
http://www.ecademy.com/account.php?id=1001
http://www.ecademy.com — connecting business people for increased Emotional and Financial wealth.

http://www.w2forum.com/
When Josh Dhaliwal and Graham Brown started Wireless World Forum in 2001, they realised that few technology and media companies were able to access insight about how their consumers were being impacted by changing technologies and markets.

We set our goal to serve our clients through our understanding of consumers. That's why we are Passionate about consumers and believe that our experience in working with over seven hundred companies in sixty countries is a key cornerstone in the strategic developments of our clients.

Working with a wide range of clients has given us the ability to see commonality and parralels in market development and share this experience with emerging sectors, such as convergent telecoms media.

W2F Limited Coda Centre
189 Munster Road
Fulham
London
SW6 6AW
United Kingdom
Telephone: (+44) 207 386 3635
Fax: (+44) 207 386 3646

FRIENDS

www.frype.com

http://sharea.com/ (LS)
Sharea.com is an online community. It's a place to meet new people as friends, colleagues, and who knows – perhaps even lovers; share your favorite audio, images and videos online; send instant messages, record media Blogs and create a simple way to stay in touch with friends who are far away.

Suite 12, 2nd Floor, Queens House, 180 Tottenham Court Road, London, W1T 7PD, UK.

www.profileheaven.com (LS)
marketing@profileheaven.com

http://badoo.com/

Badoo operates a social network, offering users a set of tools to connect to its global community. The Badoo network is free to use for all members meeting the age criteria (over 18). Currently Badoo.com has more than 6 million members worldwide.

Queens House, 180 Tottenham Court Road
London, WIT 7PD,
United Kingdom
Phone: 442071086185

everyonesconnected.com
EveryonesConnected to meet like-minded people through friends and common interests. Free to join.

http://london.citysocialising.com/Default.asp
London

www.faceparty.com

http://www.mooble.com/
Mooble.com is a flash based social networking community.

Features:

- Chat (online, video, audio) with friends without downloading a single thing.
- Join an interest group or announce an event
- Share pictures of yourself with your friends or the world
- Blogging
- Personal voice greeting
- Speed Dating

Founded in March 2006. Based in England.

http://www.listal.com/ (LS)
Social network based around entertainment and media collections.

The London-based company launched in October 2005 and currently has 9,300 registered users. Listal was created by Tom Mascord.
tom@listal.com

http://www.passado.com
With more than 4 million members Passado is Europe's largest social networking community. Passado first launched in 2001 when two school friends looking to re-connect with other friends from their past set up what was soon to become the no 1 re-union site across Europe with over 4m people re-connecting with friends from school, university or work.

Over the years, Passado has developed to include new features and functions designed to give our members lots more ways to interact with one another such as blogging, photosharing, forums, and broadcasts, and today we have a vibrant community of people expressing their opinions, sharing information and having fun getting to know each other.

If you would like to contact us here at Passado, our e-mail address is: feedback@passado.com

Postal address is:

Passado Ltd.
8-10 Quayside Lodge,
William Morris Way,
London SW6 2UZ
Great Britain

http://asmallworld.net/publicpages
Erik Wachtmeister founded a SmallWorld as a private online community for like-minded individuals. Most networking communities are open. Ours is only by invitation. Trusted members who have existing social networks of quality in the real world extend the invitations. ASmallWorld offers a retreat that intimately allows members to enhance their networks and to reconnect with old friends.

ASmallWorld also offers trusted and select information. Most of our content is produced by our members who offer travel suggestions, feedback, lively forum discussions, and other topics of common interest. Features on the website include a forum of diverse topics, listings of events around the world, a personal messaging service, suggestions and user ratings for travel and restaurants, and city-based resources.

Since its inception in 2004, aSmallWorld has quickly expanded into a global community of trusted friends and information. Members range from entrepreneurial and business opinion makers to leaders in media, entertainment, fashion, the arts, and sports.

Start building your network.

Find friends you already know in our community. Start by going to My Network and view your inviter's network. Connect to those you already know. You can also view friends of friends. Also try searching the member list for friends. However, do not try to connect to members whom you don't know. Not only does this violate the trust and privacy of our community, but if three members decline your connection request, you won't be able to send any more.

Erik Wachtmeister, Chairman and Founder

Erik is the Founder and former CEO of Viking Internet, a UK listed investment vehicle. He has held senior corporate finance positions with Ladenburg, Thalmann in New York and Los Angeles, Rothschild in New York, and Lehman Brothers in London and New York. He received his MBA from INSEAD in 1983, and his BS in Foreign Service from Georgetown University in 1977.

Louise Wachtmeister, Marketing Director and Co-Founder

Prior to aSmallWorld, Louise worked at JKL Group, which is a leading PR Company in the Nordic region. In 2001, Louise completed her master thesis on branding at the Stockholm School of Economics. Additionally, Louise is a silver and gold medalist in the Swedish National Track Championships and has a long history of political activism holding elected positions with the Stockholm City Hall and District Court. She also was the President of the largest chapter of the Conservative Youth Party in Stockholm during four years and participated actively in two elections, including the election of Sweden's entry into the European Union in 1994.

aSmallWorld Ltd
Eagle House, 110 Jermyn Street
London SW1
support@asmallworld.net

http://www.diamondlounge.com/
Diamond Lounge is a place for interesting, professional people who want to network, do business and let their hair down in total privacy.

Members pay a flat membership fee of £30/€45/$60 a month.

Diamond Lounge Ltd
94 New Bond Street
London W1S 1SJ
Tel: + 44 (0) 20 7930 7777
Fax: + 44 (0) 20 7990 7907
E-mail: -info@diamondlounge.com

http://www.outorin.org/ (LS)
An,

We cannot give you detailed information on our user, members etc., since this is a private network. We will try to answer your questions as much as possible and would also like to get more information about your proposed publication.

-Founders & management
The founding members are German and UK nationals from important aristocratic background

-Founding year & address/nationality
The site and the company were founded in 2004, and is Uk based

-Target audience & membership level (number of users)
Our target audience is international high net worth individuals and aristocrats; the sites main goal is to bring these members together and to exchange potential lifestyle and business leads.

The site will be limited to ten thousand members, who are evaluated in respect to their credentials and background; each member has a rating. Members who are able to prove their background with social and financial references are favored. We are the only gated online community bringing these individual together, so they are able to network on a serious social and business level.

-Top three countries in which the community is used
Germany, UK, Middle East

-Main technical features and possible features in the near future
E-mail, Auction, Chat, Forums, Networking Features, City, and Travel Guides etc.

-Languages in which the service is available
Currently only in English

Best regards,

OutOrIn Management

contact@outorin.org

Out or In, has the strictest membership criteria of any Gated Community Site on the Internet. The Site access is free for any applicant fulfilling the necessary criteria. Some of the criteria necessary to be granted site access include the following:

- Minimum Age for any Applicant is 25 years.
- Applicants need to be based in a major city.
- Male applicants need to be members of at least one private "Members Only" Club.
- Applicants need proof to have attended a reknown prestigious university or boarding school.
- Applicants need to have a strong network of social contacts on the highest level.

DATING

http://www.manjam.com/ gay men
Manjam is a unique social network for dating, work, and travel. Promote yourself, your talents and lifestyle through a network of like-minded people.

Powered by Juxmedia Ltd
BM 2558, London,
WC1N 3XX,

United Kingdom
Tel: +44 (0) 870 4323 087
Fax: +44 (0) 870 4321 389

dblock@dblock.org
Daniel Doubrovkine is CEO

http://www.bentlads.com/default.aspx gay men
All three from Juxmedia Ltd, BM 2558, London, WC1N 3XX, United
Kingdom

http://www.ohlalaguys.com/
Dating for gay men.

Powered by Juxmedia Ltd, BM 2558, London, WC1N 3XX, United Kingdom
Tel: +44 (0) 870 4323 087
Fax: +44 (0) 870 4321 389

http://www.outeverywhere.com/ lesbians & gay men
Based in the UK

http://www.someonejewish.com
Someonejewish.com is an online communication venue operated and owned
by JMT Ventures Limited - 5th Floor, Grosvenor House, 1 High Street,
Edgware, Middlesex HA8 7TA, UK

SomeoneJewish is the UK Jewish dating service where you can find, schmooze,
and meet other Jewish people. SomeoneJewish is 100% dedicated to Jewish
dating and Jewish singles.

http://quechup.com
03 November 2005: Quechup is the first of many websites being launched
by iDate Corporation. Quechup is already growing fast in the U.K. and

is rapidly starting to attract members from around the world. What makes Quechup.com stand out against other dating sites is its unique integration of mobile technology, allowing members to receive profiles and notifications through their mobile phones. Where previously such sites confined people to being in front of a computer, Quechup allows them to take the experience with them via their mobile phone, in order to be more convenient and useful to people's busy lifestyles. Mobile services currently include notifications and alerts direct to members' mobile phones through SMS (Short Messaging System) or, if they choose, via MMS (multimedia message service) technology, which allows for photos, members' profiles, sound clips, and, in the future, video to be sent direct to members' mobile phones. Once the services are well established, iDate plans to take mobile integration one step further, allowing members to SMS each other directly via Quechup, while keeping their mobile numbers private, something especially important to women using online dating services.

Attention! This site sends invitation e-mails to your entire addressbook without your consent when you try to check who of your contact is already using this service.

SPECIAL INTEREST

Books

http://www.booktribes.com/ (LS)
Launched in December 2006.
Everyone knows the best way of discovering new books is through word of mouth. Trouble is that it's booksellers and publishers who seem to have the loudest voices in deciding what we should read. It's no secret that publishers pay big book chains to give prominence to titles they want to push. Online booksellers have their own agendas too. Things aren't much better when it comes to radio and television bookclubs where they tell you what your next book is to be. Sorry, but how weird is that?

Isn't it time there was a place where a reader can speak to reader? A place where you can find people with shared – or wildly different – tastes. Where you can see who loves what and who's reading what, right now in real time.

Where you can click your favourites, badmouth duds, rate, review, and tag over two million titles. Where groups decide what they are going to read. Where you can keep quiet ... or start or join debates and message other members with top tips or whatever you damn well like, frankly. A place, above all, of honest opinions – not marketing spin.

This place is Booktribes.

Booktribes is new. It's dedicated to the joy of reading. And it's entirely independent. We're not tied to any bookseller, publisher, internet search engine or anything. We're not trying to sell you books; only to make it easier for you to savour them. Our main aim is to put our users in charge of what they read and what they think about what they read. To cut out the hype and get to the real deal. The site is a work in progress. If you're not happy with the way we're doing things, we'll do them differently. That's a promise, so be brutal with your comments. You don't need to spare our feelings.

Our other main aims are:

A – to help you find great new ideas about what to read in a way that's never been possible before – the biggest personal recommendation network anywhere. Our search engine is not perfect, but it's already pretty cool and pretty clever. For starters, we have a database of 2.5m books and rapidly growing numbers of reader recommendations. It will get better the more people join;

B – to give you your own personal book space where you can rate books, write about what you like and don't like, and share your comments with other readers;

C – to put you in touch with those who share your reading tastes – or maybe don't .

Mike Dixon - mike.dixon@booktribes.com

Fashion

http://osoyou.com/
Fashion network to be launched in the summer of 2007 by Dawn Bebe.

OMG Ltd
22 Stukeley Street
London
WC2B 5LR

http://iqons.com/ (LS)
IQONS is a new on-line fashion community that aims to have the same impact on fashion as MySpace had on music. Launched in January 2007. Founded by Rafael Jimenez, Suran Goonatilake, and Diane Pernet.

Dear An,

Thanks for your patience !
Here is a brief overview of IQONS.com:

> *-Founders & management: Rafael Jimenez and Suran Goonatilake (cofounders)*
> *-Founding year & address/nationality: February 2007 in London/Paris*
> *-Target audience & membership level (number of users): fashion, design, and creative industries professionals and aficionados (about 10,000 members)*
> *-Top three countries in which the community is used: USA, UK, France*
> *-Main technical features and possible features in the near future: fashion networking, showcasing (your portfolio), catwalk rating (forum), 15 Minutes of Fame, instant messaging, events posting, editorial content, competitions...*
> *-Languages in which the service is available; English only (for now)*

For more information please see our "about" attached.
Best regards,

Nick
PR Manager
Iqons.com
+33670697689
nick@iqons.com
www.iqons.com/niq

Iqons.com is an online social network focused on fashion and style for everyone from star designers to fashion addicts. On Iqons, you can display your style and your work, get feedback from the people who are at the top of the fashion industry, and tap into the latest, coolest products and trends. Our aim is to 'set fashion free' of geography and 'who-you-know'; Iqons is the world's first truly interconnected 'fashion ecology' comprised of designers, retailers, models, PRs, photographers, hair and makeup artists, stylists, show producers, magazines, bloggers, manufacturers, head-hunters, aficionados… and basically anybody with an interest in fashion.

How does Iqons actively promote talent?

1. Iqons offers a mechanism for its members to 'connect to the highest echelons of fashion'. Influential, highly respected people from the fashion industry, who we refer to as Featured Iqons, will review and comment on the work showcased by members of the site. By doing so, members get their much needed validation, which allows them to further promote their work and reach larger audiences.

2. 15 Minutes Of Fame is the feature that puts the spotlight on a different member each day, drawing all our homepage visits to his or her Portrait page. Sign Up to receive the Iqons Weekly Newsletter to find out in advance who will be featured next.

3. IQONS creates Projects with influential and respected partners in the fashion industry for our members to participate in. The first Iqons Project is "You Wear It Well / Got A Minute?", a collaboration with Diane Pernet and Dino Dinco's itinerant Fashion-Film Festival "You Wear It Well". Members are invited to submit sixty second video-clips about fashion, style, or beauty to community rating. The winning videos will be shown on the homepage twice daily for the whole next month, and the best ones will take part in the original travelling festival, now in its second edition. Other forthcoming projects for 2007 include recycling/ethical design, modelling, photo-styling… etc.

Meet the Iqons Team

Rafael Jimenez – Co-Founder and Creative Director

Rafael was previously with the avant-garde fashion house Comme des Garcons, where he led varied ground-breaking initiatives leading to the birth of the Guerilla Stores. These stores would open for one year in unusual locations and be run by partners with no previous experience in retail. This concept rose in response to the slick, "marbled-floor" environment habitually used in fashion.

Dr Suran Goonatilake OBE – Co-Founder

Suran is the Chairman and co-founder of Bodymetrics, a company pioneering the use of body-scanning and virtual reality technologies in fashion. At Selfridges, in Oxford Street, and in Harrods, Knightsbridge, customers can get their body scanned and order perfect-fitting designer jeans and women's luxury suits. He was previously a co-founder of the Centre for Fashion Enterprise (CFE), a non-profit initiative that finances and nurtures high-growth fashion designers. The CFE pioneered a new model of building luxury fashion companies and drew upon lessons Suran learnt in technology start-ups and practises from the film and music industries. As a PhD student at University College London, Suran, along with three other students, founded Searchspace, an enterprise software company that provides software to half of the world's largest banks, which in May 2005 was acquired by Warburg Pincus, one of the world's largest buy-out funds. Suran also has interests in film and TV – recently an executive producer of Luxury Unveiled, a TV series on iconic fashion brands such as Chanel, Cartier, and Dunhill, and also an executive producer of a British comedy with Ewan McGregor, 'Scenes of a Sexual Nature'. In June of 2005, Suran was made an officer of the Order of the British Empire (OBE) in the Queen's birthday honours list for his services to Entrepreneurship.

Colin McDowell – Iqonographer

Colin is one of the most authoritative fashion commentators in the world. The author of sixteen books, he is the Senior Fashion Writer for The Sunday Times Style section and founder of Fashion Fringe, the project dedicated to seeking out and supporting the fashion talents of the future.

Diane Pernet – Co-mentor

Diane has pioneered the Web as a medium for fashion communication through her highly influential blog, A Shaded View on Fashion. Her blog is mandatory reading for fashion lovers everywhere, whether they are a new designer starting their career in New York or an established magazine editor tracking street fashion in Seoul.

Lee Daley – Independent Non Executive Director and Strategic Advisor

Lee brings a long and prestigious background in the world of advertising and brand consultancy to Iqons. Currently transitioning from a role as CEO of Saatchi & Saatchi UK to Commercial Director for Manchester United, he has run businesses in New York and London, including Red Cell – a global network for WPP with operations in the US, Asia, Latin America, and Europe. His business experience has taken him around the world working on brands such as L'Oreal, MTV, Nokia, and Coca-Cola.

Fairfax House, 15 Fulwood Place, London WC1V 6A, United Kingdom
nick@iqons.com

Films

http://myfilms.com
Myfilms is a film-centric social network supported by the UK Film Council, the government-backed strategic agency for film in the UK, and funded through the National Lottery. The site is part of a major UK Film Council initiative to increase the viewing of non-mainstream films at the cinema by tackling the three main barriers: access, awareness, and information.

The Digital Screen Network is already improving access to non-mainstream films by creating a network of 240 screens across the UK that will show these films on a regular basis. The UK Film Council's Prints and Advertising Fund makes available £2 million per year to help British distributors raise awareness of non-mainstream films and now myfilms aims to provide audiences with a better film experience through a wider range of films.

theteam@myfilms.com

Food & Beverage

http://www.foodcandy.com/ (LS)
Owned by Vestris Inc., a British Virgin Islands company. Vestris Inc. is a registered British Virgin Islands company at Trident Chambers, P.O. Box 146, Wickhams Cay, Road Town, Tortola, British Virgin Islands.

Top 5 things to do:

1. Join, upload a picture and complete your profile.
2. Recommend your favorite restaurant and discuss your cooking.
3. Make new foodie friends in your city and around the world.
4. Let the world know you exist by syndicating your food blog.
5. Invite your friends to join.

http://www.bottletalk.com/ (LS)
Bottletalk is a free online social networking service for people who love wine. Bottletalk makes it easy to: store details of the wines you have indulged in and what you thought of them in your personalized area, share your wine experiences with friends, family and other wine lovers, rate, and tag wines for easy reference, discover new wines you'd like to drink and store these in your 'wanted' section, buy wines easily from online retailers.

The Loft
2 Blake Mews
Kew
Richmond
TW9 3GA
United Kingdom
contact@bottletalk.com

Gaming

http://3b.net/
Founded in 2003, 3B is an international software development and services company dedicated to creating the next generation 3D online experience.

3B provides a platform that enables users to socialize, shop, and browse within a 3D environment.

3B's online social experience enables users to hang out and chat in customizable 3D spaces called villages. These spaces are built to display their MySpace pages, their friends' pages, their favorite websites, their flickr photos and more. In addition to creating a personalized avatar which they can dress and design, the user can personalize their village by choosing a 3D theme for their space and changing some of the elements inside the village.

Some examples of 3D themes available include art gallery, auto, beach, emo, girly, the lounge, New York, party, prom, retro cafe, sky lounge, soccer, spa, techno, hiphop, weddings, football, and basketball.

3B International has subsidiaries in London, England and Cape Town, South Africa. Nicky Morris is the CEO.

Good Causes

http://www.bottomup.net/
'BottomUp', the first on-line social network entirely focused on triple-bottom-line sustainable development using a 'bottom-up' approach, can facilitate Micro-Finance Institutions and Co-operatives to organize and mobilize people and resources, and protect, and enable this form of economic organization to operate within legal frameworks and under the internationally recognized Co-operative values, and principles.
BottomUp' extends the power of social networking to promote social development through active engagment with micro-finance organisations and co-operatives
BottomUp' is a 'community interest company' regulated in the UK and must by law re-invest its profits back into social enterprises like, for example, micro-finance funds.
'BottomUp' actively seeks partnerships with micro-finance organisations and co-operative ventures to provide social networking and on-line training services and to re-invest its profits back into social enterprises of those partner organisations...please contact us to explore and discuss potential opportunities.

BottomUp Ltd,
2nd Floor
145–157 St. John Street
London EC1V 4PY
England

Music

http://www.dischorde.com/
www.dischorde.com is a new take on the music and networking site. You can collect friends and browse music as usual on some inferior websites, but once you've started listening and rating the music you find on site, our 'affinity engine' will learn your tastes and begin suggesting new music you might enjoy and new people who share your preferences. If you let us know where you live, we can match your favourite bands and genres to live gigs that are on in your area and selectively send you information about those that are of most interest to you. Once you're signed up, you'll be able to buy tickets, stream and download music, chat in forums, via instant messenger and by on-site e-mail, read music news and reviews, upload your own tracks and pictures, and set up a shop to buy and sell stuff.

Sign up as an artist, and we've got an instant online music sales solution for you. Instantly start earning money from people downloading your music from the site, as well as getting featured on the main page once your talent is recognised and you top the 'most listened' charts. Both artists and venues can list their gigs, news of which will automatically go out to their fans and people in the area, who can buy tickets online.

We've got big plans for the future and will be expanding into new areas like viral video, flash games and other new art forms as time goes on, so keep checking back to see what's new on the site, and other offerings from the Insomnia group.

Insomnia Ltd.

3 West End,
Redruth, Cornwall, TR15 2RZ

http://www.yourspins.com/ (LS)

YourSpins is a new kind of music community for fans who want to immerse themselves in a world of remixes. Within YourSpins, you'll be able to share your mixes of top songs with others, rate, and comment on other mixes — and chat, mail, and IM other people too. Plus you can make your own unique ringtones to be sent to your phone. Each user gets their own homepage, with all their mixes and ringtones listed. Soon, we'll introduce blogs for each user, but for now, all mixes can be exported to your own blog by pressing 'Blog this mix' on the mixpage.

Digimpro Ltd.
Westbourne Studios - Unit 110
242 Acklam Road
London
W10 5JJ
UK
Chris Leonard
talk2us@yourspins.com

http://bandwagon.co.uk
Music

http://www.last.fm/

Last.fm is the flagship product from the team that designed the Audioscrobbler music engine. More than ten million times a day, Last.fm users "scrobble" their tracks to our servers, helping to collectively build the world's largest social music platform.

Last.fm taps the wisdom of the crowds, leveraging each user's musical profile to make personalised recommendations, connect users who share similar tastes, provide custom radio streams, and much more.

Founded by Felix Miller, Martin Stiksel, and Richard Jones, we are a London-based company with a music-obsessed team of developers and creative professionals from around the world.
Contact: office@last.fm

Telephone and Post
London Office: +44 (0) 20 7780 7080
Last.fm Ltd.
Karen House
1–11 Baches Street
London, UK
N1 6DL

Parents

http://www.raisingthem.com/
This project was conceived, like many others no doubt, around a dinner table. The discussion was focusing on the difficulty in finding playdates where both the parent and the children enjoy themselves. One of the guests suggested to use one of these "online parent matching sites". He was serious and truly believed that such sites existed. They did not... and that is how we decided to create My Playdate, which enventually evolved into Raising Them!

How does Raising Them work?
Once you've registered with Raising Them, you'll invite people you know to join your parenting network. Your friends will come to Raising Them and invite their friends. As your network grows, you'll have more opportunities to interact easily with everyone you know, make new acquaintances, and use the network's collective knowledge to enrich your life.
Social networks are the heart and soul of Raising Them; the larger they are, the more powerful they become. Best of all, everyone in your network has been invited, approved and recommended by someone else inside your social circle.

Who can use Raising Them?
Anyone who is caring for one or more children. If you are going to the local playground every day and you are wishing that you knew another parent there to help you or that your child had a regular friend to play with, then this service is for you. Have you recently moved to a new city or a new neighborhood and are finding it difficult to meet other parents and/or kids? Are you looking for parenting advice or playgroups for your child? Does one of your children have special needs and do you want him or her to meet

other kids with the same needs? There are countless reasons why you would benefit from using Raising Them.

Enjoy!
Vero Alaimo
RaisingThem Co-Founder.

http://littlelegends.biz/ (LS)
Little Legends is a free community tool for parents and caregivers in the UK.
info@littlelegends.bizz

Religion

www.totallyjewish.com
Since 2000 Totally Publishing has been developing an international portfolio of publications and online services that target the world's affluent and influential Jewish communities. Today Totally Publishing owns and operates two leading Jewish newspapers and the popular online brand TotallyJewish, which supports websites operating in the high growth sectors of online classifieds, dating, travel, and directories.

T: +44 (0)20 7692 6962
F: +44 (0)20 7692 6689

Based in the UK.

Sports

http://www.isporty.com/
Formerly known as Tired and Tested. Sportsite aimed at the UK market.

Chris Ward

Chris Ward has previously founded two successful and award winning marketing and internet businesses, working with many of the UK's most well known entertainment names and brands in the process, including leading to its public relations success the website, Friends Reunited.

In 2003, after ten years, Chris finally sold both Beatwax and Firstmovies and left his CEO role at both companies late in the year. Chris then set out to achieve more with his body than his brain and to help raise funds for two cancer charities. He cycled from Lands End To John O'Groats, climbed the Three Peaks, started bike racing and cycled up the Alps, learnt to ski and competed in the New York and Vienna marathons.

Russell Fraser

Russell Fraser is co-founder of Scanners, a successful Broadcast Media business.

The company has top Advertising Agencies, Marketing, and PR Agencies, Record and Music Publishing Companies among its clients.

Russell's first love has always been sport, especially football. He has been involved in the organisation and administration of sport clubs for over twenty years and has successfully run several teams. He has been a FA representative for the teams he has managed and has also served on League committees as a board member for eight seasons. Russell still regularly plays and organises football.

London-based.

Travel

http://travelhiker.com/

Travelhiker.com is a place for people of all ages who love to travel to share information, advice, experiences, and photos from their travels—all for free. Members can create their own travel diary to share with friends and family or simply browse those of others for inspiration. The review section (of hotels, bars, restaurants and local attractions) from members provides an invaluable source to help you research your trip; and if you cannot find exactly what you are looking for, why not contact another member who has been to your destination—either directly via e-mail or in the forum? Whether you are on a gap year or just going away for the weekend, you should be able to find useful information from Travelhiker.com's members. It is also possible to find someone to share a trip with—this could be a lift share from one town to another, anywhere around the globe or perhaps you are looking for a companion to share a longer trip with.

Travelhiker.com was founded by James Holmes in 2006. A resident of Harrogate in the United Kingdom and graduate of Oxford University, James has worked in the United Kingdom and Canada and travelled throughout Europe, Australia, and the United States.

http://www.travelowl.co.uk
Orbital Park, Ashford, Kent, TN24 0GA
TravelOwl is the latest part of the Orbital Marketing Services Group to launch and works in close association with our sister company BP Travel Marketing Services. The launch of TravelOwl begins an exciting period of online development and shows our commitment to the UK Travel Industry.

Miscellaneous

http://www.umyup.com/
UmYup is a web service that allows homeowners who are thinking about moving to exchange property details with a view to find out who might be interested in buying their home and previewing details of properties they might want to buy before they come on the market.

Everyone using the UmYup service is a homeowner who is thinking about moving – that makes them both a seller and, in all probability, a buyer as well.

How does UmYup work?

A user anonymously discloses (selected) details about their home in order to test the market and attract prospective buyers whilst at the same time is privy to the same type of information about the properties of every other user on UmYup. Users can then use the UmYup correspondence service to communicate securely with other users about their properties.

Users can set up search profiles within their account. As new users join UmYup, and new properties are added to the database, existing users looking for properties of that type will be automatically alerted by the system via e-mail bulletins.

Free and Advanced access

The basic service is available free to all users who sign up for the service. For a small fee, a user can upgrade their account to become Advanced Access users. This allows them to see a wider range of details about properties and to communicate with other users.

More About UmYup

UmYup has evolved as a response to the need for a targeted, consumer led exchange in the UK housing market. Until now, there has been no meaningful mechanism available that will harness valuable information, on an individual basis, which will allow buyers and sellers to interact and connect anonymously to buy and sell houses.

The site will allow:
- direct "c2c" - person to person contact via our secure platform for the specific purpose of exchanging information about future and current house buying intentions;
- anonymous interaction with other house buyers and sellers, until both parties get to the point where they might want to progress negotiations;
- "price discovery" about one's own property – gauge the demand and interest online to allow a user to set the optimal price for house selling;
- view properties before they are ever "on the market" and potentially bypass the traditional estate agent mechanism in the UK – extremely powerful information for any house buyer;
- the rating of other users to make the experience more valuable and enjoyable;
- photo exchange;

- potential savings of 1-2% + VAT of the value of house, when an UmYup bargain occurs and no estate agent is involved.

The UmYup social network and exchange platform means you could sell and buy securely and with minimum hassle — there is no need to have your home on the market, even to sell it. UmYup will alert buyers to new properties as they occur, so you could find your dream home within hours of the seller thinking about selling.

Managing Director Andy Brown.

www.expats-abroad.com
Expats Abroad is run by two British expats in Spain, and if you are currently living overseas, we hope you will use our site to find other expats living in your community. If you work overseas, keep in touch with all your old friends no matter where they are currently living. If you are thinking about moving overseas, you can receive relocation advice and information from other expats via our chat room and forums by registering.

http://my.mashable.com/
Online community around Pete Cashmore's Web 2.0 blog.
Contact: petecashmore@gmail.com

http://vingo.tv/
VingoTV (www.vingo.tv) is "SocialTV" delivered to any Internet connected device and targeted specifically at the global expatriate communities. It has been founded by Australian and French expatriate Entrepreneurs Steven Barker and Seb Peypoux. Located in London, UK, VingoTV launched its Alpha version of the website in November 2006. In a month, more than 1,500 users have already signed up.
VingoTV aggregates international TV content rights in order to stream that content — live and on demand — over the Internet while providing the interactive networking tools that will allow TV to become social.
VingoTV platform allows users to do five things — stream, timeshift, placeshift, geoshift, connect.

§ Stream: Watch live TV online.

§ Timeshift: Record their favourite programmes for later viewing.

§ Placeshift: Watch live or recorded programmes from any internet connected computer anywhere in the world.

§ Geoshift: Watch any local content regardless of the original geographical broadcast region making local content truly global.

§ Connect: Socialise with groups of people who share your TV viewing preferences (i.e. other Arabic speakers in London , Stratrek fans globally, Japanese football fans in England).

The targeted market is the global expatriate community (there are more than 80m expatriates all around the world) with an initial focus on the Polish expatriate community.
Currently the website is available in English and Polish, but in the near future VingoTV will also be available in French, Italian, German, Russian and other languages serving the expatriate communities who would like to watch their favorite Local TV content and connect with fellow expats using their native language.

http://www.gottabet.com/
With Gottabet.com, we wanted to combine the power of online communities with the fun of having dares, challenges, and bets among friends. There's a competitive spirit in each of us, challenges everywhere and sometimes you just gottabet on it!

Wim Vernaeve – Co-founder
Bertrand Bodson – Co-founder
Peter Vandenberk – VP of Development
Richard Taylor – VP of Technology
Philip Wilson – VP of Engineering
Kenneth Lee – Software Developer
Adam Perfect – Web Developer

Gottabet.com
Coppergate House
16 Brune Street
E1 7NJ London
United Kingdom

http://www.biddingbuddies.com/ (LS)
BiddingBuddies is the only social networking website designed and built exclusively for eBay members, certified, and integrated with the eBay platform. Founded in 2005, biddingBuddies was created by combining expertise in eBay's Application Programming Interface (API) with social networking experience and software from leading provider, Sparta Social Networks. BiddingBuddies is a member of the eBay Developers Program and is certified by eBay as an eBay Compatible Application.

Jim Beggs founded biddingBuddies after discovering the power of both eBay and social networking. He developed the idea of a "people-centric" eBay, where relationships, reputations, trust, security, and sales are enhanced through networking with others. With a strong background in software development in the UK and North America, Jim runs the biddingBuddies team from his hometown of Belfast, N. Ireland. Jim holds a BSc Degree in Electrical & Electronic Engineering from Queen's University Belfast, and an MSc in Satellite Communications Engineering from the University of Surrey, England.

biddingBuddies.com,
c/o Internet Venues Ltd
145-157 St.John Street
London
EC1V 4PY
United Kingdom

Tel: +(44) (0) 797 464-2338
E-mail: support@biddingbuddies.com

http://videomodelpics.com/

Social network for models, actors, dancers, musicians, photographers, agents, directors and extras. They create profiles on the site, with the opportunity to get jobs and share media like videos, blog entries, and pictures. admin@videomodelpics.co.uk

http://www.thebuttonclub.com/ (LS)
The Button Club community provides members with access to exclusive events and entertainment.

The Club's objective is to empower, connect, and inspire members through events in Theatre, Film, Fashion, Art, Music, Sport, and Travel.

To become a member you will either be invited in by an existing member or you can apply for membership by filling out an application for consideration by management.

Katja Wunder
Co-founder and Director

Telephone: +44 (0) 700 340 1310
83 Lexham Gardens, London, W8 6JN
Or E-mail: enquiries@thebuttonclub.com

http://trustedplaces.com/
What is trustedplaces?
Trustedplaces is a community of real people, like you and me, who all have opinions on places they have experienced in their daily lives. By being part of the community you can share your opinions on places that you know, trust, and recommend – or even avoid – with all of your friends and their friends too. Discovering great new places is both fun and easy as you tap into all the recommendations shared by the community – it is also great value as you enjoy special offers from participating businesses.

What can you find on trustedplaces?

- Trusted recommendations and reviews from your friends, their friends or new people you haven't met yet

- Tools to make it easy for you to record and share your favourite places so that you will never forget them
- Special offers from places that want to get closer to the trustedplaces community

... you can also:

- Let the world know your opinion
- Ask the community important questions like "Where can I find the best Mojito in London?"
- Connect with people you already know or make new friends that share the same interests as you

Who we are and what we believe in?

We are a small team in London, supported by a few people in the rest of Europe, that brings together many different professional and cultural backgrounds. We believe that the web is transforming people's lives and giving them true power when it comes to choice. This is why we decided to build trustedplaces – to enable word of mouth to spread faster and to a much larger audience, allowing people to make better informed decisions based on what their peers experience and believe.

Contact: info@trustedplaces.com

MOBILE

http://www.pinppl.com (LS)

Pinppl is an application that allows RIM and Blackberry users to create a profile, upload pictures, and tag people who they like. (mososo)

Pinppl is designed, developed, and maintained by a guy named Paul Anthony, based in London, in the UK. He can be reached at PIN: 203EAE43, or by e-mail at: paul@pinppl.com.

http://www.wayn.com/ (LS)
http://en.wikipedia.org/wiki/WAYN

Annika Erskine
Marketing Manager

123 Aldersgate Street / Floor 3
London EC1A 4JQ

Tel: +44 (0) 20 7336 8088
Fax: +44 (0) 20 7336 7995
Mob: +44 (0) 7984 032 560
E-mail: annika.erskine@wayn.com

http://mywap.o2.co.uk/index.php3?jsid=F826D34AB7423EEFFB3571
B7ADCCD6BF.c4

Mywap is probably the world's leading mobile social software application
with nearly 1.7m users, mainly in the UK, but also from other places around
the world, particularly Eastern Europe where they seem to be skipping a
generation of technology and moving straight to the mobile web.

The service is run by O2, a UK mobile operator, based on a third party white
label platform. Mywap allows users to create their own mobile internet site
or moblog including pictures, text, links to other sites and components such
as guestbooks. Vitally, the resulting site can be created and updated from a
mobile, so it doesn't require access to a PC to use it, which goes some way
to explaining the service's popularity.

People are using this functionality to create sites bigging up their favourite
football teams, pop groups or tv shows as well as personal stories and pages.
It's fair to say that there's a fair bit of pirated content on mywap, but this
clearly doesn't account completely for the popularity of the service, given
the range of different sites available.

http://www.playtxt.net/

Playtxt is a new kind of online community. Playtxt is global, location
based and mobile. Who What Anywhere is a mantra to help you interactive
more easily with your circle of friends while you discover and share local
information on your mobile phone, across the world. It recognises two
hundred thousand places in 3527 regions in 238 countries. Use playtxt on
the web, by SMS and soon by mobile using our free J2ME based location
based instant messenger, which you can download to your mobile. Sign up
now, its completely free!

SCOTLAND

BUSINESS

http://www.businessbuzz.org/

FRIENDS

http://www.shetlink.com/
The online community for the Shetland Islands

TESTIMONIAL

Social and business online networking in the UK
David Long — founder and managing director — ClikOnThis.com

The rise in popularity of online networking in the UK is rapidly changing the way in which people interact, both at a social and at a business level. Whether it's the early phenomenon of Friends Reunited (www.friendsreunited.co.uk), which arguably introduced online networking to the masses. Or the rising popularity of business network sites such as Ecademy (www. ecademy.com) or LinkedIn
(www.linkedin.com).

And it's not just the adults who are getting in on the act! It seems that social networking is now a thing for the school playground, with sites such as www.bebo.com aimed at the teen market and even the under 10's are catered for with sites such as www.clubpenguin.com

But is all this networking a good thing? And what is the right time and place to network?

In early 2007, the US site www.facebook.com opened it's pages to non college users. It seems that the UK marketplace appetite for networking knows no bounds as the UK is now the largest user of Facebook! The site is destined to only increase in popularity —

just as long as it can survive the court case in Boston, USA regarding possible copyright infringement.

However, companies need to be aware of the potential dangers of staff using networking sites like Facebook. Because the site encourages the sharing of messages and photographs it is not unusual to find pictures of your work colleagues on their latest weekend away or at the ever so slightly over the top party. Whilst this might be great for entertaining and amusing their friends, is it really portraying the right image for your business?

But, when used properly, the business networking sites have the potential to provide tangible business benefits. Recruiters are using sites such as LinkedIn.com to find potential new candidates, whilst job-seekers use the same site to find new job opportunities and to research potential new employers.

I have been working with a client recently to help them understand how to utilise the business networking sites to their commercial advantage. Employees now have personal profiles as well as business orientated profiles so that they can split their personal and business lives. Customers are actively being encouraged to join these networks and to connect online with other customers. New customers are actively being sought and found with the help of the growing network. The company is also using the forums to seek out market feedback about new services and products and to provide information and guidance to others.

In summary, online networking is becoming a serious tool for business professionals who are migrating from the social sites to more specific business sites. But the passion and appetite for networking needs to be acknowledged in the board room to ensure that it´s done for the right reasons, and in the right way.

Regards

David

NEW DEVELOPMENTS

http://wiki.mozilla.org/Labs/The_Coop

"The Coop" is a Mozilla Labs project to experiment with adding social tools to the web browser. We want to create a fun and easy way to share links with your friends and to browse the set of links that friends have shared with you. We also want to make it easy to "subscribe" to a friend in order to make it easy to keep track of the pictures, movies, blog posts and status information that they might be posting on a variety of services.

The Coop is a Firefox addon in development that will let users keep track of what their friends are doing online and share new and interesting content with one or more of those friends. It will integrate with popular web services, using their existing data feeds as a transport mechanism.

Users will see their friends' faces and by clicking on them will be able to get a list of that person's recently added Flickr photos, favourite YouTube videos, tagged websites, composed blog posts, updated Facebook status, etc. If a user wants to share something with a friend, they simply drag that thing onto their friend's face. When they receive something from a friend, that friend's face glows to get the user's attention.

http://pulse.plaxo.com/

Plaxo Pulse is another good example of how a company starts as a service in one domain (in the case of Plaxo an online address book), and then gradually evolves into a more allround service by adding social networking tools. With Plaxo Pulse, users can now automatically keep tabs on how their friends & acquaintances are doing. Or to put it in their own words: Pulse is the easiest way to share photos, recommendations, links, videos, bookmarks, comments – or just about anything – with your friends, family, or business network. Have you checked your Pulse?

http://www.linqia.com/

Linqia is the first independent community and group meta search engine enabling people to find and join any community or group on the web. It was founded by Maria Sipka (Starfish Community Group S.L.) in Barcelona,

Spain, in October 2007. Maria is also the founder of The Community Girl (http://communitygirl.ning.com).

http://www.internetaddressbook.com/
The Internetaddressbook is a new service from the Netherlands (started September 2006) that brings together all your online identities in one place – social networking URLs, instant messaging IDs and web addresses. You create an account, then add your IDs from Fotolog, Facebook, Webshots, Gaia Online, Photobucket, and the usual suspects (including MySpace, of course). There's also a live search that finds people across multiple social networks – the results seem pretty good, but it works best when the user is already registered. They're also working on a "wanted" section, where you can list people you're looking for. What's more, you can add people you know to your contacts. Bringing together multiple social networks is definitely a growing trend, with more people having accounts on lots of different sites.

http://www.shareyourpage.com
Share Your Page is a relatively new service which aims to join all social network sites (such as Piczo, MySpace, Hi5...). List your page here and get lots of hits to your personal page from people just like yourself. In the same way you can search through our listings, make friends and chat. We are essentially a social networking site – but with a difference in that we allow users to promote other sites they might have. ie. Get lots more hits to your profile!

http://www.profilelinker.com/
ProfileLinker is an innovative web utility that allows you to link your social network profiles in one central location.
You can also search for users across several networks, get message alerts from your favorite social networks, get your horoscope, weather, sports news, and more.

http://www.nthebook.com
Manage your identity with an NtheBook profile.
Let us be your guide down the path where preparation meets opportunity. There are over 40 million searches a month for individuals on the internet. If someone were to look you up, what would they find? With an NtheBook

Profile, you can control and manage what people find. NtheBook enables you to create a profile that is available across a number of online search engines including: Google, AOL, MSN, Yahoo! and Ask Lynn Mitchell, NtheBook.com founder and CEO.

Contact Information:
NtheBook
Rachel Molokin
www.nthebook.com
Rachel.Molokin@NtheBook

Corporate Office
8282 South Memorial Drive
Suite 300
Tulsa, OK. 74133
Fax: 918-592-3536
E-mail: support@NtheBook.com

http://profilactic.com/
Profilactic is a digital life aggregator that makes it easy to keep up with all of the content you and your friends create online.

We built Profilactic.com for anyone who contributes content to more than a few social networking sites like MySpace, Facebook, Flickr, Digg, etc. It can be a real chore to keep all of your profiles up-to-date and follow up on all of the content you create or comment on. Profilactic gives you the services and tools to make using all of your favorite social networking sites easier.

The site was built by four guys based in Louisville, Kentucky. We all have day jobs and families, so this is something we work on in our spare time. Fortunately, our day jobs involve writing software, so we *should* be pretty good at this stuff.

The public beta release of Profilactic, which launched on January 19, 2007, consists of five key areas: Profile, Mashup, Clippings, Friends, and Friends' Mashup (which you can read more about below). We also have supporting features like Badges and RSS feeds that allow you to take Profilactic with you. Of course, we will be adding tweaks, enhancements, and new features throughout the beta, so chances are that the list you just read is already slightly out-of-date.

What sites do you currently support?
We have a list of about thirty default sites that we currently support in the beta (with more rolling out over time).

43 Things, 43 People, Bebo, Blinklist, Blue Dot, ClaimID, Consumating, Del.icio.us, Digg, Flickr, GameSpot, Instructables, Jaiku, LiveJournal, MP3.com, MSN Spaces, MySpace, Newsvine, Slide, TV.com, Vimeo, Vox, Webshots, Yahoo! 360, YouTube, Multiply, iLike, Pandora, Last.fm, and Zooomr.
However, you can add an unlimited number of "custom" sites to your Profilactic account. So, basically, we support *every* site.

Contact: feedback@profilactic.com

http://loopster.com/
Connecting social networks among themselves.
Loopster allows you to find what's new with the people you care about, no matter which online service they use.

Loopster enables you to import your friends from various social networks, connect them together, and watch how they change.

http://mugshot.org/
Created by Red Hat

Mugshot offers several activities:

- Mugshot Page – Pull together activity from all your online accounts at one place on the web.
- Web Swarm – Share web links with individuals or groups in real time and get live feedback when people visit those links.
- Music Radar – Show off the music you listen to using services like iTunes, Rhapsody, Yahoo! Music, and others on your web site, blog or MySpace page.

- Stacker - Keep track of what your friends are doing online, on the web or live on your desktop.
- Groups - Create public or private groups around shared interests.

http://www.naymz.com/

Naymz is an online provider of reputation/identity management and promotion services for people, groups, and businesses. Naymz provides a simple and user friendly experience for those who are concerned with promoting an accurate and positive picture of their personal or professional reputation and identity.

By signing up for a free Naymz account you start to take control of what information others find about you online. Start by creating a Naymz profile page, which you can personalize to include information about you and links to your content on the Web:

- Social networks (MySpace, Friendster, FaceBook)
- Blogs (Blogger, TypePad, Xanga)
- Classmates and Reunion sites
- Photo Albums (Flickr, Webshots)
- Personal or Professional Bios
- Other interests (Del.icio.us, YouTube, Amazon Wish list)

After you create your account, Naymz handles the rest. We promote your page at the top of the major search engines. Now when people search for your name on Google, Yahoo! or MSN, your Naymz profile is the first thing they'll see.

http://socialnetwork.in/

What is this site for?

- To help you aggregate links to all of your profiles into one page and widget (widget coming soon!), including social networks, chat, VOIP, and other communities.
- To help you aggregate links to all the social sites you wish to monitor.

- To help you aggregate links to all your friends on various social and chat networks.
- To provide a simple means for you to rate social and chat networks using a 1–10 scales and comments.

http://otherego.com/ (formerly www.rantiq.com)
OtherEgo.com began from one young entrepreneur's vision to create a different type of social network, a social network where users could easily share their favorite websites and internet profiles inside one page. Starting from scratch, and about forty books later, the owner learned how to create dynamic and interactive webpages. This began in January 2006 and was completed as Rantiq.com in November 2006. It was then redesigned in March 2007 as OtherEgo.com. (See the history section below on how we reached this point.)

Learning from the highly complex Rantiq.com website, we changed our focus to simplicity and easy navigation. Instead of just sharing links, we figured out a way to have websites load inside a single profile page. This is a unique feature of our social network. We also included simple privacy controls allowing you to hide specific sections from the public. Instead of an all-on or all-off solution, that most social networks are using, OtherEgo.com users can select which part of their profile to hide/show.

History

Our entrepreneur's journey really began during the end of 2005, when an idea popped up of having a social network that shares other social network profiles and websites. This would make it a lot easier for friends to know if you are a member of other networks.

In January 2007, our entrepreneur decided to quit his job, move back home, and learn how to obtain the skills needed to create something like this. As a first attempt, the result ended with Rantiq.com (which is no longer online). Rantiq.com was a full blown social networking application, allowing customization, highly complex privacy settings, and numerous profile sections for members to share their information.

30/3/2007 Otherego was officially launched.

Founder and CEO Enoch Lee

Based in Sacramento, California.

http://profilefly.com/
Profilefly.com is a site that makes it easy to share and promote all of your:

Profiles – Social Networks, Blogs, Photo Sites, Professional, Love & Dating
Contacts – E-mail & Instant Messengers
Bookmarks – Video links, Cool Sites, News, & more

How do I get started?
The first step is to Sign Up. After you've created an account, you can quickly make your profile by filling in some basic information, and adding your pic. After you've added your information, you're ready to start sharing your Links.

How do I add my Links?
In your profile, click "Edit Links". Remember, you must be logged in. You'll then walk through a serious of quick steps to add all of your Profiles, Contacts, and Bookmarks. Once there added, your information is ready to be shared.

How do I see my friend's Links?
When you find a friend who's content you'd like to see, click "Add to my directory". Whenever that person adds a link, you'll see it right in the feed located in your profile.

What is the Profilefly Widget & how do I use it?
A widget is an item you can place in your other profiles like Myspace, and it will automatically display the links you've shared there as well. To add a widget, login and grab the widget code located here. Then paste it in your other profiles to share your Bookmarks without every having to update them!

http://zoolit.com/
Zoolit is a shareable Web page that lists all your personal sites. Your Zoolit Landing Page is always current and up to date, providing the world with all of your personal Websites, Social Networks, Blogs, contact info, and Photo and Video Sharing sites.

When you add, change or delete a Website address, simply make the change on your Zoolit Page and its updated everywhere you have your Zoolit Button or Link. Zoolit is super simple to set up and use, and it is completely free.

http://socialurl.com/
Meta-network service, manage your identities in one spot (SocialURL is also a social network itself).

SocialURL is a fun and trouble-free way to manage your online identities. Here at SocialURL we will put everything into one location. Just imagine – a profile jam packed with your photos, friends, and even links that direct others to your additional profiles. Connecting with others from one platform certainly becomes effortless with the help of our website.

SocialURL is free! With a few simple clicks of the mouse, you will straightforwardly be able to set up a basic account.

Connect with others around the globe.
Search for old classmates and love matches.
Share hundreds of photo albums online, control who sees them, or keep them private.
Organize to-do lists and bookmark favorite sites.
Build a social web full of your additional profiles – including EBay, Facebook, Myspace, LiveJournal, Yahoo360, YouTube and more.
Upload your YouTube videos to one profile.
Track every single visitor that views your online identity.

http://www.hypeit.com (before Spokeo)
On May 5 2007 Spokeo refocused the site from a social news reader to a community centered on sharing interesting stories.

harrison@hypeit.com

www.konnects.com
Konnects, Inc. is an online business networking platform designed to give the power of online social networking to business professionals. Konnects has created over 350 city business networks around the globe, and over eighty unique industry networks. Konnects partners with existing organizations to create unique online business networks which can then be promoted on the Konnects network of sites. Organizations can choose to remain private or allow the general public to join at their discretion.

The patent pending Konnects solution is unique in that it allows individual users to join multiple online business networks, without having to re-create their profile. Each network contains its own community of professionals who engage in discussions, share interests, contacts, referrals and more... As an individual joins multiple networks they can widen their contact base and engage in targeted communities of professionals that share common interests. Konnects enables you to get connected to more than 320 communities around the world and over eighty industry specific communities. Subscription-based service.

Konnects Inc.
P.O. Box 1642
Tacoma, WA 98042-1642

Create your own social network

http://www.ning.com/
Marc Andreessen and Gina Bianchini founded Ning in October 2004 to give everyone the opportunity to create social networks. Two years later, Ning powers over thirty thousand social networks and counting.

From eBay sellers in Upstate New York to bead store owners in Maine, aspiring hip hop artists in New Jersey, pop culture junkies in New York City, college professors in Germany, young deviant artists in North Carolina, and even a few big media companies in LA, with Ning anyone can create the perfect social network for them.

What makes this all possible is the Ning Platform.

As a platform, you don't have to appeal to Ning for the features you want. If you have the time and the inclination, you can build them yourself. It's the software equivalent of Home Depot.

Platforms give everyone the freedom to create.

Why Did We Build Ning?

When we started, we wanted to enable a diversity of social networks the same way the web browser enabled millions of different websites.

We are committed to relentlessly improving our platform and the social networks powered by it, so if you don't see something you're looking for, let us know. There's a good chance it's right around the corner.

ceo@ning.com

NB Readers of this book are invited to join http://worldwidenetworking.ning.com, the community for founders & top networkers, created by the author An De Jonghe.

http://www.collectivex.com/
CollectiveX is a simple tool that enables you to quickly and easily set up a private website for sharing and networking within your group.

Founded by Clarence Wooten. CollectiveX was launched in 2006 and is based outside of Washington, DC in Columbia, Maryland. The company is funded by Wooten, other private investors and the state of Maryland.

CollectiveX, Inc.
9861 Broken Land Parkway
Suite 250
Columbia, MD 21046
Phone: 410.715.1400

Press Contact:
Mike DiLorenzo
Phone: 617.758.4143
press@collectivex.com

http://www.me.com/
Once upon a time in a land by San Francisco Bay, a small group of people with very different backgrounds decided to come together and build me.com The site's official launch date was October 23, 2004, and the team was immediately greeted with a surge of members. Happily, the storm never stopped.
We're still a relatively young company, so it makes sense that we're always full of big ideas. We're planning and implementing new features all the time. We're hardworking, beer-chugging, brainstorming… anyway, Mary Poppins aint got nothin' on me.
A humongous thanks from the me.com team goes out to you, the members who make yourselves at home here and give the site soul. We pledge to continue working toward the goal of providing a positive, life-changing experience for you here, on me.com you, after all, do bring out the best in me.

Sincerely,

me.com
50 West San Fernando, Suite 320
San Jose, California 95113
Tel: 408.93…
Fax: 408.275.9430

http://post282.com/
Post282 is a place where you can create your own private community website for chatting with friends, sharing images and movies, and posting links to cool stuff you find on the web. Post282 is not about making new friends and meeting people. This site is about staying in touch with people you already know. Your community is private – only you and your friends can access it, post to it and read what others are posting. As a community administrator you control who has access to your site.

Post282 is owned and maintained by Rob O'Leary and Garrett Killeen. Rob designed, built, and runs the system. Garrett works on design, testing, and administration.

rob@post282.com

garrett@post282.com

admin@post282.com

http://www.lifesterblog.com/
LifesterBlog is a free blogging and social networking site. It allows you to customize your blog, share posts, photos, videos, music and books, and connect with friends. You can also control your privacy.

In English and Chinese.

admin@lifesterblog.com

Some examples of how companies have incorporated social networking in their strategy

http://www.starwoodhotels.com/sheraton/guestbook/index.html
Sheraton has redesigned its website to include travelstories from their guests: people can send in their experience (obviously when they have stayed at a Sheraton hotel) and upload the picture or video that goes with it. It is not a real social network as such since only the barest of personal information about the guest is included (first name plus the initials of their last name) and guests or visitors cannot interact between themselves, but the onset is given. Also, Sheraton very cleverly includes a prominent link to the hotel in question under every guest story, making it easy for visitors to check out the hotel in question right after reading a raving review by another guest.

How It Works

1. Tell us where you traveled.
2. Upload your photo or video.

3. List your contact information: First name, Last name initial, and e-mail address.
4. Share your story—in your language.
5. Agree to the terms.
6. Smile. Welcome to the neighborhood.

http://www.thecoca-colacompany.com/presscenter/nr_20070606_ sprite_yard.html
The Sprite Yard creates an entertaining social experience beyond the value of traditional online destinations by providing consumers constant mobile, social and brand connectivity through mobile devices such as cell phones and personal digital assistants (PDAs).

Launched in China on June 1, 2007 and on June 22, 2007 in the US.

http://www.dellideastorm.com/
In 1984, Michael Dell had $1000 and an unprecedented idea – bypass the middleman and sell custom-built PCs directly to customers. This idea led to the creation of what is now Dell Inc. and the birth of Dell's direct model. Twenty three years later, we believe more than ever that the best way to understand and serve our customers is to talk to you directly, wherever you may be located. The only difference between 1984 and 2006 is that we now have millions of global customers in more than one hundred countries.

It is with this mindset that we created Ideastorm. The name is a take-off on the word "brainstorm," and it is our way of building an online community that brings all of us closer to the creative side of technology by allowing you to share ideas and interact with other customers and Dell experts. You can suggest new products or services you'd like to see Dell develop or tell the world how you feel about major trends in technology and society. We hope this site fosters a candid and robust conversation about your ideas.

Our commitment is to listen to your input and ideas to improve our products and services and the way we do business. We will do our best to keep you posted on how Dell brings customer ideas to life.

www.salesforce.com

Appspace- An "enterprise-level MySpace" will be launched in April 2007. According to Salesforce: "Just as MySpace brought together individuals on the consumer web, AppSpace will bring together companies and their customers on the Business Web."

IdeaExchange- Empowering the Community to Collectively Design

Introduced in October of 2006, the IdeaExchange (http://ideas.salesforce.com) is an online community where the salesforce.com community can create, comment on and promote new feature ideas. In less than six months, IdeaExchange has seen incredible growth in traffic and influence with more than 2,500 new ideas posted, more than 42,000 promotions and more than 3,700 comments.

http://www-142.ibm.com/software/sw-lotus/products/product3.nsf/wdocs/connectionshome

IBM Lotus Connections is social software for business that empowers you to be more innovative and helps you execute more quickly by using dynamic networks of coworkers, partners and customers. It includes profiles, communities, blogs, bookmarks & activities.

Interestingly enough, IBM has chosen to offer the possibility to submit their webpage on Lotus Connections to Digg and Del.icio.us, thus maximizing on the social networking opportunities.

http://savannahnow.com/ (LS)

Hello An,

Glad to participate.

Here is the brief text for www.savannahnow.com (Savannah, Georgia, USA)

Founders & management

Darryl Kotz — Executive Director of Online — Savannahnow.com/Savannah Morning News (Savannah, Georgia, USA)

Heather Nagel Doughtie and Felicia Haynes — Morris Digital Works (interactive arm of Morris Communications, Augusta, Georgia, USA)

Founding year & address/nationality
Launched May 24, 2006 — Savannah, Georgia, USA

Target audience & membership level (number of users)
Target audience is locally focused 18–55 — 150,000 + registered users

Main technical features and possible features in the near future
Drupal based system allows for blogs, personal member pages, post audio, add friends, create groups, post photos, add events to calendars and post comments.

Future enhancements include video, Spanish language feature.

Languages in which the service is available
English only today/Spanish in the future

I am also attaching a word doc with a little more detail and links in case you need screen shots.

We also recently won the Newspaper Association of America — Digital Edge award in our category for Best Visitor Participation, based on the social networking aspects of our site.

I hope this helps, please let me know if you need anything else.

Take care and talk soon.

Darryl

Darryl Kotz
Executive Director of Online
Savannahnow.com Savannah Morning News
P. 912.652.0375 M. 912.332.2955
E. darryl.kotz@savannahnow.com

Welcome to Savannahnow.com! This is a new kind of community website that joins with the Savannah Morning News in a mission of helping build a stronger community. With your help, we will work to provide a friendly, safe, easy to use place on the Web for everyone in the community to post news items, create a unified community calendar, and share photos, recipes, and opinions.

This is a place where you can take the lead in telling your own story. As a registered Savannahnow.com user, you get your own weblog, your own photo gallery, and the ability to post entries in special databases such as events and recipes.

In return, we ask that you meet this character challenge: be a good citizen and exhibit community leadership qualities. It's a simple and golden rule. Act as you would like your neighbors to act.

Anybody can be a leader. You're a leader every day in what you do and what you say — regardless of whether you *want* to be a leader. Your words have power.

Here are some suggestions:

- Lead by example. Demonstrate how you would like others to behave.
- Every time you post, ask yourself: Am I helping make a better place to live? Am I helping people get to know and understand one another better?
- Ask follow up questions when someone seems to disagree with you. Maybe they're right. It happens.
- Ask for help, and accept help. Helping others builds bonds of friendship.

Please note, by posting to Savannahnow.com, you grant us permission to use, on a royalty-free basis, any posted content in Savannah Morning News or any affiliated publication of Savannah Morning News whether in print or online. Please keep this in mind when posting content.

Additionally, we may edit items selected for the newspaper. We ask that you keep your Savannahnow.com account information up-to-date so that we can contact you if necessary.

The mailing address for the Savannah Morning News is:
P.O. Box 1088, Savannah, Ga., 31402-1088.

Executive director of online
Darryl.kotz@savannahnow.com
Online community coordinator
Jennifer.wozniak@savannahnow.com

http://www.pallmall.pl/login.php
Hi An,

The PallMall website is different than other SN because of legal regulations. It is a huge project of a consumer community made for a tobacco brand. As in Poland there is no legal possibility to promote cigarettes, British American Tobacco focussed on direct marketing communication. A web based community is one of the most interesting applications; however, it has to be strictly controlled due to legal issues. To gain access to the website you have to be at least 18 years old, a Polish citizen, and have sent to BAT a signed questionnaire in which you state you understand the danger of smoking tobacco, you are an adult, a conscious tobacco user, and agrees to receive marketing communication from BAT. Also, a copy of the ID with visible name and date of birth is needed.
Inside the service there is always a visible health warning. We have also included features to monthly check the validity of the e-mails and cell phones given via tokens.

The Pall Mall website is huge success for BAT and is kind of a benchmark for other markets. It is also one of the projects I am especially proud of — it was big challenge to create a huge community in such a restricted place:

Regards,
Piotr

Piotr Wrzosinski

Conclusion

How is Web 2.0 changing your daily life?

Although I am not a *Trekkie* (Star Trek fan) who believes technology will take over our life completely, I am convinced that the social network phenomenon (and Web 2.0 as a whole) is more than a fad. It has entered into the lives of millions of users already and will continue to become integrated in our lives. In the following paragraphs, you will read in which segments of the economy, social networks have played a role.

Politics

Politics are probably not the first thing which springs to mind when thinking of social networks. Nevertheless, they have proven to be a new source to win and mobilize voters in ways we have not seen in recent years. Not surprisingly, the USA has taken the lead with networking sites of the Democrats and the Republicans where you can pledge your allegiance, get involved in fundraising groups, discuss party strategy on forums etc. Some individual candidates have created a personal social networking site as well, such as presidential candidate Obama. The USA has even social networking sites where users come together—virtually speaking that is—to discuss politics online: a discussion forum as you will but with the benefit of actually "seeing" your adversary...This creative use of social networking has been limited to the US to the best of my knowledge, but I would love to see this spread to other parts of the world. Europe, for instance, could certainly use a social network to connect all of its member states and their inhabitants: it would be a cost-effective way to make Europeans feel more connected and to overcome cultural and linguistic barriers. Keeping in mind that the website of the European Union is by far the largest website in terms of number of pages of the whole EU, it could also be a more practical way of communicating.

Marketing

Marketeers agree that word-to-mouth references are still the best way to convince a prospect to try a new service or product. In that respect, Web 2.0 social networking sites become the new form of Tupperware party: anyone can join, you hang out with your friends and meanwhile business is getting done. If we take a closer look at the more clever ways in which marketeers use social networking sites today, we say that to have acces to certain services, a member needs to sign up his friends as well (e.g. by downloading his address book into the system). This is an incredibly fast and inocuous way for marketeers to gain access to a potential wealth of new clients.

Recruitment

In a tight market (shortage of qualified candidates), everything counts, including the reputation of a company or its managers on the Internet. Jason Goldber, the CEO of Jobster, has understood this message well and signs each message Jobster sends to one of its members. As the spokesperson for Jobster he is also the face and combines many speaking engagements with a seemingly personalized message online.

Candidates are fed up with waiting for an answer. The message 'Your cv is being sent to the appropriate department' does not win you any brownie points.

By contrast, the company that is at the forefront (fast to adopt new media), communicative (get the message out before your prospect starts wondering what your message is) and personal will win the race to their future employees' heart. Another interesting development in the recruitment market is the rise of the "hybrid" platforms: jobboards that add social networking to their offering in order to increase the interaction between candidates and employers, thus improving their success rate. Jobster (www.jobster.com) is probably the best known example, but new initiatives are following. Among them iHipo (www.ihipo.com), which stands for "International High Potentials," and Hipo India (www.hipoin.com) by the same company. Started in June and September 2007 respectively, the team is a good example of how e-recruitment becomes more internationally focussed and similar to webdevelopment teams: with different nationalities (a Dutchman, a German and a Singaporian) who are working together around the globe. At the moment, the service is still free for both candidates and clients, but eventually employers will pay a fee to search the database and to place ads. The founders assured me they would charge less than Monster or Linkedin though. Also, in future, high potentials will be able to upgrade in order to get the contact details of registered recruiters, to receive premium content etc. The company is autofinanced in the case of iHipo, but it will be looking for VC funding for its Indian counterpart.

Customer service

Companies will feel the need to put a name and a face to their customer service people. What made MySpace a huge hit to begin with? Tom! People relate to people, and with our current technology, nothing is easier. Consider including a chat button to connect with a customer service employee. If you're offering a toll-free number, this will definitely come cheaper!

Media/Communication

While the influence of traditional media is diminishing, your publicity dollars are too if you are still spending them on printed media and television. While I am not one of those people who claim the printed press is dead – I did write this book, remember?—I do believe the best way to ward off a possible threat is to absorb it and turn it into something of your own. A nice example that illustrates this point is Savannah Now, the online community edition of the newspaper with the same name. Although 'only' a local newspaper, the team behind it has created an extremely user-friendly site that is inviting and so simple your grandmother could use it. Savannah Now has even claimed a price with their site.

Amazon is another example of how a website can attract bookworms to connect online and exchange book reviews between themselves. Who said on and offline media do not mix?

Sales

What would happen if you'd stop letting your internal sales team make those cold calling calls and instead put them to work in the social networking field? Personally, I believe your results would not be worse, quite the contrary even. Social networks offer the opportunity to work the inside angle because you have access to the names of many more people than you can find in (subscription) business directories. On top of which you find loads of free background information on your target: where did he/she go to school, where did he/she work before, what are his/her interests/hobbies…This is information which a seasoned sales professional can obtain when he has done his homework before a cold call. Now you have it at the fingertips of your junior inside sales who can decide before making the call, whether it is worthwhile pursuing or not.

Travel

The travel industry has been one of the most active industries so far in the world of Web 2.0. There are a lot of travel social networking sites out there (a good many of which are covered in this book) and more are yet to come.

Mostly they are founded by globetrotters who enjoy sharing the experiences they've had in particular countries, hotels, and such. Their primary objective is to exchange travel impressions, much in the way you used to sit down and watch a holiday video with your friends. The business world is catching up though: Sheraton hotels have included a social networking element in their website, for guests to interact and share their stories. How long will it take before travel social networking sites offer the possibility to not only swap travelstories but to click right through to book a flight to the destination you just chatted about?

Banking

Although one of the industries with the most money to burn, banks are traditionally known as being—hmm—conservative with respect to new ideas. So far I came across only one bank that has tried the social networking field and that is Fortis bank with its join2grow.biz project. The idea behind it is to build a platform for young entrepreneurs (a potentially lucrative demographic group a few years from now) and to let them interact with retired professionals who want to share their expertise. It is a smart idea which merits brownie points for taking the lead, although the execution could still be improved. Still, I see potential for other applications as well. For example a platform where you could lend money to 3rd world countries or charities (similar to Kiva) for those banks aiming to attract the socially conscious investor.

Good Practises for Social Networks & General Remarks

Many networks use an internal mailsystem to keep control of how their users interact with one another and to gain insight in their objectives. However, the process of logging in to your account (entering your password and login every time) can result in users getting annoyed and finally dropping out altogether. Especially users who are member of several networks at once, tend to be time-conscious.

Although social networks have become mainstream, it still takes goodwill and trust to sign up for (yet another) social network. One of the ways in which to establish trust is by clearly presenting the people behind the project (which most networks do) but also by indicating where the company is located physically, how one can reach them by e-mail (not just by filling our an anonymous template) and by telephone or fax and possibly even the company's credentials (registration or VAT number). This is a sore point in which many websites fail. A positive exception to this rule are the French websites: many give a clear overview which establishes their credibility. Whether this is due to French legislation or their own initiative is unknown to me, but I would recommend it to all online communities.

The identity and culture of a network seems to determine the intensity of interaction between users and the type of interaction. For example, within Linkedin it is quite acceptable to contact someone you don't know personally, if there is a business motive behind it, the general idea being that if you didn't want to receive business opportunities, you wouldn't create a profile on Linkedin. On Ecademy contact is much more up close and personal: people really try to help one another and contact is often continued offline during the Ecademy meetings.

Survey

Over one thousand people from sixty-one countries took part in the online survey which was held from January 07 till October 07 on www.titans-consulting.com/adj/. While the survey has no pretense of being scientific, I believe it offers some insights in who, why and where people are using social networks today.

Who was Joe Average who filled out this survey?

Answer: Male, between 30 and 40 years old, in a relationship, with children, from Belgium, the USA or the UK. Surprisingly enough only 27% of women participated, though they are generally regarded as being the larger group of users of social networks.

Which social networks are most popular?

Answer: The top ten is equally shared by professional as well as social (friendship) networks. However Linkedin clearly takes the lead when it comes to business networking, or networking as such, in the demographic group we have queried.
The top 10 consisted of (in order of importance): Linkedin, Xing, Ecademy, Facebook, MySpace, Viadeo, Ryze, Hi5, Orkut, 360 Yahoo.

Why do users join a social network? What is their number one reason?

Answer: Here I admit I was surprised: a whopping 89% put "professional use" as their number one reason to join an online community! Fifty-three percent uses it to socialize and to stay connected with friends, and a meager 16% is interested in joining a social network if it caters to his/her hobby. Keeping in mind the old predjudice (from people who are not using social networks obviously) that online communities are predominantly used by teenagers who like to chat (socialize), our survey states the opposite. Also, it makes you wonder about the surge of specialized networks (niche networks) and their chances of survival if they offer no business advantage.

Is it important that you can use your own language?

Answer: Even with globalization and the increasing use of English, the majority seems to think it is important to be able to use one's mother tongue when interacting online (40%). Thirty-one percent feels it is convenient but not necessary; 28% doesn't feel it is important. If you're launching a network today, wouldn't you want to score points with your potential users by offering them the possibility to use their mother tongue?

Would you rather pay a membership fee to have an ad-free network or do you prefer a free account with advertising?

Answer: Twenty percent of the users is willing to pay for the privilege to have an ad-free community, while 80% is not. I guess it would be interesting to calculate how much money you could earn with – say—Google Adwords (the preferred partner for most small networks) and by attracting 20% of your estimated public and charging them a membership fee...

Would you join a network because someone famous is a member?

Answer: Twenty percent of you would! When A Small World (a so-called "gated community" which is invite-only) reportedly counted Paris Hilton and Tom Cruise amongst its members, everyone and his poodle wanted to join. One Korean network has used this trick successfully by openly anouncing which celebrities were members, but strangely enough I haven't seen this marketing trick anywhere else.

How much time do you spend on your social network(s)?

Answer: The majority visits his/her site(s) several times a day (37%) or once a day (18%). Twenty-two percent visits several times a week. That adds up to 77% of all respondents who are intense networkers – much more than what most surveys seem to suggest. The fact that many people were introduced to this survey through one network or another obviously embellishes the results but even so, I'm wondering whether social networking is establishing itself as an accepted business practice (similar to prospecting) which people can do during business hours instead of a tool to find a new date?

Would you consider joining a network outside your own country?

Answer: Three quarters of all participants consider themselves true cosmopolitans, while 13% is only interested in local communities, and 13% would go as far as neighbouring countries.

What are the top three things you do when turning on your PC?

Answer: While e-mail and surfing the Internet occupy the first two places, checking your social network profile comes in third with 44%! It has become considerably more important than Internet banking, online shopping or gaming, adding to the notion that for a growing group of Internet users, social networking has become an integral part of their online identity and habits.

Do you participate in offline (face to face) meetings?

Answer: While a majority doesn't participate in offline meetings (54%), the difference with those who do is quite slim, suggesting that social networks can establish further contact with and between members if they choose to do so. This being said, a vast majority of online communities do not organize face to face meetings, probably because this demands an organisation (logistics, time, money, volunteers) which not all networks have access to.

Do you use video networks?
Answer: Eighty-one percent off all participants do not use video networks. Is video networking a hype or has the business world yet to discover/ appreciate the power of video? I am guessing the latter is probably correct.

LITERATURE/REFERENCES/CREDIT

Riley, Emily *Social Networking Sites* JupiterResearch. 2007

Stamet, L.Y, Waasdorp, G.J.M.. *The International Recruitment Manual* Intelligence Group & Stepstone. 2006

Wildbit *Social Networks Research Report* Wildbit, LLC. 2005

Van Stegeren, T. *Ontwikkelt Web 2.0/sociale software zich ook bij ons tot (serieus) massamedium? Een overzicht* De nieuwe reporter. 2006

Online Sources

http://www.frankwatching.com/archive/2005/05/26/Linkdossier_Social_networking

http://www.businessweek.com/technology/content/sep2006/tc20060911_501990.htm

http://www.businessweek.com/globalbiz/content/nov2006/gb20061128_985082.htm?chan=globalbiz_europe_today

http://en.wikipedia.org/wiki/List_of_social_networking_websites

http://yasns.pbwiki.com/

http://www.forrester.com/Research/Document/Excerpt/0,7211,40306,00.html

http://www.emarketer.com/Articles/Print.aspx?1004325&src=print_article_graybar_article

http://mashable.com/2006/06/24/uk-social-networks-myspace-bebo-and-piczo-in-the-lead/

http://onlinepersonalswatch.typepad.com/news/2006/03/ultimate_list_o.html

http://www.symantec.com/ciodigest/articles/200703/playing_leapfrog.html

http://www.readwriteweb.com/archives/top_spanish_web_apps.php

http://www.watblog.com/index.php?tag=%20india%202.0

http://socialnetworking.knowhow-now.com/

http://www.cutuli.it/index.php/category/social-network/

http://africansocialnetwork.blogspot.com/

http://socialsoftware.weblogsinc.com/2005/02/14/home-of-the-social-networking-services-meta-list/

http://realsocial.com/

http://www.businessweek.com/technology/content/sep2006/tc20060911_808191.htm?campaign_id=rss_tech

http://www.socialnetworking.jp/archives/2004/09/sns_20.html

http://www.allthingsweb2.com/mtree/SOCIAL_NETWORKING_2.0/

http://www.mathdaily.com/lessons/Social_network

http://www.lesreseauxsociaux.com/

http://en.wikipedia.org/wiki/MoSoSo

http://freetopia.blogspot.com/2005/09/mobile-social-applications-mososo.html

http://www.theglobeandmail.com/servlet/story/RTGAM.20061206.WBmingram20061206154826/WBStory/WBmingram/

http://www.econsultant.com/web2/videos-hosting-sharing-searching-services.html

http://www.japantoday.com/jp/feature/1137

http://hq.andrewshuttleworth.com/hq/files/ExecutiveAnswer-Networking.pdf

http://www.techcrunch.com/tag/Connexion/

http://ontmoeten.net/

http://philippineinternetreview.blogspot.com/2006_12_01_archive.html

http://momb.socio-kybernetics.net/section/invitation

http://www.loogic.com/index.php/web20/

http://wwwhatsnew.com/2006/11/29/1000-aplicaciones-web-20-clasificadas/

http://www.linknrank.com/categories.php

http://www.listio.com/

http://www.killerstartups.com/?category=SocialNetworking&all=1

http://money.cnn.com/galleries/2007/biz2/0707/gallery.web_world.biz2/jump.html

http://bd.english.fom.ru/report/map/ocherk/eint0701/

Glossary

A

AJAX: AJAX stands for Asynchronous JavaScript and XML. Ajax allows content on Web pages to update immediately when a user performs an action, e.g. with Google Maps the user can change views and manipulate the map in real time

Avatar: icon or representation of a user on a social network or virtual reality.

B

Blog: short for web log; online journal

C

Chat: online instantaneous text-based conversation between users

Community: group of people who connect online and share certain interests

Crowdsourcing: outsourcing a task to a large, undefined group of people on the Internet in the form of an open call.

Cul-de-sac: Editorial content area for online marketeers, without the risk of negative content

D

E

F

Folksonomy: "folk" and "taxonomy" – the product of collaborative tagging

Forum: place on the Internet where you hold discussions, post topics and ask questions

G

Gated community: private social network, by invitation only.

H

I

Instant messaging: also called IM, is the exchange of text messages through a software application in real-time. It usually offers the possibility to check whether your contact persons are online when you log on.

J

K

L

M

Mashups: new breed of web applications that are made by mixing two or more websites together to offer a new service. The term originally was used on the hiphop scene.

Message board: also called discussion forum; online bulletin board where you can read, leave and respond to posted messages.

MMORPG: stands for "massively multiplayer on-line role-playing game," online video games where a large number of players interact with one another in a virtual world.

MoSoSo: abbreviation for Mobile Social Software – software that lets you network through your mobile phone or laptop.

N

O

OpenID: system for single sign-on. With OpenID, users do not need to sign in with a username and pasword.

P

Podcasting: comes from i-Pod and broadcasting: creating audio files that are available on your website, which people can then download to their MP3 players or PC. Podcasts are delivered through RSS feeds; once you subscribe you will automatically receive updates (like **blogs**).

Portal: Website that offers a broad array of resources and services, such as e-mail, forums, search engines, and on-line shopping malls.

Q

R

S

Social bookmarking: activity that allows users to save and categorize a personal collection of bookmarks and share them with others.

Soft launch: web site that is implemented in stages rather than all at once

Stealth mode: secretive phase until the site is ready to launch

T

Tagging: adding bookmarks to webpages, articles etc

Taxonomy: classification of things, e.g. websites

U

User-generated content: content that is created by the public instead of by professionals. Examples are blogs, wikis, etc.

V

Vlog: video blog

W

Web 2.0: Internet applications that focus on the users: content is made for users, by users

Web 3.0: the next step of the Internet (sometimes referred to as the Semantic Web) that will combine artificial intelligence with the use of databases, letting the Internet suggest solutions to your queries instead of simply listing possible answers for you to chose from.

Widget: Widgets display information and invite the user to act, for example buttons, pop ups, badges etc. Sometimes called snippets.

X

Y

Z

Alphabethical Index

A

B

C

E

F

N

P

T

W